Exodus

Judaism, Christianity, and Islam – Tension, Transmission, Transformation

Edited by Patrice Brodeur, Alexandra Cuffel,
Assaad Elias Kattan, and Georges Tamer

Volume 11

Exodus

Border Crossings in Jewish, Christian and
Islamic Texts and Images

Edited by Annette Hoffmann

DE GRUYTER

ISBN 978-3-11-064275-9
e-ISBN (PDF) 978-3-11-061854-9
e-ISBN (EPUB) 978-3-11-061708-5
ISSN 2196-405X

Library of Congress Control Number: 2019947120

Bibliographic information published by the Deutsche Nationalbibliothek
The Deutsche Nationalbibliothek lists this publication in the Deutsche Nationalbibliografie;
detailed bibliographic data are available on the Internet at http://dnb.dnb.de.

© 2021 Walter de Gruyter GmbH, Berlin/Boston
This volume is text- and page-identical with the hardback published in 2019.
Printing and binding: CPI books GmbH, Leck

www.degruyter.com

Table of Contents

Annette Hoffmann
Introduction —— 1

Wolfgang Oswald
The Way Out of Vassalage – The Exodus Narrative (Ex 1–14) and Ancient International Law —— 15

Kära L. Schenk
The Exodus Narrative and Divine Warfare in the Dura-Europos Synagogue —— 29

Jessica N. Richardson
Through Water and Stone: The Brescia Sarcophagus *Crossing of the Red Sea* —— 49

Kristine M. Larison
"Prolific Writing": Retracing a Desert Palimpsest in the South Sinai —— 77

Silvan Wagner
Bewegung in der *Altdeutschen Exodus* als Heilsempfang und Übersetzung —— 93

Sara Offenberg
Purim Like Yom Kippurim: Between the Texts and Images of the *London Miscellany* and R. Eleazar the Preacher's Commentary on Exodus —— 109

Rella Kushelevsky
The Crossing of Boundaries and Liminality in the Rabbinic Aggadot on the Death of Moses and on "Those to Die in the Wilderness": Analogous Aspects —— 131

Mika Natif
Between Heaven and Earth: The Illustration of the Death of Moses in Rashid al-Din's *Jami al-Tawarikh* (World History) —— 145

Angelika Neuwirth
The Prophet Muhammad's Visionary Journey to Jerusalem – a Spiritual Exodus —— 163

Susanne Talarbadon
The Paradigm of a Second Exodus in Jewish Tradition —— 183

Ute Holl
„Du hast die Greuel gesehen...". Zum Exodus als ästhetischer Unterscheidungskraft —— 199

Bibliography —— 223

Index —— 245

Photo Credits —— 253

Annette Hoffmann
Introduction

Scientific debates in the humanities centring on border crossings and cultural exchanges between Judaism, Christianity, and Islam have dramatically increased over the last decades.¹ Within this context, however, little attention has been paid to the Book of Exodus.² This seems surprising, given that the story of Israel's migration from Egypt and its journey to the Promised Land via the Red Sea – the threshold and border to Asia – and then the Sinai desert, is not only a master narrative of a border crossing in itself, but also plays a prominent role in the Abrahamitic religions.³ Pesach, which commemorates the eve of the Exodus,⁴ is one of the highest Jewish holidays, and Moses is one of Allah's most important prophets. Muhammad met him during his night journey. The Crossing of the Red Sea has been typologically equated with baptism, the moment of entry into

---

1 See for instance: *Multicultural Europe and Cultural Exchange in the Middle Ages and Renaissance*, ed. James Peter Helfers, Turnhout 2005; *History as Prelude: Muslims and Jews in the Medieval Mediterranean*, ed. Joseph V. Montville, Lanham/MD 2011; *Judaism, Christianity, and Islam in the Course of History: Exchange and Conflicts*, ed. Lothar Gall/Dietmar Willoweit, Plymouth 2011; *Beyond Religious Borders: Interaction and Intellectual Exchange in the Medieval Islamic World*, ed. David M. Freidenreich/Miriam Goldstein, Philadelphia 2012; *Interpreting Scriptures in Judaism, Christianity and Islam: Overlapping Inquiries*, ed. Mordechai Z. Cohen/Adele Berlin, Cambridge 2016; *Entangled Histories: Knowledge, Authority, and Jewish Culture in the Thirteenth Century*, ed. Elisheva Baumgarten/Ruth Mazo Karras/Katelyn Mesler, Philadelphia 2017.
2 The few exceptions are: Katrin Kogman-Appel, *Jewish Book Art Between Islam and Christianity. The Decoration of Hebrew Bibles in Medieval Spain*, Leiden/Boston 2004. In her book Kogman-Appel discusses not only the description of the Tabernacle in Exodus, but also a group of Haggadot, which contain Exodus cycles; see ibid., 182–202; *Jewish Biblical Interpretation and Cultural Exchange. Comparative Exegesis in Context*, ed. Natalie B. Dohrmann/David Stern, Philadelphia 2008. In the latter volume, however, only Adele Berlin's article considers the innerbiblical interpretation of the Book of Exodus, see: Adele Berlin, "Interpreting Torah Traditions in Psalm 105", in: ibid., 20–36.
3 This common ground has been emphasized by the theologian Eckart Otto in: *Mose. Geschichte und Legende*, München 2006, without exploring the topic further. The same can be said about the more educational rather than purely scientific book written by Christfried Böttrich/Beate Ego/Friedmann Eißler, *Mose in Judentum, Christentum und Islam*, Göttingen 2010. The book is divided into three parts, which introduce the role of Moses in the three monotheistic religions.
4 Pesach commemorates the sparing of the firstborn: "and when I see the blood, I will pass over you, and the plague shall not be upon you to destroy you, when I smite the land of Egypt" (Ex 12:13).

Christianity,[5] or the Harrowing of Hell, Christ's descent into the underworld; both antitypes again pertain to border crossings. Christ himself has been identified with the Pesach lamb, which was sacrificed to mark the doors (transit areas) of the Israelites' houses with blood on the one hand, and to wash away Adam's sin on the other. Sea and desert are spaces of liminality and transit in more than just a spatial and geographical sense. Their passage includes a transition to freedom and initiation into a new divine community, an encounter with God and entry into the Age of Law, or even a violation of Law. Moses died just before crossing the Jordan River, which separated him from the Promised Land – a border crossing that he was not permitted to make. In short, the Exodus – even in the wider sense of its conception – is predominantly a story of Passover(s).[6]

Border crossings, however, cannot occur without borders. The latter demarcate geographical, chronological, political, or social entities and/or identities, which have been identified as different from each other. Demarcating borders and passing over them is a daily human practice, as Martin Heintel and others have recently underlined.[7] Borders have increasingly become the subject of theoretical debates and research, especially in the wake of the so-called "spatial turn" of the eighties and nineties,[8] giving way to the recent Border Studies,[9]

---

[5] For the baptism as an initiation rite, see Arnold van Gennep, *Les rites de passage*, Paris 1981 (first published in 1909), 133–135.

[6] The broader sense of Exodus considers the whole way of the Israelites, which leads from Egypt to the Jordan River in the land of Moab. The whole way, as Chrisoph Dohmen and Matthias Ederer have recently pointed out, is constituted by a series of departures, see Christoph Dohmen/Matthias Ederer, "Wie Exodus zum Exodus wurde. Ein Buch und sein Thema", in: *Exodus. Rezeption in Deuterokanonischer und Frühjüdischer Literatur*, ed. Judith Gärtner/Barbara Schmitz, Berlin/Boston 2016, 1–16, in particular 1 and 10–14.

[7] See Martin Heintel et al., "Grenzen – eine Einführung", in: *Grenzen. Theoretische, konzeptionelle und praxisbezogene Fragestellungen zu Grenzen und deren Überschreitungen*, ed. Martin Heintel/Robert Musil/Norbert Weixlbaumer, Wiesbaden 2018, 1–15, 2.

[8] See for instance Doris Bachmann-Medick, *Cultural Turns. Neuorientierungen in den Kulturwissenschaften*, Reinbek 2006, 284–328; *Spatial Turn. Das Raumparadigma in den Kultur- und Sozialwissenschaften*, ed. Jörg Döring/Tristan Thielmann, Bielefeld 2008; Stephan Günzel, *Raum. Eine kulturwissenschaftliche Einführung*, Bielefeld 2017.

[9] See for instance Christian Wille, "Räume der Grenze – eine praxistheoretische Perspektive in den kulturwissenschaftlichen Border Studies", in: *Praxeologie. Beiträge zur interdisziplinären Reichweite praxistheoretischerAnsätze in den Geistes-und Sozialwissenschaften*, ed. Friederike Elias et al., Berlin 2014 (Materiale Textkulturen, 3), 53–72; *A Companion to Border Studies*, ed. Thomas M. Wilson/Hastings Donnan, Chichester 2016.

which complement the Global Studies of the 21st century.¹⁰ Borders and processes of border crossing, however, often imply conditions of liminality, a term shaped by the ethnologist Victor Turner as early as the 1960s. Following Arnold van Genneps' *Rites de Passage*, Turner describes different liminal stages, which are commonly characterized by ambiguity and indefiniteness, as an intermediate state of tripartite transition processes.¹¹ Turner mentions the wilderness as a typical space for limial states.¹² The "initiatory aspects of Sinai" in Turner's sense of ritual have, moreover, already been analyzed by Ilana Pardes in her *Biography of Ancient Israel*.¹³ Several elements of the Exodus story correspond to rites of passage described by van Gennep: the marking of thresholds with blood, for instance, or the passage through water, which alludes to washings as disjunction rituals.¹⁴

The Crossing of the Red Sea, the miraculous parting and closing of the waters, is certainly not only a border crossing, a flight out of the state of vassalage, the demonstration of God's power, but it is also a border demarcation between two different peoples: the Egyptians and the Israelites, or the saved and the drowning. This dichotomy has often been visually expressed. In the fourth-century fresco in the catacomb of Via Latina in Rome, for instance, a blank interspace between the Egyptians and the Israelites is emphasized at the image's center, interrupted only by the arm and staff of Moses in the act of closing the waters (fig. 1). In a similar yet opposing way, the Italian painter of an Exultet roll from 1136 depicted the sea shore as a black bold line that diagonally divides the entire picture into two distinct parts: that of the saved and that of the drowning people (fig. 2). The miracle at the sea, moreover, constitutes a frontier within the Exodus narrative, namely between the Israelites' exit from Egypt and their wanderings in the wilderness, or between deliverance and guidance into the Holy Land, as Christoph Dohmen and Matthias Ederer have recently pointed out.¹⁵ Yet at the same time, upon closer inspection, in the story of Exodus seemingly binary entities often reveal a complex nature. Moses above all, who closes the waters by

---

10 See among others: *An Introduction to Global Studies*, ed. Patricia J. Campbell/Aran MacKinnon/Christy R. Stevens, Chichester et al. 2010, in particular XVIII–30.
11 Van Gennep, *Les rites de passage* (as in n. 5); Victor W. Turner, "Liminalität und Communitas", in: *Ritualtheorien. Ein einführendes Handbuch*, ed. Andréa Belliger/David J. Krieger, Opladen/Wiesbaden 1998, 247–260.
12 *Ibid.*, 252.
13 Ilana Pardes, *The Biography of Ancient Israel. National Narratives in the Bible*, Berkley/Los Angeles/London 2000, 65–99, in particular 68.
14 Van Gennep, *Les rites de passage* (as in n. 5), 29.
15 Dohmen/Ederer, "Wie Exodus zum Exodus wurde" (as in n. 4), 6.

crossing the border with his staff, has a double identity: he is an Israelite, but he grew up in Pharaoh's court and was later also identified as an Egyptian by the Midianite women.[16] Thus, with the protagonist's entry into the story, the narrative immediately turns into an account of a border crossing. Moses' ambiguity, his liminal status, is already encapsulated in the image of him floating in a casket between two riverbanks (fig. 3).

Fig. 1: The Crossing of the Red Sea, fresco, 4th century. Rome, Catacomb of Via Latina

Since the tragic history of the SS Exodus 1947 with 4,500 Holocaust survivors on board, who – just like Moses and those who were destined to die in the wilderness – were not permitted to enter Palestine, the term "Exodus" (gr. ἔξοδος, way out) has also become an epitome for refugee movements. In recent times an increasing number of publications titled "Exodus" have examined refugee flows and immigration issues following mainly illegal frontier crossings all over the

---

16 "They said, 'An Egyptian helped us against the shepherds'" (Ex 2:19).

Fig. 2: The Crossing of the Red Sea, Exultet roll, 1136. Paris, Bibliothèque Nationale de France, Ms. nouv. acq. fr. 710, n. 4

Fig. 3: The Finding of Moses, *Jâmi' al-tawârîkh* of Rashid al-Din, Tabriz, ca. 1314–1315. Edinburgh, University Library, Arab. Ms. 20, fol. 9r

world, from Indochina to Mexico.[17] In this sense, the topic reveals its actual relevance. As of late, this is even more true in light of the fate of lifeboats in the Mediterranean, such as the "Aquarius", "Lifeline", "Diciotti", and others, which immediately remind us of the SS Exodus. Some of the articles in this volume, to a greater or lesser extent, hint at the timeliness of this issue. Migrations and cultural exchange processes are being increasingly accompanied by perceptions of difference and acts of demarcation, which exhort to keep historical memory alive.

The impact and memory of the Exodus story in post-biblical texts and images lend themselves to intercultural comparative examination. Such an approach has partly been taken in exhibitions and edited volumes on the figure of Moses, for instance Jane Beal's book *Illuminating Moses* (2014) or the cata-

---

17 See for instance Tessa Morris-Suzuki, *Exodus to North Korea. Shadows from Japan's Cold War*, Lanham/MD et al. 2007; Paul Collier, *Exodus. How Migration is Changing our World*, Oxford et al. 2013; Angelos Dalachanēs, *The Greek Exodus from Egypt. Diaspora Politics and Emigration, 1937–1962*, New York 2017.

logue *Moïse. Figures d'un Prophète* (2015).[18] These studies, however, draw exclusively on Jewish and Christian literature and art. While the figure of Moses has always played a central role in Jewish and Christian Studies, in Islamic Studies the scholarly interest in biblical topics and their representation in general, and the Exodus in particular, has notably risen in recent years.[19] This increased attention invites further debate on Jewish, Christian, and Muslim interactions. Moreover, the Book of Exodus, or more precisely the Fourth Commandment ("You shall not make [...] an idol"), has been addressed in relation to the image controversy and to historical debates about Jewish, Christian, and Muslim cultures and their interactions, as for instance in the volume *Images of the Divine and Cultural Orientations* (2015), which opens up fundamental questions on image theory.[20]

On the other hand, in Theology and Egyptology, seminal studies on Moses and the Book of Exodus have repeatedly brought to the fore the story's dichotomies, such as Jan Assmann's *Moses der Ägypter* (2000) and *Die mosaische Unterscheidung* (2003), establishing the distinction between true and false as core issues of monotheistic religion.[21] Assmann has even spoken about a Mosaic

---

18 *Illuminating Moses: A History of Reception from Exodus to the Renaissance*, ed. Jane Beal, Leiden et al. 2014 (Commentaria; 4); Jean-Christophe Attias/Anne Hélène Hoog, eds., *Moïse. Figures d'un prophète*, exhibition catalogue (Musée d'Art et d'Histoire du Judaïsme, Paris), Paris 2015.
19 See Brannon M. Wheeler's groundbreaking book: *Moses in the Qur'an and Islamic Exegesis*, New York 2002; ʿAbd-Elṣamad Elschazlī, *Der Dialog zwischen Mose und Pharao über Gott im Koran und bei ausgewählten Korankommentatoren*, Göttingen 2015; see further Rachel Milstein's studies, which concentrate on Arabic and Persian bible illustration in general, but also reveal a special interest in the figure of Moses; see Rachel Milstein, "The Iconography of Moses in Islamic Art", in: *Jewish Art*, vol. 12/13, 1986/1987; ead., *La Bible dans l'art islamique*, Paris 2005, 87–92; *Biblical Stories in Islamic Paintings*, ed. Naʿama Brosh with Rachel Milstein, Jerusalem 1991. Similar interests in the role of biblical figures in the Islamic tradition are pursued for instance in Carlos A. Segovia, *The Quranic Noah and the Making of the Islamic Prophet. A Study of Intertextuality and Religious Identity Formation in Late Antiquity*, Berlin/Boston 2015 (JCIT, 4). Segovia proposes a typological reading of the Qur'anic Noah narratives and underlines that Muhammad is "repeatedly modelled in the Qur'ān upon various biblical figures", see ibid., 15. A second book by Segovia on *The Quranic Jesus* appeared recently in the same series: id., *The Quranic Jesus. A New Interpretation*, Berlin/Boston 2018 (JCIT, 5).
20 *Images of the Divine and Cultural Orientations. Jewish, Christian, and Islamic Voices*, ed. Michael Welker/William Schweiker, Leipzig 2015; see also the series of lectures organized in 2010 by Barbara Schellewald and Vera Beyer: https://www.geschkult.fu-berlin.de/en/e/kosmos_ornatus/news/Vortragsreihe.html.
21 Jan Assmann, *Moses der Ägypter. Entzifferung einer Gedächtnisspur*, München/Wien 1998, and id.: *Die mosaische Unterscheidung: oder der Preis des Monotheismus*, München/Wien 2003.

dialectic (2013).²² His more recent book *Exodus* (2015) instead highlights the idea of covenant and its foundation as the crux of the Exodus narrative.²³ Yet, Assmann states that in order to enter this covenant (between God and Israel) the exodus from Egypt was necessary, leading back to the "antagonistic tension between Egypt and Israel". Likewise, binary (or sometimes triangular) perceptions of the story are implicit in many studies on Exodus, for instance in the work of Joachim Krause, who analysed the intertextual relationships in the Book of Joshua between the Exodus from Egypt and the "Eisodus" into the Holy Land (2014),²⁴ or in that of Kristine De Troyer, who focused on the concepts of "Doing Good and Bad" in Exodus (2016).²⁵

In dialogue with these studies, but also diverging from them, this volume contains eleven contributions on transitional processes as a core theme of the Exodus narrative. These articles have been written by leading specialists in biblical and Rabbinic literature, in the Qur'an, and in Jewish, Christian, and Islamic art and film history. By bringing these studies together, the volume takes a twofold approach. On the one hand, it concentrates on topics regarding border crossings in Exodus, offering a common basis upon which to address comparative problems, and, on the other, it permits a study of interreligious, transcultural phenomena. The Jewish, Christian, and Islamic Exodus traditions did not grow in parallel – neither in texts nor in images – but rather interdependently. Thus, the chosen title "Border Crossings" does not simply address the narrative's content, but it also includes aspects of the migration of textual and visual motifs: the use of Jewish sources in Christian and Islamic texts, for instance, or Jewish adoptions of Christian iconography or Muslim means of expression and vice versa. How do Jewish, Christian, and Islamic texts and images read and retell the transitional aspects in the Exodus story, and on what levels do the different traditions interact? What differences and similarities can be found in the pat-

---

22 Jan Assmann, "Monotheismus und Gewalt. Eine Auseinandersetzung mit Rolf Schieders Kritik an 'Moses der Ägypter'", in: *Die Gewalt des einen Gottes. Die Monotheismus-Debatte zwischen Jan Assmann, Micha Brumlik, Rolf Schieder, Peter Sloterdijk und anderen*, ed. Rolf Schieder, Berlin 2014, 36–55.
23 Jan Assmann, *Exodus. Die Revolution der Alten Welt*, München 2015. The "Gott-Israel-Verhältnis", the relationship between an acting God and Israel is also discussed by Barbara Schmitz, "Gotteshandeln. Die Rettung am Schilfmeer als Paradigma göttlichen Handelns (Ex 13,17–14,31; Ex 15; Jes 43,14–21; Weish 10,15–21; Jdt)", in: *Exodus. Rezeption in Deuterokanonischer und Frühjüdischer Literatur*, ed. Judith Gärtner/Barbara Schmitz, Berlin/Boston 2016, 33–69.
24 Joachim J. Krause, *Exodus und Eisodus: Komposition und Theologie von Josua 1–5*, Leiden et al. 2014 (Vetus Testamentum, Supplements, 161).
25 Kristine De Troyer, "Doing Good and Bad: Links between Exodus and the Deutero-canonical Books", in: *Exodus*, ed. Gärtner/Schmitz (as in n. 4), 89–99.

terns of interpretation? What correlations can be observed between the concepts in texts and those in images within these various cultures? What role do the different media play? By raising these questions, the volume aims to stimulate discussion and contribute to a deeper understanding of contact points between Judaism, Christianity, and Islam, set against the background of a common narrative central within each tradition.

The volume opens with a contribution that considers the story of Israel's exodus at the time of its scriptural composition. *Wolfgang Oswald* underlines the fact that the search for the historicity of the Exodus event led to the question of the historicity of the Exodus narrative being neglected. The oldest, pre-priestly part of the narrative (Ex 1–13), Oswald maintains, is neither a historical report, an adventure story, or a religious confession. It reworks a probably older Judean exodus tradition and deals with the legitimacy of dissolving one's state of vassalage. According to an antique legal construction, the so-called 'sacral release', this dissolution is only possible by symbolically entering into the vassalage of God. The subject of the narrative, thus, is not the geographical wandering of Israel from Egypt, but the stepping out of the state of vassalage and entering into that of independence. It concerns a "social status" in the framework of what can be called 'international law'. Thus, the border crossing addressed by the story was, as Oswald shows, originally juridical.

Kära L. Schenk's article focuses on the depiction of the Exodus in the third-century CE synagogue of Dura-Europos. It discusses spatial and narrative ambiguities in the painting that make it unclear whether Moses and the Israelites are just leaving Egypt or if they are already at the bank of the Red Sea. Pointing, furthermore, to a much-debated detail of fire and hail raining down, Schenk proposes that the image must be connected with a midrashic reworking of the Exodus narrative. In this adaptation, the Israelites' God fights against the Egyptians with divine weapons. In relation to this reading of the image, Schenk raises the question of how the Exodus narrative, in which Israel's enemies were the Egyptians, might have been understood in the contemporary world of a Jewish community living on the eastern border of the Roman Empire. In contrast to the opinions of some scholars that specific iconographic details in the painting suggest a polemic response to Roman authority, Schenk argues that in the image a more nuanced mode of communication is at work, in which the narrative had a flexible polemical target.

In her article on the Brescia Sarcophagus, *Jessica N. Richardson*, discusses how the material and aesthetic qualities of the stone, a red onyx, in which the Crossing of the Red Sea has been sculpted, are conceptually and artistically used to emphasize the subject's transitional aspects in its early Christian funerary context. From the typological pairing of the Crossing with the rite of baptism, to Easter liturgy, and the mystery of salvation, Richardson displays the whole complexity of the theme, analyzing in detail the relationships between the material and the image in question. The idea of water, the Red Sea, represented in a reddish stone picks up several elements of the narrative, the wall of water, raising on both sides of the Isrealites, the Pharaoh's army "sinking like a stone", or the enemies becoming "immoveable as a stone". Through the stone's particular color and its natural undulating veins, which subtly turn into carved waves, the metaphorical and allegorical *transitus*, which also link to the Easter sermon of Brescia's own fourth-century bishop, Gaudentius, are highly concretized and dramatized.

Kristine M. Larison's article is dedicated to the thousands of Nabatean inscriptions carved between the second and third centuries CE into the stones of South Sinai, writings that found their way into the history of the Exodus narrative through their perception and reception in later times: up to the eighteenth century, Christian travellers have interpreted them as examples of early Hebrew. They were believed to have been produced by the Israelites, who retraced the words of the Divine Law during their wanderings through the wilderness. Thus, they took part in the process of shaping the holy site. Pilgrims left their names and prayers in physical proximity to these 'Holy Scriptures' refiguring the liminal space of the desert into a holy textbook or palimpsest. Larison's contribution raises fundamental questions about the transformations of holy sites and memorialization, traditions of beliefs and processes of translation, the acquisition of knowledge, comprehension, and (in)communicability, and migration routes.

Translations are always border crossings connected with processes of transformation and reinterpretation.[26] *Silvan Wagner* analyzes the so-called "old German Exodus", a vernacular re-narration of the biblical text dated to around 1200, which scholars have either dismissed in terms of any theological ambition or inserted into the theological context of crusade. According to Wagner, both valuations concur that a possible autonomous theological approach to the Exodus was sought in terms of differences in content in relation to the text of the Vulgate, to which, however, the "old German Exodus" adheres rather closely. How-

---

[26] This has also been perfectly demonstrated for the Book of Exodus by Joachim Schaper, who analyzed the Exodus in the Septuagint in relation to the Hebrew original text, summarizing that the Greek Book of Exodus is a "work of Religion", a "Religionswerk [...], das Spuren recht subtiler interpretativer Manöveraufweist, die nicht ohne Wirkung auf die Entwicklung der jüdischen und christlichen Literaturen und Glaubenswelten geblieben sind", see Joachim Schaper, "Exodus – die LXX-Fassung und ihre Rezeption in der deuteronkanonischen und frühjüdischen Literatur", in: *Exodus*, ed. Gärtner/Schmitz (as in n. 4), 17–31, the quotation is on 29.

ever, by transporting the original narrative into the vernacular language, the "Exodus" sets the events in a courtly lay context and thus offers a new perspective, namely in terms of the circumstance of translation, which is broached in the text itself. In the "old German Exodus" the chief motive of the narrative, the Israelites' movement in space, is charged with the meaning of a *translation veritatis*, and it is paralleled with the act of translation into another language, which, at the same time, creates a conjunction of spatial and spiritual movement.

Sara Offenberg analyzes the visual program of the London Miscellany, a manuscript produced in France in the late 13th century, focusing on its connection to R. Eleazar's commentary on Exodus. Moreover, *gematriot* containing commentaries on periscopes in Exodus were also written in the margins of the manuscript. By discussing text and image relationships and the complex phenomena of intertextuality, Offenberg shows how some of R. Eleazar's ideas, which circulated among the Hasidei Ashkenaz, entered the full-page illuminations of the manuscript. The miniaturist, probably a French Christian painter, was likely guided by a Jewish patron or scribe. The series of images was, moreover, intended to display the three deeds that the Israelites had to fulfil upon their arrival in the Holy Land. Finally, the London Miscellany displays messianic aspirations as expressed in Eleazar's Commentary on Exodus.

As *Rella Kushelevsky* shows, the statement that Moses died in the steppes of Moab, at the edge of the wilderness, on the one hand, and that of the Promised Land, on the other, illuminates a liminal aspect in the depiction of Moses' death. Like Moses, those who left Egypt were not allowed to enter the Promised Land either and instead had to die in the wilderness. Kushelevsky interprets the wilderness motif and its function as a space that fashioned the liminal experience of the Israelites on their way from Egypt to the Land of Israel, before becoming a people. She analyzes the metonymic presentation of the wilderness in the Mishnah Bava Batra and in midrashim upon Moses' death and the concealment of his grave, showing that in these texts the liminal figures of Moses and those who were destined to die in the wilderness are themselves characterized as metonyms of the wilderness through which they passed. The wilderness is understood as a formative expanse, the act of hiking through it is transformed into a "rite de passage", the apex of which is the experience of death before birth into a new community.

The representation of Moses' death in the Ilkhanid World Chronicle of Rashid al-Din, the Jami al-Tawarikh, is the focus of *Mika Natif*'s study. The miniature follows the story according to which Moses is led by God to Mount Nebo in order to see the Promised Land from afar and to die alone afterwards on the top of the mountain near God, in an undefined place. In a close reading of text and image, Mika Natif shows how the miniature depicts Moses' liminal status between life and death. The physical form of the dead Moses, his posture, and also the surrounding landscape embody ideas of transition and portray the loss of his carnal body. In the image, Moses originally appears as someone who transcends spheres, an agent between the divine and earthly realms.

Angelika Neuwirth emphasizes that in the Qur'an, Muhammad's night journey to Jerusalem is designated as an "exodus", whereas Moses is to stage a collective "night journey" made explicit through a temporal determination: "by night". Observing this strikingly identical use of terms, Neuwirth asks how this analogy is to be understood. As she underlines, in the Qur'anic rendering of the biblical story the historical event of the Exodus is less important than its typological significance as a prototype of the Prophet's night journey. A central aspect is the promised deliverance, the exit from a site of oppression, which is not physical, but spiritual. With this typological bond sanctity moves on an extended Sinai-Mecca axis, which in a way 'biblicizes' the Meccan sanctuary. Moses' liberating exodus was denied to Muhammad and his community in the hostile Mecca, but as Neuwirth shows, his visionary journey to the center of the Holy Land was equally perceived as an experience of liberation, which can be repeated through prayer, and it culminated in a Mattan Torah.

The paradigm of the Second Exodus is discussed by *Susanne Talabardon*. Presented repeatedly in different layers of the Bible, it was shattered in the face of historical reality. In particular, Rabbinic tradition, attempting to downplay national restorative strivings, left the universal undertones of the Second Exodus paradigm for an emerging Christianity to exploit. In the course of medieval discussions, the return to Zion remained an individual project, at best. Others preferred to establish Diaspora towns or regions as proper places to live. In early modern times, as Talarbadon shows, settlement projects in the Holy Land re-emerged, accompanied or countered by Second Exodus projects in Diaspora regions.

Ute Holl concludes the volume with a study in musicology and film history, discussing Arnold Schoenberg's opera *Moses and Aaron* and its film adaptation produced by Danièle Huillet and Jean-Marie Straub. As Holl illustrates, both works present the relationship of political release, law, and violence as a moment of aesthetic experience. With his twelve – tone technique, that is, through the equipatition of tones in space, Schoenberg creates a smooth and undirected soundscape, which is both liminal and desertlike. Huillet and Straub moreover translate this tonal sound into a film without establishing shots, which usually serve to procure orientation, thereby dissolving cultural and spatial orders in being and transferring the audience to the same state of disorientation experienced in a liminal space such as the desert.

The majority of the contributions in this volume were initially presented at the homonymous interdisciplinary conference held in December 2010 in Heidelberg. This conference, funded by the Fritz-Thyssen-Foundation, was organized within the framework of the "Images of Alterity" project, led by Lieselotte Saurma and Anja Eisenbeiss, in cooperation with the Kunsthistorisches Institut in Florenz, Max-Planck-Institut.[27] Other articles were added at a later stage. This book developed over a long period of time, and I am extremely grateful to all the authors for their continuous work, patience, and enthusiasm. Special thanks go to Gerhard Wolf for his encouragement and substantial support of the project, and to Jessica N. Richardson and Vera-Simone Schulz for their precious advice. Furthermore, I would like to thank Giosuè Fabiano, Davide Ferri, Maximillian Hernandez, Rebecca Milner, Michaela Scharnreithner, and Kristen Streahle for their essential help during the editorial process; the entire team of DeGruyter, who carefully followed the book through the production phases; and last, but certainly not least, the editors of the series, especially Alexandra Cuffel, for their critical feedback on the texts.

---

27 The project "Images of Alterity" was part of the Heidelberg Cluster of Excellence "Asia and Europe in a Global Context. Shifting Assymetries in Cultural Flows".

Wolfgang Oswald
The Way Out of Vassalage – The Exodus Narrative (Ex 1–14) and Ancient International Law

My contribution to this volume interprets the Exodus Narrative in its historical context from the historical-critical perspective of bible scholarship.[1] However, I will do so in a way that might contradict some expectations, since I will not ponder the historical event of the exodus from Egypt, nor will I discuss its dating or speculate on the historical identities of the Pharaohs appearing in the narrative. Although such speculations are quite popular, mostly among lay people but to some extent also among scholars, they are misguided, as they ignore particular features of the text. The Exodus Narrative does not mention any date for the narrated events and the Pharaohs appearing in the narrative are anonymous. The story is designed in a way that makes it impossible to locate the narrated events in a specific historical context, and the very first task of historical-critical exegesis is to take this aspect seriously. However, although the narrated story is not historical, the narrative itself is a historical datum. It was written by an author or group of authors for a certain purpose and a specific audience. This is this historical dimension of the text I will concentrate on. Hence, in the following I will seek to understand the intentions expressed in the Exodus Narrative.

The title of the second book of the Hebrew Bible in the Christian tradition is intended to convey the content of the first part of the book, namely chapters 1 to 15: "Exodus", or: "way out". But where does Israel exit from? The answer should be clear: Egypt. While this seems plausible at first glance, it is problematic upon closer inspection. Viewing the situation in such a simplistic manner would give us a travel story, a sort of adventure novel comparable to the novels of German writer Karl May ("Durch die Wüste" / "Through the Desert"). But this would not be fitting for the text in question, since only few verses describe the departure process. The biblical narrative does not focus on the external circumstances of the journey but rather on something else, indicated in the Book of Exodus itself. It is instructive to learn how the events of the exodus are summarized, for example in the Decalogue (Ex 20:2): "I am Yahweh your God, who brought you out of

---

[1] For an extended version of this article with detailed arguments and full references see Wolfgang Oswald, "Auszug aus der Vasallität – Die Exodus-Erzählung (Ex 1–14*) und das antike Völkerrecht", in: *Theologische Zeitschrift*, 67, 2011, 263–288.

the land of Egypt, out of the house of servitude." The first definition of the point of departure is geographical-political: the land of Egypt, but without the more precise statement "out of the house of servitude" it would be insufficient and even misleading. It is not a question of leaving a country, but rather of leaving a certain social status. The journey merely illustrates the actual process, which is juridico-political. The issue is not the journey as such, but the legitimacy of this journey, and hence the legitimacy of the change of status. The story deals with the juridical and political circumstances rather than with the physical migration.[2]

Before turning to discuss this aspect further, I shall first briefly outline the literary history of the Exodus Narrative. There is unanimity among scholars that Ex 1–15 was not written by one single author but rather it should be considered as a composite literary work. The minimum consensus is that an older non-priestly narrative should be discerned from a later one indicating a priestly origin. In the following pages, I will focus solely on the older non-priestly part, contained in Ex 1–14. It is worth pointing out, however, that the priestly passages of the narrative do not significantly alter the juridico-political constellation prevailing therein, thus there is no need to devote much time to this matter. The distinction between the earlier non-priestly and the later priestly account – when discussing the encounter between Israel and Egypt at the Reed Sea in terms of international law – will be considered in the third part of this paper.

Leaving aside this debate on literary history, the main goal of the Exodus Narrative is to demonstrate that under international law subjected peoples have the right to terminate their vassal status. This concern is only dealt with in the Exodus Narrative as neither the preceding Joseph Narrative nor the following wilderness stories take up this subject. Hence, we shall concentrate on the Exodus Narrative and seek to determine its juridico-political dimension precisely. In particular, this article analyzes the juridical status of Israel at the beginning of the narrative, its change of status, and its juridical status at the end of the narrative.

The Juridical Status of Israel at the Beginning of the Exodus Narrative

Thus far we have used vague terms such as "social status" or "juridical status". We could also have used the term "dependency status", but that would require

---

[2] David Daube, *The Exodus Pattern in the Bible*, London 1963 (All Souls Studies, 2), 13.

us to explain what kind of dependency we are talking about. In the Ancient Near East, as well as in the Mediterranean Antiquity, there were many forms of social and political dependency, but it is by no means clear which one applies to Israel at the beginning of the Exodus Narrative. Moreover, there was a variety of forms, including transitional ones, and a lack of consistent and unambiguous terminology.

The issue of ambiguity becomes apparent when looking at the use of the Hebrew verbal root '*bd*, which designates the status of the Israelites before the exodus. The First Commandment of the Decalogue cited above uses the Hebrew term *beyt 'abadim*. The translations differ to some extent: "house of bondage" (KJV), "servitude" (Luther), "house of servitude" (LXX, Vulgate, Buber/Rosenzweig), "house of slavery" (NRSV, NASB), "house of slaves" (Elberfelder, Zürcher, Einheitsübersetzung).

All nominal and verbal derivations of the root '*bd* express a "dynamische(n) Relationsbegriff"[3]. An *'ebed* is somebody who has a duty of loyalty and/or duty of work towards somebody else. Israelites deprived of their rights are referred to as *'abadim* of the Pharaoh (Ex 5:15), in the same manner as the high-ranking and influential court officials of the Pharaoh (Ex 8:5). The same is true in the book of Jeremiah, for instance. The slaves to be manumitted (Jer 34:9) and the counselors of the king (Jer 36:24) are equivocally called *'abadim*.[4] The designation of the Israelites as *'abadim* and of their occupation as *'abad* only purports a relationship of dependency on the Pharaoh. On the other hand, from the commission of Moses onwards it is clear that in the future there shall be a dependency on the God of Israel: "Let my son (= Israel) go that he may serve ($\sqrt{'bd}$) me!" (Ex 4:23).

In the case of the Israelites in Egypt the obvious choice may be the translation "slave", but the term "slave" in its proper sense designates an individual. A master owns a slave, a rich master probably owns several slaves, a plurality of persons, but not a collective such as a town, a tribe or a people. Moses Finley writes:

---

[3] Ingrid Riesener, *Der Stamm 'bd im Alten Testament, Eine Wortuntersuchung unter Berücksichtigung neuerer sprachwissenschaftlicher Methoden*, Berlin 1979, 268 (Beihefte zur Zeitschrift für die alttestamentliche Wissenschaft, 149).
[4] The same unspecific usage is true for the Greek terms δουλεια / δουλος and the Latin *servitus* / *servus*, cf. Leonhard Schumacher, *Sklaverei in der Antike, Alltag und Schicksal der Unfreien*, München 2001, 66, and Norbert Brockmeyer, *Antike Sklaverei*, Darmstadt 1979, 85–97 (Erträge der Forschung, 116).

> It can sparsely be disputed, first, that helots were 'collective bondsmen', that is to say, they were a whole population (or populations) subjected to bondage, whereas debt-bondsmen and slaves fell into bondage individually, one by one.[5]

In the case of the Israelites it is a collective dependency, so the term "slavery" is not really appropriate. The Israelites living under Egyptian dominion are neither debt slaves nor purchased slaves. Equally, they are not prisoners of war, since prisoners of war were usually individually submitted to service or sold as slaves but not kept as a collective.[6]

Along with the individual forms, there were several collective forms of dependency. In a broader sense, all towns, villages, tribes, and peoples belonging to a kingdom were in some way subjugated to the monarch. However, a distinction should be made between collectives, which were traditionally part of the kingdom, and those who came under rule by conquest. The latter were often led by governors or vassal kings and were obliged to do corvée and/or pay tributes.

Ex 1:11 provides a first indication of how the status of the Israelites under Egyptian dominion could be classified among the many forms of dependency:

> 1:11 Therefore they [the Egyptians] set corvée masters (*sarey missim*) over them to oppress them with heavy labor (*siblot*). They built supply cities, Pithom and Rameses, for the Pharaoh.

The word *missim* (singular *mas*), which only occurs here in the plural form, always means "forced labour/corvée" of a collective, and it is sometimes metonymically applied to the labouring collective itself. Performers of such corvée may be a tribe (Issachar, Gen 49:15), a town (anonymous, Dt 20:11; Beth-Shemesh, Jdg 1:33; Jerusalem, Lam 1:1), a people (Canaanites, Jos 16:10; 17:13; Jdg 1:28, 30, 35; IKgs 9:15–21; IIChr 8:8; Ammonites, IISam 12:31), or even an entire kingdom, as in the late language of Est 10:1. The epigraphic evidence from the neo-Assyrian empire emphasizes this picture.[7]

---

5 Moses I. Finley, *Ancient Slavery and Modern Ideology*, Princeton 1998 [1980], 139.
6 Schumacher, *Sklaverei* (as in n. 4), 65–90.
7 Prism Nineveh A of King Esarhaddon, II, 80–82; III, 10–19, Otto Kaiser (ed.): TUAT I, 396 (Borger); see also Rykle Borger, *Die Inschriften Asarhaddons, Königs von Assyrien*, Graz 1956, 48–49 (Archiv für Orientforschung, Beiheft 9). See further the Kalah/Nimrud prism of Sargon II., 37–40 (TUAT I, 382), the annals of Sargon II., 16–17 (TUAT I, 379) on Samaria and the Cyprus stele of Sargon II., II 51–65 (TUAT I, 385–386).

Detailed descriptions show that only a small group, and not the whole population, was required to do corvée at one time. 1Kgs 5:27–28 gives an impression of how such labour was executed:[8]

> 5:27 King Solomon conscripted forced labor out of all Israel; the levy numbered thirty thousand men. 28 He sent them to the Lebanon, ten thousand a month in shifts; they would be a month in the Lebanon and two months at home; Adoniram was in charge of the forced labor.

The people or town subjected to this kind of corvée were local static bodies. To carry out corvée their masters did not deport anyone, and the workers were not prisoners or slaves. The conscripted workers of Solomon had to leave their homes temporarily due to the specific nature of the task, but they returned home once their job was done.

The difference between collective and individual dependency becomes apparent in the warfare laws of Deuteronomy. Dt 20:10–15 commands how to deal with towns outside the land:

> 20:10 When you draw near to a town to fight against it, offer it terms of peace. 11 If it accepts your terms of peace and surrenders to you, then all the people in it shall serve you at forced labor.

However, if the town denies the offer, it shall be captured and looted, the male citizens are to be killed: "You may, however, take as your booty the women, the children, livestock, and everything else in the town, all its spoil." (Dt 20:14a). Subsequently, the female war prisoners may be treated like individual slaves. Any of the victorious combatants has the right to take home one of the female war prisoners as his wife. By contrast, the citizens of the surrendered town remain in their residences and then carry out corvée for the Israelites.

Even more instructive is Lam 1:1 where the deprived state of Jerusalem is at issue:

> 1:1 How lonely sits the city that once was full of people! How like a widow she has become, she that was great among the nations! She that was a princess among the provinces has become a vassal.

---

[8] A similar depiction appears in *Prism Niniveh A of Esarhaddon*, see Eckart Otto, "Mose und das Gesetz. Die Mosefigur als Gegenentwurf Politischer Theologie zur neuassyrischen Königsideologie im 7. Jh. v. Chr.", in: *Mose, Ägypten und das Alte Testament*, ed. id., Stuttgart 2000, 43–83, 60 f (Stuttgarter Bibelstudien, 189), and Borger, *Inschriften* (as in n. 7), 60–61.

The initial verses of the first lamentation describe the city of Jerusalem after its capture. The city is left behind "lonely" and abandoned, while the people, the citizens of Jerusalem and the Judeans, were deported to exile (Lam 1:3–5). The status of the deported is not designated by the term *mas* (corvée), neither here nor elsewhere. Instead, the term *mas* is applied to the city left behind. But how can a city devoid or almost devoid of people execute corvée? Of course, the term *mas* is used here metaphorically, but metaphors are meant to succinctly put complex issues into words.

It is uncertain whether the text refers to the situation after the first capture of Jerusalem in 597 BCE or to the situation after the second capture in 587 BCE. Likewise, it is uncertain how Jerusalem rendered the imposed service.[9] The term *mas* here only refers to the juridico-political status, without expressing its practical consequences. The New Revised Standard Version draws the right conclusion despite the lack of clarity and translates *mas* with a politico-legal term: "She [the city of Jerusalem] has become a vassal."

The fact that the term *mas* is used in connection not with deported peoples but with the left-behind city is unambiguous, and for our purpose important. Returning to the Exodus Narrative, the expression used in Ex 1:11 ("corvée masters") seems appropriate, since the story is about a collective, the people of Israel. This people is led into dependency in the place of its sojourn, and right there, where they had been living before, they have to provide forced labour for Egypt.

It is noticeable, and indeed requires explanation, that Israel as a whole is subjugated to corvée. Historical analyses regularly conclude that this depiction cannot be congruent with the historical facts. Rather, those who were residing in Egypt may be defined as "Menschen, die zu den Vorläufern und Vorfahren des späteren Israel gehören".[10] Rainer Albertz speaks about an "Exodusgruppe" as some sort of "Großgruppe".[11] Only over time would the people as a whole have identified themselves with those Egyptian-based precursors and reinterpreted the exodus event as the deliverance of the whole nation.

We cannot verify whether this was ever the case since the Hebrew Bible provides no evidence for an understanding of the exodus, which does not pertain to Israel as a whole. In order to interpret the Exodus Narrative two facts are to be taken seriously: first, in all instances Israel as a whole is at issue. Second, the Israelites do something, which is usually done at a place of residence: they pro-

---

9 See the commentaries on Lam 1:1.
10 Herbert Donner, *Geschichte des Volkes Israel und seiner Nachbarn in Grundzügen*, vol. 1: *Von den Anfängen bis zur Staatenbildungszeit*, Göttingen ³2000, 98 (ATD Erg. 4/1).
11 Rainer Albertz, *Religionsgeschichte Israels in alttestamentlicher Zeit*, vol. 1: *Von den Anfängen bis zum Ende der Königszeit*, Göttingen 1992, 73 (ATD Erg. 8/1).

vide collective forced labour to their overlord. This constellation fits the Judeans of the seventh and sixth centuries very well. There is epigraphical evidence for conscripted labour at the time of King Manasseh, whose workers had to build storehouses in Nineveh.[12] However, the corresponding account in 2Kgs 21:1–18 does not mention it. Following the decline of the Assyrian overlordship, Judah quickly became an Egyptian vassal. This period began, as Bernd Ulrich Schipper has convincingly shown, under Pharaoh Psammetichus I around 615 BCE, thus in the final years of King Josiah.[13] In the aftermath of the campaign of Pharaoh Necho II and the killing of King Josiah, a heavy penalty was imposed on the country and King Jehoiakim took severe measures against the population to collect the tribute (2Kgs 23:33–35). It seems likely that Necho II also commandeered Judean citizens to take part in the building of infrastructures for the shipping canal through the Wadi et-Tumelat. This could explain why the cities of Pithom and Ramses are mentioned and why they are defined as supply cities (Ex 1:11).[14] Finally, one has to think of the Babylonian overlordship, which followed the Egyptian one after the battle of Carchemish in 605 BCE. This period is referred to in the aforementioned words of Lam 1:1 – Jerusalem, the vassal city.

But what does all this mean for the Exodus Narrative? It consistently speaks about Israel as a whole, about the nation as a subject of Egypt, and about the specific form of dependency commonly imposed upon a collective: conscripted labour or corvée respectively. Putting the Egyptianizing setting of the story aside for one moment and focusing on the juridical constellation in terms of the international law modeled in the story, the inevitable conclusion is that the situation of the Judeans of the seventh and sixth centuries is at issue. In other words, the Exodus Narrative reworks the presumably older exodus tradition in a way that allows subjugated Judeans to provide corvée or to pay a penalty tribute in their own country to find a way out of their hardship. Which of the historical overlords appears in the guise of the unnamed Pharaoh – the Assyrian,[15] the Egyptian,[16] or the Babylonian?[17] It could be any of them, but the most

---

12 See Otto, *Mose* (as in n. 8), 59–61.
13 Bernd Ulrich Schipper, "Egypt and the Kingdom of Judah under Josiah and Jehoiakim", in: *Tel Aviv*, 37, 2010, 200–226.
14 See John Van Seters, "The Geography of the Exodus", in: *The Land that I Will Show You. Essays on the History and Archeology of the Ancient Near East in Honour of J. Maxwell Miller*, ed. John Andrew Dearman/Matt Patrick Graham, Sheffield 2001, 255–276 (Journal for the Study of the Old Testament, Supplement Series, 343).
15 See Otto, *Mose* (as in n. 8), 47–67.
16 See Wolfgang Oswald, *Staatstheorie im Alten Israel, Der politische Diskurs im Pentateuch und in den Geschichtsbüchern des Alten Testaments*, Stuttgart 2009, 73–85.

probable seems to be the Egyptian one, for three reasons: first, the overlord of the Exodus Narrative is an Egyptian. Second, the Israelites take part in the works for one of the supply cities, Pithom, which was reconstructed for this purpose in the late seventh century.[18] Third, it is remarkable that of the three hegemonies presented in the book of Kings the Egyptian one is by far the most severe, with the killing of King Josiah, the deportation of King Joahas, the alteration of King Eljakim's name to Zedekiah, and the draconic penalty for the nation.

The Change of Israel's Juridical Status through the Termination of Dependency

How can a people abandon such a dependency, which they experienced as unjust and cruel? The answer is clear: it cannot and it must not. International law of Antiquity does not allow dependents to legally terminate a relation of dependency. Whenever the kings of Israel or Judah revolt against a foreign overlordship it is referred to as a "rebellion" ($\sqrt{mrd}$, 2Kgs 18:7; 24:1, 20) or "conspiracy" ($\sqrt{qšr}$, 1Kgs 15:27; 2Kgs 17:4 and passim), despite the authors, at least in the case of the Judean kings, clearly side with the "rebel" (2Kgs 18:5). Obviously, there is no terminology connoting legitimacy for such a case. Accordingly, none of the ancient vassal treaties known to us contain any sort of opt-out/release clause. It is the exclusive prerogative of the overlord to terminate any dependency.[19]

---

17 See Meik Gerhards, *Die Aussetzungsgeschichte des Mose, Literar- und traditionsgeschichtliche Untersuchungen zu einem Schlüsseltext des nichtpriesterlichen Tetrateuch*, Neukirchen-Vluyn 2006, 252 (Wissenschaftliche Monographien zum Alten und Neuen Testament, vol. 109).
18 See most recently Andrew Collins, "The Biblical Pithom and Tell el-Maskhuta, A Critique of Some Recent Theories on Ex 1,11", in: *Scandinavian Journal of the Old Testament: SJOT*, 22, 2008, 135–149. On the archaeological evidence for the Judean presence in Pithom see John S. Holladay, "Judaeans (and Phoenicians) in Egypt in the Late Seventh to Sixth Centuries B.C.", in: *Egypt, Israel, and the Ancient Mediterranean World, Studies in Honor of Donald B. Redford*, ed. Gary N. Knoppers/Antoine Kirsch, Leiden 2004, 405–437, here 423–424.
19 Texte aus der Umwelt des Alten Testaments (TUAT), Alte Folge, 3 vols., ed. Otto Kaiser, Gütersloh 1982–1997, vol. I/1, 18–19; Martha T. Roth, *Law Collections from Mesopotamia and Asia Minor*, Atlanta ²1997, 16 (Writings from the Ancient World, 6/Society of Biblical Literature, 39). Compare with the prologue of the law code of Lipit-Eshtar of Isin (ca. 1934–1924 BCE): TUAT I/1, 24–25; Roth, ibid., 25, and the Esarhaddon inscription Ass. A. II 37–III 15: Eckart Otto, "Programme der sozialen Gerechtigkeit, Die neuassyrische *(an-)durāru*-Institution sozialen Ausgleichs und das deuteronomische Erlaßjahr in Dtn 15*", in: *Zeitschrift für altorientalische und biblische Rechtsgeschichte*, 3, 1997, 26–63, 46. See also Borger, *Inschriften* (n. 7), 2–3, and the Cyrus Cylinder (TUAT I, 409). More evidence is provided by Otto, *Programme* (as above),

The overlord entitled in the case of the Israelites to command release from dependency is, according to ancient international law, the Pharaoh alone. This is why Moses addresses the Pharaoh with the request "Release my people!" (Ex 5:1; 7:16, 26; 8:16; 9:1, 13; 10:3). Throughout the Hebrew Bible, it is the prerogative of the master to release any dependent subject: King Cyrus releases the deported Israelites from Babel (Is 45:13), and Israelite landlords are to release their slaves in the seventh year (Dt 15:12). No Judean or Israelite king, not even the most powerful one, would have had the right to ignore this prerogative of the overlord, and in any case they would have been under the spell of the treaty oath. The solution introduced by the Exodus Narrative is to bring in firstly the non-royal but also unsuccessful figure of Moses, and secondly and most successfully, Yahweh, the God of Israel, as opponents of the Pharaoh. However, the legitimacy of the God of Israel to challenge the Pharaoh's prerogative is not just a pretention; rather it is demonstrated in the form of the so-called plagues.

Several passages are important for our understanding of the plague narrative and they start with the so-called "recognition formula" in which the objective of the plagues is clarified: the Pharaoh shall recognize the might of Yahweh. While the Pharaoh is sovereign over his country alone, Yahweh owns the whole world (Ex 9:29) and there is nobody like Yahweh on the whole earth (Ex 9:14). Furthermore, Yahweh is like a master in the middle of the land of Egypt (Ex 8:18). The "signs" (Ex 8:19; 10:1–2), as the proverbial plagues are called in the narrative, are meant to signify Yahweh's overlordship over the whole earth, over the entire creation, and hence Yahweh's supremacy over the Pharaoh. As the plagues and the final victory at the Reed Sea evidence this supremacy the exodus has not only been successful, but, more importantly, the duty of loyalty towards the overlord as demanded by international law has not been breached. This god is permitted to do what a vassal king never can. Therefore, termination of the dependency relationship by Israel is not only legitimate but, what is more, it is legal in terms of international law.

To support this main line of narrative argumentation there is a second one intended to demonstrate the legitimacy of the exodus. The plagues also have a temporary effect on the Pharaoh, in so far as they lead him to issue some sort of release edict for the Israelites. Shortly before the exodus, after the killing of the Egyptian firstborn, the Pharaoh declares: "Go, serve the Yahweh, as you said!" (Ex 12:31).

44–46, and Moshe Weinfeld, *Social Justice in Ancient Israel and in the Ancient Near East*, Jerusalem 1995, 78–80.

The legal nature of the Exodus Narrative finally becomes apparent in its final scene. At this point we have to consider the literary history of the text. Elements such as the walls of water (Ex 14:22) and "all of Pharaoh's horses, chariots, and chariot drivers" (Ex 14:23) belong to the priestly layer of the text. Likewise, the terrific showdown when "the waters returned and covered the chariots and the chariot drivers, the entire army of Pharaoh [...]" (Ex 14:28) was only introduced by the priestly writer. The priestly text turns the encounter between Israel and Egypt into a military confrontation, which it had not been previously. The older pre-priestly narrative, what we call the Exodus Narrative, shows no interest in military details and any vividness is entirely lacking. There is no army on one side and no group of refugees on the other, but simply Egypt and Israel, that is two nations. The final statement reads: "And Israel saw Egypt dead on the sea shore." (Ex 14:30) This does not mean that so many Egyptians were dead and so many horsemen and charioteers had drowned, but rather: Egypt as such is dead, Egypt as a political power does not exist anymore. The legitimate overlord, the God of Israel Yahweh, gains predominance over the oppressor, who in turn loses his power.

The Juridical Status of Israel at the End of the Exodus Narrative

How has the juridical status of Israel actually changed? Is it not purely theoretical, given that the new overlord of Israel is said to be its God, Yahweh, and since this god like any god – at least for modern readers – is not a factor in real politics? However, closer inspection shows that the basic principle of this legal constellation is well attested in the Ancient Near East and Mediterranean Antiquity as a real political phenomenon.

As mentioned above, we know of a large number of royal decrees granting a town or a people release from taxes, tributes or corvée, but these decrees are not uniform. Release from this type of obligation may be granted in such a way that the released population is dedicated to serve its god, i.e. the temple of its god. As a general rule this legal construct obliges a collective to pay tributes or to render corvée for a certain temple rather than the king.

A decree of the Kassite King Kurigalzu II (ca. 1345–1324 BCE) can be understood in this sense:

(The king) who established freedom (*andurārum*) for the people of Babylon, freed her people from forced labor (*ilku*) for the sake of the god Marduk, who loves his dynasty.[20]

Moshe Weinfeld summarizes this conventional procedure as it appears from the epigraphical evidence:

> This socio-legal reality, whereby a whole collectivity is freed from the yoke of the king by taking upon itself the yoke of a god, is known to us from Mesopotamian documents dating from the middle of the third millennium B.C.E. [and onwards].[21]

Besides this practice, mainly attested in the ancient Near East, another one is encountered in sources from early Greece, the so-called sacred manumission. Although this custom pertains to individual slaves and not to collectives, it is relevant for our case. Sacred manumission means that a slave is not just released in terms of civil law, rather a deity participates in the procedure. The person to be manumitted is either sold to the deity for a symbolic or real amount of money, or he or she is consecrated to the deity. In some cases, the deity appears as a witness to the release. Furthermore, it is attested that the deity – mediated by a priest – signs the sale contract on behalf of the slave who is not capable of holding rights.[22] All these variations, which are not mutually exclusive, have one goal: they shall make it impossible to re-enslave the manumitted person.

> Der Sinn [...] ist in der besonderen Absicherung des Freilassungsaktes gegen dessen Mißachtung durch die Schutzautorität des Gottes und der für ihn handelnden Priester zu sehen.[23]

---

20 Translation according to Weinfeld, *Social Justice* (as in n. 19), 80, compare Niels Peter Lemche, "Andurārum and Mīšarum: Comments on the Problem of Social Edicts and their Application in the Ancient Near East", in: *Journal of Near Eastern Studies*, 38, 1979, 11–22, 20. Compare further the "Advice to the Prince": Wilfred G. Lambert, *Babylonian Wisdom Literature*, Oxford 1969 (reprint Winona Lake 1996), 110–115. An overview of liberation acts pertaining to temple cities is provided by Weinfeld, *Social Justice* (as in n. 19), 97–101. Another prominent example of this type of release edict is the edict of Artaxerxes in Ezra 7:12–26.
21 Weinfeld, *Social Justice* (as in n. 19), 233.
22 Karl-Dieter Albrecht, *Rechtsprobleme in den Freilassungen der Böotier, Phoker, Dorier, Ost- und Westlokrer, untersucht mit besonderer Berücksichtigung der gemeinschaftlich vorgenommenen Freilassungsakte*, Paderborn 1978 (Rechts- und staatswissenschaftliche Veröffentlichungen der Görres-Gesellschaft, N.F. 26), 324. Note in this context the term "to ransom" (√פדה) in Dt 7:8; 9:26; 13:6; 15:15; 21:8; 24:18.
23 Albrecht, *Rechtsprobleme* (as in n. 23), 323: "The aim (of the sacred manumission) is the enhanced protection of the act of manumission by the protective authority of the deity and the priests acting on behalf of it against any disregard."

Contrary to later Roman practice, freedmen in Greece almost never attained the civil rights of a polis citizen. Instead, they were without legal protection and always in danger of being re-enslaved.[24] For that reason, from the 5th century, temples became more and more engaged in the process of manumission as a religious assurance against re-enslavement. This was also a problem in ancient Judah, as can be understood from the story of revoked manumission in Jer 34 (esp. 34:11).

There are two interesting pieces of evidence from the Jewish colony in Elephantine, Upper Egypt. One is part of a testation of manumission and states: "And you are released from the shade of the sun and (so is) Jeh(o)shima your daughter and another person does not have the right to you and to Jeh(o)shima your daughter but you are released to God."[25] The other one is an adoption document which likewise contains a number of provisions in order to prevent re-enslavement: "And an individual does not have right to brand him or make him a slave, but he shall be my son."[26]

Affiliation with the deity is intended to compensate for the absence of legal security, not in a merely symbolic way but in a direct juridical and political sense, since violation of the status of a freedman, or disregard for the affiliation with a deity, was under sanction. To be in a God's possession meant *de iure* to be a servant of this god, but *de facto* it meant to be free in relation to the citizens of a polis.

Summary

In the light of the practices outlined above, the legal construction of the Exodus Narrative acquires a sharper profile. The argument of the narrative is not a direct adaption of one of these legal remedies, but rather the complete spectrum of legal practices associated with the release from dependency makes up the traditio-historical background on which the Exodus Narrative draws. At the same time, the Exodus Narrative transforms these traditions in order to make its own point. In the edicts from the Ancient Near East the king is, unquestionably,

---

24 Albrecht, *Rechtsprobleme* (as in n. 23), 209–215.
25 Bezalel Porten/Ada Yardeni, *Textbook of Aramaic Documents from Ancient Egypt*, vol. II: Contracts, Jerusalem/Winona Lake 1989, B3.6, lines 9–10, 73, compare *Texte zum Rechts- und Wirtschaftsleben*, ed. Bernd Janowski/Gernot Wilhelm, 263–264 (Texte aus der Umwelt des Alten Testaments, Neue Folge, 1).
26 Porten, *Textbook* (as in n. 25), B3.9, lines 8–9, 85, compare *Texte* ed. Janowski/Wilhelm (as in n. 25), 264–265.

always the sovereign, who establishes order and righteousness by granting freedom to cities and peoples and subsidies to temples and their deities.[27] The Exodus Narrative, on the contrary, depicts the god of Israel whose people are to be released as the one who acts as sovereign, whereas the king who is to release the people loses his sovereignty. The effect is the same, but the distribution of roles is different and so are the claims of legitimacy.

The preponderance of the divine impact, however, does not mean that in the Exodus Narrative the procedure of release from dependency loses its juridical character. It does not advocate some sort of spiritual dominion nor spiritual release from bondage. The manifold practices of sacred manumission and temple-oriented obligations rather show that the Exodus Narrative applies legal constructs in common use that can be politically enforced. The legal claim brought forward time and again in the negotiations with the Pharaoh and finally implemented at the Reed Sea constitutes and reinforces the freedom of Israel: its people are liberated from executing corvée for the foreign overlord and, due to the relationship of service to its god, saved from a return to dependency.

In real politics, release edicts were enforced by military and/or political power, whereas in the world of the authors and addressees of the Exodus Narrative there was no real political power capable of enforcing the Israelite/Judean claim for release. Therefore, in the world of the narrative there are only two possibilities to attain success: either through the Pharaoh's insight, which is the purpose of the plague story, or through God himself, which is the case in the sea miracle.

The author of the Exodus Narrative was realistic in acknowledging that under the overlordship of Pharaoh Necho II, under whose reign it was presumably written (see above), the "manumission" of Israel could not be enforced by military means. Nowadays, justified international legal claimes are executed by means of a UN mandate, a possibility unknown to ancient people. In the Exodus Narrative the God of Israel fulfills this function.

---

27 Stefan M. Maul, "Der assyrische König – Hüter der Weltordnung", in: *Gerechtigkeit. Richten und Retten in der abendländischen Tradition und ihren altorientalischen Ursprüngen*, ed. Jan Assmann/Bernd Janowski/Michael Welker, München 1998, 65–77.

Kära L. Schenk
The Exodus Narrative and Divine Warfare in the Dura-Europos Synagogue

The painted cycle of images on the walls of the Dura-Europos synagogue, originally located in eastern Syria and dated between 244 and 245 CE, represents the most extensive example of Jewish pictorial narrative in the ancient world.[1] The synagogue's decoration included a prominent depiction of the Exodus from Egypt. I argue that this image should be understood as a battle scene in which Israel's divine king defeats the Egyptians. The Exodus panel is part of a larger narrative sequence encompassing the upper and middle level of panels in the synagogue, and it is one of many references to battle in the synagogue's decoration. Whereas some have argued that the use of Roman imagery in such battle scenes was designed to equate the Romans with the ancient enemies of

---

[1] For the initial report on the synagogue and its frescoes, see Carl H. Kraeling, "The Synagogue", in: *The Excavations at Dura-Europos Conducted by Yale University and the French Academy of Inscriptions and Letters*, ed. Michael I. Rostovtzeff et al, New Haven/CT 1936, 337–83. For a more comprehensive discussion of the site and the synagogue, see Carl H. Kraeling, *The Synagogue: The Excavations at Dura–Europos*, Final Report VIII, Part I, New Haven/CT 1956. In addition to Kraeling's final report, the following studies consider the question of the decorative cycle as a whole: Michael I. Rostovtzeff, *Dura-Europos and Its Art*, Oxford 1938; Robert Comte du Mesnil du Buisson, *Les Peintures de la synagogue de Doura-Europos 245–256 Après J.-C.*, Rome 1939; André Grabar, "Le theme religieux des fresques de la synagogue de Doura (245–256 apres J.-C.)", in: *Revue de l'histoire des religions*, 123 (2–3), 1941, 143–192 and 124 (1), 1941, 5–35; Isaac Sonne, "The Paintings of the Dura Synagogue", in: *Hebrew Union College Annual*, 20, 1947, pp 255–362; Eleazar L. Sukenik, *The Synagogue of Dura-Europos and Its Paintings*, Jerusalem 1947; Rachel Wischnitzer, *The Messianic Theme in the Paintings of the Dura Synagogue*, Chicago 1948; Erwin R. Goodenough, *Jewish Symbols in the Greco–Roman Period*, 13 vols, New York 1953–68 (Bollingen Series, 37), esp. vols. IX–XI; Joseph Gutmann, "Programmatic Painting in the Dura Synagogue", in: *The Dura–Europos Synagogue: A Re-Evaluation (1932–72)*, ed. Joseph Gutmann, Missoula/MT 1973, 137–154; Kurt Weitzmann and Herbert Kessler, *The Frescoes of the Dura Synagogue and Christian Art*, Washington, DC 1990, 151–183; Warren Moon, "Nudity and Narrative: Observations on the Synagogue Paintings from Dura-Europos", in: *Polykleitos, the Doryphoros, and Tradition*, ed. Warren Moon, Madison 1995, 283–316 [originally published as Warren Moon, "Nudity and Narrative: Observations on the Frescoes from the Dura Synagogue", in: *Journal of the American Academy of Religion* 60, 1992, 587–658]; Annabel J. Wharton, "Good and Bad Images from the Synagogue of Dura Europos: Contexts, Subtexts, Intertexts", in: *Art History*, 17, 1994, 1–25; Id., *Refiguring the Post Classical City. Dura Europos, Jerash, Jerusalem and Ravenna*, Cambridge 1995, 38–51; Shula Laderman, "A New Look at the Second Register of the West Wall in Dura Europos", in: *Cahiers Archeologiques*, 45, 1997, 5–18; Steven Fine, *Art and Judaism in the Greco-Roman World: Toward a New Jewish Archaeology*, Cambridge 2005, 172–183.

Israel (the Egyptians in the case of the Exodus), I will argue that the synagogue decoration co-opts Roman imagery in order to present Israel's divine king, rather than the Roman emperor, as the victor in the narrative. The ultimate polemic function of the narrative relates to its focus on Jerusalem, the contested former site of the Jewish Temple that was occupied by the Romans in the third century.

The Exodus as a Battle Scene

The Exodus panel, based on the events described in the fourteenth chapter of the Book of Exodus, is located on the upper right corner of the west wall in the assembly hall in the Dura-Europos Synagogue. I will argue that the panel is divided into two main sections: the moment when the Egyptians overtake the Israelites at the shore of the Red Sea (to the right, fig. 1) and the parting of the Red Sea, when the Israelites crossed over in safety while the Egyptians drowned (to the left, fig. 2). In doing so, I will challenge key aspects of Carl Kraeling's 1956 final report on the synagogue[2] in order to emphasize the significance of divine participation in this unconventional battle scene.

Moses is the dominant character in the right half of the panel (fig. 1), identified by an Aramaic dipinto as "Moses, when he went out from Egypt and cleft the sea."[3] He dwarfs the figures behind him, a row of twelve men who represent the tribal leaders of Israel. A group of still smaller armed men stands beneath the leaders. The image follows a translation in which the text of Ex 13:18 is rendered "and the children of Israel went up *armed* out of the land of Egypt," rather than "to the *fifth* generation."[4] A row of figures beneath the soldiers themselves consists of civilians, carrying silver to indicate the "plundering of the Egyptians" (Ex 11:2; 12:35–36), and the unleavened dough that they were to take with them out of Egypt (Ex 12:34).[5] Finally, one Israelite leads his son by the hand; perhaps, as Kraeling suggests, this is the son to whom the narrative should be recounted during the feast of Unleavened Bread (Ex 13:3–8).[6]

---

[2] Kraeling, *The Synagogue: The Excavations* (as in n. 1), 74–86, for a full discussion of the Exodus narrative at Dura.
[3] Ibid., 78 and 269.
[4] This translation is found in the Jerusalem Talmud (Y. *Shab.* 6:4), in Targum Onkelos on Genesis, and referred to as a possible translation in the Mekhilta. "To the fifth generation" is found in the Septuagint, Josephus, and other of the Targumin, as well as in Christian texts (such as Eusebius).
[5] Kraeling, *The Synagogue: The Excavations* (as in n. 1), 79.
[6] Ibid., 79–80.

Fig. 1: The Exodus from Egypt, right side of painted panel, 244–245, Dura-Europos Synagogue

Fig. 2: The Exodus from Egypt, left side of painted panel, 244–245, Dura-Europos Synagogue

Another armed group appears directly above. Although Kraeling saw no difference between the two groups of soldiers, identifying both "armies" as Israelite soldiers flanking the elders in their midst, [7] the division between the army above, on the one hand, and the elders, second army, and civilians, on the other, is clear because the legs and feet of the first army's soldiers are visible behind the three groups massed together below. I propose that this second army represents the Egyptians pursuing the Israelites to the shores of the Red Sea. Exodus 14:10–11a records that "[…] the Israelites looked up, and there were the Egyptians, marching after them. They were terrified and cried out to the Lord. They said to Moses, 'Was it because there were no graves in Egypt that you brought us to the desert to die?'" In response to their complaints, Moses answered, "Do not be afraid. Stand firm and you will see the deliverance the Lord will bring you today. The Egyptians you see today you will never see again. The Lord will fight for you" (vs. 13–14). The idea that the Israelites have been overtaken by the shores of the Red Sea sets up my reading of other elements on the right side of the painting. Here, I draw on ideas from Andre Grabar's early suggestions in connection to midrashic sources.[8]

For instance, one way to identify the structure on the right side of the panel is simply to think of it as Egypt in general, with the open doors suggesting the Israelites' flight from Egypt. Kraeling proposed that the statue mounted over the doorway, holding a globe and flanked by winged victories, was a Roman imperial image designating the structure as one of the "royal" cities of Pharaoh.[9] However, in a second possible interpretation that Kraeling had rejected,[10] Grabar had argued that the structure could be understood in light of a reading of Exodus 14:9, which describes how the Israelites were encamped by the Red Sea, specifically "by Pi-hahiroth, in front of Baal-Zephon." The text of the Mekhilta and of the Targum Pseudo-Jonathan interpret Pi-hahiroth as the location where they had camped and Baal-Zephon as an idol of the Egyptians.[11] Grabar thus argued that the structure in the Dura panel represents the city of Pi-hahiroth, with the statue over the gate representing the idol Baal-Zephon.[12]

---

7 Kraeling, *The Synagogue* 1956 (as in n. 1), 80–81.
8 Grabar, Le theme religieux des fresques, 123 (2–3), 1941 (as in n. 1), 146–148.
9 Kraeling, *The Synagogue* 1956 (as in n. 1), 78.
10 Ibid., 77.
11 Mekhilta, *Beshallah* 3:8–10 (ed. Lauterbach, I:205–206). The fifteenth-century Alba Bible (Madrid, Palacio de Liria, no. 399) of Castile represents an intriguing parallel to this imagery. Under the advisement of R. Moses Arragel of Guadalajara, the illuminators of this Christian book included a number of midrashic legends in their illustrations of the text. These include the depiction of Ba'al Zephon as an idol at the edge of the sea (fol. 68 v). See Carl Otto Nordström, The *Duke of Alba's Castilian Bible. A Study of the Rabbinical Features of the Miniatures*, Uppsala1967, 88–93 and fig. 41.
12 Grabar, Le Thème, 123 (2–3), 1941 (as in n. 1), 147–148.

If the gate locates the armies specifically at Pi-hahiroth at the shore of the sea, it may help to explain the position of the pillars of cloud and fire in the panel. The pillars, shown in the panel as Corinthian columns of red and black, represent the divine presence in the Exodus narrative. Whereas normally, according to the text of Exodus, one of these pillars went ahead of the Israelites to guide them (first through the sea and then through the Sinai Wilderness), in the image the pillars are located to the right, "behind" the Israelites. However, it is just at the moment that the Egyptians overtake the Israelites, and that Moses is commanded to lift his staff and part the sea, that the pillars withdraw behind the Israelites to protect them from the approaching Egyptians (Ex 14:19–20). This reading would integrate the pillars into the scene with Moses and the Israelites at the Red Sea in a more meaningful fashion.

Finally, the withdrawal of the pillars behind the Israelites to protect them at Pi-hahiroth would also explain the function of the red and white spots depicted above them. Both Kraeling[13] and Kurt Weitzmann[14] have argued that these elements represent the seventh plague against the Egyptians mentioned earlier in the Exodus account. But it would be arbitrary to show only this plague. I would propose instead that the fire and hail are aligned with the pursuing Egyptian forces to suggest the divine power that fights against them, as promised by Moses. Exodus 14:24 recounts how when the Egyptians tried to follow the Israelites into the sea, "the Lord in the pillar of fire and cloud looked down upon the Egyptian army, and threw the Egyptian army into panic." The Mekhilta elaborates on the contrast between divine power and the Egyptians against which the Lord would fight in Exodus 14 by using the poetic description of Psalm 18:13: "'His thick clouds' as against their squadrons; 'hailstones,' as against their catapults; 'coals,' as against their missiles; 'fire' as against their naphtha."[15] Targum Pseudo-Jonathan likewise expands on the same passage to recount how "the Lord looked forth with anger upon the hosts of the Egyptians from the column of fire, to hurl upon them flakes of fire and hail, and from the column of the cloud and confounded the hosts of the Egyptians." Although Kraeling pointed out that the Exodus relates how the Lord threw the Egyptians into a panic *when they entered the sea*,[16] the Mekhilta specifies that Moses caused the Israelites to see the hail and fire *at the moment when they cry out to him* at Pi-hariroth: "And so also here Moses prayed *at that moment* and God caused them to see

---

13 Kraeling, *The Synagogue: The Excavations* (as in n. 1), 75.
14 Weitzmann, *The Frescoes of the Dura Synagogue* (as in n. 1), 39–41.
15 Mekhilta, *Beshallah* 3:105 (ed. Lauterbach, I:212).
16 Kraeling, *The Synagogue: The Excavations* (as in n. 1), 77–78, and see 77, note 226.

squadrons upon squadrons of ministering angels standing before them. And thus it says: 'At the brightness before Him, there passed through His thick clouds, hailstones and coals of fire' (Ps 18:13)".[17] Thus, there are three armies aligned at the shores of the Red Sea: the terrified Israelites, who will not actually be called to fight; the Egyptians who pursue them; and the divine hosts of heaven (represented by the fire and hail) through whom the Egyptians will come to grief in the "battle" proper, as they falter in the sea.

The next half of the panel (fig. 2) represents the final outcome of the "battle" between the armies. A vertical line before Moses marks the beginning of the Red Sea. In this body of water the Egyptian army is engulfed by waves and surrounded by leaping fish. The drowning Egyptians are utterly helpless; they are shown without the weapons, horses and chariots that the Exodus text mentions and many seem to have been stripped of their clothing as well.[18] A second image of Moses (whose name is given again in Aramaic) is now shown looking backward over the sea as he extends his staff to indicate the means through which the army has been drowned. Moses is then shown a third time to the left, accompanied by a third Aramaic dipinto, "Moses, when he cleft the sea." He seems to touch the water below him with the end of his staff and, above, the Israelite "army" crosses through the sea on dry land, over twelve individual paths made for each of the tribes. A strip of sea with fish below indicates the wall of water on one side of the Israelites and a corresponding strip in the poorly preserved upper area seems to demarcate the wall on the other side. Kraeling read the events as out of order: the Egyptians are drowned first, and then the Israelites cross.[19] However, we might see the final half of the panel as taking place within one large representation of the sea. To the far left, the Israelites are not making their first tentative entry into the sea from the shore but are now crossing over on the dry bed in the middle of the sea. This same sea is closing in behind them, engulfing and drowning the pursuing Egyptian army. The twelve tribal elders, now carrying standards, lead a victorious army out of the sea.

---

17 Mekhilta, *Beshallah* 3:104–106 (ed. Lauterbach, I:212–213).
18 The nakedness of the defeated enemy was a standard convention for representing their complete humiliation as far back as Sumerian representations of battle such as the Standard of Ur or the Stele of the Vultures. For a description of these battle narratives, see Irene Winter, "After the Battle Is Over: 'The Stele of the Vultures' and the Beginning of Historical Narrative in the Art of the Ancient Near East", in: *Pictorial Narrative in Antiquity and the Middles Ages*, ed. Herbert L. Kessler/Marianna S. Simpson, Washington DC 1985, 16–21 (Studies in the History of Art, 16). As Kraeling has noted, the nakedness of the drowning Egyptians in particular is a theme found in Exodus Rabbah, an Amoraic midrash, as well. Kraeling, *The Synagogue: The Excavations* (as in n. 1), 83, see note 248.
19 Kraeling, *The Synagogue: The Excavations* (as in n.1), 86.

Above Moses' head, the hand of God reaches down to indicate the power through which this act of redemption has been accomplished. The motif of the divine hand does not appear in the prose account of Exodus 14, but makes multiple appearances in Exodus 15, a poem sung by the victorious Israelites. Verses 3–6 are particularly relevant:

> The Lord is a warrior;
> > the Lord is his name.
> Pharaoh's chariots and his army he cast into the sea;
> > his picked officers were sunk in the Red Sea.
> The floods covered them;
> > they went down into the depths like a stone.
> Your right hand, O Lord, glorious in power –
> > your right hand, O Lord, shattered the enemy.

The divine hand appears again over the third image of Moses. Here, however, the hand is turned with the palm turned towards the viewer and seems to have a demonstrative function, indicating the outcome of the narrative in the victory of Israel's army. Although the figure of Moses is larger than all the others in the panel, his heroic presence is qualified through the inclusion of the columns, fire and hail, and divine hand, indicating the real power that defeated the Egyptians. Without creating an "image" of Israel's god, the painters of the Exodus scene have used symbolic means to present him as the main actor in the battle.

The Exodus and Divine Warfare in the Dura Synagogue's Decoration

The Exodus panel is part of a larger decorative cycle painted on the walls of the Dura Synagogue's assembly hall (see view of west wall, fig. 3). In its final phase, the synagogue's decoration included a Torah shrine (fig. 10) and central images (constituting the so-called "reredos" or central images and the "wing panels" flanking to the right and left) and the three levels of narrative panels on the surrounding walls (see plan of synagogue decoration, fig. 4, for location of panels to be discussed). However, approximately one third of the decorative cycle has been destroyed and the Exodus panel is one of only three remaining panels on the upper level. To the right of the Exodus, on the north wall, is a panel with Jacob's vision of the heavenly ladder at Bethel, drawn from Genesis and preceding the

Exodus chronologically.[20] On the other side of the central images, also on the upper level, there is a fragmentary narrative panel featuring the enthroned King Solomon.[21] If read from right to left, there is obviously a large chronological jump between the Exodus and the episode associated with Solomon. However, the panels depicting Jacob at Bethel and the Exodus on the upper level actually constitute a narrative prelude to a cycle of panels depicting the journey of the Ark of the Covenant from Sinai to Zion that encircles the middle level. The pillars, hail and fire, and miraculous hands that represented divine presence and power in the Exodus narrative disappear on the middle level to be replaced by the Ark of the Covenant. The Ark first appears in the sanctuary of the Tabernacle constructed in the Sinai Wilderness in the panel to the left of the Torah shrine and central panels. Moses and the twelve tribal representatives, who had just crossed the Red Sea in the Exodus panel, reappear in a panel to the immediate left, where they surround the miraculous well in the courtyard of the Tabernacle and offer prayer. Thus, the Exodus is not an isolated event, but part of the larger flow of Israel's historical narrative as presented on the surrounding walls. The pair of panels with the Tabernacle and Well is drawn from passages in the Pentateuch and thus presents the earliest phases of a chronological sequence that will continue on the middle level and end with an image of the Jerusalem Temple constructed by Solomon, the final destination for the Ark.[22] The narrative then continues with Solomon enthroned on the upper left. If we extend the narrative sequence backward and forward on the upper level, the pattern of the remaining panels suggests that the lost episodes would have taken place before Jacob's Vision, to the right, and after Solomon's reign, to the left. The remaining panels of the upper two levels appear to form a folded and (now) fragmentary figure-eight with episodes spanning the biblical narrative from Genesis to Kings.[23]

---

20 See Kraeling, *The Synagogue: The Excavations* (as in n. 1), 70–74 for a discussion of the panel, and for earlier references.

21 Ibid., 88–93. The precise identification of the scene is open for question; however, the association with Solomon is based on a Greek rendering of his name on the panel itself. See discussion: ibid., 279.

22 For the general structure of the middle level, see: Gutmannn, "Programmatic Painting" (as in n. 1), *passim* and, more recently, Kära Schenk, "Temple, Community, and Sacred Narrative in the Dura-Europos Synagogue", in: *Association for Jewish Studies Review*, 34 (2), 2010, 195–229. For the identification of the final panel as the Temple in Jerusalem, see in particular ibid., 217–221.

23 Many publications consider the overall structure of the synagogue decoration (or lack thereof). See, in particular, Gutmann, "Programmatic Painting" (as in n. 1); Wharton, "Good and Bad Images" (as in n. 1) and Fine, *Art and Judaism* (as in n. 1), 172–183. To my knowledge, I am the only one to propose that the remaining panels on the surrounding walls of the upper two levels

Fig. 3: Dura-Europos Synagogue, composite view of west wall of assembly hall, 244–245

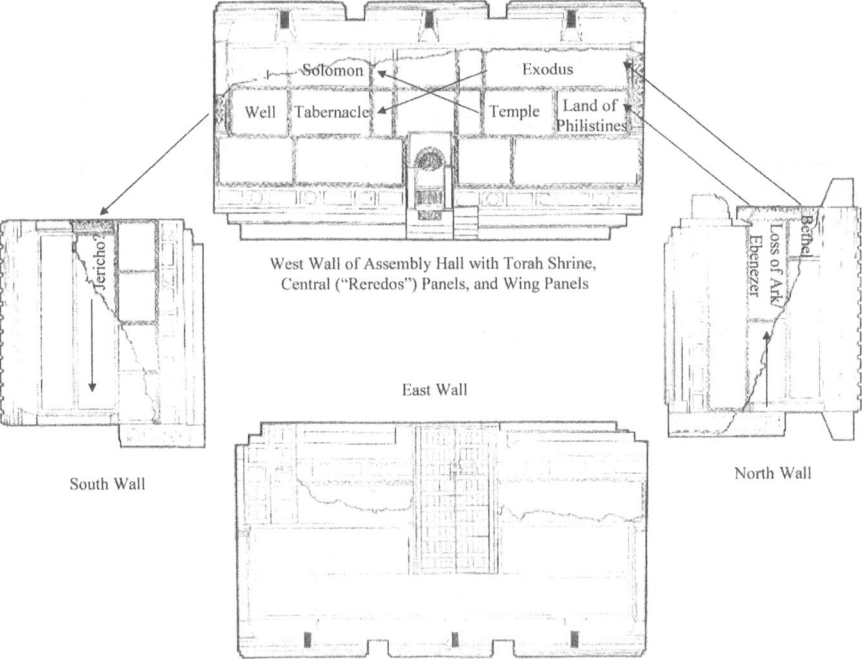

Fig. 4: Four plans of the Dura-Europos Synagogue wall paintings, grouped together and modified through the addition of labels

Some of the remaining episodes on the middle level continue the theme of divine warfare found in the Exodus. For instance, around the corner on the south wall and to the left of the panels set in the Sinai Wilderness on the middle level,

---

form a chronological continuous series, intersecting at the center of the west wall, which might plausibly be reconstructed as a selective history of Israel from Genesis to the Exile.

we see the tail-end of a procession with the Ark in a panel that has only been partially preserved (fig. 5). I would identify this fragmentary procession as the Battle of Jericho. Though several Ark-related processions have been suggested for the panel, only two episodes (the Battle of Jericho and the Crossing of the Jordan) would fit chronologically between the scenes in the Sinai Wilderness to the right and the next remaining narrative after the lacuna in middle level (the Battle of Ebenezer).[24] A detail in the fragmentary procession may link the panel with Jericho. Kraeling has noted that one figure in the procession carries a lulav bundle for the feast Sukkot and removes the willow branch from the bundle, pointing it toward the ground.[25] According to the Mishnah, there were processions around the altar every day of Sukkot while the Temple stood. On *Hoshanah Rabbah* (the seventh and last day of the feast), participants would make seven processions around the altar, blowing the *shofar* as part of the procession.[26] The Tosefta describes how participants would beat the willow branches against the ground after finishing the seventh circuit on the seventh day.[27] The ceremony suggests a correlation to the Battle of Jericho (Jsh 6:3–4), where seven priests were each to blow a *shofar*, circling Jericho once a day for six days and seven times on the seventh day as they carried the Ark of the Covenant. This connection is made explicit in the Jerusalem Talmud when, in reference to the sevenfold circuits on the feast's seventh day, it notes, "This is a memorial to Jericho."[28]

If the victorious battle was once shown on the south wall, it would represent an inversion of the scene shown on the opposite wall of the middle level, where

---

24 The object carried in procession is generally identified as the Ark of the Covenant. However, Wischnitzer has also suggested that the panel represented the movement of Joseph's bones from Egypt. See: *The Messianic Theme* (as in n. 1), 53–55. Kraeling argued that the panel depicted the consecration of the Temple under Solomon; see Kraeling, *The Synagogue* 1956 (as in n. 1), 113–117, and Kurt Weitzmann argued that the panel presented David dancing before the Ark as it was brought into Jerusalem; see Weitzmann, *The Frescoes of the Dura Synagogue* (as in n. 1), 94–98. Gutmann proposed that the panel once depicted the crossing of the Jordan. See Gutmann, "Programmatic Painting" (as in n. 1), 141. As far as I know, I am the only one to suggest Jericho as a serious possibility.
25 Kraeling, *The Synagogue: The Excavations* (as in n. 1), 117, note 396.
26 M. *Suk.* 4:5; Y. *Suk.* 4:1–3; The Babylonian Talmud records differing opinions as to whether the participants placed the branches at the altar and then made the processions or, instead, made the processions while carrying the branches and then stacked them before the altar. B. *Suk.* 43b.
27 Whereas the Mishnah refers only to beating the palm branches (*lulavim*) at the conclusion of this rite (M. *Suk.* 4:6), the Tosefta specifically refers to the "beating of willows" (T. *Suk.* 3:1d), a custom practiced on *Hoshanah Rabbah* to this day.
28 Y. *Suk.* 4:3:6b.

Fig. 5: Battle of Jericho(?), painted panel, 244–245, Dura-Europos Synagogue

the Ark narrative resumes with panels drawn from the book of Samuel.[29] The first clearly identifiable panel is the Battle of Ebenezer (fig. 6), in which two wicked priests decided to take the Ark into battle with the Philistines, believing that this talisman would bring them victory. But the Philistines defeated the Israelites, captured the Ark, and carried it off the battle field. The capture of the Ark is represented in the next panel (fig. 7), which is clearly paired with the scene on the opposite wall (fig. 5) that I have identified as the procession of the Ark during the Battle of Jericho. At Ebenezer, the priests Ark believed that the Ark would automatically grant them victory. Although they looked back to battles like Jericho as a precedent for their expectations, their own attempts to use the Ark as a tool rather than relying on divine power and initiative resulted in defeat.

However, as the narrative continues around the corner on the west wall, subsequent episodes affirm the divine power represented by the Ark in a way that distinguishes this power as greater than the might of both the Israelites and

---

29 For a discussion of the narrative sequence on this part of the west wall, see Kraeling, *The Synagogue: The Excavations* (as in n. 1), pp 93 f.

Fig. 6: Battle of Ebenezer, painted panels, 244–245, Dura-Europos Synagogue

Fig. 7: Loss of the Ark of the Covenant, painted panels, 244–245, Dura-Europos Synagogue

the Philistines. Here, the Philistines place the Ark in their temple only to wake on two successive mornings to find the idol of their god Dagon fallen and (on the second morning) broken (fig. 8). To the left of the panel, the Philistines send the Ark away on a cart and the milk kine draw it back towards Israel. In its wake, the Ark leaves behind the empty Philistine temple and pedestal, as well as two images of the broken idol on the ground. Whereas the scene of battle on the north wall is a more conventional conflict between two human armies (Israelite and Philistine), Kraeling has also pointed out that the two destroyed idols are accompanied by a number of scattered liturgical elements in a way that is similar to the scattering of a defeated enemy's weapons after a battle.[30] If this is the case, then the Ark has defeated the idol in "battle," ultimately victorious even as the Philistines had initially claimed victory in the scene before. This image of divine (rather than human triumph) is shown directly below the Exodus scene and echoes the theme of divine warfare that I explored in the previous section.

Fig. 8: The Ark in the Land of the Philistines, painted panel, 244 – 245, Dura-Europos Synagogue

The theme of warfare between Israel and surrounding nations would certainly have had resonance for a community that had mounted two major revolts against the Romans in the first and second centuries and suffered crushing defeats in both cases. Given recent events, some scholars have speculated that

---

30 Kraeling, *The Synagogue* 1956 (as in n. 1), 103.

Roman details in the Dura synagogue paintings might connect Israel's historical and contemporary enemies as part of an intentionally constructed pictorial polemic. For instance, Warren Moon has observed that the gate in the lower right hand corner of the Exodus scene (representing either Egypt or the last stop in Egypt) is depicted using Roman iconographical sources, which he describes in the following manner: "Winged Victories, as we see them here, lightly perched on globes, are a familiar Roman symbol for world dominion; Mars, carrying orb and spear, completes the triumphal message."[31] Moon goes on to argue that the use of such Roman elements in connection to Egypt creates a link between the Egyptians in the narratives and the Romans who had more recently defeated Israel in battle and destroyed their temple in Jerusalem. Moon also argues that the Philistine idol toppled by the Ark in the panel below would have been read in connection to imperial cult statues and that the destruction of the idol hinted at a kind of anti-imperial polemic as well.[32] This reading has been repeated, though not unequivocally endorsed, by Jaś Elsner,[33] who writes of the synagogue painting's "active and aggressive commentary on local religion, in which the pagan Durenes – possibly even the Romans – appear in the role of contemporary Philistines [...]."[34]

However, the significant problem with this argument is that Roman iconographical sources do not seem to have been used in an internally consistent manner to suggest a polemic function. Winged nikes appear as the acroteria on the Tabernacle of Aaron, for instance, where their presence presumably does not imply an imperial reference or critique. It is more likely that the elements were drawn from among the repertoire of standard architectural decoration that the artists themselves included to depict the gate of a city. Moreover, though the Philistine idol in the paintings may have resembled some of the cult statues in the city of Dura,[35] a connection to imperial cult statues in the

---

[31] Moon, "Nudity and Narrative" (as in n. 1), 294.
[32] Ibid., 299.
[33] Jaś Elsner, "Cultural Resistance and the Visual Image: The Case of Dura Europos", in: *Classical Philology*, 96 (3), 2001, 282–283.
[34] Jaś Elsner, *Roman Eyes: Visuality and Subjectivity in Art and Text*, Princeton/NJ 2007, 277–278.
[35] Dagon shows some resemblance to the depiction of the god Aphlad in his posture, in the standard that he holds, and in his garment. See plate I/1 in Susan B. Downey, *The Stone and Plaster Sculpture. The Excavations at Dura-Europos Conducted by Yale University and the French Academy of Inscriptions and Letters*, Final Report III, Part I, Fascicle 2, Los Angeles 1977. He is also similar to depictions of Arsu, ibid., pl. XI/42. An image of the Palmyrene god Iarhibol, though cuirassed, resembles Dagon because he is standing and holding a staff and is beardless;

city is weak both in terms of the appearance of the idol[36] and the theme of the narrative, which is unrelated to ruler cult. In the multicultural environment of the city of Dura, it is difficult to determine that "Roman details" must have a Roman political target, any more than the Persian clothes worn by Aaron and his sons in the Tabernacle, or by kings (Israelite or other) throughout the synagogue decoration must have served to praise or condemn Persian power or culture. Along these lines, there is little to suggest that the Israelite characters in the paintings were portrayed using a specifically "Jewish" set of iconographical or stylistic elements that would set them apart in a corresponding fashion. For instance, the Israelite elders who emerge triumphantly from the Red Sea (fig. 2) carry standards quite similar to the *vexilla* of the Roman army in numerous triumphal monuments (see fig. 9). In this way, the Israelites, too, resemble Romans. We do not find a systematic language of defamation in the paintings, equating the use of Roman (or Persian) motifs with the biblical enemies of Israel.

If we are to think of Roman iconographical borrowings in terms of polemic function, we should instead consider how the message of Roman triumphal monuments has been appropriated and subverted.[37] In such monuments the re-

---

ibid., pl. XII/47. Dagon is closest in appearance to some examples of unidentified gods wearing civilian dress, but carrying a staff and sword. See ibid., pl. XV/52–53 and pl. XVI/54.

36 There were statues to the emperor at Dura. Susan Downey describes an inscription, probably from the late second century CE from the Temple of Zeus Megistos, which "apparently records a dedication to an unknown emperor, whose statue probably stood on the podium". Ibid., 149. In the Temple of Bel, she found a late second century CE plinth to support "a statue or statues" along with a fragment of a life-sized bronze foot and silver radiate crown. The plinth was inscribed with a dedication by the XX Palmyrene cohort and, according to Downey, was large enough to support, "at least two statues, perhaps of Septimius Severus and his sons or of Caracalla and Geta," 150. According to Thomas Pekáry, images in the wall painting from the temple dedicated to Bel may have depicted imperial statues. See:"Das Opfer vor dem Kaiserbild", in: *Bonner Jahrbücher*, 186, 1986, 91–103, here 101–102. However, none of these images is similar to the figure of Dagon in any particular fashion.

37 Thus, André Grabar's assessment that "[...] la décoration de Doura me semble avoir été ordinée sur le modèle des grande compositions triomphales de l'art monarchique [...]" may be correct, at least broadly speaking. See Grabar, "Le thème" (as in n. 1), 34. We know that the Romans had been commissioning monuments at Dura since their arrival in the second century CE: the remains of a triumphal arch before the city walls attest to their presence at this time. Moon notes that "The Triumphal arch erected by Trajan's troops c. 115–17 A.D., on the desert road west of the city gate, is one of the most important fixed points for the chronology of the city, as A.R. Bellinger has proven," in: "Nudity and Narrative" (as in n. 1), 285. For the arch, see *The Excavations at Dura-Europos*, Report IV, New Haven/CT 1931, 56–65 and Robert O. Fink, "An Addition to the Inscription of the Arch of Trajan (Rep. IV, no. 167)", in: *The Excavations at Dura-Europos*, Final Report VI, New Haven/CT 1949, 480–482. The Mithraeum at Dura is also associated with the coming of the Romans. For the Dura *mithraeum*, see "The Mithraeum", in:

Fig. 9: *Profectio* and *Adventus* (above), Galerius Crowned by an Eagle (below), detail, north face of south pier from the Arch of Galerius, 300, Thessalonica

peated focus of the narrative is the figure of the emperor himself.[38] In the Arch of Galerius, for instance, the narrative panels (fig. 9) showing the *profectio* and *adventus* (above) and Galerius crowned by an eagle during his combat with the Per-

---

The Excavations at Dura-Europos. Preliminary Report of the Seventh and Eighth Seasons of Work 1933–1934 and 1934–1935, ed. Michael I. Rostovtzeff/Frank E. Brown/Charles Bradford Welles, New Haven/CT 1939, 62–134. In addition, see Pekáry, "Das Opfer" (as in n. 36), *passim* for a discussion of the paintings added to the Bel Temple in 239 CE for Julius Terentius, tribune of the Twentieth Palmyrene Cohort that was stationed at Dura. For a close Roman parallel to the Dura synagogue outside the city of Dura itself, consider the imperial monument in Luxor, Egypt. For Luxor, see Johannes Deckers, "Die Wandmalerei des tetrarchischen Lagerheiligtums im Ammon-Temple von Luxor", in: *Römische Quartalschrift*, 68, 1973, pp 1–34; Iole Kalavrezou-Maxeiner, "The Imperial Chamber at Luxor", in: *Dumbarton Oaks Papers*, 29, 1975, 227–251; and Johannes Deckers, "Die Wandmalerei im Kaiserkultraum von Luxor", in: Jahrbuch *des* Deutschen Archäologischen Instituts, 94, 1979, 600–652.

38 Richard Brilliant, *Visual Narratives: Storytelling in Roman and Etruscan Art*, Ithaca/NY 1984, 90–123.

sian king (below) are two of many scenes in which the emperor (or the emperor and his tetrarchic co-rulers), is enlarged to suggest his importance as the main character.[39] The oversized figure of Moses who appears three times in the Exodus panel (as well as in additional scenes in the middle level) could be understood as a Jewish answer to the figure of the emperor. However, Moses' power is qualified in the Exodus scene through the inclusion of the divine hand and it is the repeated intervention of the divine presence (represented by the columns, fire and hail, divine hand, and – especially – the Ark of the Covenant in the middle level) that ties the narrative as a whole together. Interestingly, the scene of David dancing with the Ark into the city of Jerusalem is not represented on the middle level following the Ark's departure from the land of the Philistines.[40] Rather a depiction of the Temple of Jerusalem alone, ready to receive the Ark when it arrives, appears to the left of the panel. This omission effectively deemphasizes the human agency of Israel's king and elevates the Ark itself as a central actor in the narrative. The synagogue's narrative does not connect Israel's historical and contemporary enemies so much as it presents Israel's divine king in the place reserved for the Roman emperor in comparable monuments throughout the empire.

Worship and Warfare in the Synagogue Liturgy

The most powerful aspect of anti-Roman polemic in the synagogue was the liturgical function of the decoration and its ultimate focus on the contested site of the Jerusalem Temple itself. Liturgical engagement with the Exodus narrative would have encouraged identification between contemporary Jews and biblical Israelites (regardless of their appearance in the synagogue decoration). According to the Mishnah:

> In every generation a man must so regard himself as if he came forth out of Egypt, for it is written, *And thou shalt tell thy son in that day saying, It is because of that which the Lord did for me when I came forth from Egypt.* Therefore are we bound to give thanks, to praise, to

---

39 For this panel in particular, see Hans Peter Laubscher, *Der Reliefschmuck des Galeriusbogens in Thessaloniki*, Berlin 1975, 36–38, and Sabine MacCormack, *Art and Ceremony in Late Antiquity*, Berkeley 1981, 33.

40 For David's lack of agency in the Dura synagogue paintings, see: Kära Schenk, "King David narratives, messianic politics and the Dura-Europos synagogue", in *The Eloquence of Art: Byzantine Studies in Honor of Henry Maguire*, eds. Andrea Olsen Lam and Rossitza Schroeder (Routledge, 2019), forthcoming.

glorify, to honour, to exalt, to extol, and to bless him who wrought all these wonders for our fathers and for us.[41]

The Mekhilta, which includes a lengthy exposition of each line of the Song of the Sea, assumes that Moses and the Israelites recited it antiphonally, as in the synagogue.[42] We don't know whether the congregation at Dura itself did so, but such liturgical activity would have created a link between the biblical Israelites and the congregation. The Mehkilta also emphasizes the paradigmatic character of the event: *"The Lord will fight for you.* Not only at this time, but at all times will He fight against your enemies."[43] The ultimate setting for divine victory would be the site of the Temple in Jerusalem. The Song of the Sea anticipates events to come with a reference to the conquest of the Holy Land and the building of the Temple:

> You brought them in and planted them
> on the mountain of your own possession.
> The place, O Lord, that you made yours above,
> the sanctuary, O Lord, that your hands have established.
> The Lord will reign forever and ever. (vss. 17–18)

The Mekhilta, with a similar narrative focus, emphasizes that Israel's enemies would ultimately be brought to destruction when "the Lord dwelleth in Zion" (Joel 4:20–21).[44]

I have argued that the Exodus panel was part of a larger narrative sequence constructed in the shape of a figure eight that intersected over the Torah shrine at the centre of the west wall (fig. 10). The congregation's liturgical interaction with the shrine and its decoration actually completed this narrative. Like the majority of the synagogues in the late antique period, the Dura synagogue was oriented, though the position of its Torah shrine, towards the site of the Jerusalem Temple.[45] Destroyed in 70 CE during the first revolt against Rome, the Temple was the focus of additional conflict during the Bar Kokhba Revolt of 132–135 CE. In the period contemporary with the Dura synagogue's final phase of decoration, the site of Jerusalem (now the city of Aelia Capitolina) was still occupied

---

41 M. *Pes.* 10:5.
42 Mekhilta, *Shirata* 1:86–93 (ed. Lauterbach, II:7–8).
43 Mekhilta, *Beshallah* 3:136 (ed. Lauterbach, I:215).
44 Mekhilta, *Beshallah* 1:231–233 (ed. Lauterbach, I:186).
45 Joan Branham, "Sacred Space under Erasure in Ancient Synagogues and Early Churches", in: *Art Bulletin*, 74 (3), 1992, 384–386; Rachel Hachlili, "The Niche and the Ark in Ancient Synagogues", in: *Bulletin of the American Schools of Oriental Research*, 223, 1976, 43–53, here 52.

by the Romans. A dedication text in the Dura synagogue links the shrine to the Temple by calling it a "house for the ark."[46] Just as Solomon's Temple was a "house" for the Ark of the Covenant (see I Kings 8), so the shrine served as a receptacle for the display of the Torah cabinet, also called an "ark" in both synagogue inscriptions and rabbinic texts in this period.[47] The images of the Ark of the Covenant in the narrative on the surrounding middle level are shown in the guise of the synagogue's Torah cabinet (see, for example, figs 7, 8). The placement of the Ark in the Temple (and of the "ark" in the Torah shrine) marked the completion of the narrative of the Ark's journey on the wall surrounding by enacting through liturgy King Solomon's placement of the Ark of the Covenant in the Temple. A symbolic image of the Temple is positioned on the decorative panel above the shrine, marking both the focus of prayer within the synagogue and a sign post pointing beyond the synagogue to the site.[48]

Though we do not know the exact nature of liturgy at Dura, prayers referenced in rabbinic texts seemed to function on a number of different levels in connection to the lost Temple: they recalled the lost Temple of the past; they perpetuated the sacrificial service that could no longer be offered on the site of the Temple itself in the liturgical present; and they petitioned for the hoped for return of the Temple in the messianic future.[49] There are no features of the shrine's decoration that unequivocally represent the temple as a "messianic" or "eschatological" structure. However, within the receptive context of liturgy, the generalized nature of the Temple image on the shrine would potentially have allowed for many levels of significance, including the anticipated reconstruction of the Temple in the messianic future. Any hope for the restoration of the divine presence and the Temple to the site of Jerusalem would inherently have entailed a polemic rejection of the Romans' continuing occupation of the same site. The theme of human dependence on divine power (as opposed to human valor) in

---

46 See Kraeling, *The Synagogue: The Excavations* (as in n. 1), 269.
47 See Steven Fine, *This Holy Place. On the Sanctity of the Synagogue During the Greco-Roman Period*, Notre Dame/IN 1997 (Christianity and Judaism in Antiquity Series, vol. 11), *passim* for the use of the development of the term "ark" in connection to liturgy.
48 Archer St. Clair, "The Torah Shrine at Dura-Europos: A Re-Evaluation", in: *Jahrbuch für Christentum und Antike*, 29, 1986, 109–117; Gabrielle Sed-Rajna, "Images of the Tabernacle/Temple in Late Antique and Medieval Art: The State of the Research", in: *The Real and Ideal Jerusalem in Jewish, Christian and Islamic Art*, ed. Bianca Kühnel (Studies in Honor of Bezalel Narkiss on the Occasion of His Seventieth Birthday), *Journal of the Center of Jewish Art*, 23/24, 1997/8, 42–53.
49 See Reuven Kimelman, "The Literary Structure of the Amidah and the Rhetoric of Redemption", in: *Echoes of Many Texts: Reflections on Jewish and Christian Traditions*, ed. William G. Dever/J. Edward Wright (Essays in Honor of Lou H. Silberman), Missoula/MT 1977, 171–230, particularly 190.

Fig. 10: Torah Shrine with painted "Temple panel," 244–245, Dura-Europos Synagogue

the Exodus panel and other battle scenes suggests how the restoration of the Temple to Jerusalem would be accomplished: not through direct military revolt (an option that had failed twice in previous centuries), but through obedience to and trust in Israel's divine king to defeat the occupying forces of its enemies.

Jessica N. Richardson
Through Water and Stone: The Brescia Sarcophagus *Crossing of the Red Sea**

Among the many examples of Early Christian sarcophagi representing the Crossing of the Red Sea, one in particular deserves special mention not only for its artistry and imagery, but also for its materiality (fig. 1). Today located in the Museo di Santa Giulia, Brescia, the object in question is a fragment that contains superbly carved scenes from the Old and New Testaments. Discovered following the 1945-allied bombing of the church of Sant'Afra in Brescia (today the rebuilt Sant'Angela Merici), where it had been used as a frontal for the high altar,[1] it dates from the second half of the fourth century and is made of a precious stone usually identified as African or red onyx.[2] While the Crossing of the Red Sea was a subject especially prevalent on fourth-century Christian sarcophagi, all of the known examples are in white marble.[3] Within the context of the present

---

* I am extremely grateful to Gerhard Wolf and the Kunsthistorisches Institut in Florenz – Max-Planck-Institut for their support. This article is dedicated to Angelo Turra and my entire Brescia family.
[1] The sarcophagus fragment entered the Civico Museo Cristiano, Brescia by 1949: Municipio di Brescia: *Civico Museo Cristiano: breve guida alle opere esposte*, Brescia 1949, 5; Paolo Guerrini, "Notizie e bibliografia", in: *Memorie storiche della diocesi di Brescia*, 16 (4), 1949, 185–187, at 185. See Gaetano Panazza, *La Pinacoteca e i musei di Brescia*, new edition, Bergamo 1968, tav. VII (opposite 57) and 215, n. 75. The earliest full study of the sarcophagus following its rediscovery is Antonio Mainenti, "Il sarcofago di S. Afra (frammento in onice)", in: *Commentari dell'Ateneo di Brescia* 165, 1966, 177–206.
[2] Jutta Dresken-Weiland, ed., *Repertorium der christlich-antiken Sarkophage*, vol. 2, *Italien mit einem Nachtrag Rom und Ostia, Dalmatien, Museen der Welt*, Mainz 1998, 87, no. 249, with bibliography. The sarcophagus fragment has featured in two exhibitons: Clara Stella, "Fronte di sarcofago frammentaria", in: *Milano capitale dell'impero romano, 286–402 d.C.*, exhibition catalogue (Milan 1990), ed. Maria Paola Lavizzari Pedrazzini/Maria Pia Rossignani, Milan 1990, 157–158, cat. 2b.2c; Francesca Morandini, "Fronte di sarcofago frammentario", in: *Constantino 313 d.C.: l'editto di Milano e il tempo della tolleranza*, exhibition catalogue (Milan/Rome 2012–2013), ed. Gemma Sena Chiesa, Milan 2012, 190, cat. 29. See also Guntram Koch, *Frühchristliche Sarkophage*, Munich 2000, 458. On the history of the dating of the sarcophagus, Maurizio Marchini, *Un tesoro della ecclesia di Brescia: La Confessione di fede di Tommaso sul sarcofago da S. Afra nel Museo di S. Giulia*, Brescia 2014, 17–18. The type of stone will be discussed below.
[3] Clementina Rizzardi, *I sarcofagi paleocristiani con rappresentazione del passaggio del Mar Rosso*, Faenza 1970 (Saggi d'arte e d'archeologia, 2), 32–109. Of the twenty-nine early Christian sarcophagi with representations of the Crossing of the Red Sea in Rizzardi's catalogue, the Brescia fragment (64–67, cat. 12) is the only one made of colored stone. The majority (nineteen) are

volume, it is worth considering how the deployment of a reddish, variegated, richly veined stone – an unicum in early Christian historiated sarcophagi[4] – contributed to the readings of the biblical imagery, how the material itself was harnessed to form part of the narrative effect, and ultimately to its intended messages. This article explores issues of liminality in relation to the ways the material and symbolic properties of stone were used in the Brescia Crossing, as well as in the surrounding reliefs. Furthermore, it addresses questions of transitions and crossings vis-à-vis the object's function, showing how material and representation relate to the eschatological concerns of the tomb, as well as to the religious climate of fourth-century Brescia.

The Brescia fragment originally formed one side of a sarcophagus that would have contained additional images at either end. Divided into two registers, the scenes read from left to right. The upper, larger zone presents Old Testament narratives, beginning with the scene of Moses closing the Red Sea at what was presumably the midpoint of the sarcophagus' long side (figs. 1–2). This is followed by the saved Israelites, the Column of Fire, and Moses Striking the Rock (far right, with the rock now missing). The lower register instead depicts events from the New Testament: the Raising of Lazarus, a badly damaged scene that might represent the Marys at the Tomb of Christ, and the Incredulity of Saint Thomas. There is much more space dedicated to the Crossing than to the surrounding scenes, giving it prominence. Furthermore, this image presents an exquisite use of the innate qualities of material: both its color and form are perfectly suited to the rendering of this biblical narrative. Through the technique of carving, the natural undulating veins of the reddish stone were manipulated to reflect the setting, presenting a harmonious balance between artistry and the material's natural features. Yet the depiction of the sea is the most striking element. The carefully cut reliefs, combined with the color of the stone and the particular patterns of its veining, serve to dramatize the event, calling forth associations between what is materially present, the stone, and what is re-

---

referred to generically as of "marble" (cats. 1–2, 10–11, and 15–29). For the remaining, six are of Carrara marble (cats. 3–6 and 8–9), one of Pyrenees marble (cat. 13), one of "white marble" (cat. 14), and the stone of one small fragment from the Musée d'Art Chrétien, Arles is unidentified (cat. 7).

4 With few exceptions, the majority of Early Christian sarcophagi are made of white marble. Robert Couzin, notes the intent of the *Repertorium* to study sarcophagi in colored stone – of which they include only two other examples, the porphyry sarcophagi in the Museo Clementino, Vatican: Robert Couzin, *Death in a New Key: The Christian Turn of Roman Sarcophagi*, PhD thesis, University of Toronto, Toronto 2013, 55, n. 8.

Fig. 1: Sarcophagus (fragment), Old and New Testament scenes, late fourth century, red onyx, 104.5 x 74 cm, from the church of Sant'Afra, Brescia. Brescia, Museo di Santa Giulia

presented, water, thus concretizing the metaphorical associations between the two substances.

San Faustino *ad sanguinem* – Material – Use and Reuse

In the wake of the total destruction of Sant'Afra in 1945, the Brescia sarcophagus fragment was found in the sanctuary.[5] The slab had been part of the high altar

---

5 On the rediscovery and the excavations at the site: Paolo Guerrini, "La basilica paleocristiana di San Faustino 'ad sanguinem'", in: *Miscellanea di studi bresciani sull'alto medioevo*, ed. the Comitato Bresciano per l'ottavo congresso internazionale dell'arte dell'alto medioevo, Brescia 1959, 39–44, esp. 42–43. (Reprinted from the *Giornale di Brescia* 16 February 1953); Camillo Borselli, "Gli scavi nella chiesa inferiore di S. Afra e la ecclesia Sancti Faustini ad sanguinem", in: *Commentari dell'Ateneo di Brescia*, 154, 1955 [1956], 71–86; Camillo Borselli, "Gli scavi nella chie-

Fig. 2: Sarcophagus (fragment), detail: Crossing of the Red Sea, late fourth century, red onyx, from the church of Sant'Afra, Brescia. Brescia, Museo di Santa Giulia

complex: its smooth, richly-veined back surface served as the altar frontal, while the opposite side containing the carved reliefs had faced inward, hidden from sight. The fragmentary status of the reliefs corresponds to its reuse within the setting of the altar, as its dimensions match the length and width of the side of the altar where it had been found (104.5 × 74 cm, with a thickness of 13 cm).[6] The rediscovery generated a discussion concerning its making and its early use: the sarcophagus was associated with the earlier church at the site, and with the history of Brescia's two patron saints, the second-century martyrs Faustino and Giovita.[7] San Faustino *ad sanguinem* was the first church built

---

sa inferiore di S. Afra", in: *Miscellanea di studi bresciani sull'alto medioevo*, ed. the Comitato bresciano per l'ottavo congresso internazionale dell'arte dell'alto medioevo, Brescia 1959, table II; and Giovanni Vezzoli, "Cimeli paleocristiani e altomedioevali di S. Faustino ad sanguinem", in: ibid., 9–18.

[6] Gianluigi De Silvi, "La chiesa paleocristiana dei Santi Faustino e Giovita 'ad sanguinem'", in: *Angela Merici: la società, la vita, le opera, il carisma*, ed. Gianpietro Belotti, Brescia 2004, 261–280.

[7] Fidèle Savio, "La légende des SS. Faustin et Jovite", in: *Analecta Bollandiana*, 15, 1896, 5–72, 113–159, 377–400.

on the site that was then dedicated to Sant'Afra. As the name *ad sanguinem* suggests, it is believed to be the location of the saint's martyrdom, together with that of his companion, Giovita (120 CE).[8] Gaetano Panazza proposed that the fragment had been part of a sarcophagus made for the two martyrs, that is, the tomb in which they were interred before Bishop Ramperto translated their relics from San Faustino *ad sanguinem* to Santa Maria in Silva (today San Faustino Maggiore, Brescia) in the ninth century. Panazza further suggested that the sarcophagus was commissioned at the behest of Bishop Faustinus of Brescia (r. ca. 360 – 381), thus placing its production in the second half of the fourth century.[9] The connection rested on an inscription (later deemed false) with the name Faustinus, discovered at the same time, inside a Roman sarcophagus contained within the high altar.[10] This theory initially proved attractive and gained widespread support. It provided early evidence for the promotion of the city's patron saints by the eponymous bishop (later saint) Faustinus, and gave the exquisite slab a first-rate provenance, as having housed their bodies.

While Panazza's hypothesis is no longer tenable,[11] it is reasonable to assume that the Brescia sarcophagus originally belonged to the church of San Faustino *ad sanguinem*. For in the aftermath of the bombing, amid the rubble of Sant'Afra, a second slab of the same stone was identified, without carving, which had served as the frontal of another altar (fig. 3).[12] Furthermore, it is possible to trace a remarkable history of its reuse at the site.[13] Fifteenth-century sources

---

[8] The site is believed to have served previously as a Roman cemetery: Borselli, "Gli scavi" (as in n. 5), 83–84.
[9] Tradition maintains that the fourth-century bishop Faustinus was active in the promotion of the cult of his eponymous saint, Faustino, and his companion Giovita. Gaetano Panazza, "Le manifestazioni artistiche dal secolo IV all'inizio del secolo VII", in: *Storia di Brescia*, ed. Giovanni Treccani degli Alfieri, vol. 1, *Dalle origini alla caduta della signoria viscontea (1426)*, Brescia 1963, 361–391, at 380. The earliest *passio* for the two saints dates from the eighth or ninth centuries. See Savio, "La légende" (as in n. 7).
[10] The inscription was found near a wooden casket containing bones wrapped in an Eastern silk textile (samite; today in the Museo di Santa Guilia). The pedimented tomb within which they were found, made of local *botticino* marble, survived in its entirety and was placed in the crypt. See Panazza, *La Pinacoteca* (as in n. 1), tav. VII and Vezzoli, "Cimeli paleocristiani" (as in n. 5), 10–16 and figs. 4 (sarcophagus) and 6 (inscription). For further thoughts on the authenticity of the inscription, Marchini, *Un tesoro* (as in n. 2), 13.
[11] Although it is still found sometimes in the scholarship on this artefact: Morandini, "Fronte di sarcofago" (as in n. 2), 190. For a summary of the problems with this hypothesis, Marchini, *Un tesoro* (as in n. 2), 13–15.
[12] This is now displayed beside the carved sarcophagus in the Museo di Santa Giulia (discussed below).
[13] For the reuse of sarcophagi, more generally, see n. 74 below.

refer to an *arca* or funerary monument made of "alabastrina" in the crypt that seems to have incorporated parts of the earlier sarcophagus.¹⁴ Sixteenth- and early seventeenth-century sources testify to its reuse in yet another funerary complex, the *Arca di San Felice* constructed in 1508 for the city's late seventh-century bishop, Saint Felice.¹⁵ Ascanio Martinengo, writing in 1602, provides a beautiful description of the memory of this tomb:

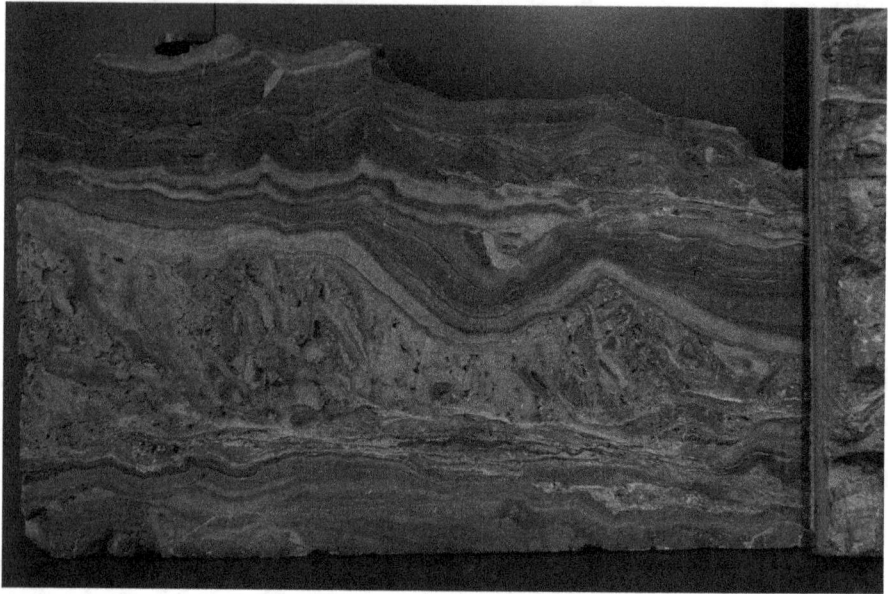

Fig. 3: Sarcophagus (fragment), red onyx, from the church of Sant'Afra, Brescia. Brescia, Museo di Santa Giulia

> It was this, an *arca* of inlaid stone, more precious than any other that can be seen, and in my opinion, it was not produced by nature in our land, but in Africa, and carved on the front with countless small figures dressed according to Longobard custom [. . .]. Once its excellence was made manifest, it was sawed in many parts, and made into the parapets before the altars of the Church of Sant'Afra that are seen today.¹⁶

---

14 Panazza, *La Pinacoteca* (as in n. 1), tav. VII and Vezzoli, "Cimeli paleocristiani" (as in n. 5), 14. See also Marchini, *Un tesoro* (as in n. 2), 14.

15 Provvisioni del Comune di Brescia dated 31 March 1508: "S. Felicis reliquiae existentes in loco vili in Ecclesia S. Aphrae ponantur in arca alabastrina, ita petente vicinia". Quoted in Vezzoli, "Cimeli paleocristiani" (as in n. 5), 14.

16 Ascanio Martinengo, *Vite de' gloriosi santi martiri Faustino, et Giovita, & di Sant'Affra et d'altri santi bresciani gli cui sacri corpi, & reliquie si conservano in diverse chiese di Brescia*, Brescia

Martinengo here comments on the age and 'style' of the reliefs at Sant'Afra, and the sawing or division of the slabs for their reuse in his own period as part of the presbytery enclosure.[17] He goes on to describe the "fiery veins" of the stone and its "diligent carving", which were deserving of its "sacred bones". What is perhaps most noteworthy is the vivid account of the stone's veining in relation to its provenance, designated as "not from our parts", but from "Africa".[18] The equisite qualities of the stone, together with the 1508 characterization of this *arca* as made of alabaster, led later writers to meditate on its physical properties and the differences between alabaster and onyx. This conversation on the material qualities of the Brescia fragment continues to this day. Indeed, a recent study has even identified it as *alabastro fiorito*.[19] Others, however, have noted its similarity to marble native to Brescia, such as *Breccia oniciata* or *Breccia damascata*.[20]

1602, 216: "Era questa una arca di pietra vergata sì pretiosa quanto alcuna altra che si possa vedere, & al mio parere non prodotta dalla natura in questi nostri paesi, ma in Africa, & scolpita nella parte dinanzi d'infinite piccole statuine vestite all'uso Longobardo, che per essere disegnata, nel moverla fù spezzata, & conosciuta l'eccellenza, segata in più parti, & fattine i parapetti che si veggono hora innanzi agli altari della Chiesa di S. Afra. L'essere questa pietra sì antica, che già cominciava ad incarolarsi, & altresì l'essere scolpita con statue con gli habiti all'uso Longobardo, oltra la fede della lama scritta dentro ritrovata, chiaramente dimostrano che fu fatta in quei tempi ch'egli morì, & fioriva l'imperio de Longobardi, l'essere così pretiosa, sì per le vaghissime e infocate vene, & portata da sì lontani paesi, come per essere scolpita con tanta diligenza, se ben con rozza arte co[n]forme a quei secoli, argomento sono, che tutte opera di quei pietosi Prencipi, ò pure della città che volesse dare sepolcro a quelle sacre ossa condegno & conforme alla grandezza, alla riputatione, & alli meriti suoi".

17 Bernardino Faino's mid-seventeenth-century guide to Brescia also relates that the "ancient marble slabs" used for the parapet of the church were from an earlier *arca*. Bernardino Faino, *Catalogo delle chiese di Brescia (Manoscritti Queriniani E. VII. 6 ed E. I. 10)*, in: *Supplement: Commentari dell'Ateneo di Brescia*, ed. Camillo Borselli, Brescia 1961, 55 and 56.

18 See n. 16 above.

19 For the 1508 reference, see n. 15 above. Roberto Bugini/Luisa Folli, "Sull'uso di marmi colorati antichi in Lombardia (Italia settentrionale)", in: *Marmora: An International Journal for Archaeology, History and Archaeometry of Marble and Stones*, 1, 2005, 145–168, at 154. On "Alabastro fiorito", Gabriele Borghini, ed. *Marmi antichi*, Rome, 2001 (Materiali della cultura artistica, 1), 142. Marchini, *Un tesoro* (as in n. 2), 16, n. 21, cites a recent *tesi di laurea* (Roberta Zani, *Il sarcofago della chiesa di Sant'Afra a Brescia*, BA thesis, Università degli Studi di Padova, Padua 2013) that refers to the stone as "rocciosa alabastrina", and he expresses the need for further analysis to prove this point.

20 Marchini, *Un tesoro* (as in n. 2), 16. Paolo Schirolli, "Il passato geologico della 'terra dei marmi': l'evoluzione del paesaggio e l'assetto attuale", in: *Il marmo bresciano: territorio, vicende, economia*, ed. Antonio Porteri/Carlo Simoni, Brescia 1997, 13–44. For local stones resembling this type, see also Andrea Botti/Maurizio Gomez Serito, *Pietre bresciane: il manuale del marmo e del porfido bresciano*, Roccafranca 2005.

The selection of this particular stone for an image of the Crossing raises further questions about how the material might have contributed to the visualisation of the subject. That is, how the natural veining and variegated colors might have evoked symbolic association and forms that were actualized through carving, how nature and artifice intersect to create the image.[21]

The Crossing of the Red Sea on Early Christian Sarcophagi

The Crossing of the Red Sea holds a special position in both early Jewish and early Christian art. It is the most prominent episode, for example, in the images found in the synagogue of Dura Europos (ca. 240 CE),[22] and it is represented twice in the fourth-century catacombs of the Via Latina in Rome (see Hoffmann fig. 1 and Schenk fig. 2).[23] The significance of the Old Testament episode and its re-interpretation within the Christian funerary context has long been noted.[24] Following the passage from Saint Paul in 1 Corinthians 10:1–2, "For I would not have you ignorant, brethren, that our fathers were all under the cloud, and all passed through the sea. And all in Moses were baptized, in the cloud and in the sea", a strong exegetical tradition relates the episode to Christian bap-

---

[21] There is a long tradition of images found within stone or the natural characteristics of the latter being manipulated to form part of an image. Amongst the many studies on this topic, see John Mitchell, "Believing is Seeing: The Natural Image in Late Antiquity", in: *Architecture and Interpretation: Essays for Eric Fernie*, ed. Jill A. Franklin/T. A. Heslop/Christine Stevenson, Woodridge 2012, 16–41.
[22] Kurt Weitzmann/Herbert L. Kessler, *The Frescoes of the Dura Synagogue and Christian Art*, Washington DC 1990 (Dumbarton Oaks Studies, 28), 38–52. See also the article by Kara Schenk in the present volume.
[23] Antonio Ferrua, *Le pitture della nuova catacomba di via Latina*, Vatican City 1960 (Monumenti di antichità cristiana, 2nd series, 8), 54–55 and 81–82; William Tronzo, *The Via Latina Catacomb: Imitation and Discontinuity in Fourth-Century Roman Painting*, University Park, PA/London 1986, 1–2, 23–24, 30, 32, 52–55, 61, 65–67. Dorothy Hoogland Verkerk, "'The font is a kind of grave': Remembrance in the Via Latina Catacombs", in: *Memory and the Medieval Tomb*, ed. Elizabeth Valdez del Alamo, with Carol Stamatis Pendergast, Aldershot 2000, 157–171. For a comparative discussion of the theme in Jewish and Christian art (focusing on Byzantine manuscripts), see Carlo-Otto Nordström, "The Water Miracles of Moses in Jewish Legend and Byzantine Art", in: *Orientalia Suecana*, 7, 1958, 78–109, esp. 87–98.
[24] For example, Jean Lassus, "Quelques représentations du 'Passage de la Mer Rouge' dans l'art chrétien d'Orient et d'Occident", in: *Mélanges d'archéologie et d'histoire*, 45, 1928, 159–181.

tism and salvation.²⁵ This message, moreover, was visually articulated through the typological pairing of Moses' closing of the Red Sea with New Testament events, such as the Raising of Lazarus.²⁶ Yet within the study of fourth-century Christian sarcophagi, the subject has had a particular fortune. Already by the second quarter of the twentieth century, the known representations of the Crossing were singled out and discussed as the "Red Sea sarcophagi", and even labeled according to their production as the "Red Sea atelier".²⁷ As Jaś Elsner recently noted, in the late fourth century, this is the only narrative theme in

---

25 All English and Latin biblical passages are take from the Douay-Rheims Bible. URL: <http://www.drbo.org/lvb/index.htm> [02.08.2018]. The passage from the Vulgate reads: "Nolo enim vos ignorare fratres quoniam patres nostri omnes sub nube fuerunt, et omnes mare transierunt, et omnes in Moyse baptizati sunt in nube, et in mari". Amongst the many studies to discuss this topic, see: Franz J. Dölger, "Der Durchzug durch das Rote Meer als Sinnbild der christlichen Taufe", in: *Antike und Christentum*, 2, 1931, 63–69; Jean Daniélou, *Sacramentum futuri: études sur les origines de la typologie biblique*, Paris 1950 (Études de Théologie Historique), esp. 152–176; Michael A. G. Haykin, "'In the Cloud of the Sea': Basil of Caesarea and the Exegesis of 1 Cor 10:2", in: *Vigiliae Christianae*, 40 (2), 1986, 135–144; Alastair John Roberts, *The Red Sea Crossing and Christian Baptism: A Study in Typology and Liturgy*, PhD thesis, Durham University, Durham 2015. URL: <http://ethesis.dur.ac.uk/10977/> [02.08.2018]. See also Dorothy Hoogland Verkerk, "Exodus and Easter Vigil in the Ashburnham Pentateuch", in: *The Art Bulletin*, 77 (1), 1995, 94–105 and Everett Ferguson, *Baptism in the Early Church: History, Theology, and Liturgy in the First Five Centuries*, Grand Rapids/Cambridge 2009, with reference to Exodus throughout. See also Robin M. Jensen, *Baptismal Imagery in Early Christianity: Ritual, Visual, and Theological Dimensions*, Grand Rapids 2012, esp. 20–22. For a fresh interpretation of this passage as "more than a mere figure for Christian baptism", Finn Damgaard, *Recasting Moses: The Memory of Moses in Biographical and Autobiographical Narratives in Ancient Judaism and 4th-Century Christianity*, Frankfurt am Main 2013 (Early Christianity in the Context of Antiquity, 13), 91. Daamgaard argues that it is "considered as an event that *united* the Iraelites with Moses and as a paradigm of Christian redemption", and that in this passage "Paul [the author] presents himself as figure parallel to Moses", ibid.
26 See for example, Shulamit Laderman/Yair Furstenberg, "Jewish and Christian Imaging of the 'House of God': A Fourth-Century Reflection of Religious and Historical Polemics", in: *Interaction between Judaism and Christianity in History, Religion, Art and Literature*, ed. Marcel Poorthuis/Joshua J. Schwartz/Joseph Turner, Leiden 2008 (Jewish and Christian Perspectives, 17), 433–456, esp. 437–439. The two episodes are found together in the paintings of the Via Latina catacomb: Tronzo, *The Via Latina Catacomb* (as in n. 23), 65–67 (with explicit mention of the pairing of the scenes in the Brescia sarcophagus on 67).
27 Marion Lawrence, "City-Gate Sarcophagi", in: *The Art Bulletin*, 10 (1), 1927, 1–45. Edmond Le Blant, *Étude sur les sarcophages chrétiens antiques de la ville d'Arles*, Paris 1878, vi–vii: Le Blant, in his study on early Christian sarcophagi in Arles, already noted the prevalence of the theme there and in examples in Rome and elsewhere. For the "Red Sea atelier": Alexander Coburn Soper, "The Latin Style on Christian Sarcophagi of the Early Fourth Century", in: *The Art Bulletin*, 19 (2), 1937, 148–202.

historiated Christian sarcophagi that "has the distinction of developing an iconography that occupies the full visual field of the main front of the coffin exclusively and without being juxtaposed against varieties of other Old and New Testament (or apocryphal) scenes".[28]

Drawing on a rich scholarly tradition, in her 1970 monograph, *I sarcofagi paleocristiani con rappresentazione del passaggio del Mar Rosso*, Clementina Rizzardi identified three reasons for the representation of the Crossing within the Christian funerary context of the fourth century: liturgical, historical, and baptismal. The first, proposed initially by Edmond Le Blant, related the imagery to a prayer made on behalf of the defunct for the salvation of the soul. This prayer, the *Commendatio animae*, links the Israelite's journey or liberation at the hands of Moses to Christian salvation ("Libera, Domine, animam eius, sicut liberasti Moysen de manu Pharaonis regis Aegyptiorum"). While these verses are not attested to before the ninth century, a prayer attributed to Saint Cyprian of Antioch (d. 304) and dating from either the second or third century – probably adapted from an ancient Hebrew prayer –, expresses a similar conceit.[29] Comparable prayers were recited during the Christian Liturgy of the Dead.[30] The incipit to Psalm 113 *In Exitu Isräel de Aegypto*, which would have been sung during the transfer of a corpse to its burial, metaphorically recalls the mystical journey of Christians, prefigured by the Israelites, towards the Heavenly Jerusalem.[31]

The second explanation for the imagery discussed by Rizzardi relates Moses' defeat of Pharaoh in the Crossing to the Emperor Constantine's victory over Maxentius at the Milvian Bridge in 312 CE. The point is made explicit by Eusebius of Caesarea (d. 339/340) in the *Ecclesiastical History*:

> "Pharaoh's chariots and his host hath he cast into the sea, his chosen horsemen, even captains, they were sunk in the Red Sea, the deep covered them"; in the same way also Maxentius and the armed soldiers and guards around him "went down into the depths like a

---

[28] Jaś Elsner, "'Pharaoh's Army Got Drownded': Some Reflections on Jewish and Roman Genealogies in Early Christian Art", in: *Judaism and Christian Art: Aesthetic Anxieties from the Catacombs to Colonialism*, ed. Herbert L. Kessler/David Nirenberg, Philadelphia/Oxford 2011, 10–44, at. 12.
[29] Karl Michel, *Gebet und Bild in frühchristlicher Zeit*, Leipzig 1902 (Studien über christliche Denkmäler, 1), 53–54. Rizzardi, *I sarcofagi* (as in n. 3), 21, quoted as: "Padre santo, Dio eterno, esaudisci la mia preghiera, come tu hai esaudito gli Israeliti, allorché uscirono dall'Egitto".
[30] Le Blant, *Les sarcophages* (as in n. 27), XXVI.
[31] Rizzardi, *I sarcofagi* (as in n. 3), 19–22.

stone", when he turned his back before the God-sent power that was with Constantine, and was crossing the river that lay in his path [...].³²

The parallel drawn between Maxentius and Pharaoh likened Constantine to Moses. The Crossing image on sarcophagi, according to this hypothesis, would have evoked the victory of the emperor wrought by the Christian God.³³ The idea, first promoted by Erich Becker, was sustained further by the fact that most of the known examples were from Rome or from cities, like Arles, politically linked to Constantine.³⁴

As noted, the typological pairing of the theme of the Crossing with baptism – the third reason for the theme identified by Rizzardi – ultimately relates to the passage in First Corinthians and its interpretation and amplification in the works of later Christian authors.³⁵ The association, elaborated in the writings of Origen, Tertullian, Ambrose, and Augustine, amongst others, was expressly connected to the Easter celebration. The biblical narration of the Crossing of the Red Sea was evoked during the Easter Vigil, when most catechumens were baptized. Within this major liturgical celebration, it related to both the Resurrection of Christ and to the individual desire for salvation through the rite of bap-

---

32 Eusebius, *Ecclesiastical History*, book 9, pt. 9. Eusebius: *Ecclesiastical History*, vol. II: books 6–10, trans. by John Ernest Leonard Oulton, Cambridge, MA 1932 (Loeb Classical Library, 265), 361.
33 Rizzardi, *I sarcofagi* (as in n. 3), 22–24.
34 Erich Becker, "Protest gegen den Kaiserkult und Verherrlichung des Sieges am Pons Milvius in der christlichen Kunst der konstantinischen Zeit", in: *Konstantin der Große und sein Zeit*, ed. Franz J. Dölger, Freiburg im Breisgau 1913 (Römische Quartalschrift für christliche Altertumskunde und Kirchengeschichte, supp. 19), 155–190. Thomas F. Matthews, *The Clash of Gods: A Reinterpretation of Early Christian Art*, Princeton 1999, 76, states, "Becker made an ideological muddle of the subject," as "in Early Christian literature Moses is not a type of the emperor but of Christ". For further discussion of the imperial associations of the imagery: Galit Noga-Banai, "The Sarcophagus of Louis the Pious at Metz: A Roman Memory Reused", in: *Frühmittelalterliche Studien*, 45, 2011, 37–50. Recently, Noga-Banai has revived the argument for the Constaninian reference and the Roman ideological significance of the Crossing: Galit Noga-Banai, *Sacred Stimulus: Jerusalem in the Visual Christianization of Rome*, Oxford 2018 (Oxford Studies in Late Antiquity), 76–85. For the figure of Moses in Eusebius' *Vita Constantini*, Damgaard, *Recasting Moses*, 153–181. Damgaard traces the sources for Eusebius' comparison to Flavius Josephus' *Jewish Antiquities* (first century CE, where Moses' crossing of the Red Sea is compared to Alexander the Great's crossing of the Pamphylian Sea) and the *Oratio ad Sanctorum Coetum*, a speech credited to Constantine that the emperor himself may have delivered in Rome at Easter in 314. See Damgaard, *Recasting Moses* (as in n. 25), 163–166.
35 Rizzardi, *I sarcofagi* (as in n. 3), 24–31.

tism.³⁶ The image of the Crossing on sarcophagi was thus a visual means of expressing liminal moments linked to the Sacraments, and Christian victory on several fronts: initiation into Christian life through baptism and the salvation of the soul through the Resurrection of Christ.³⁷

Scholars have placed the Red Sea sarcophagi in two categories based on their imagery and formal characteristics. The first group, dating from the Constantinian and Post-Constantinian period (up to 340), presents the Crossing as one of a number of episodes from the Old and New Testaments carved on the surface of the sarcophagi, which is usually divided in two horizontal registers, with the scenes often defined by an arcaded colonnade.³⁸ The sarcophagi in the second group, instead, date from the so-called Theodosian period (that is, roughly the time of the Emperor Theodosius, r. 379–395) and present the Crossing as part of a continuous narrative of Exodus.³⁹ This division, however, does not necessarily hold true. The Brescia fragment fits somewhere between these poles.⁴⁰ While both Old and New Testament scenes are found together in relation to the Crossing (as in the first group), the upper register, or what survives of it, presents a continuous narrative focussed on the Crossing (as in the second group).⁴¹ The fragment thus seems to present a visual fusion of the two types initially recognized by scholars.

In the majority of the sarcophagi that present the Crossing as part a continuous narrative related to Exodus several distinctive features emerge. The scene is at the centre on the long side of the sarcophagi, revealing its privileged place. The moment selected, however, is not the parting of the Red Sea, but its closing by Moses, at the will of God, with his staff (Ex 14:26–29). This formal arrange-

---

36 See n. 25 above.
37 See Arnold Van Gennep, *The Rites of Passage*, trans. by Monika Vizedom/Gabrielle L. Caffee, Chicago 1960. On "Baptism as a boundary-crossing rite" in Early Christian ritual, Richard E. Demaris, "Water Ritual", in: *The Oxford Handbook of Early Christian Ritual*, ed. Risto Uro et al., Oxford 2019, 391–408, at 398–399. On baptismal "iconography" on early Christian sarcophaghi (without mention of Brescia Crossing), Robin M. Jensen, *Living Water: Images, Symbols, and Settings of Early Christian Baptism*, Leiden/Boston 2011 (Supplements to Vigiliae Christianae. Texts and Studies of Early Christian Life and Language, 105), 43–85.
38 Lawrence, "City-Gate Sarcophagi" (as in n. 27).
39 Of the twenty-nine, fourth-century sarcophagi catalogued by Rizzardi, she identified seven in which the scene of the Crossing is combined with other Old and New Testament scenes. Rizzardi instead placed the remaining twenty-two sarcophagi in the second category. In the latter, the scene occupies the entire register, "dando vita al vero e proprio sarcofago di Passaggio". Rizzardi, *I sarcofagi* (as in n. 3), 136.
40 Rizzardi, *I sarcofagi* (as in n. 3), 64–67, cat. 12, dated it to the 340s.
41 Elsner, observing the variations in the marble examples, justly states that the "key point" is that "the Red Sea theme was highly adaptable". Elsner, "Pharaoh's Army" (as in n. 28), 18–19.

ment is reflected in five of the most complete surviving examples, the marble sarcophagi today located in Aix-en-Provence (Musée des Beaux Arts), Arles (St-Trophime [fig. 4] and Musée d'Art Chrétien), Rome (Museo Pio Cristiano Vaticano [fig. 5]), and Split (Archaeological Museum).[42] In each instance the representation of the Red Sea at the centre allows for a formal division between the Egyptians (left) and the Israelites (right). Visually, the water is emphasized as an important barrier and a point of transition between the fallen Egyptian soldiers and the saved Israelites. Its central location dramatizes the moment of transition in relation to water – the salvation of the Israelites by Moses' closing of the sea – and its Christian reinterpretation in the rite of baptism.

Fig. 4: Sarcophagus, Carrara marble, ca. 380–390, 240 x 62 cm. Arles, church of St-Trophime

The later fourth-century sarcophagi, moreover, have been singled out because of their arrangement and how the figures relate to one another. The overcrowded scenes of battle extend across the long surface of the sarcophagus forming a tightly constructed narrative that reads from left to right. In addition to this mode of representation and the organization of the episodes across the surface, Elsner links these images to another potential 'transition', what he terms "visual antiquarianism". Not only has the Old Testament episode been absorbed within

---

42 Rizzardi, *I sarcofagi* (as in n. 3): Aix-en-Provenance, 32–38, cat. 1; Arles, St-Trophime, 39–44, cat. 3; Arles, Musée d'Art Chrétien, 48–52, cat. 5; Rome, 96–100, cat. 26; Split, 105–109, cat. 29.

the context of Christian salvation. Elsner highlights the significance of the "Theodosian rendering" of the theme, and places these objects within the larger debates on early Christian art and Late Antique culture more generally:

> The Red Sea sarcophagi come to the question of genealogy at a later moment than Constantine – in roughly the 380s. [...] They combine this with a persistent classicism in relation to their referencing of the arts of the Roman past that is at the very least highly aggressive. If Jewish subject matter signals Christian triumph, then the clothing of it in the forms of Roman art signifies that this triumph is over Rome.[43]

Elsner here offers a further perspective on the interpretive possibilities of the transitional aspects of the Crossing of the Red Sea on fourth-century sarcophagi, one linked to the historical context of representation and to their production.[44]

Thus, the various meanings ascribed to the theme of the Crossing on these late fourth-century sarcophagi all relate to transitional border crossings, the symbolic and typological significance of baptism, death and Resurrection, expressed also in the writings of Christian exegetes, and transitional moments within the early history of Christianity and its visual language. Coeval to these works, the Brescia fragment suggests a new perspective on the multivalent readings of the Crossing, one based on materiality, that is, the relationship between material and form, how the innate qualities of the stone relate to the representation itself.

Sea and Stone, Water and Rock

Within the larger Exodus account that unfolds across the long side of the white marble sarcophagi of the later fourth century, water is the main protagonist (figs. 4–5). The Red Sea, represented at the centre of the pictorial field is the transitional element of the narrative. In these sarcophagi, it is consistently represented as a series of relatively abstract horizontal wavy lines at the lower centre or, like in the Vatican sarcophagus (fig. 5), as an articulated backdrop of the drowning Egyptian army, with the figures superimposed, interrupting the deeply cut, rippled surface of the stone. Notwithstanding its particular significance in relation to the Crossing, water features prominently in the imagery found on early

---

43 Elsner, "Pharaoh's Army" (as in n. 28), 29.
44 Elsner "Pharaoh's Army" (as in n. 28), esp. 19–28. The explicitly Christian quotations of Roman works – his argument pertains specifically to the women and children and their genesis in monuments from Rome and Benevento – and the classicizing way in which they are depicted became a means for expressing Christian triumph.

Christian sarcophagi.⁴⁵ A brilliant visualization of the confluence of water and stone is found on the short side of the fourth-century sarcophagus in Santa Maria dei Miracoli presso San Celso, Milan (fig. 6). Here in the scene of Moses/Peter striking the Rock (Ex 17:6), the two substances are pictured in tandem. The rough-hewn stones pilled along the outer left border of the slab 'contain' a horizontal band of strigillated waves, literally enclosed in the upper right corner of the surface by the very rocks from which they spew. It is at this precise point of intersection of stone and water that we find Moses'/Peter's rod, touching simultaneously both substances, and emphatically calling attention to the transformation miracle.⁴⁶

The idea of water, particularly the sea, as a transitional substance related to baptism and salvation might take on a special meaning when represented in stone. There is a long tradition of writing that links the sea to marble. The Old Testament draws analogies between stone and water. For example, in Job 38:30 we read: "The waters are hardened like a stone, and the surface of the deep is congealed" ("In similitudinem lapidis aquae durantur, et superficies abyssi constringitur"). The passage of the Crossing in Exodus 14:15–22 presents the "mare Rubrum" (as it is described in Ex 13:18) as the salvific source of transition, one capable of changing form:

> And the Lord said to Moses: Why criest though to me? Speak to the children of Israel to go forward. But lift thou up thy rod, and stretch forth thy hand over the sea, and divide it: that the children of Israel may go through the midst of the sea on dry ground. And I will harden the heart of the Egyptians to pursue you: and I will be glorified in Pharao[h], and in all his host, and in his chariots, and in his horsemen. And the Egyptians shall know that I am the Lord, when I shall be glorified in Pharao[h], and in his chariots and in his horsemen. And the angel of God, who went before the camp of Israel, removing, went behind them: and together with him the pillar of the cloud, leaving the forepart, stood behind, between the Egyptians' camp and the camp of Israel: and it was a dark cloud, and enlightening the night, so that they could not come at one another all the night. And when Moses had stretched forth his hand over the sea, the Lord took it away by a strong and burning wind blowing all the night, and turned it into dry ground: and the water was divided.

---

45 Moreover, it has been proposed recently that the profuse rendering of the geometric motif of the strigil on sarcophagi is an overt reference to waves of the sea. Elizabeth L. Fischer, *Streams of Living Water: The Strigil Motif on Late Antique Sarcophagi Reused in Medieval Southern France*, MA thesis, University of North Carolina, Chapel Hill 2011. On this motif, see Janet Huskinson, *Roman Strigillated Sarcophagi: Art and Social History*, Oxford 2015.

46 On Peter's water miracle and its relationship to Moses' miracle in Exodus: David R. Cartlidge/J. Keith Elliot, *Art and the Christian Apocrypha*, London/New York 2001, 163–164. On the conflation of Peter and Moses in fourth-century art, with reference to this miracle, see Noga-Banai, *Sacred Stimulus* (as in n. 34), 79–80, esp. 79, n. 74.

Fig. 5: Sarcophagus, detail: right portion of sculpted relief showing the Crossing of the Red Sea by the Hebrews and the drowning of Pharaoh's Host, ca. 380–390, marble, 233 x 68 cm (entire sarcophagus). Vatican City, Museo Pio Clementino

> And the children of Israel went in through the midst of the sea dried up: for the water was as a wall on their right hand and on their left.

The Red Sea is described as a "wall of water" ("erat enim aqua quasi murus" in the Vulgate). Stone, moreover, is used metaphorically to describe how the Egyptian army sank. The so-called Song of Moses and Miriam that follows the Exodus passage just quoted, describes Pharaoh's chariot and army: "The depths have covered them, they are sunk to the bottom like a stone" (Ex 15:5).[47] The victory, attributed to the Lord, continues with the evocative description of the tumultuous swirling waters that pile, surge, and congeal: "And with the blast of thy anger the waters were gathered together: the flowing water stood, the depths were gathered together in the midst of the sea" (Ex 15:8).[48] Describing the enemies, it continues: "Let fear and dread fall upon them, in the greatness of thy arm: let them become immoveable as a stone" (Ex 15:16).[49]

---

47 "Abyssi operuerunt eos; descenderunt in profundum quasi lapis".
48 "Et in spiritu furoris tui congregatae sunt aquae: stetit unda fluens, congregata sunt abyssi in medio mari".
49 "Irruat super eos formido et pavor, in magnitudine brachii tui: fiant immobiles quasi lapis".

Fig. 6: Sarcophagus, detail: Moses striking the rock, marble, late fourth century. Milan, Santuario di Santa Maria dei miracoli presso S. Celso

In his 2007 article charting the associations between the marble and the sea in Antiquity and the Middle Ages, Fabio Barry discusses the explicit links between marble as matter and liquid. He also points out the metaphorical connections, present in the Latin language itself between *mar* (sea) and *marmor* (marble).[50] Greco-Roman classical authors such as Aristotle and Theophrastus made these connections explicit, and such associations had a particular resonance in Early Christian thought and visual culture (and beyond).[51] For example, in the

---

[50] Fabio Barry, "Walking on Water: Cosmic Floors in Antiquity and the Middle Ages", in: *The Art Bulletin*, 89 (4), 2007, 637–656 (see 632 for specific mention of the Brescia sarcophagus). See also Fabio Barry, *Painting in Stone: The Symbolism of Colored Marbles in the Visual Arts and Literature from Antiquity until the Enlightenment*, PhD thesis, Columbia University, New York 2011, 46–61 ("Antique Theories of the Generation of Stones"), for further references by Roman writers. See, more recently, Barbara Baert, "Marble and the Sea or Echo Emerging (A Ricercar)", in: *Espacio, tiempo y forma*, ser. VII, Historia del arte, 5 (2017), 35–54.

[51] Barry, "Walking on Water" (as in n. 50). For discussion of these associations in the later medieval periods in the West and in Islam, see Marcus Milwright, "'Waves of the Sea': Responses to

fourth century, the marble-sea metaphor is explicit in the writings of the Emperor Julian the Apostate (r. 361–363). In his *Misopogon* (or *Beard-hater*) of 362, he compared the frozen waters to "blocks like marble [...] the white stone that comes from Phrygia".[52] White marble and colored stone also had a host of symbolic meanings in classical Roman times. Moreover, the use of vividly colored marble or other stones could relate explicitly to the carved subject matter.[53] The imagery on the white marble Red Sea sarcophagi might have triggered associations with the object carved on its surface, establishing an intimate relationship between material and representation. In the Brescia crossing the relations between stone and sea, materials and representation, are most eloquently articulated. Here, the stone itself, both its physical aspect and the many associations the material would have held at the time of its making, became the means for expressing transition.

The Brescia Fragment, Color and Form

In the Brescia fragment, Moses, with his extended hand and presumably his rod (which no longer survives in the relief), closes the Red Sea. The drama is heightened by the surface space dedicated to the event. In contrast to the coeval exam-

---

Marble in Written Sources (Ninth-Fifteenth Centuries)", in: *The Iconography of Islamic Art: Studies in Honour of Robert Hillenbrand*, ed. Bernard O'Kane, Edinburgh 2005, 211–221.

52 Julian, *Misopogon*, 341: "As I was saying then, the winter was more severe than usual, and the river kept bringing down blocks like marble. You know, I suppose, the white stone that comes from Phrygia; the blocks of ice were very like it, of great size, and drifted down one after another; in fact it seemed likely that they would make an unbroken path and bridge the stream". Julian, *Orations 6–8. Letters to Themistius, To the Senate and People of Athens, To a Priest. The Caesars. Misopogon*, vol. 2, trans. by Wilmer C. Wright, Cambridge, MA 1913 (Loeb Classical Library, 29), 421. The links are made explicit also by the late fourth-century Latin writer Rufus Festus Avienus in his *Periegesis seu Descriptio orbis terrarum*. URL: <http://www.documentacatholicaomnia.eu/04z/z_0300-0400__Avienus._Rufus_Festus__Periegesis_Sive_Descriptio_Orbis_Terrarum__LT.pdf.html> [11.08.2019]. See also Barry, "Walking on Water" (as in n. 50), 651, n. 46.

53 Lorenzo Lazzarini, "Rosso *Antico* and Other Red Marbles Used in Antiquity: A Characterization Study", in: *Marble: Art Historical and Scientific Perspectives on Ancient Sculpture*, conference proceedings (Malibu, J. Paul Getty Museum, 1988), Malibu 1990, 237–252. On the use of colored marble in Roman antiquity: Rolf Michael Schneider, "Coloured Marble: The Splendour and Power of Imperial Rome", in: *Apollo*, 154 (473), 2001, 3–10; Marilda De Nuccio/Lucrezia Ungaro, eds., *I marmi colorati della Roma imperiale*, exhibition catalogue (Rome 2002–2003), Venice 2002; and Mark Bradley, "Colour and Marble in Early Imperial Rome", in: *The Cambridge Classical Journal*, 52, 2006, 1–22.

ples in white marble, the representation of the sea extends vertically and horizontally and partly covers the Egyptian army. Furthermore, unlike these sarcophagi, in which the sea is represented as a series of abstract wavy lines, the water is depicted as a translucent cloth through which the drowning figures emerge. Directly to Moses' right and under his extended arm, are the profiled heads of two submerged horses, their reins just visible beneath the "wall" of water, to use the biblical metaphor. The figures materialize as if behind a thin veil. What we witness in this scene is the very moment of Moses' closing, the beginning of the miracle. The horses, fully sunken, are the first to suffer, while Pharaoh and his army have not yet been entirely enveloped by the rising water. This allows another drama to unfold horizontally across the upper surface of the scene: Moses gazes toward Pharaoh (probably the larger figure at the far left) and two soldiers. The soldier at the far right, his head slightly and eloquently bent, glances toward the ensuing water. The space between Moses and the soldiers is not carved. Here the stone's smooth surface, with its natural rippling, multicolored horizontal patterns, connects these figures, creating a heightened tension between, quite literally, the heads of the two nations.

Moses is the pivotal figure between the saved Israelites (viewers' right), and the Egyptian army (viewers' left). The veining of the stone and its articulation through soft, subtle carving emphasizes his central positon. The carving mimics and at times follows these natural lines in the stone, which move with dramatic force from soft pink to a bold red and take on a particular form in the area selected for the representation of Moses closing the water. The multicolored horizontal veining that begins at the left edge of the fragment takes a downward turn just as it passes Moses' (missing) rod, swiftly descending towards his feet, which are immersed partly in the water. The carved flowing water follows the veining of the stone to this shore, coming to a seemingly abrupt end in the area around Moses' left foot. Here and to the right, the veining is particularly intense and the stone is polished but not carved: its natural appearance provides the desert-like or even rocky setting for the next scenes.

The stone's veining is used also in other carved scenes to create spectacular visual effects, both mimetic and metaphorical. For example, the Column of Fire, which served to provide light to the Israelites, is located to the right of the Crossing. It demarcates the youthful Moses of the Crossing and the fragmentary image of the bearded, elderly Moses striking water from the rock (far right). In other fourth-century Red Sea sarcophagi, shafts of columns often contain carved patterns (fig. 4). Instead, in the Brescia fragment, the churning veins of the stone object itself define the shaft. This visual mimesis contains also a potential symbolic interpretation. Originally, the Column of Fire may have had carved flames issuing from its capital.⁵⁴ Yet it is worth considering also the shifting shades of the stone above the capital. Here the veining reaches a lighter and relatively consistent tone, extending horizontally left and right, as if a spell of brightness breaks the sky. Could this be a reference to the light issued by the column's flame, which served to guide the Israelites through the darkness of the desert? Thus, just as the stone seems particularly suited to the representation of the Red Sea, others scenes also flirt playfully between material and representation, drawing associations between color-light, liquid and stone.

Aquarum muri: The Easter Exodus Sermons of Bishop Gaudentius

In his analysis of several white marble examples, Elsner notes that "the Red Sea crossing sarcophagi represent not the text of Exodus as a manifestly or meaningfully *Jewish* scripture, but rather Exodus as a site of Christian exegetic and interpretative investment".⁵⁵ One church father often mentioned in relation to these sarcophagi, and discussed by Elsner, is Saint Ambrose, bishop of Milan from 374 to 397.⁵⁶ Ambrose's use of the Old Testament passage for exemplary purposes in his writings on baptism provides an ostensibly close milieu, both chronologically and geographically, in which to place the imagery of the Brescia sarcophagus fragment.⁵⁷ Yet an even closer setting exists. Here we must turn to one of Ambrose's younger associates, that is, to Brescia's own fourth-century bishop, Gaudentius, and also to his writings. Remarkably, Gaudentius' Easter sermons not only survive, they exhibit a preoccupation with the very same biblical passages that fill the stone slab. Moreover, as discussed by Giancarlo Bruni, in the Easter sermons of Gaudentius, the Exodus narrative and, in particular, the Red Sea, provided a means for expressing the concept of *transitus*, as it related

---

54 As described in the biblical passage and as seen, for example, in the Via Latina catacombs.
55 Elsner, "Pharaoh's Army" (as in n. 28), 32. See also Giancarlo Bruni, *Pasqua primavera della storia: teologia del tempo nei testi omiletici di Gaudenzio di Brescia*, Rome 2000 (Scripta Pontificiae Facultatis Theologicae "Marianum", 55), 123, n. 41 for further references to the association of the Red Sea with baptism in liturgical-patristic writings, East and West.
56 Elsner, "Pharaoh's Army" (as in n. 28), 32. On Saint Ambrose, see Ferguson, *Baptism in the Early Church* (as in n. 25), 634–647.
57 See, for example, Saint Ambrose's *De sacramentis* (On the Sacraments: six sermons delivered to the newly baptized during Easter week), book 1, chap. 6: Saint Ambrose, *'On the Mysteries' and the Treatise, 'On the Sacraments'*, by an Unknown Author, trans. Tim Thompson, ed. James H. Srawley, New York 1919 (Translations of Christian Literature, ser. 3, Liturgical Texts), 83–84.

to the Christian sacraments and to the salvific power of Christ wrought through the Resurrection, and ultimately to the Eucharist.[58]

Gaudentius was appointed Bishop of Brescia by Saint Ambrose at some point before 397, although a precise timeline of his life and works has yet to be established.[59] His twenty-one extant sermons (or Tractates) are important testimony to the liturgical practice of late fourth- and early fifth-century Brescia.[60] Tractates 1–10 offer a complete cycle of sermons delivered in Brescia between the Easter Vigil though the first Sunday after Easter, likely in the 390s or the first years of the fifth century.[61] The Crossing of the Red Sea features prominently in these sermons. For example, in Tractatus One, the First Sermon on Exodus, delivered on the observance of the Paschal Vigil, the night prior to baptism, Bishop Gaudentius explicitly linked the Crossing of the Red Sea to this consequent sacrament:

> The blessed and perfect Exodus, therefore, is completed in us when the true Moses, our Lord Jesus, God by nature and not by appointment, taken from the water of the Jordan, leads us by the rod of His cross through the water of baptism. He leads us from the captivity of the devil, that Pharaoh, and snatches us away from all the Egypts of his darkness.[62]

In this passage, the Red Sea of Exodus prefigures the water of baptism. Bruni highlights the complexity of the associations in this passage between the two

---

[58] Bruni, *Pasqua primavera* (as in n. 55), esp. 121–145.
[59] He was probably ordained bishop between 388 amd 396, see Dominic Keech, *Gaudentius of Brescia on Baptism and the Eucharist*, Norwich 2013 (Joint Liturgical Studies, 76), 12.
[60] See Bruni, *Pasqua primavera* (as in n. 55), esp. 9, n. 2, with further bibliography. See also Alfredo Brontesi, *Ricerche su Gaudenzio da Brescia*, Brescia 1962 (Monografie di storia bresciana, 56; Memorie storiche della diocesi di Brescia, 29, fasc. 3/4), 117–131 and 173–177.
[61] These formed part of the first fifteen Tractates sent by Gaudentius, with a dedicatory epistle, to the imperial delegate Benivolus. Benivolus together with Ambrose opposed the Arian legislation of Justinian II during the crisis of 385–386. He later became a member of Gaudentius' congregation. For Latin transcriptions and an Italian translation of all 21 Tractates: Gabriele Banterle ed. and trans., *Delle varie eresie, San Filastrio di Brescia; Trattati, San Gaudenzio di Brescia*, Milan/Rome 1991 (Scrittori dell'area Santambrosiana, 2) (Hereafter Gaudentius, *Tractates*, ed. Banterle). See also Gaudenzio di Brescia, *I sermoni*, trans. Carlo Truzzi, Rome 1996 (Collana di testi patristici, 129). The English translations, used in this article, are found in Stephen L. Boehrer, *Gaudentius of Brescia: Sermons and Letters*, PhD thesis, The Catholic University of America, Washington, DC 1965 (Studies in Sacred Theology, 2nd series, 165).
[62] Gaudentius, Tract. I, 13. Boehrer, *Gaudentius of Brescia* (as in n. 61), 54. Gaudentius, *Tractates*, ed. Banterle (as in n. 61), 254: "Exodus ergo beata atque perfecta consummator in nobis, quando uerus Moyses de Iordanis aqua sumptus, et natura, non positione deus, dominus noster Iesus, uirga crucis suae per acquam nos baptismi de captiuitate Faraonis educit diaboli ac de omni tenebrarum eius Aegypto eripit [. . .]". See Bruni, *Pasqua primavera* (as in n. 55), 124–127.

"intermediaries," Moses, who with his wooden rod divides the water, and Jesus as the "true Moses". Jesus emerges from the waters of the Jordan, and leads with the "rod of His cross," indicating that he entered the water to consecrate it. Furthermore, the bond drawn between Moses' "rod" and the wood of the cross established the latter as a "sign of the power of protection", in that baptism was the means for the liberating power of the Crucifixion".[63] In short, as Bruni discusses, Exodus was the interpretative key used to understand events that take place in the "*here* and *now* of the celebration".[64] Furthermore, as noted by Celestino Corsato, in Gaudentius, the Red Sea, the Jordan, the cross, and baptism are strictly connected through the scriptural-typological category of Exodus, in a progression toward the mystery of salvation.[65] This message, moreover, was directed at both neophytes and seasoned penitents alike:

> This exposition is most appropriate to the faithful. Only the first-born of the devils have been killed for the catechumens. But, for those who merit to approach the grace of heavenly baptism the entire army of the devil is drowned and killed. Thus truly and rightly those reborn in Christ hear: "This month shall be the first of the months for you; it is the first in the months of the year". This explanation is fitting also for penitents whom the darkness of sin and the blindness of this Egypt has once again possessed. For if they cry to the Lord, regaining their senses and running from the evil works of darkness, they will follow the light of heavenly mercy and will return to eternal light and salvation. [...] For when a man returns to the light of truth and justice he understands that he has been wandering about in the darkness of Egypt.[66]

---

[63] Bruni, *Pasqua primavera* (as in n. 55), 88–89, 121–123. "Il rapporto battesimo-croce è posto: nell'uno opera la Potenza liberatrice della seconda" (at 123).

[64] Bruni, *Pasqua primavera* (as in n. 55), 124: "il testo dell'Esodo fornisce la chiave di lettura di quanto sta avvenendo nel *qui* e *ora* della celebrazione". Bruni (123) further states that: "Gli *effetti* sono presto detti. I neofiti escono dalle acque battesimali liberi dalla schiavitù del diavolo, di cui il faraone era allegoria, e dalla notte del mondo, di cui le tenebre dell'Egitto erano allegoria. Una uscita dalla oscura mondanità e dall'agente nascosto che la suscita; neofiti chiamati a divenire figli della luce dediti a una esistenza luminosa. Così, ad esempio, a conclusione del *Discorso* diciottesimo".

[65] Celestino Corsato, "Il battesimo nei 'Tractatus' di Gaudenzio di Brescia", in: *Sul sentiero dei sacramenti: scritti in onore di Ermanno Roberto Tura nel suo 70° compleanno*, ed. Celestino Corsato, Padua 2007, 203–234, at 221–222: "Mar Rosso, Giordano, croce, battesimo sono strettamente connessi, attraverso il legame della categoria scritturistico-tipologica dell'esodo, nella progressione di quel 'mistero della salvezza' che si adempie pienamente in Cristo e che viene comunicato agli uomini attraverso i sacramenti/misteri: l'acqua battesimale – una volta santificata nel Giordano da Cristo su cui è disceso lo Spirito Santo e resa efficace dal sangue prezioso del legno della croce – fa 'uscire' uomini nuovi liberati e 'rinascere' figli luminosi adottati e 'risorgere' creature vivificate".

[66] Gaudentius, Tract I, 20–22. Boehrer, *Gaudentius of Brescia* (as in n. 61), 55–56. Gaudentius, *Tractates*, ed. Banterle (as in n. 61), 256: "Oportunius autem congruit expositio ista fidelibus,

Thus in Tractatus One, the darkness representative of Egypt is juxtaposed with the light that will be given through baptism, establishing the latter as the means to salvation though a series of complex relations realized in Christ and brought about in the initiation rite soon to take place.

In later Tractates, Gaudentius returns to the allegorical associations of the Red Sea, explicitly linking the waters to baptism, as well as to the Eucharist. In Tractatus Seven, the seventh sermon on the Exodus, he writes:

> St. John the Evangelist, not without lament, records this: "He came unto His own and His own received Him not." In other words, He came to those whom He had liberated from the slavery of Egypt, whom He had led with dry step through the Red Sea, in whose sight He had drowned Pharaoh and the Egyptians when He let fall the walls of the surrounding waters, whom He had filled with heavenly manna in the desert, for whom He had produced springs form the dry rock, to whom He had entrusted the words of the law, to whom in the voice of the prophets He had prophesied His coming in the flesh, to whom in particular He came, saying: "I have not been sent except to the lost sheep of the house of Israel".[67]

Later in Tractatus Ten, the Eighth Sermon on Exodus, Gaudentius again concerns himself with the "walls of water" and recalls Moses' miraculous production of water from stone:

> He divided the Red Sea and the water of that fluid element lined into the firmness of walls. For "the waters solidified as a wall; the waves solidified in the middle of the sea", as the faith of this triumphal canticle in Exodus testifies. He divided the Red Sea, I say, which is called Erythrean by the Greeks, that He might prepare both a passage for His people and a pitfall for the pursuers. For after the Israelites had passed with dry step through the bottom

---

nam catecuminis adhuc tantum primitiua daemonum sunt interfecta; his uero, qui ad gratiam merentur baptismi caelestis accedere, totus exercitus diaboli summergitur ac necatur, ut uere ac merito audiant in Christo renati: *Mensis hic uobis initium mensuum, primus est in mensibus anni*. Congruit et paenitentibus haec explanatio, quos iterum tenebrae criminum et Aegypti huius caligo possederat. Nam si ingemescant ad dominum resipiscentes et fugientes ab operibus nequissimis tenebrarum, lumen caelestis indulgentiae consequentur et ad aeternam lucem redient ac salutem. Scriptum est enim: *Cum conuersus ingemueris, tunc saluus eris et scies, ubi eras, cum confidebas in illis. Scies*, inquit, *ubi eras*. Tunc enim se homo in erroribus Aegypti tenebrarum fuisse intellegit, cum ad lucem ueritatis regreditur atque iustitiae".

67 Gaudentius, Tract. VII, 16. Boehrer, *Gaudentius of Brescia* (as in n. 61), 95. Gaudentius, *Tractates*, ed. Banterle (as in n. 61), 304–306: "Vnde sanctus euangelista Iohannes non sine querela commemorat: *In propria uenit et sui eum non receperunt*, id est ad eos uenit, quos de seruitute Aegypti liberarat, quos per mare Rubrum uestigio sicco transduxerat, in quorum conspectu Faraonem et Aegyptios resolutis aquarum circumstantium muris obruerat, quos manna caelesti satiauerat in deserto, quibus de rupe arida fontes produxerat, quibus eloquia legis crediderat, quibus aduentum suum secundum carnem uaticinio praenuntiauerat prophetarum, ad quos praecipue uenerat dicens: *Non sum missus nisi ad oues perditas domus Israhel*".

of the sea, and all the Egyptians had hastily entered after them in the same course, God immediately restored the proper fluidity, which He had taken away, to the standing waters; and He destroyed the armed troops of horsemen and the Pharaoh himself with his horse chariots and all of his army in the overwhelming waves. The walls of water [*aquarum muri*] that had protected the believing people overturned the enemy force in this fitting downfall. He who had rained down fire on those guilty of abominable sacrilege rained down food of manna to His worshippers in the desert. […] "He broke open the rock and waters flowed" for many thousands of men thirsting in the desert.[68]

The parallels made by Gaudentius between the Crossing and Christian salvation – the "passage" (*transitus*) wrought by the waters of the "Rubrum mare" and those of baptism – offer an evocative context for the Brescia sarcophagus fragment. The imagery in the fragment resonates with the words articulated in the bishop's sermons. The figures and animals have been rendered to appear as if beneath a veil of water. This not only recalls the biblical passage in Exodus (the "wall of water"), but the vivid descriptions of Gaudentius just quoted. In the stone slab, the transitional aspects of the Old Testament narrative and its Christian 'reading' are given full force through the material itself. Here the sea and its undulating waves are the main protagonists, a metaphorical and allegorical *transitus* as expressed also by Bishop Gaudentius. Moreover, it is noteworthy that Gaudentius connects the event to Moses striking the rock and that this too is visualized in the Brescia fragment. While we cannot be certain which came first, the sarcophagus imagery or the sermons, it is safe to assume that the Old Testament episodes on the sarcophagus did not require typological visual pairing (that is, the New Testaments scenes below) for the multiple associations of the Christian context to be understood.

---

[68] Gaudentius, Tract. X, 3–6. Boehrer, *Gaudentius of Brescia* (as in n. 61), 135–136. Gaudentius, *Tractates*, ed. Banterle (as in n. 61), 354–356: "Ipse diuisit Rubrum mare, quando in murorum firmitatem liquentis elementi unda diriguit; *gelauerunt* enim *tamquam murus aquae, gelauerunt fluctus in medio maris* sicut testatur in Exodo fides illius cantici triumphalis. Ipse ergo, inquam, diuisit Rubrum mare, quod a Graecis nuncupatur Erythreum, ut et plebi suae transitum et persqeuentibus foueam praepararet. Egressis namque Israhelitis per fundamenta maris sicco uestigio et Aegyptiis omnibus eodem meatu post illos properanter ingressis confestim proprium liquorem stupentibus aquis deus, qui abstulerat, reddidit, et armatas acies equitum ipsumque Faraonem pariter cum quadrigis curruum totoque eius exercitu undis obruentibus enecauit; aquarum muri, qui credentem populum tuiti fuerant, hostilem manum propria ruina prosternunt. Ipse pluuit mannae cibum cultoribus suis in heremo, qui ignem pluuerat nefando sacrilegio criminosis, ipse pluuit manna placidus, qui flammam pluuerat indignatus. Sed quoniam singula per ordinem replicare propositus primi ac septimi dierum tractatus non capit, necessaria breuitate praeteriens pauca perstringam. Ipse *disrupit petram et fluxerunt aquae* tot milibus hominum sitientibus in deserto […]".

However, the Brescia fragment does present a unique combination of Old and New Testament imagery, which surely was intended to be viewed in tandem. As recently discussed in detail by Maurizio Marchini, it is the only Red Sea sarcophagus to contain an image of the Incredulity of Saint Thomas (far right, lower register).[69] Marchini convincingly relates this episode to Bishop Gaudentius' promotion of the saint's cult in late fourth-century Brescia.[70] In making this connection, he is the first scholar to link concretely the sarcophagus imagery to the work of Gaudentius. Taking the imagery at face value, a series of parallels are immediately recognizable. Just below the image of the Red Sea is the resurrected Lazarus. Here, the analogy between the images of Moses and Christ is equally palpable, both work miracles, one with his rod the other with his "wand". As Thomas Matthews discussed in detail, Moses provided a precedent for Christ as miracle-worker or "magician" and such images clearly highlight this association.[71] Just below the Column of Fire, with its clear metaphorical meaning of brightness and truth, is the figure of Thomas. He reaches to touch Christ's wound, as the Saviour's right arm points to the Column, the source of light, depicted directly above. Hence, while the ways in which the slab's imagery relates to the writings of the city's bishop are crucial, the sarcophagus creates a series of visual connections that, like Gaudentius' sermons, were intended undoubtedly for reflection, most appropriately on an object intended for Christian burial.

The consistent use of metaphors of light and shadow/darkness in relation the Exodus narrative as realized in its typological pairing in the New Testament found throughout the Easter sermons betrays Gaudentius' debt to Neoplatonic philosophical thinking.[72] It also finds a poignant pairing in the visualization of these scenes in the Brescia fragment. We cannot rule out the possibility that the stone was selected not only for the allusions it could create in relation to the "mare Rubrum", but also to light, to the shifting colors of its veining. Thus, two preoccupations in relation to the Crossing found in Gaudentius' Easter sermons are visibly manifest in the stone slab. Namely, the parallels he repeatedly drew between the Red Sea as "wall of water" and the shadow-light metaphors of the narrative as it relates to Christian salvation. The typological reading of biblical events as moving from a state of darkness (Egypt) to one of rebirth and

---

[69] Marchini, *Un tesoro* (as in n. 2), esp. 38–40 and 45–93.
[70] Although Saint Thomas features briefly in the Easter sermons (Tract. IX, 9), it is in Tract. XVII, 6–9 (his sermon delivered at the consecration of the basilica dedicated to the *Concilium Sanctorum*, Brescia) that his meditations on the saint are most pronounced.
[71] Matthews, *The Clash of Gods* (as in n. 34), 72–77. See also n. 46 above.
[72] Corsato, "Il battesimo" (as in n. 65), 229–230.

light (through Christ), are visualized in the Brescia sarcophagus fragment, through execution and the placement of the scenes, as well as in the shifting colors that 'move' in harmony with the carved scenes.

Material Liminalities

The idea of *transitus*, as expressed in the Bishop Gaudentius' sermons finds an extraordinary visual parallel in the imagery of the Brescia sarcophagus fragment. Not only do we witness a direct iconographic pairing of Old and New Testament episodes; just as in his sermons, the Red Sea is given centre stage. Its particular importance is emphasized through both its position and the space given to its representation. What the carvings seem to indicate is a deep reflection on the material in relation to the images, that is, the intricate interplay between color and form and the symbolic associations of the stone's surface in relation to this scene and its surrounding imagery.

Whether the sarcophagus was carved in Brescia looking at local models is a question we cannot answer. Regardless, the elegant, classicizing style of its imagery surely would have found comparanda in the many remains of the fourth-century Roman city. As suggested by Marchini, perhaps the Brescia sarcophagus originally served to inter a member of the Christian elite, although this remains a hypothesis.[73] The later history of the fragment and the ways it might have been interpreted and reused are equally complex. What is certain is that its material and artistry were highly prized from the earliest writings and that there was a strong memory of its reemployment as part of an *arca* for one of the city's holy bishops, Saint Felice. The reuse of the slab within a saintly context and the visibility of its carvings suggest its special status at that time, one recognized in the early modern sources. The descriptions considered it "precious" for its carving and its material, even questioning its provenance and the very nature of its composition. The modern re-interpretation of the sarcophagus fragment at the site, as the stone for the high altar with its images hidden from view, might argue for a reuse linked to its material value alone.[74]

---

[73] Marchini, *Un tesoro* (as in n. 2), 22–23.
[74] The reuse of antique Roman sarcophagi in later periods was commonplace, see for example: Isa Ragusa, *The Re-use and Public Exhibition of Roman Sarcophagi during the Middle Ages and the Early Renaissance*, BA thesis, New York University, New York 1951; Bernard Andreae/Salvatore Settis, eds.: *Colloquio sul reimpiego dei sarcofagi romani nel medioevo*, conference proceedings (Pisa, Scuola Normale Superiore, 1982), Marburg 1984; and the discussion in Jaś Elsner/Wu Hung, "Editorial", in: *RES: Anthropology and Aesthetics*, 61/62, special issue: *Sarcophagi*, 2012,

The meaning of the term materiality has been the subject of much debate within the history of art and a number of related disciplines. Tim Ingold argues that the properties of materials are "not attributes but histories".[75] For the Brescia slab, these histories might be all that was read into the stone around the time of the creation of the images, as well as the object's physical perigrinations and its reuse at the site. These would include also its modern display in the Museo di Santa Giulia. In this 'final' setting, the contemporary viewer cannot help but create associations between the historiated fragment and its 'relative', the uncarved slab from the same sarcophagus displayed next to it (fig. 3). The latter, in its smooth, unworked state, also evokes associations of images, but of another kind. Michael Ann Holly has described materiality as "the meeting of matter and imagination".[76] In addition to its "histories," the carved sarcophagus fragment might be read in terms of the imaginative recreation of the biblical narratives in relation to the stone, one that continues to astonish and surprise the viewer, even today. In this object, matter and imagination combine in a unique way. They comment upon a series of typological and allegorical associations that permeated Christian ideas on Exodus, the Red Sea, and baptism within (but also beyond) fourth-century Brescia. In the sarcophagus fragment, the liminal setting that separated the Egyptians from the Israelites and the Israelites from the Christians, so eloquently expressed by Bishop Gaudentius in his Easter sermons, was accentuated and amplified through the medium of the red stone.

5–21, esp. 7 (with further bibliography). For recent studies on the reuse of Red Sea sarcophagi in particular: Dorothy Verkerk, "Life after Death: The Afterlife of Sarcophagi in Medieval Rome and Ravenna", in: *Roma Felix – Formation and Reflections of Medieval Rome*, ed. Éamonn ó Carragáin/Carol Neuman de Vegvar, Aldershot 2007, 81–96. Jaś Elsner, "The Christian Museum in Southern France: Antiquity, Display, and Liturgy from the Counter-Reformation to the Aftermath of Vatican II", in: *Oxford Art Journal*, 32 (2), 2009, 181–204 (with mention of Brescia sarcophagus, 199, n. 64). Galit Noga-Banai, "The Sarcophagus of Louis the Pious" (as in n. 34), 37–50.
75 Tim Ingold, *Being Alive: Essays on Movement, Knowledge, and Description*, London/New York 2011, 19–32.
76 Michael Ann Holly, "Notes from the Field: Materiality", in: *The Art Bulletin*, 95 (1), 2013, 15–17, at 15.

Kristine M. Larison
"Prolific Writing": Retracing a Desert Palimpsest in the South Sinai

The rocky terrain of the South Sinai is crisscrossed by pathways used for trade and pilgrimage over centuries of travel across the peninsula's formidable high desert. These routes are also delineated by numerous inscriptions carved into the surrounding stones. Some of this writing, such as the Egyptian stelae at Serabit El Khadim, predates the Christian era while other inscriptions represent a dominant Arabic population in the region after the seventh century. I focus here on the afterlife of Nabataean inscriptions interpreted by Christian travelers as early Hebrew that was produced by the Israelites during their wilderness sojourn. The Exodus narrative gave meaningful form to these mysterious texts. It also provided a destination for many pilgrims at Mount Sinai, located among the granite massifs at the centre of the peninsula and home to an Orthodox monastic community since the beginning of the fourth century AD.[1] The Monastery of St. Catherine, as it is known today, commemorates Moses' theophanic encounter with the divine in two distinct events both associated with the same mountain – the miraculously Burning Bush and the Giving of the Law.[2]

According to at least one sixth-century account, the Nabataean inscriptions seen in "all the stopping places of the desert" were carved by the Hebrews as they copied and retraced the words of the divine Law received on Mount

---

[1] On the innovative nature of Christian pilgrimage to Sinai, see Rudolf Solzbacher, *Mönche, Pilger und Sarazenen: Studien zum Frühchristentum auf der südlichen Sinaihalbinsel – Von den Anfängen bis zum Beginn islamischer Herrschaft*, Altenberge 1989 (Münsteraner Theologische Abhandlungen, 3), esp. 38–40, 70. For Jewish traditions that place Sinai/Horeb in northwestern Arabia rather than the Sinai Peninsula, see Allen Kerkeslager, "Jewish Pilgrimage and Jewish Identity in Hellenistic and Early Roman Egypt", in: *Pilgrimage and Holy Space in Late Antique Egypt*, ed. David Frankfurter, Leiden 1998 (Religions in the Graeco-Roman World, 134), 99–225, esp. 146–213.

[2] These two moments from the life of Moses appear in the sixth-century program of mosaics decorating the eastern wall of the monastery church at Sinai. The bibliography concerned with the Monastery of St. Catherine at Sinai is vast. For an introduction to the art and architecture of the monastery, as well as its history, see *Sinai: Treasures of the Monastery of Saint Catherine*, ed. Konstantinos A. Manafis, Athens 1990. More recent scholarship is collected in *Approaching the Holy Mountain: Art and Liturgy at St. Catherine's Monastery in the Sinai*, ed. Sharon E. J. Gerstel/Robert S. Nelson, Turnhout 2010 (Cursor Mundi, 11).

https://doi.org/10.1515/9783110618549-005

Sinai.³ This "prolific writing" refigured the desert as a textbook of holy scripture. It also inspired mimetic practice, as generations of Christian pilgrims left their own names, prayers, and invocations on the same rocks where they found these earlier inscriptions. Even though later travellers could not read or decipher the mysterious writing, it still signified, demanding a form of response through pious imitation. Archaeological surveys of the South Sinai have noted inscriptions in Greek, Arabic, Coptic, Syriac, Hebrew, Thamudic, Armenian, Georgian and Latin all dated to the Late Antique and Byzantine periods. There are also signatures added by modern travelers, written in Russian, German, English, French and Danish. Many of these inscriptions appear in close proximity to the Nabataean texts that preceded them. Some rocks carry inscriptions in seven or more languages.⁴

I propose that we trace a textual palimpsest in the South Sinai by paying closer attention to these voices now preserved as inscriptions written in stone. The brief texts, a sort of desert graffiti, offer their own gloss on Christian pilgrimage and travel in the region by giving meaningful shape to an otherwise strange and confounding landscape. While narrative pilgrimage accounts have a rich history of translation and study, whether for academic purposes or by individuals intending to follow in their footsteps (literally or figuratively, as armchair travellers enjoying vicarious pilgrimage), Sinai's rock inscriptions deserve more sustained analysis than they have thus far received. In what follows I offer a point of departure, arguing the importance of these desert inscriptions not only as a means of charting human movement through a harsh and demanding environment, but also as a way of transforming the landscape through such an encounter. The texts are anchored to a meaningful topography, even if their brief, formulaic prose reveals little beyond names and ethnographic origins for their authors. By the time Christian monks and holy men came to occupy the Sinai Peninsula in the second half of the fourth century AD, the Nabataeans' presence and their script had been forgotten. Sinai's rock inscriptions came to function as

---

3 Cosmas Indicopleustes, *Christian Topography*, V.53, trans. by Daniel F. Caner in: *History and Hagiography from the Late Antique Sinai*, Liverpool 2010 (Translated Texts for Historians, 53), 250–251.

4 For an overview of inscriptions found along the road systems of the South Sinai, see Uzi Dahari, *Monastic Settlements in South Sinai in the Byzantine Period: The Archaeological Remains*, Jerusalem 2000, 12–15 and Beno Rothenberg, "An Archaeological Survey of South Sinai", in: *Palestine Exploration Quarterly*, 102, 1970, 4–29, esp. 19, 22–29.

visual signifiers above and beyond their ability to convey specific verbal or linguistic meaning.[5]

Inscriptions in Stone: The Nabataean Mystery

The Nabataean inscriptions scattered across the South Sinai were written between the second and third centuries AD, after the Nabataean kingdom and its majestic rock-cut capital at Petra had become subjects of the Roman empire under Trajan.[6] The Nabataeans were Arab merchants who rose to prominence in the second century BC after taking control of the spice trade passing through the Arabian Peninsula. By the first century AD, they penetrated the South Sinai and may have been the first to cut passable tracks across the peninsula. Nearly 3,000 Nabataean inscriptions from the South Sinai have been recorded and published to date, although the total number is estimated somewhere between 7,000 and 10,000 inscriptions.[7] These are located "in remote wadis, on rock outcrops and summits, near isolated water sources, on sandstone as well as hard igneous rock [...]"[8] They are frequently accompanied by drawings of camels and other quadrupeds (horses, donkeys, goats and gazelles), animals familiar to the indigenous nomadic groups of the Sinai Peninsula (fig. 1).[9] And while the Nabataeans were prolific road-builders as well as accomplished merchants and traders, the way in which samples of this desert graffiti permeate the wadis and furthest rest-

---

[5] This material is drawn from my doctoral thesis, *Mount Sinai and the Monastery of St. Catherine: Place and Space in Pilgrimage Art*, University of Chicago 2016. I wish to thank my advisor, Robert S. Nelson, and the members of my dissertation committee, Rebecca Zorach and Jaś Elsner, for their support throughout this project. I take full responsibility for any errors remaining. I also thank Annette Hoffmann for her generous invitation to contribute to this volume.

[6] Caner, *History and Hagiography* (as in n. 3), 6–8. On the Nabataeans more generally, see Glenn Warren Bowersock, *Roman Arabia*, Cambridge, MA 1983; Fergus Millar, *The Roman Near East, 31 B.C. – A.D. 337*, Cambridge, MA 1993, and Fahad Mutlaq Al-Otaibi, *From Nabataea to Roman Arabia: Acquisition or Conquest*, Oxford 2011.

[7] Jane Taylor, "Language, Script and Graffiti", in: *Petra and the Lost Kingdom of the Nabataeans*, Cambridge, MA 2002, 168. The most comprehensive publication of Nabataean texts is the *Corpus Inscriptionum Semiticarum (CIS)*, pars II: *Inscriptiones Aramaicas continens*, ed. Académie des inscriptions et belles lettres, Paris 1902. However, the CIS II does not include Nabataean inscriptions discovered in the Sinai during the 1960s and 1970s by Israeli archaeologists. The greatest concentration of these were found in Wadi Haggag. See Avraham Negev, *The Inscriptions of Wadi Haggag, Sinai*, Jerusalem 1977 (Qedem, 6), esp. 73–80.

[8] Ze'ev Meshel, "Were the Sinai Rock Inscriptions Really Inscribed by 'Nabateans?'", in: *Sinai: Excavations and Studies*, Oxford 2000 (BAR International Series, 876), 143–151, esp. 144.

[9] Ibid., 148; Taylor, "Language, Script and Graffiti" (as in n. 7), 167.

ing-places of the peninsula as well as the relatively late date of the Sinai inscriptions (in comparison with the height of Nabataean power and influence during the first centuries BC and AD), has prompted some scholars to question whether the authors were, in fact, Nabataean, or if the Nabataean language and script were adopted and put to use by local inhabitants, predecessors of today's Bedouin.[10] The Nabataeans never really established permanent settlements in the South Sinai, nor is there an explanation for why the inscriptions stop being produced after the third century AD.[11]

As monastic settlements expanded in the South Sinai between the fourth and sixth centuries, a new interpretation was given to the looping, calligraphic letters of the Nabataean script, discovered throughout the peninsula by its Christian visitors. Sinai's rock inscriptions are mentioned by two early travellers in the region, the Spanish noblewoman and pilgrim Egeria, who visited Sinai and the Holy Land in AD 381–384, and Cosmas Indicopleustes, an Alexandrian merchant and amateur theologian writing in the late 540s. Both of their accounts participate in the larger cultural project of transforming Byzantine Palestine into the Christian Holy Land in this period. Egeria is the first known pilgrim to have reached Mount Sinai, but it is clear from her description that the surrounding area was already carefully mapped out according to Old Testament events. As she concludes her tour around the Mountain of God (Holy Sina), Egeria states, "And so in that way each and every thing was shown to us that the books of Moses record had been done in this place".[12]

The one surviving manuscript of her *Travels* has lost pages at both the beginning and end of the text, so that Egeria's account starts with her arrival at the foot of the holy mountain at Sinai.[13] Abridged portions of the missing text have been transmitted through Peter the Deacon's guide *On the Holy Places*

---

[10] For a brief overview of scholarly viewpoints, see Avraham Negev, "New Dated Nabatean Graffiti from the Sinai", in: *Israel Exploration Journal*, 17 (4), 1967, 250–255, esp. 253–255.

[11] By contrast with the relative abundance of Nabataean archaeological remains in northern Sinai, the citadel at Pharan was the only permanent settlement located in the southern part of the Peninsula. Dahari, *Monastic Settlements in South Sinai* (as in n. 4), 6–7. Jebel Serbal and Jebel Moneijah, both in close proximity to Pharan, functioned as important religious centres supporting Nabataean temples on their peaks. However, for Ze'ev Meshel, the absence of traditional Nabataean gods (as well as the rarity of official titles or kings' names) in the inscriptions further distanced the writers from Nabataean culture and identity. Meshel, "Sinai Rock Inscriptions" (as in n. 8), 150. For more on the Nabataeans in the Sinai Peninsula, see Javier Teixidor, "Les Nabatéens du Sinaï", in: *Le Sinaï durant l'antiquité et le Moyen Age: 4,000 ans d'histoire pour un desert*, ed. Dominique Valbelle/Charles Bonnet, Paris 1998, 83–87.

[12] Egeria, *Travelogue*, V.8, trans. by Caner, *History and Hagiography* (as in n. 3), 225.

[13] See John Wilkinson, *Egeria's Travels*, 3rd edition, Oxford 1999, 1, 167.

Fig. 1: Francis Frith, Inscriptions on the granite rocks in Sinai, Albumen print from The *Queen's Bible*, 1862–1863

(1137), which includes the staging posts along Egeria's route from Jerusalem.[14] It is through *De locis sanctis* that we discover Egeria's remarks on the Nabataean writing that she saw near Pharan: "The mountains have been carved out all around their sides. These vaults have been made in such a way that if you wanted to hang a curtain, they would make most beautiful bedchambers; and each bedchamber has been decorated with Hebrew letters".[15] Egeria's observations accord with her tendency to interpret any archaeological remains that she came across as proof of the scriptural narrative that served as her primary guidebook.[16]

Cosmas Indicopleustes, whose *Christian Topography* develops an elaborate model for understanding the cosmos based upon the Hebrew Tabernacle, offers more detailed descriptions of the "prolific writing" that could be found throughout the Sinai desert.[17] His account blends first-hand experience with invented history, attempting to explain the significance of the strange inscriptions that he, too, had witnessed:

> When they received the Law from God in writing and were taught letters for the first time, God used the desert like a quiet school, allowing them to hew the letters on stone for forty years. For that reason one can see, at all the stopping-places in that desert (I mean, the [desert] of Mount Sinai), that all the rocks of the area that have broken off from the mountains have been inscribed with carved Hebrew letters. I can attest this myself, having travelled in those places on foot.[18]

And again:

> But as for the Israelites themselves, once they had acquired letters for the first time, they constantly put them to use with prolific writing, so that all those places are still full of carved Hebrew letters, preserved to the present day for the sake of unbelievers, I think.

---

[14] Ibid., 4; Caner, *History and Hagiography* (as in n. 3), 211–212.

[15] Peter the Deacon, *De locis sanctis* (Y 14), trans. by Caner, *History and Hagiography* (as in n. 3), 216.

[16] Egeria does this, for example, by identifying ancient beehive tombs in the plain of El Raha as the Graves of Craving (PD, Y 17; Egeria, *Travelogue*, I.1 and V.10) and with the foundations of "small round houses" made of stones that she believes to be remains of the Israelites' desert encampments (Egeria, *Travelogue*, V.5 and X.4).

[17] Cosmas Indicopleustes, *Christian Topography*, V, selections trans. by Caner, *History and Hagiography* (as in n. 3), 250–251. For the entire treatise, see Cosmas Indicopleustes, *Topographie chrétienne*, ed. Wanda Wolska-Conus, 3 vols., Paris 1968–1973 (Sources chrétiennes, 141, 159, 197).

[18] Cosmas, *Christian Topography*, V.53, trans. by Caner, *History and Hagiography* (as in n. 3), 250–251.

Whoever wishes can go and look in those places, or may ask and learn that we have told the truth.[19]

Cosmas provides the additional testimony of "certain Jews, who had read them [the carved inscriptions]", in order to verify his own claims.[20] He also speculated on a chain of linguistic transmission that began with the art of writing given to Moses before being passed on to all nations through the Greek and Phoenician alphabets.[21] This theory was not original to Cosmas Indicopleustes or even to the sixth century in particular. Clement of Alexandria referred to the same idea in his *Stromata*, stating that: "Moses was the first wise man, and the first that imparted grammar to the Jews, that the Phoenicians received it from the Jews, and the Greeks from the Phoenicians".[22] However, in Cosmas' account, we find a concrete link posited between the tablets of stone given at Sinai and the remaining physical trace of this grammatical pedigree that might still be seen in the mysterious inscriptions scattered throughout the wilderness, the "quiet school" of the desert.[23] The practice of writing these texts was thus understood as a process of copying letters first inscribed on the rocks and stone of the Sinai by the very hand of God (see Ex 31:18; 32:16).[24]

This extra-biblical explanation for the Nabataean inscriptions was revived in the scholarly debates of eighteenth-century travellers, specifically by the enthusiastic Robert Clayton, Bishop of Clogher, who translated and published the diary of the Franciscan 'Prefetto' of Egypt, *A Journal from Grand Cairo to Mount Sinai, and back again* (London, 1753). The Prefetto and his party encountered the same group of inscriptions in the Wadi Mukattab, or "Valley of Writ-

---

19 Ibid., V.54, trans. by Caner, *History and Hagiography* (as in n. 3), 251.
20 Ibid., V.53, trans. by Caner, *History and Hagiography* (as in n. 3), 251.
21 "The Hebrews were the very first to be instructed by God. After receiving letters through those stone tablets and studying them for forty years in the desert, they passed them on, around that time, to their neighbors, the Phoenicians, and first to Cadmus, King of Tyrians. From him the Greeks received them, and thereafter all the nations in succession". Ibid., V.54, trans. by Caner, *History and Hagiography* (as in n. 3), 251.
22 Quoting Eupolemus' *On the Kings in Judea*. See Clement of Alexandria, *Stromata*, I.23.153; URL:<http://www.earlychristianwritings.com/text/clement-stromata-book1.html>[19.03.2017]. The patristic precedent for Cosmas' theory was noted by Caner, *History and Hagiography* (as in n. 3), 251 n. 30.
23 The nature of his eyewitness account is emphasized in both passages quoted above. Cosmas says, after his initial description of the carved letters in V.53, "I can attest this myself [...]" and in V.54, "Whoever wishes can go and look [...]".
24 Only the first set of stone tablets were written by God. After Moses broke the tablets in anger because of the golden calf, he was required to supply the second set of stone tablets and to rewrite the words of God's covenant by himself (Ex 34:1, 4, 27–28).

ing", that had likely impressed Egeria and Cosmas Indicopleustes centuries earlier (fig. 2). "And though we had in our company persons, who were acquainted with the Arabic, Greek, Hebrew, Syriac, Coptic, Latin, Armenian, Turkish, English, Illyrican, German, and Bohemian languages, yet none of them had any knowledge of these characters".[25] In a footnote, Clayton suggests that the inscriptions were written in ancient Hebrew, "which the Israelites having learned to write at the time of the giving of the law from *Mount Sinai*, diverted themselves with practising it on these mountains during their forty years abode in the wilderness".[26] He expanded this proposal in his remarks "On the Origin of Hieroglyphics" appended to the Prefetto's travel diary, where he also cited the commandment given in Deuteronomy 6:6–9 as evidence for why the Israelites might inscribe the words of the law throughout the Sinai desert.[27]

> But after the delivery of the law upon *Mount Sinai*, and the Israelites were ordered to write some of the words of the law on the posts of their doors, and on their gates, everyone who had the least genius would endeavor to learn and to practice the art of literary writing. And accordingly we find from the aforementioned Journal, that in the wilderness of *Kadesh*, where, soon after the giving of the law, the children of Israel wandered for forty years, there are whole mountains which are engraved, with inexpressible labor, with characters at present unknown, but which, there is great reason to suspect, were the ancient Hebrew characters [...].[28]

The Bishop of Clogher was so excited by the possibility of recovering what he believed was ancient Hebrew that he dedicated his translation of the Prefetto's *Journal* to the London Society of Antiquaries, asking them to "make some enquiry" into the Sinai inscriptions by outfitting "a suitable person" to make copies of as many of the inscriptions as possible so that they might be accessible for further study.[29] Clayton even offered to help finance the expedition.[30] While the im-

---

25 Robert Clayton, *A Journal from Grand Cairo to Mount Sinai, and back again. Translated from a manuscript, written by the Prefetto of Egypt*, London 1753, 45.
26 Ibid., 46.
27 Clayton also developed at length the possible transfer of "literary writing" from the Israelites to other nations. In this way, his commentary reiterated the theories stated by Cosmas Indicopleustes, although he did not acknowledge any connection to the sixth-century text. N. N. Lewis and M. C. A. MacDonald point out that the first printed edition of Cosmas' work appeared at the beginning of the eighteenth century in *Collectio Nova Patrum et Scriptorum Graecorum*, vol. II, 113–345, ed. Bernard de Montfaucon. N. N. Lewis/Michael MacDonald, "W. J. Banks and the Identification of the Nabataean Script", in: *Syria* 80, 2003, 41–110, esp. 42.
28 Clayton, *A Journal from Grand Cairo* (as in n. 25), 69–70.
29 Ibid., 3–4.
30 Minutes of the Society of Antiquaries from 30 April 1752 include a letter from Robert Clayton to the Archbishop of Canterbury that allows for the payment of £100/year for a total of five years

WADY MOKATTEB.

Fig. 2: Wady Mokatteb, lithograph by Day & Haghe illustrating Léon de Laborde's *Journey through Arabia Petraea, to Mount Sinai, and the excavated city of Petra...*, London 1836

mediate collection of Sinai inscriptions never took shape quite as he envisioned, Clayton's efforts stimulated scholarly interest in their significance across Europe.[31] It was the cumulative, if piecemeal, work of various travelers and scholars

---

"paid in such a manner as the Society shall direct". Lewis/MacDonald, "W. J. Banks" (as in n. 27), 43 n. 10. The amount of £500 was also specified by Carsten Niebuhr, who visited Sinai in 1762. See Taylor, "Language, Script and Graffiti" (as in n. 7), 148.

31 The London Society of Antiquaries declined to take part. It was the king of Denmark, Frederick V, who finally supported an expedition to Arabia between 1761–1767 with a primary objective of recording and deciphering the Sinai inscriptions. This failed to take place, except for twenty texts copied by the team's astronomer and surveyor, Carsten Niebuhr. See idem, *Travels through Arabia, and other countries in the East performed by M. Neibuhr*, trans. by Robert Heron, Edinburgh 1792, I: 197, 200–202. It took nearly a century for another such expedition to be organized and this, too, hardly counted as a success. Lewis/MacDonald, "W. J. Banks" (as in n. 27), 43–44.

who passed through Sinai and took note of the inscriptions they saw there that finally allowed the mysterious writing to be deciphered.[32] In 1840 Eduard Beer, a professor at the University of Leipzig, successfully identified the characters of the alphabet used in the Sinai inscriptions and offered the first translation of these texts.[33] He also pointed toward their source in the region of Arabia Petraea, proposing a connection with the Nabataean kingdom based in the Negev.[34] Unfortunately, Beer died in 1841, at the age of 36, and did not get to see his scholarly insights confirmed. The paleographic connection between the Sinai inscriptions and the Nabataean capital at Petra was conclusively demonstrated by M.A. Levy in 1860.[35]

The first word recognized by scholars in the Nabataean script was *šlm*, the Aramaic-Hebrew-Arabic word for peace.[36] These three letters are the most frequently occurring combination in the inscriptions, followed by the word *dkyr*, "let be remembered".[37] The content of the thousands of Nabataean inscriptions found across the Sinai Peninsula is fairly simple and repetitive. Most consist of formulaic petitions giving little more than a name, patronymic, and the request to be remembered and blessed. The most common phrases are "Remember so-

---

[32] The process of documenting the Sinaitic inscriptions and identifying their linguistic origins over the course of the eighteenth and nineteenth centuries has been summarized by Jane Taylor in several publications and by N. N. Lewis and M. C. A. MacDonald. See Taylor, "Language, Script and Graffiti" (as in n. 7) and ead., "The Writing on the Rocks", in: *Al-Ahram Weekly Online*, 620, 9–15 January 2003, URL:<http://weekly.ahram.org.eg/Archive/2003/620/heritage.htm> [19.03.2017]; Lewis/MacDonald, "W. J. Banks" (as in n. 27).

[33] Eduard Friedrich Ferdinand Beer, *Inscriptiones Veteres litteris et lingua hucusque incognitis ad Montem Sinai magno numero servatae quas Pocock, Niebuhr,... aliique descripserunt*, Leipzig 1840. The publications consulted by Beers are listed in his introduction. Taylor, "Language, Script and Graffiti" (as in n. 7), 149–150; Lewis/MacDonald, "W. J. Banks" (as in n. 27), 46–47.

[34] At the time, there were no known samples of Nabataean script with which to compare the texts from Sinai, although the first publication of inscriptions from Petra became available in 1855. See Lewis/MacDonald, "W. J. Banks" (as in n. 27), 46 n. 40. As argued by Lewis and MacDonald, the situation might have been remedied earlier if the research notes and inscriptions copied by William John Banks during his travels in the Near East between 1815–1819 had been more widely circulated. Banks produced a near-perfect copy of the Turkmaniyya tomb inscription at Petra and clearly recognized the correspondence between this elegant script and the Sinai rock graffiti. Ibid., 47, 49–50.

[35] M. A. Levy, "Über die nabathäischen Inschriften von Petra, Hauran, vornehmlich von Sinai-Halbinsel und über die Münzlegenden nabathäischer Könige", in: *Zeitschrift der Deutschen Morgenländischen Gesellschaft*, 14, 1860, 363–484, 594.

[36] Also translated "be secure". See Lewis/MacDonald, "W. J. Banks" (as in n. 27), 63–68, passim.

[37] Both words were translated by E. F. F. Beer, although the use of *šlm* had already been noted by Edward Wortley Montagu on his trip to Sinai in 1766. Ibid., 44.

and-so the son of so-and-so", and "May so-and-so the son of so-and-so be secure" or "May so-and-so be secure in well-being".[38] This example from Wadi Mughara is one of only seven Nabataean inscriptions that includes a specific date; it reads, "Be remembered Ha'lit the son of Ḥalisat in welfare. In the year 161 [AD 267/8]".[39] The character of the texts is primarily religious and, considering the limited range of dates between which the Nabataean inscriptions were created,[40] existed as a rather brief and locally circumscribed phenomenon.[41] The work of collecting and publishing inscriptions in the South Sinai pursued over the last century has allowed for an impressive body of analysis regarding personal names, the use of titles, and family relationships as revealed by the accumulation of such prayers and petitions written across the desert.[42]

Therefore, the interpretation first supplied by Cosmas Indicopleustes, although he was mistaken about who exactly carved these examples of desert graffiti into Sinai's rock and stone, was actually not too far off the mark. He asserts, "This was also what certain Jews who had read them told us, saying that what was written went thus: 'Departure of so-and-so, from the tribe of so-and-so, in the year such-and-such, in the month such-and-such', just as some of us also write in lodging places".[43] His translators may have recognized aspects of the general formula being employed (Nabataean does indeed belong to the greater linguistic family of Semitic languages), but as Comas pointed out, leaving one's name behind in lodging places or at stops and resting points along a route of travel was also common practice. The Piacenza pilgrim, who visited Sinai in the late sixth century, similarly acknowledged writing the names of

---

38 Ibid., 63–68, passim; Meshel, "Sinai Rock Inscriptions" (as in n. 8), 148.
39 Negev, "New Dated Nabatean Graffiti" (as in n. 10), 251–252.
40 There are only seven texts that provide dates as part of the inscription. These range between AD 150–267. Meshel, "Sinai Rock Inscriptions" (as in n. 8), 150; Avraham Negev, *Nabatean Archaeology Today*, New York/London 1986, 115. See also Negev, "New Dated Nabatean Graffiti" (as in n. 10), 250–255.
41 The work that Avraham Negev has done on personal names reveals a distinctive subset of local names commonly used in the Sinai but not found elsewhere. Geographical names are also limited, whereas occupations noted in the inscriptions are often consistent with the known resources available to and supporting an indigenous population.
42 Because the inscriptions usually contain both the writer's name and that of his father, including even his father's father at times, some genealogies can be established going back for several generations. Negev, *Nabatean Archaeology Today* (as in n. 40), 116. See also id., *Personal Names in the Nabatean Realm*, Jerusalem 1991 (Qedem, 32).
43 Cosmas, *Christian Topography*, V.53, trans. by Caner, *History and Hagiography* (as in n. 3), 251.

his parents on a bench at the house in Cana where Christ's first miracle took place.⁴⁴

Although the authors of these simple blessings eventually ceased using the Nabataean script to offer their petitions for peace and good memory,⁴⁵ this impulse to memorialize one's name (and transitory existence) within the desert landscape did not stop with the advent of Christian monasticism and pilgrimage in this region. Instead, Christian travellers rewrote the meaning of the Nabataean texts with the addition of their own.⁴⁶ I suspect these later inscriptions were never intended to efface previous texts, but represented a desire to associate their prayers with those already inscribed in the Sinai wilderness. Ze'ev Meshel clarifies this pattern of pious imitation in his archaeological analysis by emphasizing that, while Nabataean inscriptions can be found alone without inscriptions in other languages nearby, the addition of later Christian writing almost always appears in concentrations where Nabataean inscriptions are also present.⁴⁷ The archaeological data therefore suggests an intentional layering of texts, one on top of another, in the application of Sinai's rock graffiti over the centuries.

Bridging the linguistic gap of incommunicability, the inscriptions foreground the importance of physical proximity. Through the reiterative act of writing on stone, subsequent travellers came into material contact with Sinai's past and the presumed former occupants of its venerable history. The desert inscriptions also reflect the physical conditions of their environment – not just in their accumulation along well-travelled routes and/or popular resting places in the wadis of the South Sinai, but also in adhering to the sides of rocks and mountains most often in shade (where nomadic shepherds and pilgrims might gain protection from the forceful heat of the sun).⁴⁸ This practical aspect of locating the Sinai

---

44 Piacenza Pilgrim, *Travelogue*, 4, trans. by John Wilkinson, *Jerusalem Pilgrims before the Crusades*, 2ⁿᵈ ed., Warminster 2002, 131.
45 As stated above, there is some scholarly debate as to whether or not the authors were themselves Nabataean or simply using and adapting the Nabataean language. Most accept that it was likely a combination of "travellers, pilgrims, and local inhabitants of Sinai in the early centuries AD" who wrote the surviving inscriptions. Lewis/MacDonald, "W. J. Banks" (as in n. 27), 46.
46 The notion of Kulturkampf introduced by Beno Rothenberg seems to have been overdetermined. Avraham Negev responded to his assertions, stating that "in no case do the Byzantine-Christian inscriptions overlap or cover Jewish inscriptions or Symbols". Instead, the two types of inscriptions are probably contemporaneous with one another. Idem, *Inscriptions of Wadi Haggag* (as in n. 7), 73–74; cf. Rothenberg, "An Archaeological Survey" (as in n. 4), 19–20.
47 Meshel, "Sinai Rock Inscriptions" (as in n. 8), 144–145. As Rothenberg states, "the Nabataean inscriptions are the oldest and also the most conspicuous along the whole road". Id., "An Archaeological Survey" (as in n. 4), 19.
48 Negev, *Inscriptions of Wadi Haggag* (as in n. 7), 78.

inscriptions has been noted by archaeologists in their survey work as well as by other travellers. When John Lewis Burckhardt copied several of the inscriptions that he came across in 1816, he described the cliffs of Wadi Mukattab as "so situated as to afford a fine shade to travellers during the mid-day hours".[49] (See fig. 2).

I propose that alongside early documents like Egeria's pilgrimage account and the unique philosophical treatise of Cosmas Indicopleustes, which both interpret a misrecognized Nabataean script as ancient Hebrew according to the Exodus narrative, the physical proximity of later inscriptions adhering next to these earliest samples of desert graffiti offers material evidence for the continued Christianizing interpretation of the unknown letters in later centuries. Granted, we do not have other historical sources confirming this association between the time of Egeria and of Cosmas and later European travel accounts that date from the seventeenth and eighteenth centuries; the entire medieval period exists as a lacuna with regards to Nabataean inscriptions in the South Sinai Peninsula.[50] But the ongoing practice of pilgrimage graffiti placed in juxtaposition to these early, unreadable inscriptions are texts that should be able to speak for themselves, giving voice in a multitude of names and languages to their perceived value and importance. It was enough that the Nabataean letterforms offered a physical trace of human presence and past activity. As such, even though inscrutable, they conveyed meaning and can be incorporated into a Christian rereading of Sinai's stark landscape and mountainous terrain.

---

[49] John Lewis Burckhardt, *Travels in Syria and the Holy Land,* London 1822, 621.
[50] Taylor, Lewis and MacDonald all point to the Prefetto of Egypt as the first modern account of the Sinai inscriptions, after introducing their history of the Nabataean graffiti with Cosmas Indicopleustes. However, there were at least a few earlier mentions of the inscribed rocks found in/around the famed Wadi Mukattab. Raymond Weill attributes the distinction of first noting these inscriptions to Pietro della Valle, who passed through the Sinai Peninsula in 1615–1616. Id., *La presqu'île du Sinai: étude de géographie et d'histoire,* Paris 1908, 288. Weill also lists a number of other travelers in the seventeenth and early eighteenth centuries who were attentive to the strange letter forms of the ancient script (Monconys, Neitzschitz, Thévenot, and Morrison), although more as a matter of curiosity than representatives of sustained scholarly or archaeological interest. Ibid., 289, 293. The shift in how these inscriptions were treated really occurs with Egmond van der Nijenburg, who copied a number of examples of Nabataean graffiti during his travels through Sinai in 1721, and with Robert Clayton's translation of *A Journal from Grand Cairo to Mount Sinai and back again* (1753), which publicized the Prefetto's pilgrimage account from 1722. Richard Pococke arrived sixteen years later than the Franciscan superior but mentions this account in his own, *A Description of the East and Some Other Countries,* which was published between 1743–1745.

In Conclusion: Charting the Sinai Landscape Through Texts

This essay has focused on the history of reception and Christian interpretation of Nabataean inscriptions from the South Sinai Peninsula in relation to a scriptural past sought by many of its travellers and pilgrims after the monastic settlement of Mount Sinai and surrounding areas in the fourth century. I have so far only alluded to the presence of Christian inscriptions added to the same rocks and stones occupied by Nabataean writing as evidence for the continued visual significance and material meaning of the Nabataean graffiti in later periods. But the later inscriptions have much to add to our understanding of pilgrimage and travel through the Sinai. These can be found along the major pilgrimage routes leading to Mount Sinai and the Monastery of St. Catherine from both eastern and western sides of the peninsula and, in some cases, help to indicate which roads were more popular and/or well-travelled in certain periods. In conclusion, I gesture towards the diversity of languages and cultural identities that have accumulated in the inscriptions of the South Sinai and offer a brief acknowledgment of what these texts can add to our understanding of Sinai's history.

As mentioned previously, inscriptions from to the Early Christian and Byzantine periods include texts written in Greek, Arabic, Coptic, Syriac, Hebrew, Thamudic, Latin, Armenian and Georgian. Although the Greek inscriptions are the most numerous, these have not received any systematic study.[51] Michael Stone's survey of Armenian language inscriptions, a total of 113 (along with twenty Georgian examples), has led to a reconsideration of the route approaching the Sinai monastery from Jerusalem to Aila (Elat).[52] Until publication of this epigraphic evidence, the western route from Palestine to Mount Sinai was assumed to be the preferred one based on early pilgrimage accounts such as that of Egeria.[53] Following the coast of the Mediterranean from Palestine to Pelusium, it then

---

51 Philip Mayerson, "The Pilgrim Routes to Mount Sinai and the Armenians", in: *Israel Exploration Journal*, 32 (1), 1982, 44–57, esp. 46 n. 4 and Michael E. Stone, "Sinai Armenian Inscriptions", in: *Biblical Archaeologist*, 45 (1), 1982, 27–31, esp. 31.
52 The inscriptions have been published as *The Armenian Inscriptions from the Sinai*, ed. Michael E. Stone, Cambridge, MA 1982.
53 Michael E. Stone, *Armenian Inscriptions from Sinai: Intermediate Report*, Sydney 1979; Stone, "Sinai Armenian Inscriptions" (as in n. 51), 31; and Mayerson, "Pilgrim Routes to Mount Sinai" (as in n. 51), 46 n. 4. Avraham Negev made the same observation based on more general evidence, stating that "the western routes leading from Egypt to the same Holy Mountain, crossing the large wadies Mukattab and Feiran are almost void of Christian inscriptions, although Nabatean graffiti entirely cover the rocks there". Idem, *Inscriptions of Wadi Haggag* (as in n. 7), 79.

turned southward to Clysma and traced the eastern shore of the Gulf of Suez before going inland. It was also the longer route, with some twenty-five stations along the way. The eastern road was more direct and shorter overall, with a total of eighteen stations. It went directly south from Jerusalem to Elusa and then Elat before entering the South Sinai.[54] The concentration of Armenian inscriptions along the eastern pilgrimage route corresponds with the seventh-century report given by Anastasius of Sinai of hundreds of Armenian pilgrims visiting the Sinai monastery together at a time.[55] They also draw our attention to locations whose significance has been forgotten over time, such as Wadi Haggag where the accumulation of Christian texts might indicate a site of particular religious interest.[56] For example, Avraham Negev proposed that Wadi Haggag and the spring at Ain Huderah might have been an alternate identification for the biblical site of Hazeroth (where Aaron and Miriam opposed Moses and Miriam was struck with leprosy; see Nm 11:35–12:16 and Nm 33:17–18).[57] If one subset of inscriptions yields such useful data for comparison with other surviving historical accounts, the value of further documenting the content, locations, and range of dates available for other language groups among Sinai's rock graffiti cannot be underestimated.

More recently, the Middle Eastern Culture Center in Japan (MECCJ) is in the process of collecting and analyzing Arabic inscriptions in the South Sinai alongside other archaeological data from the area of Rāya/al-Ṭūr on the Red Sea.[58] Al-Ṭūr (Raithou) was an important port for trade and pilgrimage from Late Antiquity onward, while the adjacent site of Rāya (located eight km south of the city) flourished between the eighth and twelfth centuries in particular. The MECCJ surveys focus on nearly 2,000 inscriptions found at Mt. Nāqūs, where the legend of a buried monastery and musical sand attracted a number of scholars and

---

54 See Dahari, *Monastic Settlements in South Sinai* (as in n. 4), 9–11.
55 Numbering seventy-three in all, as compared to five examples of Armenian graffiti identified on the western approach to Mount Sinai. Stone, "Sinai Armenian Inscriptions" (as in n. 51), 30; Mayerson, "Pilgrim Routes to Mount Sinai" (as in n. 51), 57. On the large groups of Armenian pilgrims visiting Mount Sinai, see Anastasius of Sinai, *Tales of the Sinai Fathers*, I.4 [Nau 38], trans. by Caner, *History and Hagiography* (as in n. 3), 176–177.
56 Stone, "Sinai Armenian Inscriptions" (as in n. 51), 28–29; cf. Mayerson, Pilgrim Routes to Mount Sinai (as in n. 51), 45, whose numbers were derived from the *Intermediate Report* published by Stone in 1979.
57 Negev, *Inscriptions of Wadi Haggag* (as in n. 7), 1, 76–77.
58 Mutsuo Kawatoko/Risa Tokunaga, "Arabic Rock Inscriptions of South Sinai", in: *Proceedings of the Seminar for Arabian Studies*, 36, 2006, 217–227. For a full description of the archaeological work being done by the MECCJ, see *Archaeological Survey of the Rāya/al-Ṭūr Area on the Sinai Peninsula, Egypt, 2004*, ed. Mutsuo Kawatoko, Tokyo 2005.

tourists in the nineteenth century.⁵⁹ The greatest number of Arabic inscriptions at this site, however, date to the ninth and tenth centuries, corresponding to the period in which Rāya served as one of the most important international ports in the Arab Islamic world.⁶⁰ While the majority of Arabic inscriptions at Mt. Nāqūs are Muslim, Arabic inscriptions found elsewhere in the South Sinai are predominantly Christian in origin, especially in Wadi Mukattab. At this site, a total of seventy-seven out of 112 Arabic inscriptions were incised by Christians.⁶¹ This concentration of graffiti offers a glimpse of routes travelled and preferred by a completely different demographic from that of the Armenians.

By comparing the addition of later pilgrim writing to the earlier Nabataean inscriptions, I wish to emphasize the reciprocal nature of experience and interpretation that has come to characterize Sinai's commemorative landscape. Visitors brought with them expectations based upon readings of scripture, biblical commentaries, and the accounts of previous travellers. These helped to shape their understanding of what they saw. Yet through their physical encounter with the holy places at Sinai, visualizing the figures and events of its sacred past, touching and tasting phenomena unique to this desert environs (such as the samples of manna given to pilgrims by monks and holy men), individuals were themselves transformed. Their experiences, memories, and interpretations were added to accumulating layers of meaning at the site – new layers of strata continuously laid down in the ongoing definition of Sinai's sacred topography. We still have much to learn from the voices they left behind.

---

59 Kawatoko/Tokunaga, "Arabic Rock Inscriptions" (as in n. 58), 218.
60 The Arabic texts fall into three categories; invocations (beginning "O God, forgive [...]"), professions of faith, and commemorations of visits. Ibid., 221. Besides 966 Arabic inscriptions, the MECCJ survey counted 432 inscriptions written in Greek, eight in Coptic, seventy-one in Latin, one in Nabataean, eleven in Russian, and six in Modern Hebrew, along with a number of tribal marks and drawings (including ninety crosses). Ibid., 219.
61 See Kawatoko/Tokunaga, figure 9, for a table displaying the number of Arabic inscriptions found at various sites in the South Sinai (identifying a total of 249 inscriptions outside the Rāya/al-Tūr area). Ibid., 224–225.

Silvan Wagner
Bewegung in der *Altdeutschen Exodus* als Heilsempfang und Übersetzung

Das Thema des Exodus nimmt für die Geschichte der deutschsprachigen Literatur eine gewichtige Stellung ein: Die alttestamentarischen Bücher Genesis, Exodus und Judith werden in der Epoche zwischen 1050 und 1170 in die frühmittelhochdeutsche Volkssprache nacherzählend übertragen, eine Epoche, die nicht zuletzt mit diesen Bibelparaphrasen Grundlegendes für die deutschsprachige Literatur leistet:

> Die Leistung läßt sich am prägnantesten dadurch charakterisieren, daß es der Volkssprache in diesen rund hundert Jahren gelingt, literarisch zu werden. Dies gilt zunächst in einem ganz wörtlichen Sinn: Sie verbindet sich nunmehr endgültig dem Buchstaben, der Schrift, derart daß wir seit dieser Zeit (und erst seit ihr) von einer kontinuierlichen Geschichte der deutschen Literatur sprechen können. Aber auch in einem tieferen Sinne kommt in dieser Zeit die deutschsprachige Literatur zu sich selbst. Am Anfang der Epoche steht die Volkssprache, soweit sie der Aufzeichnung für wert befunden wird, noch ganz im Dienste der Theologie, des Glaubens. [...] Am Ende der Epoche beginnt die Literatur sich als eigenständige Vermittlerin von Erkenntnis zu verstehen [...]. Gleichsam das Siegel auf diese Entwicklung wird der Durchbruch zur reinen Fiktionalität im höfischen Roman sein.[1]

Die frühmittelhochdeutsche Paraphrase des zweiten Buchs Moses, etwas irreführend als *Altdeutsche Exodus* bezeichnet, wird ungefähr im letzten Drittel dieser Epoche verortet[2], und ich möchte im Folgenden zeigen, dass der Text eine prägnante Wegmarke im Literarisierungsprozess darstellt: Die volkssprachliche Dichtung tritt ihrem Publikum – ungeachtet ihrer erst kurzen Erfahrung – in der Altdeutschen Exodus mit erstaunlicher Selbstbewusstheit und Eigenständigkeit entgegen, wobei gerade auch dem Thema des Exodus – der Bewegung aus der Fremde in die Heimat – eine zentrale Stellung zukommt. Diese Behauptung be-

---

1 Gisela Vollmann-Profe, *Geschichte der deutschen Literatur von den Anfängen bis zum Beginn der Neuzeit. Band I: Von den Anfängen zum hohen Mittelalter*, Teil 2: *Wiederbeginn volkssprachlicher Schriftlichkeit im hohen Mittelalter (1050/60 – 1160/70)*, Königstein 1986, 15 – 16.
2 Die Datierung ist – wie bei den meisten volkssprachlichen Texten dieser Epoche – nur recht ungenau möglich: Vogt verortet die Entstehung des Textes um 1100, Pinower setzt die Zeit zwischen 1120 – 1130 an, Menhardt plädiert sogar für eine Verortung um 1170, vgl. Ursula Henning, Art. „Altdeutsche Exodus", in: *Verfasserlexikon*, vol. I, 2. Aufl., Berlin/New York 1978, Sp. 276 – 279, hier Sp. 276. Die Datierung wäre auch auf der Basis der hier vorgestellten Ergebnisse neu zu diskutieren, was jedoch den Rahmen der Möglichkeiten sprengen würde.

darf freilich einer genauen Begründung, denn für eine moderne Lektüre drängt sich ein entsprechender Eindruck nicht gerade auf.

Die *Altdeutsche Exodus* ist in zwei Handschriften überliefert, wobei die Wiener Handschrift fragmentarisch ist, die Millstätter Handschrift hingegen den vollständigen Text enthält. In beiden Handschriften ist die *Altdeutsche Exodus* mit der Altdeutschen Genesis, einer Übertragung des ersten Buchs Moses, zusammen überliefert. Die *Altdeutsche Exodus* ist nicht gerade ein Lieblingskind der Forschung. Sie steht deutlich im Schatten der *Altdeutschen Genesis*, die im Vergleich zum Vulgatatext vor allem durch zahlreiche eingeschobene Auslegungen eine deutlich veränderte Version mit eigenständigen theologischen Tendenzen präsentiert.

Vor dieser Folie erscheint die *Altdeutsche Exodus* zunächst tatsächlich als unspannend, da sie sich vergleichsweise eng an den Vulgatatext hält und auf den ersten Blick keine innovativen theologischen Deutungen anbietet.[3] Gerade aber der Aspekt, dass sie auf eine allegorische Auslegung verzichtet, kennzeichnet sie als Text, der das Erzählen selbst und nicht die religiöse Botschaft oder theologische Deutungen dominant setzt und damit eine „neue Autonomie"[4] gewinnt. Die ältere Forschung spricht der *Altdeutschen Exodus* deswegen allerdings auch jedweden theologischen Ehrgeiz ab[5] und ordnet den Text zusammen mit der *Genesis* im Rahmen der klösterlichen Lektionen ein. In den Worten Edward Schröders:

> Die ‚Exodus', für das Osterfest gedichtet, setzt die ‚Genesis' fort, die für die vorösterliche Zeit zur Vorlesung bestimmt war. In welchem Kreise? Nun darüber kann kein Zweifel sein: im Kreise von Ordensgeistlichen, eher von Chorherren als von Mönchen.[6]

Auf diese Einordnung wird noch zurückzukommen sein. Die jüngere Forschung – vor allem Dennis Green – hat das Augenmerk auf die dennoch existenten Unterschiede zwischen der *Altdeutschen Exodus* und der Vulgata gelegt[7] und spricht etwa davon, dass sich eine Kreuzzugstheologie in der volkssprachlichen Fassung

---

[3] Vgl. Hartmut Freytag, *Die Theorie der allegorischen Schriftdeutung und die Allegorie in deutschen Texten besonders des 11. und 12. Jahrhunderts*, Bern/München 1982, 80.
[4] Henning, *Exodus* (vgl. Anm. 2), Sp. 277.
[5] Vgl. Henning, *Exodus* (vgl. Anm. 2), Sp. 277.
[6] Edward Schröder, „Zur ‚Exodus': Termin und Publicum", in: *Zeitschrift für deutsches Altertum und Literatur*, 72, 1935, 239–240, hier 240.
[7] Vgl. dazu detailliert Dennis H. Green, „The Millstätter Exodus and its Bibical Source", in: *Medium Aevium*, 38, 1969, 227–238.

niederschlägt.⁸ Diese These einer eigenständigen theologischen Lesart der Exodusgeschichte in der mittelhochdeutschen Fassung kann auf der Basis der doch recht marginalen Unterschiede zum Vulgatatext als Gesamtdeutung jedoch nicht überzeugen.⁹

Gemeinsam ist beiden Urteilen der älteren und jüngeren Forschung, dass ein etwaiger eigenständiger theologischer Ansatz der *Altdeutschen Exodus* in der inhaltlichen Differenz der Erzählung zum Vulgatatext gesucht wird. Dies ist eine naheliegende, doch keineswegs notwendige Vorgehensweise, kann doch derselbe Inhalt in einen anderen Zusammenhang gestellt andere Bedeutung erlangen. Der andere Zusammenhang, in den die *Altdeutsche Exodus* das biblische Geschehen stellt, ist die Volkssprache bzw. die Übertragung aus dem Lateinischen ins Mittelhochdeutsche. Was angesichts der heutigen Übersetzungspraxis eher marginal erscheint, stellt für hochmittelalterliche Verhältnisse allerdings einen gravierenden Eingriff dar: Was heute die Öffnung eines Textes für einen anderssprachigen, aber grundsätzlich gleichen Leserkreis bedeutet, ist im Hochmittelalter der Wechsel vom klerikal-lateinischen zum laikal-volkssprachlichen Publikum.¹⁰

Von dieser Perspektive aus muss auch die Einordnung der *Exodus* durch Edward Schröder hinterfragt werden, der als Publikum selbstverständlich den

---

8 Green stellt die *Altdeutsche Exodus* dabei in den Zusammenhang des *Rolandsliedes* und der *Älteren Judith* und hebt das feudale Setting der Texte hervor, das bei der *Exodus* die alttestamentarische Thematik überforme: „We saw that this work treated an Old Testament theme, but described the Israelites in feudal, knightly warfare of the present (or, more exactly, crusading warfare) was treated in Old Testament terms"; Dennis H. Green, *The Millstätter Exodus. A Crusading Epic*, Cambridge 1966, 236.
9 Green stützt sich in erster Linie auf die Schilderung der zweiten und achten ägyptischen Plage, die in der Schilderung der *Altdeutschen Exodus* als Kampf gegen eine unritterliche Heerschar von Kröten und gegen eine ritterliche Heerschar von Heuschrecken inszeniert sind. Vollmann-Profe relativiert jedoch seine Interpretation des Gesamttextes als verdecktes Kreuzzugsepos: „Diese Einlagen dürften kaum als ironische Distanzierung vom Stil heldenepischer Dichtung gedacht gewesen sein, auch nicht als Signale, die ‚Exodus' als allegorisch verhülltes Kreuzzugsepos zu verstehen, was ebenfalls in der Forschung ventiliert wurde. Man wird sie wohl eher als witzig-spielerische Verbeugung vor dem adeligen Publikum interpretieren dürfen, beispielsweise – vom Autor her betrachtet – als kleine Kabinettstückchen, vergleichbar etwa den Kadenzen eines Solokonzerts"; Vollmann-Profe, *Geschichte* (wie Anm. 1), 92. Zur Kritik an Greens Interpretation ausführlich vgl. Edgar Papp, „D[enis] H[ovard] Green, The Millstätter Exodus. A Crusading Epic [Rez.]", in: *Beiträge zur Geschichte der Deutschen Sprache und Literatur*, 89, 1967, 356–363.
10 Auch Vollmann-Profe betont, dass „der ‚Exodus'-Dichter vor allem erzählen will"; Vollmann-Profe, *Geschichte* (wie Anm. 1), S. 91, und sich dabei „immer wieder, wenn auch bescheidene, Freiräume" schafft; ibid., 92.

hohen Klerus ansetzt. Die Selbstverständlichkeit, die Schröder kaum begründet[11], ist allerdings keineswegs gegeben: Die volkssprachliche Form, die vielfältige Parallelen auch zur frühhöfischen Literatur aufweist[12], verweist auf ein laikales Publikum.[13] Dafür spricht auch, dass die *Altdeutsche Exodus* außer der Vulgata keine weiteren lateinischen Vorlagen verwendet und sich damit nicht in den theologisch-gelehrten Diskurs stellt:

> Obwohl das Buch Exodus nicht selten ausgelegt wurde und nicht nur in Exoduskommentaren, sondern auch in zahlreichen Predigten, läßt sich aus dem Bereich dieser lateinischen Literatur keine direkte Quelle für die Altdt. Exodus als eine offenbar spezifisch volkssprachliche Dichtung des Buches Exodus nachweisen.[14]

Im Folgenden möchte ich die *Altdeutsche Exodus* konsequent aus volkssprachlich-höfischer Perspektive lesen. Dabei lässt sich, so denke ich, eine neue laientheologische Fokussierung der Exodusgeschichte herausarbeiten, die ich als Leitthese der Analyse voranstellen möchte: In der *Altdeutschen Exodus* wird das

---

11 Sein einziges wirkliches Argument, dass nämlich in der *Exodus* nicht übersetzt würde (und deswegen ein klerikales Publikum anzusetzen sei), fällt in sich zusammen, wenn man die Übertragung des Begriffs „Adonai" in V. 1141 bedenkt. Schröders Selbstverständlichkeit wird noch tradiert etwa bei Helmut Birkhan, *Geschichte der altdeutschen Literatur im Licht ausgewählter Texte*, Teil II: *Mittelhochdeutsche vor- und frühhöfische Literatur*, Wien 2002, 32.

12 Schon Otto Pniower hat Parallelen zum *Annolied*, dem *Alexander*, der *Kaiserchronik*, dem *Rolandslied* und der französischen *Chanson de Geste* herausgearbeitet: „der verf. der Exodus folgt, wie jeder bei der oberflächlichsten vergleichung sieht, dem grundtext ganz sclavisch und gestattet sich zusätze nur da, wo er heeresausrüstungen, aufzüge udgl. schildern oder in die geleise der volksmässigen heldendichtung einlenken kann"; Otto Pniower, „Die Abfassungszeit der Altdeutschen Exodus", in: *Zeitschrift für deutsches Altertum und Literatur*, 33, 1889, 73–97, hier 78. Pinower arbeitet vor allem die geistige Nähe zum *Rolandslied* heraus und die Freude des Dichters der *Exodus* „an der schilderung kriegerischer ausrüstung und ritterlicher aufzüge" (ibid., 80), so dass es gerade vor diesem Hintergrund verwundert, dass er auf die rein religiöse Ausrichtung des Textes besteht und nicht ein frühhöfisches Publikum in Erwägung zieht. Diese Spannung schlägt sich auch in seinem Aufsatz nieder; vgl. ibid., 81, 85, 87, 90.

13 Vgl. auch Henning, *Exodus* (vgl. Anm. 2), S. 278; Vollmann-Profe, *Geschichte* (wie Anm. 1), 92. Dennis H. Green, „The Millstätter Exodus and its Biblical Source", in: *Medium AEvum*, 38, 1969, 227–238, arbeitet heraus, dass alle Veränderungen zur biblischen Vorlage den Erzählcharakter der *Altdeutschen Exodus* stützen. Auch Hansjürgen Blinn geht – gerade auf Basis seiner differenzierten zahlenallegorischen Untersuchung – von einem laikalen Publikum aus, dem freilich die zahlenallegorischen Feinheiten verborgen bleiben, vgl. Hans-Jürgen Blinn, *Die Altdeutsche Exodus. Strukturuntersuchungen zur Zahlenkomposition und Zahlensymbolik*, Amsterdam 1974, 290–292.

14 Hartmut Freytag, *Die Theorie der allegorischen Schriftdeutung und die Allegorie in deutschen Texten besonders des 11. und 12. Jahrhunderts*, Bern/München 1982, 80.

Hauptmotiv der Erzählung, die räumliche Bewegung, aufgeladen mit der Bedeutung des Heilsgewinns und darüber parallelisiert mit dem Übersetzungsvorgang in die Volkssprache. Vor allem in Prolog und Epilog wird diese Verknüpfung von räumlicher und geistiger Bewegung vorbereitet, sie schlägt sich aber auch in Spuren der Erzählung vom Exodus nieder.

Spuren einer eigenen Lesart des Exodusgeschehens – mehr kann an der *Altdeutschen Exodus* nicht aufgezeigt werden; die *Altdeutsche Exodus* ist selbst kein theologischer Text, sondern erzählende Literatur[15], die kein theologisches Konzept explizit entwickelt, sondern lediglich auf ein solches mehr oder weniger konsequent zurückgreift.

An exponierter Stelle, im Prolog der Erzählung vom Exodus, wird das Thema der Übersetzung eingeführt, so dass von Anfang der Dichtung an der Erzähler und seine Tätigkeit des Übersetzens zentral gestellt ist:

Ich tâte iw gerne chunde,	Ich würde euch
wan daz mich irrent sunde,	(zumal mich Sünden belasten)
ettewaz uon den bûchen,	sehr gerne etwas aus den Büchern erzählen,
dâ wir inne sculen sûchen	in denen wir nach der
des himeliskin chuniges êre	Ehre des Himmelskönigs und nach
und sîniu werch uil hêre,	seinen herrlichen Werken suchen sollen,
diu er wîlen worhte	die er vormals
durch Abrahâmes liebe, der in uorhte,	mittels Abrahams ehrfürchtiger Zuneigung
an der isrâheliskin diete,	an den Israeliten ausführte,
die er lôste ûzzer nôte. (VV. 1 – 10)[16]	die er aus ihrer Not erlöste.

Dieser Selbstentwurf des Erzählers passt viel eher in einen höfischen Rezeptionsraum als zur klösterlichen Lesung, da sich hier ein wissender Erzähler einem Publikum gegenüberstellt, das den Inhalt der angesprochenen Bücher nicht in der Weise wie der Erzähler präsent hat. Auch der später wieder aufgegriffene[17] Bezug auf die Ehre Gottes als König des Himmels ist für ein höfisches Publikum sofort anschlussfähig, ebenso wie das Handeln des Herrschers *durch* einen ihm in Liebe und Furcht zugetanen Vasallen, zu dem hier Abraham stilisiert wird.

---

15 Dies gilt allerdings auch schon für die biblische Vorlage, wie überhaupt für die meisten biblischen Bücher, die grundsätzlich von Gott erzählen und nicht über ihn und sein Verhältnis zum Menschen reflektieren. George Lindbeck fasst diesen Unterschied in der Differenzierung zwischen *first order language* und *second order language*, vgl. George A. Lindbeck, *The Nature of Doctrine. Religion and Theology in a Postliberal Age*, Philadelphia 1984.
16 Ich zitiere aus der Ausgabe *Die Altdeutsche Exodus. Untersuchungen und kritischer Text*, hrsg. von Edgar Papp, München 1968.
17 Vgl. V. 16.

Von dieser Beobachtung aus lässt sich auch ein Ergebnis Greens an der Erzählung vom Exodus selbst neu bewerten: Green hat herausgearbeitet, dass die *Exodus* das aktive Handeln Gottes im Vergleich zum Vulgatatext eher marginalisiert und dafür das menschliche Handeln von Moses und Pharao in den Vordergrund stellt.[18] Angesichts eines höfischen Umfeldes entpuppt sich dieser scheinbare Unterschied zur Bibel als kongeniale Reformulierung: Gerade der besonders mächtige Herrscher handelt in einem feudalistischen Machtgefüge nicht selbst, sondern drückt seine Macht und Ehre durch das selbstverantwortete Handeln seiner Vasallen aus.[19] Gott ist damit nicht etwa in der mittelhochdeutschen Fassung marginalisiert, sondern erweist sich gerade durch seine scheinbare Passivität als Herrscher, als Machthaber nach dem Vorbild des mittelalterlichen Feudalherrschers.

Doch zurück zum Prolog: Hat der Erzähler gerade noch Abraham als Vasallen Gottes dargestellt, so wendet er sich nun in einem Gebet direkt an Gott und stilisiert sich seinerseits als dessen Dienstmann:

Hêrre, dîner gnâdone ist sô uile,	Herr, deine Gnade ist überreich,
dû uergibist grôze sculde, da dû wile.	du vergibst große Schuld, wo du willst.
nû uerlîch mir dînem scalche	Nun verleihe mir, deinem Leibeigenen,
daz ich mûze walten	die Gnade, dass ich
ein luzel dîner lêre	einen kleinen Teil deiner Lehre
durch dîn selbes êre.	um deiner Ehre willen verwenden kann.
dû gib mir dînen wîstûm,	Lass mich an deiner Weisheit teilhaben,
daz ich muge wandilôn	so dass ich mit deutschem Mund
mit tûtiskeme munde	etwas aus der lateinischen Sprache über-
der latînisken zungen. (VV. 11 – 20)	setzen kann.

Mit dem Appell an die sündenvergebende Gnade Gottes knüpft der Erzähler an den Anfang, an die zuvor zitierten ersten zehn Verse, an, wo er sich als Sünder präsentiert hat, der durch das Erzählen Buße leisten will.[20] Nur Erzählen ist es hier nicht mehr, wofür der Erzähler Gottes Gnade erbittet, sondern ausdrücklich der Akt des Übersetzens aus dem Lateinischen in das Deutsche. Das dabei verwendete Verb – *wandîlon* – ist für unseren Zusammenhang sehr spannend, da es (wie auch noch im Neuhochdeutschen) neben der transitiven Bedeutung „verwandeln"

---

18 Vgl. Green, *Millstätter* (wie Anm. 13), 229 und 232.
19 Vgl. dazu ausführlich Peter Czerwinski, „Das Nibelungenlied. Widersprüche höfischer Gewaltreglementierung", in: Winfried Frey u. a. [Hrsg.], *Einführung in die deutsche Literatur des 12. bis 16. Jahrhunderts*, vol. 1: *Adel und Hof – 12./13. Jahrhundert*, Opladen 1979, 49 – 87.
20 Diese Bitte des Erzählers um Sündenvergebung auf Basis des Erzählens selbst findet sich etwa auch im Prolog des *Gregorius* von Hartmann von Aue.

auch die intransitive Bedeutung „reisen" transportiert.²¹ Das Hauptthema der folgenden Exodus-Erzählung, die räumliche Bewegung, taucht also zuerst im Zusammenhang mit dem Übersetzungsvorgang auf.

Daneben baut der Erzähler eine implizite Analogie des Heils auf: Abraham, der Diener Gottes, erwirkt bei den (alttestamentarischen) Israeliten Heil; der Erzähler, der Diener Gottes, erwirkt bei den (neutestamentarischen) Christen Heil;²² vorwegreifend und angewendet auf den Gesamttext kann diese Analogie ergänzt werden: Moses erwirkt das Heil durch die räumliche Bewegung des Exodus, der Erzähler durch die geistige Bewegung der Übersetzung.

Für dieses Vorhaben bittet der Erzähler am Ende des Prologs um Gottes Hilfe:

Hêrre, gehuge wole waz dû sprâche,	Herr: ‚Bedenke gut, was du sprichst',
die rede dû noch ie wâr lieze;	dieses Sprichwort hast du schon immer bewahrheitet.
suer in dînen minnon	Wer auch immer mit deinem Wohlwollen
ieht wollte redenon,	jemals sprechen wollte:
daz er ûf tâte den munt,	Du erfülltest ihn vollständig in dem Moment,
dû eruultest ime in an der stunt.	als er den Mund öffnete.
ime newurde nieht for uerborgen.	Ihm blieb nicht das Geringste verborgen.
nû sende mir sanctum	Nun sende mir den Heiligen Geist
spiritum paraclitum,	des Beistands,
der mîn gebende lôse,	der meine Fesseln löse,
sô will ich gerne chôsen;	dann werde ich sehr gerne sprechen;
der heilig geist dîn	dein Heiliger Geist
ordene die rede mîn. (VV. 21–34)	ordne meine Rede.

Die alte wie junge Forschung zur *Exodus* hat den Text oftmals der Osterzeit zugeordnet, allerdings lediglich auf der Basis einer einzigen Verszeile aus dem

---

21 Vgl. dazu den ausführlichen Artikel in *Grimms Deutschem Wörterbuch:* „die ursprüngliche bedeutung von wandeln ist, dem charakter der ableitung -alôn, -ilôn entsprechend (Wilmanns d. gramm. 2 § 75), ein wiederholtes oder abgeschwächtes wenden. ‚hin und her wenden', das vereinzelt im ahd. und mhd. im eigentlichen sinn vorkommt (A), wird übertragen zu ‚hin- und her überlegen', im bairisch-österreichischen zu ‚gerichtlich eine sache erörtern, verhandeln'. der intransitive gebrauch ‚sich hin und her wenden' erscheint schon ahd. und mhd. übertragen als ‚sich mit etwas abgeben', ‚mit einem verkehren, umgehen, verfahren'"; Jacob Grimm/Wilhelm Grimm, *Der digitale Grimm*, hrsg. von Hans-Werner Bartz, Frankfurt am Main 2005, Art. *wandeln*. Natürlich wird in der vorliegenden Textstelle nicht sowohl der transitive als auch der intransitive Wortgebrauch aktualisiert, doch erscheint es mir als signifikant, dass der Dichter hier einen Begriff wählt, der in anderer Verwendung auch eine räumliche Bewegung bezeichnet.
22 Diese Analogie wird durch die arithmetische Ordnung des Prologs gestützt: 10 Verse für Abrahams Wirken, 10 Verse für das Wirken des Erzählers.

Epilog[23], der Danksagung an den Heiligen Geist, die nach Schröder den Osterbezug der *Altdeutschen Genesis* wieder aufgreift.[24] Doch legen die auffälligen lateinischen Verse des Prologs, das abschließende Gebet an den Heiligen Geist, eine ganz andere kirchenzeitliche Verortung nahe, betrachtet man die Nähe zu den ersten beiden Strophen des Pfingsthymnus' *veni, creator spiritus*:

> veni, Creator Spiritus,
> mentes tuorum visita,
> imple superna gratia,
> quae tu creasti, pectora.
>
> Qui diceris Paraclitus,
> altissimi donum Dei,
> fons vivus, ignis, caritas
> et spiritalis unctio[25]

Der auffällige und seltene Gräzizismus *paraclitus* ist die Bezeichnung des Heiligen Geistes des Beistandes, wie er sowohl im Pfingsthymnus als auch in der *Exodus* herbeigerufen wird[26]; und auch das Thema des Prologs greift direkt das Pfingstwunder auf: Der Erzähler bittet um eine angemessene, also göttlich inspirierte

---

23 „*des sol er iemer haben gewis / uon mir gloriam laudis*" (V. 3315), was nach Schröder den Schluss des Gradale „*laus tibi domine, rex aeternae gloriae*" zitiert.
24 Vgl. Schröder, *Exodus* (wie Anm. 6), 240; Green, *Millstätter* (wie Anm. 13), 8–12 u. ö.; Freytag, *Theorie* (wie Anm. 3), 81; Birkhan, *Geschichte* (wie Anm. 11), 32; Kritik daran klingt an bei Henning, *Exodus* (wie Anm. 2), 278 und auch bei Papp, *Green* (wie Anm. 9), 357 f.: „Ich kann jedoch aus dem Dankgebet, insbesondere aus dem *hiute* (V. 3312), nur schwer eine Andeutung auf das *paschale gaudium* herauslesen"; ibid., 358.
25 Heinrich Lausberg, *Der Hymnus 'Veni Creator Spiritus'*, Opladen 1979, 207–208.
26 Auch auf zahlenallegorischer Ebene ist in diesem dritten Abschnitt des Prologs der Heilige Geist dominant gesetzt, wie es Hansjürgen Blinn herausgearbeitet hat: „Der dritte Abschnitt enthält die Bitte um Unterstützung durch den Heiligen Geist. Er umfaßt 14 Verszeilen. Sieben ist die Zahl des Heiligen Geistes. Zweimal wird er in diesem Abschnitt genannt, zweimal sieben beträgt sein Umfang. Daß es sich hier nicht um eine zufällige Übereinstimmung zu handeln scheint, wird uns bei Betrachtung der Conclusio bestätigt, in deren Mittelpunkt der Dank des Dichters für die gewährte Unterstützung steht. Dieser Dank richtet sich an den Heiligen Geist; sie umfaßt wieder 2 x 7 = 14 Verse. Der Dichter scheint also bewußt die Aufbauzahl 7 im Zusammenhang mit den Teilen seines Werkes, die den Heiligen Geist zum Gegenstand haben, zu verwenden, ja den gesamten Prolog unter die Symbolik der Siebenzahl gestellt zu haben. Denn seine 70 (= 10 x 7) Verse füllen (3 + 4 =) 7 Abschnitte. Er ist somit deutlich von der Zahl 7 als Aufbauzahl geprägt"; Blinn, *Exodus* (wie Anm. 13), 101–102. Diese fundamentale Verknüpfung der Dichtung mit dem Heiligen Geist legt ebenfalls eine Verknüpfung der *Altdeutschen Exodus* mit Pfingsten, dem zentralen Fest des Heiligen Geistes, nahe.

Übersetzung[27] der lateinischen Vorlage, und er bittet damit um eben die Gnade des Heiligen Geistes, die das Pfingstwunder auszeichnet: Die Apostelgeschichte erzählt ja gerade davon, dass mit Hilfe des Heiligen Geistes die Jünger das Evangelium in anderen Sprachen predigen konnten – und genau auf dieses Geschehen spielt der Dichter der *Exodus* an, wenn er davon spricht, dass Gott den Sprecher, der in seinem Sinne spricht, ganz erfüllt:

et repleti sunt omnes Spiritu Sancto et coeperunt loqui aliis linguis prout Spiritus Sanctus dabat eloqui illis. (Apg 2:4)	Und sie wurden alle voll des Heiligen Geistes und fingen an zu predigen in anderen Zungen, wie der Geist ihnen gab auszusprechen.

Die *Altdeutsche Exodus* bildet damit nicht nur inhaltlich, sondern auch kirchenzeitlich die Fortsetzung der älteren *Altdeutschen Genesis:* Diese ist in der Tat mit dem Osterfest verknüpft, die *Exodus* aber mit dem Pfingstfest.

Mit dieser Verknüpfung stellt der Dichter den Akt des Übersetzens in einen denkbar intensiven heilsgeschichtlichen Kontext, und die bereits skizzierte Analogie des Heils wird dadurch bestätigt: Wie Moses durch die räumliche Bewegung des Exodus den Israeliten Heil bringt, bringt der göttlich inspirierte Erzähler seinen Zuhörern Heil – Zuhörer übrigens, die in Analogie zu den Zuhörern des Pfingstgeschehens der Ausgangssprache der Übersetzung eben nicht mächtig sind.

Im Epilog – ich überspringe damit die gesamte Erzählung der Exodusgeschichte, die sich, wie bereits erwähnt, sehr eng an das biblische Geschehen hält – greift der Erzähler diese analoge Verknüpfung von alttestamentlichem und neutestamentlichem Heil wieder auf, was sich auch auf formaler Ebene widerspiegelt: Ohne deutlichen Einschnitt, wie es üblich wäre, springt der Erzähler vom Ende der Erzählung direkt in die Vortragssituation:

Dô begunde singen	Da stimmte
Moyses mit den jungelingen	Moses zusammen mit den Jünglingen
ein sanch lobesam,	einen Lobgesang an,
beidiu wîb unde man,	Damen wie Herren,
deme himeliskeh hêrren	dem himmlischen Herrn
zallen sînen êren	zu höchsten Ehren,
mit michelen minnen	dem sie in größter Zuneigung
uon disen selben dingen.	wegen des eben Erzählten zugetan waren.
mit ime sô tû wir same,	Gemeinsam mit ihnen tun wir dasselbe,

---

[27] Und nicht etwa nur die Bitte um gute Rede, wie die Forschung bislang in vager Parallele zu Psalm 50,17 gesehen hat; vgl. Henning, *Exodus* (wie Anm. 2), Sp. 277; Birkhan, *Geschichte* (wie Anm. 11), 32.

daz ŏch wir mŭzzen uarn	weil auch wir dazu bestimmt sind
uon diseme ellende	von dieser Fremde aus
heim ze deme lande,	heim in dieses Land zu reisen,
zů der himelisken Jerusalem.	in das himmlische Jerusalem.
ir sprechet alle AMEN. (VV. 3289–3302)	Dazu sprecht alle: Amen.

Im gemeinsamen Amen wird durch Erzähler und Publikum[28] performativ die Analogie zum erzählten Ende der Exodusgeschichte herbeigeführt: Wie Moses zusammen mit den Jünglingen Gott lobpreist, so lobpreist der Erzähler zusammen mit dem Publikum im gemeinsamen Amen Gott. Dabei wird auch nachvollziehbar, warum der Erzähler die biblischen Jünglinge näher bestimmt als *beidiu wîp unde man*, eine Störung, die aber die Anschlussfähigkeit des biblischen Geschehens zu einem höfischen Publikum vorbereitet, das aus adeligen Damen und Herren besteht.[29]

Nach Prolog und Epilog soll nun aber auch die Erzählung vom Exodus und seine Verwendung von Bewegung in den Blick geraten: Der Begriff *heim*, der im Epilog das Ziel der Bewegung sowohl der Israeliten als auch der Christen bezeichnet, ist innerhalb der Erzählung vom Exodus ein Zentralbegriff. Er wird exponiert eingeführt an der Figur des Josephs im *prologus ante rem*, der sich dem bereits zitierten *prologus praeter rem* anschließt:

Ein bůch heizet Exodus,	Es gibt ein Buch namens Exodus.
dar inne lesen wir sus,	Darin lesen wir,
wie Jâcobes chunne	wie das Kind Jakobs
ze lande heim sunne	in seine Heimat reist
ûzzer Egiptelande,	aus Ägypten,
dâ iz was in banden,	wo es gefangen war,
alsô ime got dâ uore inthiez,	genauso wie es ihm Gott vorhergesagt hatte,
dô er ime erscain an dem wege, dâ er intslief.	als er ihm an dem Weg erschien, wo er starb.
(VV. 35–42)	

Das Bild von Joseph *in banden* ist für unseren Zusammenhang bedeutsam, korrespondiert es doch direkt mit dem wenige Verse zuvor gezeichneten Bild des

---

28 Dies gilt zunächst für die fiktionalen Größen Erzähler und impliziertes Publikum; doch erscheint es als nicht allzu spekulativ, ein kollektives Einstimmen in ein gemeinsames (und durch den Reim angekündigtes) „Amen" auch für eine realhistorische Lesung des Textes anzunehmen.
29 Daneben ist die Formulierung natürlich auch anschlussfähig zu dem Loblied Miriams in der Bibel (2. Moses 15, 20 f.), das komplementär zu Moses' Lied die anwesenden Frauen involviert. Dieses Lied wird in der *Altdeutschen Exodus* nicht erzählt, ist aber durch die *„wîp unde man"* mit angesprochen. Neben diesem Bezug bleibt aber die Ausweitung des Gesanges der Jünglinge auf „*wîp unde man*" eine auffällige Textstörung, die auch einen Bogen spannt zu einem höfischen Publikum.

gefesselten Erzählers, der den heiligen Geist bittet, sein *gebende* zu lösen: Auch hier wird wieder über das Bild der gelösten Fessel der Akt des Übersetzens mit dem Exodus, der räumlichen Bewegung, parallelisiert.

Doch nun zur wahrscheinlich zentralen Irritation dieses Eingangs der Exoduserzählung: Warum wird hier auf Joseph Bezug genommen und nicht auf Moses, der schließlich die Hauptperson des Exodusgeschehens ist? Freilich ist dies zunächst eine Anknüpfung an das Ende der Genesis, das von der Verheißung des Exodus erzählt und vom Tod Josephs, der in Ägypten begraben wird.[30] Darüber hinaus aber schildert der biblische Bericht, dass Moses nicht in das verheißene Land einziehen wird.[31] Die Ankunft in der Heimat ist aber für die *Altdeutsche Exodus* zentral, da sie die Verbindung zwischen Exodus, Übersetzung und Erlösung darstellt; deswegen beginnt die *Altdeutsche Exodus* nicht mit Moses, sondern – verdeckt unter der Formulierung *Jacobes chunne*, die auch das gesamte Volk Israel meinen kann – mit Joseph, dessen Gebeine nach dem biblischen Bericht auf dem Exodus mitgenommen und in das Gelobte Land überführt werden.[32]

Diesen in der Bibel knapp geschilderten Handlungsaspekt weitet die *Altdeutsche Exodus* auf 18 Verse aus und verknüpft die Überführung der Gebeine Josephs dort noch einmal explizit mit dem Begriff *heim* und der eingangs zitierten Prophezeiung:

Mit susgetânen êren	Unter solchen Ehrbezeugungen
sô uûren dô die hêrren	machten sich dort die Herren auf
uon deme ellende	ihren Weg aus der Fremde,
ûzzer deme lande.	aus jenem Land.
alsô si dô chômen dare,	Als sie dorthin gekommen waren,
dâ Jôseph was begraben,	wo Joseph begraben worden war,
ûf tâten si daz grab,	da öffneten sie das Grab,
dâ der gûte inne lach.	worin der Vortreffliche gebettet war.
si nâmen sîn gebeine,	Sie nahmen seine Gebeine,
daz was heilich unde reine, [...]	(die waren heilig und unversehrt)
daz er heim chôme	damit er zusammen mit seinen Verwandten
mit den sînen mâgen. (VV. 2939–2956)	heim kommen konnte.

Wegen der räumlichen Bedeutung dieses Geschehens lässt der Prolog Joseph auch *am wege* sterben, wovon in der Vulgata nicht die Rede ist: Die Gebeine Josephs liegen bereits auf eben dem Weg, der von den Israeliten für den Exodus genom-

---

30 Vgl. 1. Moses 50, 22–26.
31 Vgl. 5. Moses 34.
32 Genealogisch ausgedrückt: Jacobs *chunne* wird sterben auf dem Zug, Jacobs *chunne* wird einziehen ins Heilige Land; zur Abarbeitung am Tod und Begräbnis Moses außerhalb des Heiligen Landes aus jüdischer Perspektive vgl. den Beitrag von Rella Kushelevsky in diesem Band.

men wird. Der Tod ist damit nicht ein Ende, sondern eine Übergangsstation in das Gelobte Land, die Gebeine Josephs werden gleichsam auf dem seinen Tod überdauernden Weg zwischengelagert und später ins Gelobte Land gebracht.

Den Tod als Übergang greift der Abschluss des Textes im bereits zitierten ersten Teil des Epilogs wieder auf, wenn er für die Christen den Einzug in das himmlische Jerusalem in Aussicht stellt. Die Analogie zwischen der erzählten und der für das Publikum in Aussicht gestellten Reise wird hier zu einer Anagogie, der eschatologischen Ausdeutung des vierfachen Schriftsinnes: Der alttestamentarische Exodus verweist nicht nur auf ein neutestamentarisches Geschehen, sondern darüber hinaus auf eine eschatologische Erwartung. Nun stehen eschatologische Erwartungen des Heils grundsätzlich in Frage: Sicherheit in Bezug auf die letzten Dinge ist schwer zu gewinnen, und umso vollmundiger ist die Verheißung des Erzählers an alle Zuhörer am Ende des ersten Epilogteils, das Versprechen, dass *wir* alle in das himmlische Jerusalem einziehen werden. Deswegen schließt der Dichter die *Exodus* auch nicht mit diesem noch ziemlich ungesicherten Versprechen, sondern setzt einen zweiten Epilogteil an, der wieder den Übersetzungsakt aufgreift – und ihn zum heilsgeschichtlichen Zentrum macht:

Ich sage gnâde meiste	Ich danke für seine übergroße Gnade
deme himeliskem geiste,	dem Heiligen Geist,
der mich sundigen man	der mich Sünder
in disen stunden uernam,	in diesen Stunden erhörte,
der mich des gewerte,	der mir die Bitte gewährte,
des ich zime gerte,	die ich an ihn gerichtet hatte,
daz ich mohte chunden	nämlich dass ich
mit tûtiskeme munde	in deutscher Sprache
die urôde sîner liute	von der Freude seines Volkes
an disem tage hiute.	an diesem heutigen Tage erzählen konnte.
nû ist chomen durch das mere	Jetzt ist durch das Meer
daz uile sâlige here.	das glückselige Heer angekommen.
des sol er iemmer haben gewis	Dafür will ich ihn für immer
uon mir gloriam laudis. AMEN	rühmen und Loben. Amen.
(VV. 3303–3316)	

Der Akt der Übersetzung fundiert hier das Heilsversprechen: Während der Erzähler im Prolog noch um die Inspiration des Heiligen Geistes für die Übersetzung gebeten hat, stellt er abschließend diesen Gnadenakt Gottes als bereits erfolgt heraus; der Akt der Übersetzung, das gerade erfolgte Erzählen in der Volkssprache ist Beweis der erfolgten Gnade des Heiligen Geistes, wofür sich der Erzähler abschließend auch bedankt. Wenn aber diese Bewegung der Übersetzung mit Gottes Hilfe erfolgreich verlaufen ist, die von der erfolgreichen Bewegung des Exodus erzählt hat, so ist die erfolgreiche Bewegung der Christen in das himmlische Jerusalem als analoges Geschehen sehr naheliegend. Und nicht nur dies: Im Prolog hatte der Erzähler seine Sündhaftigkeit ebenso herausgestellt wie die diesbezügliche Gnade Gottes; wegen seiner Sündhaftigkeit wollte er vom Exodus erzählen, wofür er ebenfalls die Gnade Gottes erflehte. Letzteres ist im Epilog gerade erfolgt, also ist die Sündenvergebung auch naheliegend, wie es der Erzähler im Epilog wieder engführt mit den Worten: *der mich sundigen man / in diesen stunden vernam:* Gott erhört und hilft Sündern, das beweist der Erzähler an seiner eigenen Person, also ist die Sündenvergebung und der Einzug ins himmlische Jerusalem auch für sein Publikum wahrscheinlich.

In diesem Abschluss werden nochmals die unterschiedlichen Bewegungen der *Exodus* zusammengeführt: Übersetzung, Exodus durch das Meer und – implizit – Einzug ins himmlische Jerusalem. Garant für die letzte Bewegung ist letztlich Christus selbst, denn *an disem tage hiute* ist Pfingsten: Nicht nur Feiertag des Pfingstwunders, sondern auch Erinnerungstag an die Auferstehung Christi, die der Inhalt der Pfingstpredigt des Petrus in der Apostelgeschichte ist. Diese Predigt des Petrus korrespondiert auch mit der heilsgeschichtlichen Deutung der *Exodus*, wobei in der Pfingstpredigt die Auferstehung der Toten auf der Basis der Auferweckung Christi nicht an Joseph, sondern an David ausgeführt wird. Nach dem Bekenntnis zu Jesus, dem Gekreuzigten, den Gott von den Toten auferweckt hat, zitiert Petrus den Psalmisten:

David enim dicit in eum providebam Dominum coram me semper quoniam a dextris meis est ne commovear. *propter hoc laetatum est cor meum et exultavit lingua mea insuper et caro mea requiescet in spe.* *quoniam non derelinques animam meam in inferno neque dabis Sanctum tuum videre corruptionem.* *viri fratres liceat audenter dicere ad vos de patriarcha David quoniam et defunctus est et sepultus est et sepulchrum eius est apud nos usque in hodiernum diem.* *propheta igitur cum esset et sciret quia iureiurando iurasset illi Deus de fructu lumbi eius sedere super sedem eius.* *providens locutus est de resurrectione Christi quia neque derelictus est in inferno neque caro eius vidit corruptionem.* *hunc Iesum resuscitavit Deus cui omnes nos testes sumus* (Apg 2:25 – 32)	Denn David spricht von ihm: ‚Ich habe den Herrn allezeit vor Augen [...]. Darum ist mein Herz fröhlich und meine Zunge frohlocket; auch mein Fleisch wird ruhen in der Hoffnung. Denn du wirst meine Seele nicht bei den Toten lassen, auch nicht zugeben, dass dein Heiliger die Verwesung sehe [...]'. Ihr Männer, liebe Brüder, lasset mich frei reden zu euch von dem Erzvater David. Er ist gestorben und begraben, und sein Grab ist bei uns bis auf diesen Tag. Da er nun ein Prophet war und wusste, dass ihm Gott verheißen hatte mit einem Eide, dass sein Nachkomme sollte auf seinem Thron sitzen, hat er's vorausgesehen und geredet von der Auferstehung des Christus, dass er nicht bei den Toten gelassen ist und sein Fleisch die Verwesung nicht gesehen hat. Diesen Jesus hat Gott auferweckt; des sind wir alle Zeugen.

Die Aspekte der Verheißung, der Erlösung vom eigenen Tod, die Unverweslichkeit des heiligen Körpers und vor allem die Parallelisierung der Auferstehung Christi mit der Auferstehung der Gläubigen finden sich in der *Altdeutschen Exodus* (gegen die biblische Vorlage) anhand der Figur Jakobs wieder – auch auf dieser heilsgeschichtlichen Ebene ist die *Altdeutsche Exodus* also engstens an das Pfingstfest gebunden. Was innerhalb der Erzählung eine räumliche Bewegung ist – die Heimführung der Gebeine Josephs – wird auf der Basis der Auferstehung Jesu eine geistliche Bewegung: Die Auferstehung der Toten ins ewige Leben.[33]

Abschließend sei die doch recht komplexe laientheologische Gemengelage in Prolog und Epilog der *Altdeutschen Exodus* zusammengefasst:

Die *Altdeutsche Exodus* erzählt und verheißt Heil im Heiligen Geist. Dieses Heil ist mehrfach an Bewegung gebunden: Zunächst an die Bewegung des ausziehenden Volkes Israel; dann an die Bewegung der Übersetzung, die darüber hinaus auch mit der Wahrheit Gottes verknüpft wird; schließlich an die Bewegung von diesem Leben in das jenseitige Leben: Sterben muss Joseph in der Erzählung, sterben müssen „wir" im Epilog um anzukommen. Der Zielort der Ankunft ist stets die Heimat (*heime*), sei es Zielort der Israeliten (das Gelobte Land), Zielort der Übersetzung (das deutschsprachige Hier und Jetzt von Erzähler und Publikum), Zielort der Christen (das himmlische Jerusalem).

Die Voraussetzung, um diesen Ort zu erreichen, ist für die Christen Sündenvergebung, was der Erzähler stellvertretend durch den Akt des Erzählens erreicht; für die Israeliten ist es der Exodus, der Inhalt des Erzählens. Die Verbindung zwischen beiden Bereichen und darüber hinaus auch die Begründung der Heilsgewissheit für die Zuhörer leistet der Akt des Übersetzens in die Volkssprache, der als göttlich inspiriert dargestellt wird und im Pfingstwunder präfiguriert ist.

Die Lesung zu Pfingsten ist für die *Altdeutsche Exodus* der ursprüngliche Sitz im Leben, nicht Ostern, wie es die Forschung bislang fast durchweg gelesen hat. Und meine Ausführungen sollten gezeigt haben, dass auch das erzählte und verheißene Heil nicht für Kleriker zugeschnitten ist, sondern für ein vulgärsprachliches, höfisches Publikum. Das Erzählen in der Volkssprache nimmt sich dabei in der Anfangsepoche der volkssprachlichen Literatur keineswegs bescheiden aus, sondern versteht sich als vom Heiligen Geist inspiriert und – mehr noch – als Grundlage eines umfassenden Heilsversprechens. Sehr viel selbstbe-

---

33 Damit korrespondiert diese christliche Interpretation des Exodusgeschehens auch mit einer jüdischen eschatologischen Lesart der Bundeslade (dem zentralen Requisit des Exoduszuges nach der Gesetzgebung), die der Ort der Translation zwischen Himmel und Erde sein kann, vgl. dazu Sarah Offenberg, „Crossing over from Earth to Heaven: The Image of the Ark and the Merkavah in the North French Hebrew Miscellany", in: *Kabbalah*, 26, 2012, 135–158.

wusster kann man sich den Beginn deutschsprachiger Dichtung kaum vorstellen.[34]

---

[34] Claudia Brinker von der Heyde ist auch in Bezug auf die ältere *Altdeutsche Genesis* zu ähnlichen Ergebnissen gekommen, vgl. Claudia Brinker von der Heyde, „Der implizite Autor als (Re) creator: Legitimations- und Erzählstrategien im Schöpfungsbericht der ‚Wiener Genesis'", in: *Gottes Werk und Adams Beitrag. Formen der Interaktion zwischen Mensch und Gott im Mittelalter*, hrsg. von Thomas Honegger/Gerlinde Huber-Rebenich/Volker Leppin, Berlin 2014, 313–325.

Sara Offenberg
Purim Like Yom Kippurim: Between the Texts and Images of the *London Miscellany* and R. Eleazar the Preacher's Commentary on Exodus*

Rabbi Eleazar ben Moshe the preacher, grandson of Rabbi Judah the Pious (d. 1217), wrote a commentary on Exodus that remains in the unpublished manuscript Oxford, Bodleian Library MS Opp. 202, from the late thirteenth century.[1] The commentary contains an extensive discussion on the war against Amalek and stories from the Book of Esther in relation to a conflation between the holidays of Purim and Yom HaKippurim (the Day of Atonement). This paper discusses a possible connection between the ideas of conflation presented in R. Eleazar's commentary and the visual program of the *London Miscellany*, British Library Add. MS 11639, also known as *The North French Hebrew Miscellany*, which was produced in northern France sometime between 1278 and 1280.[2] In both manuscripts, there is an extensive emphasis on redemption and eschatological ideas, and the discussion here shall lead to a broader view of these notions within both the texts and images.

The *London Miscellany* includes eighty-four different texts, presumably chosen to suit the needs and tastes of one particular patron.[3] The volume has 739 fo-

---

* Research for this paper was supported by the Israel Science Foundation (ISF), grant no. 326/13.
1 Adolf Neubauer, *Catalogue of the Hebrew Manuscripts in the Bodleian Library*, Oxford 1886, no. 945; Amos Geula, *Lost Aggadic works known only from Ashkenaz: Midrash Abkir, Midrash Esfa and Devarim Zuta'* PhD thesis, The Hebrew University of Jerusalem, Jerusalem 2006, 17 [in Hebrew]. There are 280 folios in the manuscript, which contains only Rabbi Eleazar's commentary, and the text is written in Ashkenazi script. I am currently working on its publication. On the family ties between R. Eleazar and R. Judah the Pious, see Ivan G. Marcus, 'Introduction', in: *Sefer Hasidim: Ms. Parma H 3280*, Jerusalem 1985, 9–31, esp. 13–18 [in Hebrew].
2 *The North French Hebrew Miscellany: British Library Add. MS 11639*, ed. Jeremy Schonfield, London 2003; George Margoliouth, *Catalogue of the Hebrew and Samaritan Manuscripts in the British Museum*, London 1899, 402–427, sign. 1056; Sara Offenberg, *Illuminated Piety: Pietistic Texts and Images in the North French Hebrew Miscellany*, Los Angeles 2013. Henceforth, the *London Miscellany*. The entire manuscript is available online: http://www.bl.uk/manuscripts/FullDisplay.aspx?ref=Add_MS_11639.
3 The manuscript begins with the Pentateuch, which is followed by liturgical texts, including the *mahzor* in the French rite and commentary on the holiday prayers. We also find here the

lios and includes Hebrew and Aramaic texts written in both French square and semi-cursive scripts.⁴ The scribe wrote his first name, Benjamin, in all three colophons, and apparently penned all of the central and marginal texts.⁵ The volume is rich in marginal illustrations and includes thirty-nine full-page illuminations of Bible stories arranged in five series, some drawn in separate quires. The work on the illuminations took place in several stages, and in the 2003 facsimile edition Yael Zirlin mapped the various ateliers and the number of hands that worked on each section of the illumination program.⁶ She was not the first to study these stages and their iconography; the manuscript's entire iconographical plan has been explained in different ways by a number of art historians.⁷

I hypothesize that some of the ideas expressed in R. Eleazar's commentary on Exodus are reflected in three series of full-page biblical stories in the *London Miscellany*. These images were all produced in the early stages of the illumination program. I do not intend to argue that there was a direct connection between the

---

Passover *Haggadah*, calendar tables, mystical writings, *halakhic* works and more. Raphael Loewe, "Description of the Texts", in: *The North French Hebrew Miscellany* (as in n. 2), 188–287.
4 Malachi Beit-Arié, "The Making of the 'Miscellany'", in: *The North French Hebrew Miscellany* (as in n. 2), 62–64.
5 Ibid., 70.
6 Yael Zirlin, "The Decoration of the 'Miscellany', Its Iconography and Style", in: *The North French Hebrew Miscellany* (as in n. 2), 75–161.
7 On the illuminations in this manuscript, see George Margoliouth, "An Ancient Illuminated Hebrew MS. at the British Museum", in: *The Jewish Quarterly Review*, 17, 1905, 193–197; Zofia Ameisenowa, "The Tree of Life in Jewish Iconography", in: *Journal of the Warburg Institute*, 2, 1939, 326–345; Jacob Leveen, *The Hebrew Bible in Art*, London 1944, 72–84; Mendel Metzger, "Illustrations Bibliques d'un Manuscrit Hébreu du Nord de la France (1278–1340 environ)", in: *Mélanges Offerts à René Crozet à l'occasion de son soixante–dixième anniversaire*, ed. Pierre Gallais/Yves-Jean Riou, Poitiers 1966, 1237–1253; Bezalel Narkiss, *Hebrew Illuminated Manuscripts*, Jerusalem 1969, 86; Zofia Ameisenowa, "Die hebräische Sammelhandschrift Add. 11639 des British Museum", in: *Wiener Jahrbuch für Kunstgeschichte*, 24, 1971, 10–48; Joseph Gutmann, *Hebrew Manuscript Painting*, New York 1978, 78–80; Gabrielle Sed–Rajna, "The Paintings of the 'London Miscellany', British Library Add. Ms 11639", in: *Journal of Jewish Art*, 9, 1982, 18–30; William Chester Jordan, "A Jewish Atelier for Illuminated Hebrew Manuscripts at Amiens?", in: *Wiener Jahrbuch für Kunstgeschichte*, 37, 1984, 155–156; Thérèse Metzger, "Les Enluminures du Ms. Add. 11639 de la British Library, un Manuscrit Hébreu du Nord de la France (fin du 13e siècle – premier quart du 14e siècle): Problèmes Iconographiques et Stylistiques", in: *Wiener Jahrbuch für Kunstgeschichte*, 38, 1985, 59–113, 281–290; Gabrielle Sed–Rajna, "Ateliers de manuscrits hébreux dans l'Occident médiéval", in: *Artistes, Artisans et Production Artistique au Moyen Age: Colloque International, Université de Rennes II – Haute-Bretagne, 2–6 mai 1983*, ed. Xavier Barral i Altet, 2 vols., Paris 1986, vol. I. 339–352; Offenberg, *Illuminated Piety* (as in n. 2); Joseph Shatzmiller, *Cultural Exchange: Jews, Christians, and Art in the Medieval Marketplace*, Princeton 2013, 133–137.

London Miscellany and R. Eleazar's commentary on Exodus. My point is rather to shed light on an idea that was circulating among the *Hasidei Ashkenaz* and to analyze how this was conveyed through both text and image in the thirteenth century. It is the aim of this paper to demonstrate that the three series of illuminations in the *London Miscellany* refer to several texts contained in the same manuscript, and to suggest that these were part of a larger escatolgical concept. My examination and analysis of these illuminations and texts lead to new conclusions regarding the possible patron of the *London Miscellany* and the reason for his interest in the manuscript's texts and images.

Commentary on Exodus in the Circles of Hasidei Ashkenaz

The *London Miscellany* comprises various texts, some of them written in the margins. One of these is a collection of numerological associations (*gematriot*) that comments on all the pericopes in Exodus, with the exception of the last two, and the beginning of Genesis.[8] The *gematriot in the London Miscellany are written in three lines on the margins of* folios 615a–634a. Approximately half of this text copied at the margins is identical to the text of *Sefer Gematriot* of Rabbi Judah the Pious found in an Ashkenazi manuscript of the late thirteenth or early fourteenth century, now located in Jerusalem.[9] *Sefer Gematriot* is one of many writings of the *Hasidei Ashkenaz*, the German Pietists, which used numerological associations in the interpretation of the Hebrew Bible and in exegesis on prayers. These texts follow twelfth- and thirteenth-century Ashkenazi traditions of textual exegesis.[10] Thus, numerological associations were frequently used in mystical writings, as they allow the inner interpretation of the text to be revealed.[11]

---

8 For the entire text, see Offenberg, *Illuminated Piety* (as in n. 2), 133–147.
9 Ms. Jerusalem, The National Library of Israel, Heb. 28° 7234. *Sefer Gematriot of R. Judah the Pious: Facsimile Edition of a Unique Manuscript*, introductions by Daniel Abrams/Israel Ta-Shema, Los Angeles 1998 [in Hebrew]; *Sefer Gematriot of R. Judah the Pious*, ed. Jacob Israel Stahl, 2 vols., Jerusalem 2004 [in Hebrew].
10 Jacob Gellis published a detailed list of the Bible commentaries in Ashkenaz, but did not mention the one in the *London Miscellany*. Jacob Gellis, *Sefer Tosafot Hashalem: Commentary on the Bible*, 9 vols., Jerusalem 1982, vol. I, 7–38 [in Hebrew]. For additional commentaries, such as that of Rabbi Ephraim ben Samson, see Abrams in: Abrams/Ta-Shema, *Sefer Gematriot* (as in n. 4), 3–4; *Rabbeinu Ephraim: A Twelfth Century Biblical Commentary*, ed. Joel Klugmann, 2 vols. Jerusalem 1992 [in Hebrew]. For more on the mystical study of the Torah, see Moshe Idel, *Absorbing Perfections: Kabbalah and Interpretation*, New Haven/London 2002 164–201; id., "On

The commentary of Rabbi Eleazar ben Moshe the preacher, written according to the pericopes in Exodus, uses numerological associations (*gematriot*) as well.[12] Like his grandfather, Rabbi Eleazar was furthermore the author of a book also referred to as *Sefer Gematriot*, a commentary on the Pentateuch based on numerological associations.[13] We find other Biblical commentary in the form of numerological associations, not only in the writings of Rabbi Judah the Pious and his student Rabbi Eleazar of Worms (d. ca. 1230),[14] but also in that of the next generation, at the end of the thirteenth century.

Angels and Biblical Exegesis in Thirteenth-Century Ashkenaz", in: *Scriptural Exegesis – The Shapes of Culture and the Religious Imagination: Essays in Honour of Michael Fishbane*, ed. Deborah A. Green/Laura Lieber, Oxford 2009, 211–244; Ephraim Kanarfogel, *Jewish Education and Society in the High Middle Ages*, Detroit 1992, 89–90, 190–191 n. 22; id., On the Role of Bible Study in Medieval Ashkenaz, in: *The Frank Talmage Memorial Volume*, ed. Barry Walfish, 2 vols., Haifa 1993, vol. I, 151–166, esp. 158, 165–166 n. 58; Ivan G. Marcus, *Rituals of Childhood: Jewish Acculturation in Medieval Europe*, New Haven/London 1996, 15–16, 45–46, 102–127; Elliot R. Wolfson, "The Mystical Significance of Torah Study in German Pietism", in: *The Jewish Quarterly Review*, 84, 1993, 43–78; Leopold Zunz, *Zur Geschichte und Literatur*, Berlin 1845, 76–81.
11 Abrams/Ta-Shema, *Sefer Gematriot* (as in n. 9), 1–2, 14; id., "From Germany to Spain: Numerology as a Mystical Technique", in: *Journal of Jewish Studies*, 47, 1996, 85–101, esp. 90–91, n. 28.
12 We find shorter versions of the commentary's text in two later manuscripts, also written in Ashkenazi script: the first is a seventeenth-century manuscript, Oxford, Bodleian Library MS Opp. 32. Neubauer, *Catalogue of the Hebrew Manuscripts* (as in n. 1), no. 947. The second is a seventeenth-eighteenth-century manuscript, Oxford, Bodleian Library MS Opp. 201, Ibid., no. 946
13 Abrams/Ta-Shema, *Sefer Gematriot* (as in n. 9), 1–2. Munich, Bayerische Staatsbibliothek, Cod. hebr. 221, fols. 83a–273a. On other manuscripts of Rabbi Eleazar ben Moshe the preacher, see Mss. Milan, Biblioteca Ambrosiana P 43 Sup; Moscow, Russian State Library, Guenzburg 352; Vatican, Biblioteca Apostolica ebr. 69; Vatican, Biblioteca Apostolica ebr. 237.
14 On the Torah commentary of Rabbi Judah the Pious, see *The Commentaries to the Torah of R. Judah the Pious*, ed. Isaac Lange, Jerusalem 1975 [in Hebrew]; Daniel Abrams, *Kabbalistic Manuscripts and Textual Theory: Methodologies of Textual Scholarship and Editorial Practice in the Study of Jewish Mysticism*, Jerusalem/Los Angeles 2010, 439–440; Gershon Brin, "An Inquiry into the Commentaries to the Torah of R. Judah the Pious", in: *Sinai*, 88, 1980, 1–17 [in Hebrew]; id., "Studies in R. Judah the Pious' Exegesis to the Pentateuch", in: *Teudah 3 = Studies in Talmudic Literature in Post-Biblical Hebrew and in Biblical Exegesis*, ed. Mordechai A. Friedman/Abraham. Tal/Gershon Brin, Tel Aviv 1983, 215–226 [in Hebrew]; id., "Linguistic Inquiries into Judah the Pious' Commentary to the Torah", in: *Leshonenu*, 44, 1980, 314–315 [in Hebrew]; Ephraim Kanarfogel, *The Intellectual History and Rabbinic Culture of Medieval Ashkenaz*, Detroit 2013, 207–238; Ivan G. Marcus, "Exegesis for the Few and for the Many: Judah he-Hasid's Biblical Commentaries", in: *The Age of the Zohar: Third International Conference on the History of Jewish Mysticism*, ed. Joseph Dan, Jerusalem 1989, 1–24; Haym Soloveitchik, "Two Notes on the Commentary on the Torah of R. Yehudah he–Hasid", in: *Turim: Studies in Jewish History and Litera-*

Let us now turn to R. Eleazar the preacher's commentary on tractate *Shekalim*. Based on the pericope *Ki Tissa*, Exodus 30:11–16, it describes the raising of money (*shekalim*) for building the desert tabernacle. The tractate is read on the first Sabbath morning of the month of Adar. Purim, which is the climax of the Adar prayers and festivities, is celebrated on the fourteenth of the month. This month contains the "four special Sabbaths", when four different additions are made to the regular weekly chapter reading. Rabbi Eleazar explains the verse from Exodus 30:12: "When you take a head count of the children of Israel according to their numbers, every man shall give atonement money for his soul unto the Lord". He makes an explicit connection between the tractate *Shekalim* and Yom Kippur, by explaining that the money (*shekalim*) mentioned in the tractate is related to the Day of Atonement, as the people of Israel redeem themselves on Yom Kippur by paying half a *shekel* in advance for the Temple in the month of Adar.[15]

A similar idea appears in two other commentaries, also written in thirteenth century Ashkenaz. One is Yitzhak bar Yehudah HaLevi's *Paneach Razah*,[16] and the other is a commentary of *Ba'al ha-Turim*, written by Jacob ben Asher (ca.1270–1340), son of Rabbi Asher ben Yehiel (*Rosh*).[17] In the *Arba'ah Turim* (*Ba'al ha-Turim*) there are frequent references to pietistic notions of *Hasidei Ashkenaz* regarding religious practices and prayer:[18] "The Torah juxtaposed Yom Kippur with [the verses that speak of] *ransom for his soul*, for on that day all the people of the nation are counted and pass before Him. For this reason, it is customary to make pledges to charity on Yom Kippur."

---

ture Presented to Dr. Bernard Lander, ed. Michael A. Shmidman, 2 vols., New York 2007–2008, vol. II, 241–251.

15 They are connected to one another by means of redemption of the soul both by atonement and by donation of money to the Temple. On fol. 242a:

כי תשא את ראש בני יש': משה פרש' זו פרש'. כי תחילת דבר היא. לענין פרש' שקלים וסמך לכאן שהזכור למעלה ענין יום הכפורים וביום הכפור' נידונין הוא ומזכירי'. הנשמות ונותנין כסף לצדקה. וסמך כסף כפורים לחטאת הכפורים שהכסף כמו כן כפרה.

16 Yitzhak bar Yehudah HaLevi, *Paneach Razah*, Warsaw 1932, 62 [in Hebrew].
17 *Baal Haturim Chumash: The Torah with the Baal Ha-Turim's Classic Commentary Translated, Annotated, and Elucidated*, ed. Avie Gold, trans. Eliyahu Touger, Brooklyn 2000–2004, 882–883.
18 Abrams, "From Germany to Spain" (as in n. 11), 92–93; Ephraim Kanarfogel, *Peering Through the Lattices: Mystical, Magical and Pietistic Dimensions in the Tosafist Period*, Detroit 2000, 46, 147; Judah Galinsky, '*Arba'ah Turim*': *Four Turim and the Halakhic Literature of 14th Century Spain*, PhD thesis, Bar-Ilan University, 1999 [in Hebrew].

Moreover, in the *Tripartite Mahzor*, Budapest, Magyar Tudomanyos Akademia, MS. Kaufmann A 384, fol. 34b,[19] produced in 1340 around lake Constance, we find on the margins a commentary on the *piyyut El Mitnase* for the tractate *Shekalim* attributed to Rabbi Judah the Pious:

> That the Lord is figuring Kippurim money for grace and charity. 'And their enemy shall be thinner'. For the money of Kippurim that came before Hamman's money a thin man and an enemy Israel were saved and he failed [...]. [Thanks] For the money of Kippurim which is charity [they] shall view the glory of the Shekhinah.[20]

This source is important because it stems from the leader of *Hasidei Ashkenaz*, that is, Rabbi Judah the Pious, Rabbi Eleazar's grandfather; therefore testifying to a concept passed down through several generations.

Three Series of Full-Page Biblical Illuminations in the London Miscellany

The first series of images, in the three early series, begins on fol. 114a and depicts the High Priest pouring the oil into the candlestick (fig. 1).[21] Two pages later, images of two kings appear: on fol. 116a King Solomon (fig. 2), and on fol. 117b King David (fig. 3).[22] An inscription over Solomon's head, written by the scribe before the blue background was painted, identifies the figure as "King Solomon". This inscription is important, since Solomon is wearing not a crown, but rather a pointed red hat. He is portrayed in this scene in a somewhat modest manner. He sits like a learned man, with a grey beard, reading from a book with the inscription "The Torah of Moses".

---

19 The entire manuscript is avalible online: http://kaufmann.mtak.hu/en/study08.htm. For more on this manuscript and the other two volumes of this Mahzor see: Sarit Shalev-Eyni, *The Tripartite Mahzor*, PhD thesis, The Hebrew University of Jerusalem, 2001 [in Hebrew].
20 On fol. 34b:
שהק' חושב להם כסף כפורים לחסד וצדקה. "וצוררם ירזה". כי לבעבור כסף כפורים שקדם לכסף המן איש צר
.. בשביל כסף כפורים שהוא צדקה יחזו כבוד השכינה..ואויב ניצלו ישר' נכשל.
21 All the inscriptions below the images were added at a later stage, in the fourteenth century. Here it reads: "This is the menorah and Aaron who pours oil into the candles."
22 Ameisenowa, "Die hebräische Sammelhandschrift Add. 11639" (as in n. 7), 39; Leveen, *The Hebrew Bible in Art* (as in n. 19), 74; Zirlin, "The Decoration of the Miscellany" (as in n. 6), 81–82, 145.

Fig. 1: Aaron lighting the candles of the Menorah, the *London Miscellany*. London, The British Library, Add. Ms. 11639, fol. 114a

Fig. 2: Solomon, the *London Miscellany*. London, The British Library, Add. Ms. 11639, fol. 116a

Fig. 3: David, the *London Miscellany*. London, The British Library, Add. Ms. 11639, fol. 117b

I suggest that this portrayal of Solomon is based on the *Midrash* and on the *Second Targum on Esther* 1.III,[23] where it is mentioned that Solomon received Moses' Torah from a dove: "Thereupon a golden dove would descend from a pillar and would open the Ark, take out the Book of the Law and place it into the hand of King Solomon in fulfillment of what Moses said: 'And it shall be with him, and he should read from it all the days of his life.'"[24] The dove is absent from the image, and we see only Solomon reading "The Torah of Moses". Therefore, what is stressed in this image is the importance of studying and contemplating the Torah. The crowned David is displayed seated on a throne and playing the harp, an iconographical convention dating from the late antique period in both Jewish and Christian art.[25]

The second and most extensive series of illuminations portrays several biblical stories in non-chronological order. The series begins with the creation of the universe on fol. 516b, and, opposite it, a scene of the fourth day of the Creation. On the following pages, three eschatological beasts appear: the bird *Bar-Yokhani*, which is related to the images on the following pages, Leviathan, and Behemoth (*shor ha-bar*, the wild ox). Portrayals of biblical scenes follow: the Judgment of Solomon, Aaron's Budding Rod, Samson, Adam and Eve, Noah's Ark, and the Binding of Isaac. The series ends with a display of the Temple implements (fig. 4), two scenes showing the High Priest (figs. 5–6), and, finally, David and Goliath. Elsewhere I have suggested that this series illustrates Yosse ben Yosse's *piyyut* "*Ata Konanta Olam be–Rov Hesed*" ("You Established a World with Great Grace"), which was recited on Yom Kippur in medieval France.[26] This *piyyut*, which was probably composed in the fifth century, falls into the category of the *Seder Avodah* (Order of Worship) liturgy, that is, poetry that describes the rituals performed by the High Priest on Yom Kippur, written as part of the Yom Kippur prayers of the *mahzor* on fols. 412b–416b.[27] The *piyyut* (a liturgical poem) is

---

[23] Beate Ego, *Targum scheni zu Ester: Übersetzung, Kommentar und theologische Deutung*, Tübingen 1996, 155, 159–166; Bernard Grossfeld, *The Two Targums of Esther*, Edinburgh 1991, 109–112.
[24] Ibid., 111–112.
[25] On illuminations of David playing the harp in Jewish art, see Sarit Shalev-Eyni, "Obvious and Ambiguous in Hebrew Illuminated Manuscripts from France and Germany", in: *Materia Giudaica*, 7, 2002, 249–271, esp. 257–259.
[26] Offenberg, *Illuminated Piety* (as in n. 2), chap. 1.
[27] On this *piyyut* see: Israel Davidson, *Thesaurus of Mediaeval Hebrew Poetry*, 4 vols., New York, 1924–1933 vol. I, 399, #8815; Daniel Goldschmidt, *Mahzor for the High Holy Days: Rosh Hashanah*, 2 vols., Jerusalem 1970, vol. II, 465–478 [in Hebrew]; Andreas Lehnard, "'Seder Yom ha-Kippurim kakh hu': Zur Entwicklung der synagogalen Liturgie des Versöhnungstages", in: *The Day of Atonement: Its Interpretations in Early Jewish and Christian Traditions*, ed. Thomas Hieke/To-

divided into two parts: the first begins with the Creation and tells the story of the temptation in the Garden of Eden, Noah, Abraham, and the Binding of Isaac, while the second deals with the High Priest's ritual on Yom Kippur.[28] The illuminations correspond not only to the *piyyut*, but also to the relevant *piyyut* commentary, which appears near the end of the manuscript on fols. 723b–732a.[29]

The series of images is not located adjacent to the relevant texts: the *piyyut* is written approximately a hundred folios prior to the images, on fols. 412b–416b, and its commentary is written at the end of the manuscript on fols. 723b–732a. However, the entire decorative program, aside from the marginal illustrations, is based on series of images that are not necessarily located adjacent to the relevant text. In addition, the texts are written as part of a larger liturgical corpus of work (*mahzor* and *piyyut* commentaries), and therefore could not be interrupted in order to contain a series of full-page illuminations next to them. Furthermore, although the texts themselves are related (the *piyyut* and its commentary), they are not written next to one another, but are separated by over three hundred folios. Gérard Genette addresses the issue of the order in which written texts are read, and refers to jumping between chapters and not reading texts in the order in which they are written.[30] Such is the case of our manuscript, which contains several texts that relate to one another. In the *London Miscellany* we find an example of a manuscript that was probably supposed to be read and browsed through,[31] and thus the location of the texts and images on distant folios should not be seen as an obstacle to our study of the manuscript as a whole. Rather, we should consider how the manuscript was intended to be used.

---

bias Nicklas, Leiden 2012, 257–269, esp. 262–264; Zvi Malachi, *The Avodah for Yom Kippur: Its Characteristics, History and Development in Hebrew Poetry*, PhD thesis, The Hebrew University of Jerusalem, Jerusalem 1974, 20–23 [in Hebrew]; Aharon Mirsky, *The Poems of Yosse ben Yosse*, Jerusalem 1977, 26–31, 178–203 [in Hebrew]; Michael D. Swartz/Joseph Yahalom, *Avodah: An Anthology of Ancient Poetry for Yom Kippur*, University Park, PA 2005, 1–40, and see the Hebrew text with English translation on 291–341; Joseph Yahalom, '*Az be-en kol*' *Priestly Palestinian Poetry: A Narrative Liturgy for the Day of Atonement*, Jerusalem 1996 [in Hebrew]; Zvi Zohar, "'Ve-mi Metaher Ethem' – Your Father in Heaven, the 'Seder Avodah' Prayer: Context, Function, and Meaning", in: *AJS Review*, 14, 1989, 1–28 [in Hebrew].

28 Goldschmidt, *Mahzor for the High Holy Days* (as in n. 27), II, xviii–xxv.
29 For the entire text of the *piyyut* commentary, see Offenberg, *Illuminated Piety* (as in n. 2), 180–195.
30 Gérard Genette, *Paratexts: Thresholds of Interpretation*, Cambridge 1997, 218 (originally published in French as *Seuils*, Paris 1987).
31 Kathryn Rudy, *Piety in Pieces: How Medieval Readers Customized their Manuscripts*, Cambridge/UK 2016.

Fig. 4: The Temple implements, the *London Miscellany*. London, The British Library, Add. Ms. 11639, fol. 522a

Fig. 5: Aaron lighting the candles of the Menorah, the *London Miscellany*. London, The British Library, Add. Ms. 11639, fol. 522b

Fig. 6: The High Priest, the *London Miscellany*. London, The British Library Add. Ms. 11639, fol. 523a

Various art historians have provided different explanations for the entire manuscript's iconographical plan and also for the series of scenes under discussion here, but they have largely disregarded the texts in the manuscript. Zofia Ameisenowa, for example, suggests that perhaps the manuscript's binder erroneously grouped these images together.[32] Mendel Metzger claims that these images contain eschatological ideas.[33] According to Gabrielle Sed-Rajna and Yael Zirlin, this series has no logical or chronological order that explains the arrangement of the images.[34] Zirlin claims that the miniatures were painted by a Christian artist who embedded Christian ideas into the images. She suggests that Benjamin, the manuscript's scribe, was probably present in the atelier, and that although he was a learned man, he could not decipher the Christian meanings of the images since the Jews were not aware of these meanings.[35] Whereas it is true that the iconography and style of the images are closely related to French Christian illustrations, we should nonetheless explore the context in which these images were created. The implication here is not that the illuminations were necessarily created by a Jewish illuminator, but that the patron or a person acting on his behalf (such as the scribe) directed the artist to design and illustrate the scenes in a particular way.

Let us examine the images of the High Priest and the texts with which they correspond. On fol. 522r, Aaron is shown lightning the Menorah (fig. 5). A similar scene is already portrayed on fol. 114v (fig. 1), but the two scenes are not identical. Here, Aaron is on the right climbing three stairs mentioned in the *Mishnah Tamid* 3.9. We see the candles lighting as Aaron pours the oil into the candlestick. In the next scene, the High Priest is portrayed standing in the centre of the medallion and raising his left hand while holding his sleeve in his right hand (fig. 6). Unusually, instead of a miter,[36] he wears a crown with the inscription "Holiness

---

32 Zofia Ameisenowa, "The Tree of Life in Jewish Iconography" (as in n. 7), 326–345, at 338.
33 Metzger, "Les Illustrations Bibliques" (as in n. 7).
34 Sed-Rajna, "The Paintings of the London Miscellany" (as in n. 7), 24; Zirlin, "The Decoration of the Miscellany" (as in n. 6), 77.
35 Ibid., 124–127. This claim is not in line with the realities of the period. See Katrin Kogman-Appel, "Coping with Christian Pictorial Sources: What Did Jewish Miniaturists Not Paint?", in: *Speculum*, 75, no. 4, 2000, 816–858; Shulamit Laderman, "Two Faces of Eve: Polemics and Controversies Viewed through Pictorial Motifs", in: *Images*, 2, 2008, 1–20, at 6–7; Sara Offenberg, *Expressions of Meeting the Challenges of the Christian Milieu in Medieval Jewish Art and Literature*, PhD thesis, Ben-Gurion University of the Negev, Beer Sheva 2008 [in Hebrew].
36 In Askenazi manuscripts, Aaron is portrayed at times with a tall miter, similar to that of a bishop. See, for example, the image in the Regensburg Pentateuch, Ms. Jerusalem, Israel Museum, 180/52, fol. 156a, Ashkenaz 1300; Tripartite Mahzor, London, The British Library, Ms. Add. 22413, fol. 3a, Lake Constance region, c. 1320. Katrin Kogman-Appel, "Sephardic Ideas in

to God" (Ex 28:36) and a blue coat with bells on its edges. This crown is mentioned in the *piyyut*'s commentary: "The high priest was splendid while raising his head wearing a miter made as a crown on a king's head."[37] The *hoshen* (breastplate) on his chest is a golden plate hanging by three chains and the inscription *hoshen* is written in black on a white background. On each side of the illumination stands a kneeling, bearded man; the one on the left is raising his hands as though pleading or in prayer, while the one on the right is holding a golden object aloft.

We shall see that the image of the High Priest follows the *piyyut* and its commentary, which elaborate on Aaron's garment. We notice the difference between Aaron's clothing on fol. 522b (fig. 5), where he wears a blue mantel over a pink garment, and on fol. 523a (fig. 6), where he wears a blue coat. In the latter illumination, the garment is portrayed in a unique manner, as mentioned in the commentary text on fol. 727a: "His appearance is like aquamarine (*tarshish*). As the appearance of the heaven (he is) wearing a light blue coat [...] woven as a beehive which is round [...] it is all woven without sewing [...] the rim of a coat of mail that it be not rent."[38] Following Exodus 28:31–34 the *piyyut* and its commentary state that the High Priest would wear an aquamarine coat that is woven like a beehive. According to the text, the neckline was round and opened like armor so it would not tear, and indeed, we notice this in the image. Thus, we can see here a representation of the text (as we saw regarding the crown), though not a precisely accurate one.

Although Zirlin sees the two men kneeling at Aaron's feet as representing Bezalel ben Uri and Aholiab ben Ahisamach, and the golden object as the *Urim veTumim*,[39] the text raises another possibility. We read in the *piyyut* on fols. 415a–415b and its commentary on fol. 730a the verse: "He will be surrounded by the prefect and the head of the father's house."[40] The *piyyut* and its com-

---

Ashkenaz. Visualizing the Temple in Medieval Regensburg", in: *Jahrbuch des Simon-Dubnow-Instituts*, 8, 2009, 245–277, at 264; Sarit Shalev-Eyni, *Jews among Christians: Hebrew Book Illumination from Lake Constance*, London 2010, 46–47.

37 My translation. On the garment of the High Priest in this *piyyut*, see Malachi, *The Avoda for Yom Kippur* (as in n. 27), 325.

כהן גדול היה נהדר כשהיה מגביה את ראשו במצנפת שהיה עשוי ככתר בראש המלך.

38 My translation.

דמותו כתרשיש. כמראה רקיע בלובשו מעיל תכלת ... ארוג ככוורת שהיא עגולה ... כולה ארוג בלי תפירה ככוורת ... שפתו פתוחה כעוגל כשריון.

39 Zirlin, The Decoration of the Miscellany (as in n. 6), 102.

40 My translation.

יקיפוהו סגן וראש בית אב.

mentary follow *Mishna Yomah* 3:9: "He came to the eastern side of the courtyard, to the north of the altar, with the prefect at his right hand and the head of the father's house at the left. There were two goats. There also was a box with two lots. They used to be [made of] boxwood, but Ben Gamla made them of gold." I suggest that the men in our image refer to this text, and the golden object could be intended to portray the golden lots. Aaron's raised hand could refer to the text in *Mishna Yomah* 4.1: "He shook the box and brought up the two lots [...] If the one 'for the Lord' came up in his left hand, the head of the ministering family said to him, 'My lord, High Priest, raise up your left hand.'" Hence, we can conclude that the raising of the left hand is meant to illuminate the text of the *piyyut*, based on the *Mishna*.

As I have mentioned, in our manuscript the *Seder Avodah* seems to be visually illustrated for the believer, in chronological order from the Creation up to the work of the High Priest, providing the believer with a visual glance into the Temple. According to Zvi Malachi, during the ritual, the members of the synagogue audience receive a realistic description of the Temple and may feel as if they are actually present there in place and time. Malachi refers to this state of mind as a "psychological reality" created by the power of thought and imagination.[41]

The *Seder Avodah* series of images portraying the work of the High Priest in the Temple and ending with David and Goliath is followed by another series of four full-page illustrations in rectangular green frames and golden backgrounds on fols. 524a–527b.[42] These illustrations are related to the war against Amalek, as two of them are based on the Scroll of Esther, and Haman is known to be a descendent of Amalek. The first scene displays Esther before Ahasuerus. The image following Esther depicts the war against Amalek at Rephidim (Ex 17:8–16), where Moses is portrayed in the centre of the scene while Aaron and Hur stand on each side of him, supporting his arms (fig. 7). On the next page, we see the beheading of the Amalekite King Agag (fig. 8). The closing image is that of Mordechai and Haman, concluding the scenes related to the war against Amalek.

In the Book of Exodus, the pericopes of *Terumah* and *Tetsaveh*, which deal with the Temple implements and the High Priest's *Seder Avodah* on Yom Kippur, come immediately before pericope *Ki Tissa* read on tractate *Shekalim*. In R. Ele-

---

41 Malachi, *The Avoda for Yom Kippur* (as in n. 27), 193.
42 Metzger, "Les Illustrations Bibliques" (as in n. 7) 1252; Zirlin, "The Decoration of the Miscellany" (as in n. 6), 103–106, 119–123, 128–129; id., "The Jewish Christian Polemic in Pictures: The North French Miscellany (BL. Add. MS. 11639)", in: *Timorah*, ed. Bracha Yaniv, Ramat Gan 2006, 61–72 [in Hebrew].

azar's commentary, he refers to *Seder Avodah* on Yom Kippur and then elaborates on the connection between pericope *Ki Tissa* and Purim. We have seen that the illuminated series of *Seder Avodah* is followed by a series dealing with the war against Amalek. In what follows, I offer a possible reason for choosing to illustrate these early series in the *London Miscellany*.

A King, a Temple, and Amalek

I would like to suggest that the three series, made in the early stages of the manuscript's production, were part of a larger concept intended to display the three deeds the Israelites were commanded to carry out upon their arrival to the Land of Israel: to anoint a king, to build the Temple, and to extirpate the seed of Amalek. We find this in the Tosefta Sanhedrin 4:3, and in the Babylonian Talmud Sanhedrin 20b the following text appears: "R. Judah says, 'Three commandments were imposed upon the Israelites when they came into the land. [They were commanded] to appoint a king, to cut off the descendants of Amalek and to build the chosen House.'" This idea also appears in *Midrash Tanhumah Ki Teze* 11, where we find that as long as Amalek still exists, the Throne of God is not complete. This notion is based on the commentary on Exodus 17:16, in which Rashi stated: "For there is a hand on the throne of the Eternal: The hand of the Holy One, blessed be He, was raised to swear by His throne, to have a war and [bear] hatred against Amalek for eternity [...] the Holy One, blessed be He, swore that His Name will not be complete and His throne will not be complete until the name of Amalek is completely obliterated."[43]

As I have shown elsewhere, the Ark of Covenant in the *London Miscellany* (part of the *Seder Avodah* series, fig. 4) also illustrates the Throne of God.[44] The scene is a conflation between the Ark of the Covenant and the portrayal of the Throne of God, the vision of the *merkavah* (chariot), based on Ezekiel 1:28. The Ark in the *London Miscellany* is deliberately depicted on its broad side, as a golden rectangular box, so we see the pole inserted into its two rings. The blue and pink bows begin at each side of the pole, bringing to mind the rainbow in Ezekiel's vision. The cherubs are not on the *kaporet* (mercy seat), but rather appear separately on either side of the Ark, with six

---

43 נשבע ... כי יד על כס יה – ידו של הקב"ה הורמה לישבע בכסאו להיות לו מלחמה ואיבה בעמלק עולמית הקב"ה שאין שמו שלם ואין כסאו שלם עד שימחה שמו של עמלק כולו, וכשימחה שמו יהיה השם שלם והכסא שלם
See also *Hizkuni* and R. Haim Paltiel's commentary on Exodus 17:16.
44 Sara Offenberg, "Crossing Over from Earth to Heaven, The Image of the Ark and the Merkavah in the North French Hebrew Miscellany", in: *Kabbalah*, 26, 2012, 135–158.

Fig. 7: The war against Amalek at Rephidim, the *London Miscellany*. London, The British Library, Add. Ms. 11639, fol. 525b

Fig. 8: The beheading of the Amalekite King Agag, the *London Miscellany*. London, The British Library, Add. Ms. 11639, fol. 526a

wings, looking like *seraphim*. Therefore, the scene illustrates a combination between both the earthly and the heavenly Temples. This idea, well known in the writings of *Hasidei Ashkenaz*, also appears in R. Eleazar's commentary on fols. 182a–184b.

The *London Miscellany* is deeply rooted in the notions of *Hasidei Ashkenaz*, and the relation between the Throne of God and Amalek is elaborated in their writings. In the *London Miscellany*, the relationship between the Throne and Amalek is articulated in a commentary on the *piyyut Anseikha Malkhi* (אנסיכה מלכי) for Rosh Hashanah,[45] which states that "the Lord's name and Throne shall be whole when Amalek is vanquished."[46] As mentioned, R. Eleazar ben Moshe the preacher discusses this issue extensively in the commentary on Exodus 17:16, and on fol. 94a mentions the connection between the Lord's throne and the extirpation of Amalek: "In the future to come, in the days of the Messiah, then the seed of Amalek shall be destroyed. By my right hand, [by] my right hand, [by] my throne, [by] my throne, [I swear that] I will exact retribution from his seed."[47] Therefore, the artistic project in the *London Miscellany* could relate not only to the texts in this manuscript, but to broader ideas circulating in thirteenth century Ashkenaz which connect the war against Amalek (manifested on Purim) not only with the salvation of the body, but also with that of the soul on Yom Kippurim.

In conclusion, the only way to make sense of the *London Miscellany*'s unique iconography and order of illustrations is by examining the relevant texts within the manuscript and other writings circulating in Ashkenaz. The images are closely based on different texts, such as *midrashim*, the second commentary on Esther, the commetary on *Seder Avodah*, and the writings of *Hasidei Ashkenaz*. The connection between the three series of illuminations is midrashic. The three series beginning with the High Priest, King David, and Solomon, and the *Seder Avodah* series followed by the war against Amalek, might be understood as part of a larger idea. Aaron might represent in the scenes a vivid display of the past and future work of the High Priest, and thus the viewer could have envisioned a messianic future. Considering the texts and illustrations in this manuscript, it seems likely that the patron of the *London Miscellany* aspired to have a mystical experience. His ordering (or copying) of a compiled miscellany, which contains vari-

---

[45] Davidson, *Thesaurus* (as in n. 27), vol. I, 310, #6823; Goldschmidt, *Mahzor for the High Holy Days* (as in n. 27), I, 233–237. The *piyyut* is written on fols. 370b–371b and the commentary of fols. 711a–712b. See Offenberg, *Illuminated Piety* (as in n. 2), 158–160.

[46] ואז יהיה שמו שלם וכסאו שלם במחיית עמלק.

[47] לעתיד לבוא בימי המשיח אז ישחית זרעו של עמלק. ימיני ימיני כסאי כסאי אין שמי וכסאי שלם עד שאפרע מזרעו. See also Rabbi Ephraim's commentary on Ex 17:14: *Rabbeinu Ephraim*, I, 235.

ous works that include mystical ideas, suggests the first owner's interest in these writings. But including some of these ideas in the illustrations indicates a deeper understanding of the texts that goes beyond the copying of a manuscript. This significant point should have a major impact on our understanding of the original intention of the manuscript's owner and his interest in the mystical texts, rather than a mere similarity between those texts. Based on the material presented here, I would like to suggest a possible reason for the importance given to Aaron's image and for the importance of *Seder Avodah* and the earthly and heavenly Temple in this manuscript. Whether the patron was named Benjamin or Aaron, or not, I suggest the possibility that he was a Cohen, hence the emphasis on the High Priest's (*Cohen Gadol*) work in the Temple. Moreover, throughout the manuscript, in most of the *piyyutim* commentaries, there seems to be a focus on the work of the High Priest and the *Cohanim* in the Temple. In the scenes, Aaron could vividly display the past and future work done by the High Priest; thus, the patron could have envisioned himself portraying this part.

This hopeful aspiration in the *London Miscellany*'s texts and images finds its parallel in the extensive messianic aspirations in R. Eleazar's commentary, where the most prominent motif in all the numerological associations is that of the Messiah and Israel's redemption. This is manifested in the images which relate to the appointed kings (figs. 2–3), the cutting off the seed of Amalek, and the building of the Temple. As the people of Israel are redeemed on Yom Kippur through the work of the High Priest and the money given to the tabernacle/temple on tractate *Shekalim*, so the readers and viewers of these thirteenth century manuscripts aspired to future redemption.

Rella Kushelevsky
The Crossing of Boundaries and Liminality in the Rabbinic Aggadot on the Death of Moses and on "Those to Die in the Wilderness": Analogous Aspects

The drama of the death of Moses and of the generation that left Egypt, whom he led in their wanderings to the Promised Land, occured at the threshold of the land for which he longed, in the liminal expanse of the wilderness to the east of the Jordan River. From the height of Mount Nebo Moses, gazed upon the land, before being gathered to God, and before he took leave of his people (Dt 32:48–54:12). In analogous fashion, the generation of those who left Egypt diminished during forty years of wandering until the generation's passing, which was decreed as punishment for their sins: Moses sinned at the Waters of Meribah, when he desecrated the sanctity of the Lord by striking the rock instead of speaking to it as he had been commanded (Nm 20:7–13), while the sin of this generation lay in their accepting the spies' slander of the land (Nm 14:1–37).

These events are described with greater intensity and detail in the Talmudic and midrashic sources. The episode of Moses' death as presented in these sources betrays a perception of his character, both as a human and as one comparable to an angel; additionally, it presents their conception of death.[1]

The Talmudic aggadah of the "wilderness dead" (BT Bava Batra 73b) casts a retrospective light on the image of the generation that left Egypt. The wilderness is the crucial setting in all of these narratives on the death of Moses and of his generation. The symbolic nature of the wilderness in the Rabbinic literature can be discerned in its semiotic function in the sources on the death of Moses and in the aggadah of the wilderness dead, signifying the period of wandering in the wilderness as a liminal phase in the people's history, in the sense formulated by van Gennep and Turner.[2] This will enable us to suggest an anthropological

---

[1] See the extensive discussion, in light of the numerous versions of the narrative of the death of Moses or his concealment with God: Rella Kushelevsky, *Moses and the Angel of Death*, trans. by Ruth Bar-Ilan, New York 1995.
[2] Liminality, in the sense given it by Gennep and Turner, is a transitional phase between different biological and social situations. In this interim state the old markers of identity have been cast off, while the new ones have yet to be acquired. See Arnold van Gennep, *The Rites of Passage*, trans. by Monika B. Vizedom/Gabrielle L. Caffee, London 1960, 65–115, 189–194; Victor Turner, *The Ritual Process: Structure and Anti-Structure*, New York 1969, 94–130.

perspective alongside and complementary to the Bible's theodicic perspective of crime and punishment on this narrative.³ This article discusses (1) the image of the wilderness in the Rabbinic sources as a liminal expanse; (2) the characteristics of "those to die in the wilderness" in the Talmudic aggadah about them, and their metonymic affinities with the wilderness;⁴ (3) the Rabbinic literature's characterizations of Moses on the eve of his death, and his metonymic affinities to the wilderness; and (4) a concluding discussion: liminality as an analogous aspect in the character of Moses before his death and in that of those to die in the wilderness, and their metonymic connection with the wilderness.

The Imagery of the Wilderness and the Generation of Those Who Left Egypt

The names of the wilderness, the arena of the Israelites' wandering on their way from Egypt to the Land of Israel, change in accordance with the route of the journey, including the wilderness of Shur, the wilderness of Sin, and the wilderness of Paran; however its characteristics in the Rabbinic literature remain constant.⁵ The wilderness is chaotic and dangerous, but also a source of inspiration and divine Providence. It contains serpents the size of the beams of an olive oil press, and scorpions "about the size of a span" – a depiction that intensifies the wilderness imagery in the Bible and gives it an almost mythical dimension, with its gigantic creatures and its tremendous and perilous expanses of mirage and wandering: "The desert of Shur was eight hundred by eight hundred parasangs, and it was full of serpents, scorpions, and evil beasts".⁶ On the other

---

3 On the forty years of the Israelites' wanderings in the wilderness, and on the decree of those to die in the wilderness as punishment for the sin of the spies, see Ex 14:26–45. On the decree of Moses' death as punishment for the Waters of Meribah, see Nm 20:7–13. See also Dt 1:34–39, which connects the punishment of Moses with the sin of the spies and the wilderness generation. For a discussion of Moses as representing the members of the wilderness generation in their sin and punishment, see Gerald J. Blidstein, *The Death of Moses: Readings in Midrash*, Alon Shvut/Israel 2008, 41–54 [in Hebrew].
4 Metonymy: a figure of speech in which one word is substituted for another on the basis of some material, causal, or conceptual relation. ("Metonymy", *The New Princeton Encyclopedia of Poetry and Poetics*, ed. Alex Preminger /T.V. F Brogan, Princeton/NJ, 1993, 783).
5 On the symbolic nature of the wilderness in the Rabbinic sources, see Avigdor Shinan, "On the Wilderness in the Rabbinical Literature", in: *"When You Went after Me in the Wilderness..."*, ed. Yair Zakovitch/Avigdor Shinan, Jerusalem 1995 (The President's Study Group on the Bible and Sources of Judaism, 3), 34–35 [in Hebrew].
6 *Tanhuma*, ed. Solomon Buber, Vilna 1885, Beshalah 17, 63.

hand, the sources portray the wondrous rescue of the Israelites from the wild animals, when the latter lay down before them without harming the Israelites (*Exodus Rabbah* 24). The wilderness is identified with Gehinnom, possibly because of its blazing heat, as implied by the Talmudic dictum: "Gehinnom has three gates, one in the wilderness, one in the sea, and one in Jerusalem" (BT Eruvin 19a). This teaching itself, however, identified the wilderness with Jerusalem, as well, and in this respect it is a place of holiness and inspiration. Specifically, because the wilderness is a no-man's-land, an extraterritorial expanse, it has the potential to receive heavenly messages. As tractate Nedarim (55a) declares: "When a person makes himself as the wilderness, which is free to all, the Torah is presented to him as a gift." In the wilderness "the manna fell for them, the well came up, the quail were provided for them, the clouds of glory encircled them, and the pillar of cloud traveled before them" (*Leviticus Rabbah* 34:8). The features of the wilderness are not unequivocal; it is an elusive phenomenon that cannot be clearly identified, because of its opposing qualities: the physical and the metaphysical that, respectively, represent death and life; danger and the possibility of spiritual elevation; illusion and revelation. These aspects are already present in the Scriptures, as they come to the fore in the recurring crises within the people, in comparison with the divine revelation at the Giving of the Torah, but they are intensified in the above wilderness depictions in the Talmud and the midrash.

The same contrasts appear in the portrayal of those who left Egypt and are fated to die in the wilderness as a consequence of the sin of the spies and their acquiescence in the slander of the land. It is said of them that "the Holy One, blessed be He, took the measure of all the generations, and found no generation worthy to receive the Torah other than the wilderness generation" (*Leviticus Rabbah* 13:2). In the Mishnah, in tractate Sanhedrin (M Sanhedrin 10:3): "Of them it is said (Ps 50:5): 'Gather Me My devout ones, sealers of My covenant through sacrifice'." At the same time, this mishnah also declares that the wilderness generation are those "who have no portion in the World to Come" (M Sanhedrin 10:3), whether the "World to Come" is the afterlife or the future Messianic era. This is a generation of giants possessing both intensive spiritual power and fierce urges, that were realized in the clear consciousness of the divine presence at the Revelation at Sinai – but that also found tangible expression in the sensual surrender to the pagan cult of the Golden Calf. The wilderness generation is therefore presented as a metonym of the wilderness, that lacks clear definition – a liminal entity in the cultural-historical phase of the journey crossing the wilderness from Egypt to the Land of Israel, from servitude to freedom. The death in the wilderness of the generation that left Egypt precedes the new experience of the collective in its land.

The Talmudic Aggadah of the Wilderness Dead

We will now examine this metonymic aspect with a close reading of the Talmudic aggadah of the wilderness dead. The aggadah in Bava Batra (73b–74a) of the wilderness dead is conveyed as notes from the journey in the wilderness related by Rabbah bar Bar Hana, a late third-century Amora, from the third generation of Amoraim. Rabbah bar Bar Hana was known for his journeys and the exaggerated tall tales of what he had seen. One of the sights to which he bore witness was the wilderness dead, who had passed away centuries before. As he describes the event:

> He [an Arab merchant from there] said to me: "Come and I will show you the wilderness dead." I went [to them] and I saw them; they looked as if intoxicated. They were lying on their backs, and the knee of one of them was raised. The Arab entered under the knee, riding on a camel with an erect spear [in his hand], and did not touch it. I cut off one corner of the azure [garment] of one of them, and we could not move away. The Arab said to me: "Perhaps you have taken something from them – return it, for we have a tradition that one who takes anything from them cannot move away." I went and returned it, and we [were able to] move away. When I came before the sages, they said to me: Every Abba [i.e., Rabbah = Rav Abba] is an ass, and every bar Bar Hana is a fool. If you wanted to ascertain whether the law follows the School of Shammai or the School of Hillel, it would have sufficed to count the threads and the joints, and tell us.

Rabbah bar Bar Hana looks at a vision of the wilderness dead, who had expired centuries before his time, stretched out throughout the wilderness, in the deep sleep of death. In their deployment in the dunes of the wilderness they are a metonym of its endless expanses, and in the portrayal of their great height they represent the rocks and hills of the wilderness: one's leg is bent, and the Arab can pass underneath it, while riding on his camel with his spear upright in his hand. Bialik (1873–1934), one of the greatest Hebrew poets in the modern era, would later develop this depiction in his poem *The Dead of the Wilderness*.[7]

The definition of the status of the wilderness dead is not absolute. They are expressly identified as "the wilderness dead", but the description adds reservations to this statement. They resemble intoxicated people who are deeply immersed in their drunken stupor, in a manner that blunts the impression of death. This is also the position of a sleeping person, with an upturned face and a bent leg. The gigantic dimensions of their bodies radiate vitality, even after hundreds of years, which also casts doubt on the fact of their death. Their *tzitziyot* (ritual fringes) that they wear are an additional ameliorating fac-

---

7 Hayyim Nahman Bialik, *Poems*, Tel Aviv 1973, 340–349 [in Hebrew].

tor, since the dead are exempt from the obligation of ritual fringes (BT Shabbat 30a), nor are corpses buried in these garments – ritual fringes are only for the living. Their status as dead is not absolute and final.[8] Rabbah bar Bar Hana seeks to utilize the opportunity that comes his way, to examine the number of knots and strings in the ritual fringes of the wilderness dead, and thereby to resolve the halakhic question on this issue, which is the subject of disagreement between the Schools of Hillel and Shammai.[9] As proof of his testimony, Rabbah bar Bar Hana cuts the corner of a ritual-fringe garment from one of the wilderness dead, which results in the wilderness dead immobilizing him where he stands. From the viewpoint of the narrator, the validity of halakhic traditions does not lie in concrete markers, but in the oral and written transmission processes. The some two hundred years since the disagreements between Hillel and Shammai and the time of the third-generation Amora are channelled to the wilderness vision seen by Rabbah bar Bar Hana, intensify it, and create a time-space narrative unit, a chronotope; and the metonymic connection between the wilderness and the living-dead resting in it tightens. Their vitality, despite their being termed "the wilderness dead", is expressed in their magical power to paralyze the Amora as long as he holds the *tzitzit* corner that he had torn from the garment. They are portrayed between mortal and immortal.

Rabbah bar Bar Hana's vision stretches between the realistic and the illusionary and fantastic, without any definite resolution, like a desert mirage that expressed the marginal consciousness typical of one who walks in its expanses, blurring the distinctions between life and death.[10] Following a convention of tall tales, the narrator chooses to base the credibility of his tale on the explicit declaration by the Amora: "I saw [*ledidi hazi li*]," which precedes the series of exaggerated tales in the discursive unit in Bava Batra; that is, I saw with my own eyes. The Amora's authority is meant to convince the reader, as well as the sages (the audience within the narrative), of the credibility of what he says.

---

8 See PT Taanit 4:7 (69c), that on the eve of every Ninth of Av the Israelites would dig pits for themselves and enter them, and in the morning they would be decreased by those who died. This depiction also expresses the liminal state of the generation that left Egypt, and their metonymic connection to the wilderness expanse.
9 See BT Menahot 41b.
10 Dinah Stein, "Different Perspectives: A Reading of Bava Batra 73a–75b", in: *Jerusalem Studies in Hebrew Literature*, 17, 1999, 18–21 [in Hebrew], in contrast, indicates another tension in the aggadah of the wilderness dead: the pre-cultural and non-institutionalized element that the wilderness dead embody in their rebellion, as opposed to the domesticated element embodied in their ritual fringes.

The sages accept his words as reliable and believe his story, albeit with criticism towards how he conducted himself.[11]

The liminal status of the wilderness dead who are revealed to Rabbah bar Bar Hana as a vision in the wilderness is consistent with the Mishnaic disagreement between those who are of the opinion that those to die in the wilderness are worthy of the World to Come and those who maintain that they have no portion in the World to Come.[12] Their identification with the wilderness as its metonym is expressed not only in their blending into the wilderness dunes and their body positions, which represent the hills and rocks of the wilderness, but also, and mainly, in the undefined states of identity that the narrative fashions. Using its rhetorical means, the aggadah reconstructs the transition from slavery to freedom, from a "mixed multitude" to a collective, through the liminal phase in which the distinction between life and death is unclear. This condition is also embodied in the various sources on the death of Moses. As their leader, he represents those to die in the wilderness, and their fate is intertwined with his.

The Death of Moses

The gap between the precise location of Moses' grave in the steppes of Moab and the very fact of his death, on the one hand, and, on the other, the statement that "no one knows his burial place to this day", indicates a liminal aspect in the Biblical description of Moses' death. It is bridged in different ways in the various sources on the theme of Moses' death – whether in the Jewish Hellenistic version of Flavius Josephus who plays down the Biblical contradictive description, or by early and late Rabbinic literary sources, as well as by the elaborated medieval narrative of *Petirat Moshe* ("The Death of Moses"), which emphasize this contradiction. In these midrashic and medival sources, Moses is depicted as someone who died and was buried, and also as one who disappeared and was concealed by God (or vice versa). All in all, the sources can be thematically classified by three main, and mutually connected motifs that appear in several variants: the motif of search, the motif of the grave, and the motif of transformation. The search motif is conveyed in the portrayals of the search through the expanses of the wilderness and the cosmos for the one who is missing. The grave motif is formulated in the disappearance of Moses' grave or, alternatively, in Moses'

---

[11] Dan Ben-Amos, "Talmudic Tall Tales", in: *Folklore Today: A Festschrift for Richard M. Dorson*, ed. Linda Degh/Henry Glassie/Felix Oinas, Bloomington/IN 1976, 25–43.
[12] See M. Sanhedrin 10, 3; BT Sanhedrin 110b.

burying of himself. The motif of transformation is expressed through the reduction of the character of Moses, whether as leader or as mortal. These three motifs, represent different aspects of a single phenomenon: the blurring of the features of Moses' identity before his death or concealment. Each of these are described in detail below.

The search motif: in the Tannaitic version brought in *Sifre* (para. 305), from the third century, the Angel of Death searches for Moses in different sites in which he was active during his life in order to take his soul, but he is unsuccessful, because Moses has been taken to God.

> The Angel went looking for him at his place, but could not find him. He went to the sea and asked it: "Moses, have you seen him?" It replied, "Since the day that He [= the Holy One, blessed be He] made Israel pass through me, I have not seen him." He then went to the mountains and the hills and asked them: "Moses, have you seen him?" They replied, "Since the day that Israel received the Torah on Mount Sinai, we have not seen him." He thereupon went to Gehinnom and asked it: "Moses, have you seen him?" It replied, "I have heard his name, but I have not seen him." He then went to the ministering angels and asked them: "Moses, have you seen him?" They said to him, "Go and ask human beings." He went to Israel and asked them: "Moses, have you seen him?" They said to him, "God has fathomed him, and has concealed him," for the life of the World to Come, and no creature knows his whereabouts, as it is said (Deuteronomy 34:6): "He buried him in the valley [in the land of Moab, near Beth-peor; and no one knows his burial place to this day]." (Translated by Ruth Bar-Ilan)[13]

This version continues with a depiction of the profound grief of Joshua, Moses' disciple, and of the Holy One, blessed be He, Himself. The locations mentioned in the above citation: the wilderness ["at his place"], the sea, the mountains and the hills, Gehinnom (that only heard of Moses, but did not see him), the ministering angels in their place, and finally, human beings in their place, reconstruct the dramatic and magnificent route of Moses' life in a historic and cosmic context. His place remains a mystery until the end of the narrative, that does not give a clear answer whether he died or was concealed: the ministering angels send the Angel of Death to the humans, who report to him of Moses' concealment with God, but their conclusion is based solely on circumstantial evidence, namely, Moses' disappearance without a trace, as Scripture puts this: "and no one knows his burial place"; and the Angel of Death's search for Moses fails. His disappearance might be on account of his being buried in some unknown location, and not a result of his concealment. Furthermore, if he had been concealed, how

---

13 *Sifre on Deuteronomy* (*Siphre ad Deuteronomium*), ed. Louis Finkelstein [Berlin 1939], New York/Jerusalem 1993, 326–327 [in Hebrew].

would the ministering angels be unaware of the place, and be forced to send the Angel of Death to them, the humans? The elliptic and subject-less statement – "He buried him in the valley" – alludes to the burial of Moses by God, that is, his concealment, but the event is not transmitted as eyewitness testimony, and the reliance on the verse that relates to his burial leaves available the possibility of his death. The ambivalence regarding Moses' death or concealment is especially stressed in comparison with the concealment of Enoch, of whom the Bible explicitly testifies (Gn 5:24): "then he was no more, for God took him." It seems that none of the suppositions regarding Moses' death or concealment can be fully verified, neither by indicating the place of his burial, nor by eyewitness testimony to his concealment. The search for Moses accordingly reaches a dead end on account of the evasive definition of Moses' identity on the eve of his death.

The wilderness is the venue of the Angel of Death's journey in search of Moses. It is there that he begins, in Moses' presumed location ("at his place"), and there it ends, in the steppes of Moab, "in the valley". Moses' disappearance and the search for him attest to the wilderness' overpowering and leveling strength, the threat of loss and death embodied in its expanses, illusion and wanderings, the danger inherent in its tremendous serpents and scorpions, as mentioned above. The Biblical depiction of the Israelites' wandering serves as a model that is transferred to the Talmudic aggadah. The Angel of Death's search for Moses reconstructs the Israelites' journeys in the wilderness, beginning with the parting of the Red Sea. Concurrently, Moses' disappearance expresses the potential for inspiration and spiritual elevation inherent in the wilderness, which finds maximum realization in Moses' concealment with God, parallel to the former's ascent to Heaven prior to the Giving of the Torah. A metonymic connection is forged between the liminal character of Moses in the accounts of his death-concealment and the imagery of the wilderness in which he was both active and buried.

The search motif recurs in a late midrashic version in *Tanhuma*.[14] Moses searches for intermediaries who will entreat for him before God: heaven and earth, the stars and constellations, mountains, hills, and the sea, and finally, "the Officer of the [Divine] Presence", who informs him that the decree has been sealed and is final.[15] The wilderness is both the start and end point in Moses' searching for advocates on his behalf. From the wilderness he turns to

---

14 *Tanhuma*, ed. Buber (as in n. 6), *Ve'ethanan* 6.
15 In *Tanhuma*, ed. Buber (as in n. 6), *Ve'ethanan* 6, Moses additionally addresses the sun and the moon.

the natural and celestial bodies as he seeks mercy; and he is buried in the wilderness after the search mission fails, as is written in the continuation of the version: "He said to Israel: 'I ask of you, when you enter the land, remember me and my bones, and say, Woe to the son of Amram, who ran before us as a horse, and whose bones fell in the wilderness'." The various natural bodies refuse to plead on his behalf, since they themselves are not everlasting. Their response to Moses is formulated with the inclusion of quotations from the book of Isaiah,[16] that contrast exile with redemption, and the transience of nature with the Lord's covenant with His people: "Raise your eyes to the heavens, and look upon the earth beneath: though the heavens should melt away like smoke, and the earth wear out like a garment, and its inhabitants die out as well"; in contrast with the wearing out of the earth, the salvation of the Lord is firm and eternal (Is 51:6).[17] The search scene in *Tanhuma* represents historical and eschatological processes of exile and redemption.[18] Exile, as long and harsh as it may be, anticipates the promised redemption. The inclusion of verses from Isaiah and their broad contexts fashion the liminal identity of the people of Israel as a chosen and separate entity in its land, and also as dispersed among the nations.[19] In the deep structure of the exposition as it was fashioned by the anonymous redactor(s) of *Tanhuma*, death is the promise of eternal life in the World to Come, parallel to the promise of redemption at the height of exile. The search scene embodies the liminal state of death/exile/wilderness, which is a condition of absence and uncertainty preceding the transition to another reality (the World to Come/redemption/the Land of Israel).

The search motif that was created to bridge the gap in the Bible between the fact of Moses' death and the enigma of the place of his grave expresses in both versions, the early version in *Sifrei* and the later one, in *Tanhuma*, Moses' liminal standing on the eve of his death at the boundary of the land, in a metonymic linkage to the wilderness in which the drama of his life and death is played out. *Tanhuma* adds to Moses' liminal identity an eschatological dimension, as

---

16 On the recitation of Biblical verses by the characters, see Jona Frankel, "Bible Verses Quoted in Tales of the Sages", in: *Studies in Aggadah and Folk Literature*, ed. J. Heinemann/D. Voy, Jerusalem 1971 (Scripta Hierosolymitana, 22), 80–99.
17 See the incorporation of Isaiah 54:10: "For the mountains may move and the hills be shaken, but my loyalty shall never move from you, nor My covenant of friendship be shaken."
18 The transition from exile to redemption is portrayed in another verse in the same chapter (51:3) in terms of the desolation of the wilderness and its blossoming: "Truly the Lord has comforted Zion, comforted all her ruins; He has made her wilderness like Eden, her desert like the Garden of the Lord."
19 This idea seemingly also emerges from *Sifre on Deuteronomy*, ed. Finkelstein (as in n. 13), para. 357, 425–427.

one who is situated in the seam between the human and the metaphysical. The liminality of Moses on the eve of his death precedes future states of exile and redemption, which entail the undermining of nature, destruction and desolation, in contrast with the tidings of the covenant with God that promises the rebuilding and flourishing of Zion.

Moses' grave: The *Antiquities* by Josephus (first century CE) states: "A cloud of a sudden descended upon him and he disappeared in a ravine."[20] The narrator comments that in the Bible, however, Moses writes of his death in the first person, since he feared lest people dare to say that he ascended to God because of his great righteousness. Moses' sudden disappearance, that is related from the perspective of those watching him – Eliezer, Joshua, and the elders – seems to be concealment. Yet, scriptural declaration of his death and burial hedges this conclusion, albeit without details of the course of events in order to prevent the mythicization of his character. Did Moses disappear, under cover of the cloud, to a burial cave, as appears in other Hellenistic Latin versions of his burial by angels in an unknown place?[21] The wording "disappeared" in the *Antiquities* does not refer specifically to either concealment or death, and leaves Moses' end open to both possibilities, and patently, not exclusively to one or the other. Moses' disappearance in a cloud "in a ravine" might be explained by the physical conditions of the wilderness, that, in its infinite and monotonous expanses, swallows those who stray in its hills, valleys, and mists that cover it from time to time. A metonymic linkage is established between Moses and the wilderness in which he disappears, that enables the projection of Moses' liminal characteristics in his concealment-death upon the wilderness generation that he led, that is the generation of knowledge that will enter the World to Come, and vice versa. The diametric contrasts in the character of Moses and in the generation that he represents, between the human and the metaphysical, coexist and fashion the meaning of the period of the wanderings in the wilderness, as discussed thus far.

At this point, the disappearance of Moses' grave, as Scripture puts it (Dt 34:6): "and no one knows his burial place", will be introduced as a variation of the search motif. A *baraita* (external mishnah) brought in the Babylonian Talmud (Sotah 14a) tells of a Roman delegation that wished to see Moses' burial place. "When they stood above, it appeared to them to be below; when they

---

[20] Josephus, *Jewish Antiquities* 4:8:48–49 (4:326), trans. by Henry St. John Thackeray, London/New York 1930, 632–633.
[21] Thus in *Life of Moses*, *Liber Antiquitatum Biblicarum*, and the reconstructed version of *The Assumption of Moses*.

were below, it appeared to them to be above. They divided themselves into two parties; to those who were standing above, it appeared below, and to those who were below, it appeared above."[22] The Talmud then cites another opinion, according to which even Moses himself did not identify the place of his burial. The disappearance of Moses' grave is transmitted in this *baraita* in terms of a mirage in the wilderness. The grave is present and absent, both at the same time, and each time is revealed elsewhere, with no possibility of clearly defining its place. This is a concretization of the Biblical verse (Dt 34:6): "and no one knows his burial place to this day."

The anomalous nature of Moses' burial as the motif that fashions his death in relation to the wilderness experience finds exceptional expression in a late midrashic collection from twelfth-century Provence, *Lekah Tov*. In this version, Moses buries himself:

> If you say, "in the valley," why is it written that he died in the land of Moab? Rather, he died in the portion of Reuben and was buried in the portion of Gad. And who buried him? He buried himself.[23]

The discrepancy in the Bible between the mention of Moses' death and his grave's disappearance from the eyes of all living creatures is explained in this midrash by Moses' burying himself without witnesses, in a manner likely to refute the very fact of his death. The setting of the wilderness emerges, not only from the mention of the portions of Reuben and Gad, that are concrete sites in Transjordan, but also from the distress and even threat engendered by the picture of a person burying himself. This articulates the existential loneliness in the endless expanse of the wilderness, and acceptance of the inevitable. The wilderness expanses are also intimated by the function of distance in the descriptions of Moses' passage, or transferal, from the place of his death to that of his burial.

In the Ethiopian version *Mota Mussah* that was published by Faitlovitch, the researcher is of Ethiopian Jewry. His soul was taken from him by a ruse: Allah sends four angels to dig a grave in the wilderness. Moses offers to help them, and descends into the grave to measure it, where he encounters the Angel of Death. The latter gives him a quince. Moses smells the fruit, and his soul departs through his nostrils. Moses, who falls victim to a seeming band of grave diggers, is ensnared by the cunning of the Angel of Death, and is tempted to smell of the

---

[22] See also *Sifre on Deuteronomy*, ed. Finkelstein (as in n. 13), para. 357, 428–429.
[23] Tobias ben Eliezer, *Lekah Tov*, ed. Solomon Buber, Jerusalem 1960 (first published Vilna 1880), Dt 34:6, 134.

fruit that he is given. Not only he fails in his attempts to delay his passing, he even unwittingly buries himself. The wilderness is a suitable arena for such an act of deception. This Ethiopian version was influenced by the Islamic adaptation of the story by Tabari (eighth century).[24] The popular Islamic parallels include the motif of wanderings in the story, which may be set parallel to the motif of the search in the Rabbinic sources (see above).[25]

Transformation: liminality, that is marked by reduction, invisibility, and the blurring of identity boundaries, is present in the sources on the death of Moses, by means of the motif of transformation, as well. Its appearances are prominent in *Midrash Petirat Moshe Rabbeinu* (The Midrash of the Death of Moses), a narrative composition of the medieval-period "rewritten Bible" genre. It apparently dates to the eleventh century in Byzantium. The text depicts two transformative situations: (1) the exchanging of standing and identity between teacher and disciple, Moses and Joshua; and (2) the replacement of human identity by a reductive nonhuman or inanimate identity.

The exchanging of standing and identity between Moses and Joshua: Moses decides to waive his leadership and attend Joshua, provided that he will enter the land:

> Moses said: For thirty-six years Joshua attended me in the wilderness [...] The righteous Moses reasoned: Perhaps I must die because the time has come for my disciple Joshua to provide for Israel and to lead them, and this is why it was decreed that I not enter the land and eat of its fruits. Of what avail is its bounty to me, if my feet will not tread upon the Land of Israel? I would rather live on and let Joshua be the leader, so that I may enter the Land of Israel.[26]

Moses served Joshua for thirty-six days, beginning in the middle of the night, while Joshua slept. A detailed scene lists all the elements in the ceremony of his serving Joshua, in the way that this had previously been done for him, in the process highlighting the dramatic change in Moses' standing and in his very identity as teacher:

> Every night Moses would arise at midnight and go to Joshua's doorway. He would take the key and unlock the door. After entering, he would take a shirt, shake it out, and place it by the top of his [Joshua's] bed. He would then take his shoes, prepare them, and place them

---

24 Following Haim Schwarzbaum, *Biblical and Extra-Biblical Legends in Islamic Folk Literature*, Walldorf-Hessen 1982, 31–34.
25 See Kushelevsky, *Moses and the Angel of Death* (as in n. 1), 140–154.
26 *Midrash Petirat Moshe Rabbenu A[lav] Ha[shalom]*, ed. Adolph Jellinek, *Bet ha-Midrasch*, vol. 1, *Heder* 1, Jerusalem 1967, 123.

by the side of the bed. [After this,] he would take his vest and his cloak, his golden helmet, and his crown of pearls, examine, clean, and polish them, and lay them out in order on a golden chair. He would then fetch a jug of water and a golden bowl and place them in front of the chair. All that time Joshua did not awaken.[27]

As far as Joshua was concerned, even if not conscious of this, Moses was "invisible". Joshua is not aware of him during all the preparations made by Moses before Joshua awakens in the morning. Also in the first meeting with the Israelites after the exchange of leaders, Moses descends from the stage, which he leaves for Joshua: "When Israel saw Joshua going at the head, they were all agitated and they stood on their feet." The venue of these events is the wilderness, and the transformation is meant to enable Moses to enter the land with a new identity, as a layman before his teacher. Even though, in actuality, his wish did not come to pass, this option remains in the background.

The transformation of human identity into a non-human or inanimate identity: In the continuation of *Midrash Petirat Moshe Rabbeinu*, the motif of transformation returns in another fashion. Moses seeks to assume reductive non-human or inanimate identities, in order to circumvent the ban on his entering the land:

> Moses implored, "Master of the worlds, let me [at least] fly like a bird in the air by the power of the Tetragrammaton. Or make me like a fish, with my arms spread like two fins and all my hair turned into scales, that I may leap over the Jordan and see the land."
>
> The Holy One, blessed be He, said to him: If I were to do this for you, I would break My vow.
>
> He [Moses] said to Him, "Master of the Universe! Carry me upon the pinions of the clouds the measure of three parasangs above the Jordan, with the clouds below me and I above, that I may see all the land."
>
> He [the Holy One, blessed be He,] said to him: Consider this, too, as My breaking My vow.
>
> He [Moses] said to Him, "Master of the Universe! Cut me up, limb by limb, and cast me over the Jordan, then revive me, that I may see the land."
>
> He [the Holy One, blessed be He,] said to him: [That would be] as My breaking My vow.
>
> He [Moses] said to Him, "Show me the sight of the land."
>
> He [the Holy One, blessed be He,] said to him: In this I will comply with your wish, as it is said [Deuteronomy 32:52]: "You may view the land from a distance, but you shall not enter it."[28]

---

[27] Ibid., 123.
[28] Jellinek, *Bet ha-Midrasch*, vol. 1, *Heder* 1, 124–125. This is a development and expansion of the early Tannaitic source in *Siphre d'be Rab* (on Numbers), ed. Hayyim Saul Horovitz [Leipzig 1917] Jerusalem 1992, para. 135, 182.

Moses is prepared to assume reductive forms of existence: a fish, a bird flying above, and even limbs, as objects thrown to the opposite bank. At the same time, and paradoxically, Moses is portrayed as a metaphysical and elevated figure, specifically because of the potential of detaching him from his fixed physical identity.[29]

The three major motifs in the various sources on the death of Moses, both the early and late sources – search, Moses' grave, and transformation – embody the lack of definition in the depictions of Moses death-concealment. Based on the metonymic links in these sources to the wilderness, which is not only the arena of the events, but an expanse charged with symbolic meanings, this is a dangerous expanse of desolation and mirage; an expanse that metaphorically represents situations of destruction and exile. Moses, in his liminal identity, represents the Israelites who, under his leadership, are making their way through the wilderness to the Land of Israel. The Talmudic aggadah of those to die in the wilderness sheds light on this interim phase in the annals of the Jewish nation from a different perspective, but by means of the same literary rhetoric of a lack of definition: the figures of the wilderness dead, whom we cannot know for a certainty whether they are dead or merely sleeping; and whether they will awaken in the eschatological End of Days, or in the World to Come.

The comparison of the aggadah of "those to die in the wilderness" and the story of Moses' death-concealment is anchored in their common aspect of liminality. This feature allows for the expansion of the Biblical story as a narrative of the crossing of boundaries, and for the identification of Moses' character on the eve of his death and "those to die in the wilderness" as additional manifestations of the liminal experience of the Israelites in their wanderings in the wilderness.

---

29 For an additional expanded discussion, see Rella Kushelevsky, "The Longings for the Land of Israel in the Midrashim on the Death of Moses", in: *Alei Siah*, 31–32, 1993, 189–196 [in Hebrew].

Mika Natif
Between Heaven and Earth: The Illustration of the Death of Moses in Rashid al-Din's *Jami al-Tawarikh* (World History)

In the Jewish Bible, the death of Moses marks the completion of the Exodus and the transformation of the Israelites from a nomadic society to a settled, established nation. It is a decisive moment that signifies a turning point in the relationship between God and his people when both entities lose their ultimate mediator between High and Low – Moses. In Moses' persona Heaven and Earth met, and he was able to bridge this unconventional border. As the exceptional person portrayed in the Torah, he possessed unique characteristics unveiled in a remarkable painting known as the *Death of Moses*, in Rashid al-Din's *World History* (*Jami al-Tawarikh*) from Ilkhanid Iran (fig. 1).[1] In addition to its painterly qualities, this illustration embodies ideas of transition, extraterrestrial border crossing, and transculturation that reflect the global concepts of the author-patron of this manuscript, Rashid al-Din.

The illustrated manuscript containing the *Death of Moses* was produced circa 1314–1315 in Tabriz, under the patronage of one of the most noteworthy personalities of the Mongol Ilkhanid period in Iran. At the time, Rashid al-Din served as one of the two head viziers (chief ministers) at the Ilkhanid court.[2] As an intellectual and a man of letters, he was commissioned by the Ilkhan rulers Ghazan (r. 1295–1304) and Uljaytu (r. 1304–1316) to write a multi-volume history of the Mongols, the origins of their tribes, and their genealogies. The second volume includes sections dedicated to the pre-Islamic kings and prophets, the history of Muhammad, the caliphate and the post-caliphate dynasties of Iran.[3] In addition, the book also contains the stories and lineages of other peo-

---

[1] Descendants of Chingiz Khan, the Ilkhans were a Mongol dynasty who ruled greater Iran from about 1260 until circa 1335. By the late thirteenth century the Ilkhanid elite had begun to convert to Islam. Reuven Amitai, "Il-Khanids: Dynastic History", in: *Encyclopaedia Iranica*, vol. 12, fasc. 6, 645–654; Dorothea Krawulsky, *The Mongol Īlkhāns and their Vizier Rashīd al-Dīn*, Frankfurt am Main et al. 2011, 123.
[2] For a discussion and interpretation of the seven paintings of Moses in the *Jami al-Tawarikh*, see Mika Natif, "Rashid al-Din's Alter Ego: The Seven Paintings of Moses in the 'Jami al-Tawarikh' ", in: *Rashid al-Din as an Agent and Mediator of Cultural Exchanges in Ilkhanid Iran*, ed. Anna Akasoy/Charles Burnett/Ronit Yoeli-Tlalim, London, Warburg Institute 2013, 15–37.
[3] Rashid al-Din composed the *Jami al-Tawarikh* between 1300 and 1310. Charles Melville, "Jāmeʿ al-Tawārīk", in: *Encyclopaedia Iranica*, vol. 14, fasc. 5, 462; David Morgan, "Rashīd al-Dīn Ṭabīb",

Fig. 1: The death of Moses, *Jami al-Tawarikh* of Rashid al-Din, Tabriz, ca. 1314–1315. London, Nasser D. Khalili Collection of Islamic Art, MSS 727, fol. 54v [reconstructed by Blair as fol. 294v]

ples with whom the Mongols were in contact, such as the Chinese, Turks, Franks, Indians, and Jews. The *Death of Moses* appears in the section devoted to a history of the Jews (History of the Children of Israel; *Tarikh-i banu Israil*).[4]

The originality of Rashid al-Din's text and his approach to the genre of world history may be linked to his connections at the court and his access to sources on the one hand, and his background and upbringing on the other.[5] He was born into a Jewish family and his father was a pharmacist. Rashid al-Din himself trained as a physician (*tabib*) and in that capacity he entered the service of the Mongols.[6] At the age of thirty, around 1277, he converted to Islam and rose in rank at the Ilkhanid court.[7] During the reign of Abu Sa'id Khan (r. 1316–1335), however, the political atmosphere changed and Rashid al-Din was accused of poisoning his previous patron, Uljaytu Khan. In 1318, at the age of seventy or seventy-one, he was executed with his son Ibrahim.[8] Until his tragic end, Rashid al-Din enjoyed a productive life, both intellectually and politically. As one of the most influential figures at the court, he established his own scriptorium and atelier – the Rab-i Rashidi – in the Ilkhanid capital of Tabriz where artists, scribes, and calligraphers produced manuscripts, some of which were illustrated.[9] He further arranged for two copies of the *Jami al-Tawarikh* – one in Arabic and one in Persian – to be made every year for distribution to cities throughout the Islamic world.[10] On account of his death and the destruction of the Rab-i Ra-

---

in: *Encyclopaedia of Islam*, 2nd edition, Brill Online 2013. URL: <http://referenceworks.brillonline.com/entries/encyclopaedia-of-islam-2/rashid-al-din-tabib-SIM_6237> [13.04.2012].

4 For the organization of the *Jami al-Tawarikh*, its content and sources, see David Morgan, *The Mongols*, Malden, MA/Oxford, UK 2007, 18–19; Melville, Jāmeʿ al-Tawārīk (as in n. 3), 462–468.
5 Melville, Jāmeʿ al-Tawārīk (as in n. 3), 462–468.
6 For further discussion of his Jewish origin, see Amnon Netzer, "Rashīd al-Dīn and His Jewish Background", in: *Irano-Judaica: Studies Relating to Jewish Contacts with Persian Culture throughout the Ages*, ed. Shaul Shaked/Amnon Netzer, vol. 3, Jerusalem 1994, 118–126.
7 Morgan, Rashīd al-Dīn Ṭabīb (as in n. 3). Dorothea Krawulsky disagrees, claiming that he was a Muslim already by the age of twenty-one. Krawulsky, *The Mongol Īlkhāns and their Vizier Rashīd al-Dīn*, Frankfurt am Main et al. 2011, 122–123.
8 David Morgan, "Rashīd al-Dīn Ṭabīb", in: *Encyclopaedia of Islam*, vol. 8, Leiden, 1994, 443–444.
9 For a discussion regarding the books that were produced by and for Rashid al-Din, see Sheila Blair, "Calligraphers, Illuminators, and Painters in the Ilkhanid Scriptorium", in: *Beyond the Legacy of Genghis Khan*, ed. Linda Komaroff, Leiden/Boston 2006, 167–182.
10 See the instructions in his *waqf* Addendum in Birgitt Hoffmann, *Waqf im mongolischen Iran: Rašīduddīns Sorge um Nachruhm und Seelenheil*, Stuttgart 2000, 256. The *waqf* Addendum was translated by Wheeler Thackston in Sheila Blair, *A Compendium of Chronicles*, London 1995, 114–115.

shidi quarter, his plan did not come to fruition. Unfortunately, illustrated copies of the *Jami al-Tawarikh* dating to the lifetime of the author did not survive well.[11]

The *Death of Moses* illustration appears in an Arabic copy of the *World History / Jami al-Tawarikh*, dated approximately to 1314–1315, which has been celebrated for its ninety innovative paintings. It appears that the book was produced under the author's supervision and probable patronage, for it corresponds to stipulations specified in his endowment deed.[12] Presently divided between the Edinburgh University Library and the Khalili Collections in London, the volume possesses an unprecedented number of illustrations devoted to the figure of Moses.[13] Following his life cycle from infancy to death, the visual program portrays him in sequential scenes: floating in a box on the Nile to be found by the pharaoh's wife (Asanath), hearing God's voice on Mount Sinai, watching the pharaoh and his army drown in the Red Sea, punishing Korah and his followers, defeating the giant Og, ordering the execution of the worshippers of the Golden Calf, and facing his death. This concentration of seven paintings has no match in any copy of the *Jami al-Tawarikh* or other contemporary historical and legendary texts featuring Moses.[14] The number of Moses illustrations is striking even within the context of the Edinburgh-Khalili volume itself. For example, in the section dedicated to the pre-Islamic prophets, Abraham and David are each depicted only once, in contrast to seven representations of Moses.[15] Rachel Milstein, who has analyzed the figure of Moses in Islamicate painting and book art, argues that in fourteenth-century illustrated manuscripts, his representations are usually linked to the struggle against unbelievers, idolaters, and infidels.[16] The seven

---

11 For a study of Rashid al-Din manuscripts of the *Jami al-Tawarikh*, see the work of Kazuhiko Shiraiwa, especially: *Rashid al-Din's Compendium of Chronicles: a bibliography of extant manuscripts*, Tokyo 2000 [in Japanese].

12 Blair, *Compendium of Chronicles* (as in n. 10), 30; and ead., "Patterns of Patronage and Production in Ilkhanid Iran. The Case of Rashid al-Din", in: *The Court of the Il-Khans, 1290–1340*, ed. Julian Raby/Teresa Fitzherbert, Oxford 1996, 39–62, here 53–54.

13 MS Edinburgh, Edinburgh University Library, MS Arab 20, and MS London, Nasser D. Khalili Collection, MS 727. The manuscript bears the *hijri* date of 714 (1314–1315 CE) at the end of the section on India, in fol. 281v of the Khalili manuscript. Blair, *Compendium of Chronicles* (as in n. 10), 16, 20–21.

14 For a discussion regarding the number and placement of illustrations in the *Jami al–tawarikh*, see Blair, *Compendium of Chronicles* (as in n. 10), 42–33; Robert Hillenbrand, "The Arts of the Book in Ilkhanid Iran," in: *The Legacy of Genghis Khan*, ed. Linda Komaroff/Stefano Carboni, New Haven 2003, 134–162, here 147–149.

15 The illustrations of Abraham and David are housed at the Edinburgh University Library, MS Arab 20, E7 and E21.

16 Rachel Milstein, "The Iconography of Moses in Islamic Art", in: *Jewish Art*, vol. 12/13, 1986/1987, 199–212, here 200.

Jami al-Tawarikh illustrations, however, focus on the political, religious and judicial nature of the biblical leader of the Israelites, not on his performance of magic and wonders.[17]

Moreover, among the innovative scenes included in this cycle, the *Death of Moses* is unusual. In a contemporary manuscript of the *Jami al-Tawarikh* (MS H.1654), a different moment from the end of the leader's life was chosen to be illustrated (fig. 2).[18] The painting in H.1654 shows Moses anointing Joshua, his successor, and thus emphasizing historical continuity, while the Khalili picture focuses on the tranquil sense of harmony surrounding Moses at the time of his death (figs. 1, 2).[19]

The final image in the Moses cycle of the Edinburgh-Khalili Arabic volume shows the recumbent patriarch with his eyes closed, surrounded by trees and hills that separate him from the group of Israelites on the left (fig. 1). This scene is of particular interest because it involves the last moments of his departure from his people and this world, as well as the completion of the Exodus and the beginning of the Israelites' journey to the Promised Land. Negotiating conflicting ideas, the picture is unique: it has no parallel among illustrated manuscripts of the *Jami al-Tawarikh* or related paintings dealing with Moses in Islamicate visual culture. The work stands apart in both its exceptional subject matter and its idiosyncratic composition. Complex visual hermeneutics may shed light on the distinguished cultural persona of the patron-author of this manuscript and his time. In order to grasp the multi-layered iconography of its content and the implications of this image, we will have to go beyond the borders of Persian painting and explore possible links with other religious visual expressions that may have played a role and shaped the production and understanding of this work of art.

The Moses of the Edinburgh-Khalili illustrations is shown as the person who brings the law, leads the nation, administers justice, and governs according to

---

17 The paintings have been published and analyzed in Natif, Rashid al-Din's Alter Ego (as in n. 2).

18 MS H.1654 is housed at the Topkapi Saray Museum, Istanbul. The painting is further reproduced in Karl Jahn, *Die Geschichte der Kinder Israels des Rašīd ad-Dīn*, Vienna 1973, pl. 29. On the complexity of this manuscript, see the article by Güner Inal, "Some Miniatures of the *Jāmi al-Tavārīkh* in Istanbul, Topkapı Museum, Hazine Library no. 1654", in: *Ars Orientalis*, 5, 1963, 163–176.

19 In the Persian manuscript H.1654, Moses is portrayed only in two episodes, and he does not get the same attention and emphasis he receives in the Edinburgh-Khalili volume. See Jahn, *Die Geschichte der Kinder Israels* (as in n. 18), pls. 24, 29.

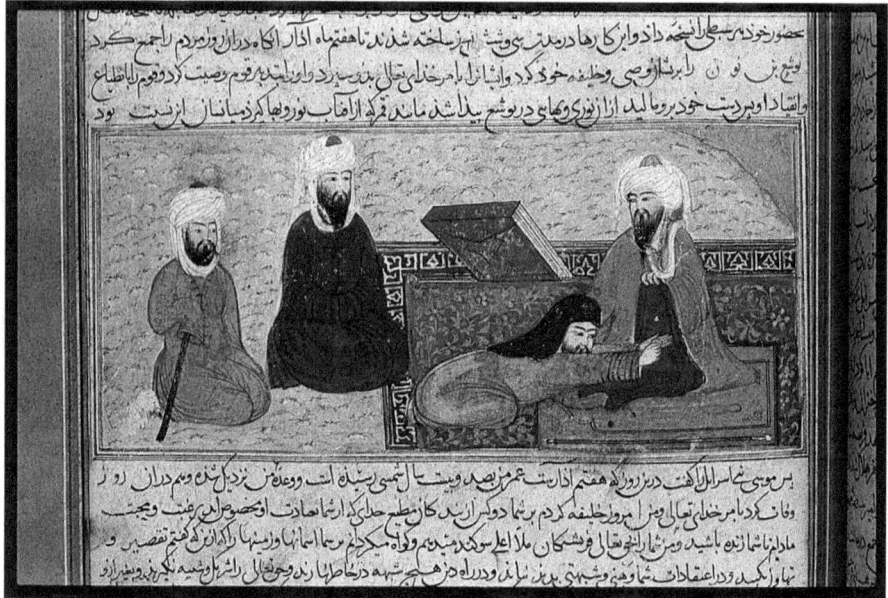

Fig. 2: Moses anointing Joshua, *Jami al-Tawarikh* of Rashid al-Din. Istanbul, Topkapi Palace Library, MS H.1654, fol. 286r.

God's rule.[20] Furthermore, he is a man who speaks directly and freely to God and dies in a state of perfect harmony, buried by God himself. I have argued elsewhere that these paintings reflect a very specific image of Moses, one that can be linked to the concept of the Prophet-king and to Maimonides' view of Moses as the Perfect Man.[21] In the present article, I explore how the depiction of Moses' death establishes his place in the divine chain of prophets who possessed hereditary authority. Chosen by God, these special individuals passed on the divine legacy until its culmination with Muhammad.[22] Linking the iconography of Moses' death with Muhammad's birth binds the two figures together as the transmitters of the same unchanged divine message (figs. 1, 3). Therefore, the moment represented in the *Jami al-Tawarikh* painting is not one of death but

---

[20] This is not a popular image of Moses in fourteenth-century Arabic and Persian illustrated manuscripts. Most commonly, he is portrayed fighting idolatry and performing miracles. See Milstein, "The Iconography of Moses in Islamic Art" (as in n. 16).
[21] Natif, Rashid al-Din's Alter Ego (as in n. 2), 13–18.
[22] On the prophets' divine legacy and hereditary authority see Uri Rubin, "Prophets and Caliphs: The Biblical Foundations of the Umayyad Authority", in: *Method and Theory in the Study of Islamic Origins*, ed. Herbert Berg, Leiden 2003, 73–99.

of continuity and miraculous transition. As a Jew converted to Islam, a vizier of the Ilkhans, a physician, a man of science and learning, Rashid al-Din may have held Moses as an ideal figure and a model to be followed, similar to Muhammad.²³

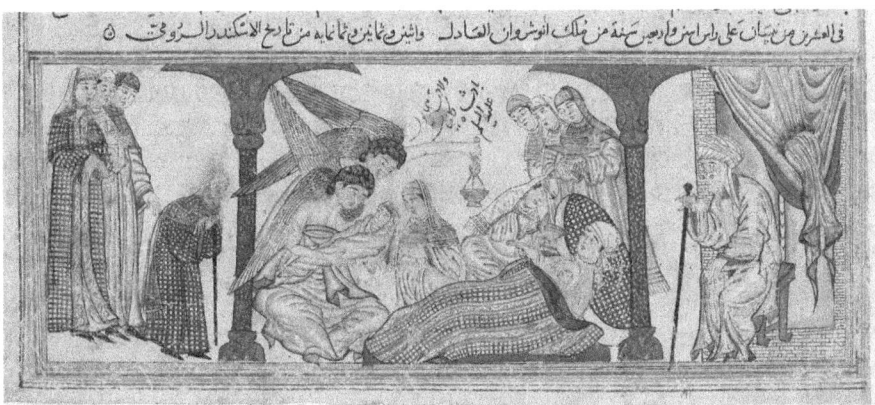

Fig. 3: The birth of the Prophet Muhammad, *Jami al-Tawarikh* of Rashid al-Din, Tabriz, ca. 1314 – 1315. Edinburgh, University Library, Arab. Ms. 20, fol. 42r [reconstructed by Blair as fol. 44r]

The pictorial invention and exquisite quality of the *Jami al-Tawarikh* images have long been recognized by historians of Islamic art as a breakthrough in Persian painting. I believe that the originality of the Moses illustrations further reflects the novelty of the text, which differs from other Islamicate histories. In the section on the Children of Israel, Rashid al-Din states that he has attempted to bring forth the Jewish perspective of the biblical stories, conveying the notion of how these people narrated their own history.²⁴ Hence, his image of Moses as the perfect man stands apart from the one projected by the Qur'an and several Muslim theologians. According to Brannon Wheeler, some Muslim theologians' disapproval of Moses is used to draw a distinction between the Hebrew Bible

---

23 Several Late Antique philosophers also linked Moses to Plato and other Greek thinkers. Robbert van den Berg brings the following famous quotation attributed to Numenius, who supposedly said, "What is Plato, but Moses speaking in Attic Greek?" (Numenius, frg. 8.13). See Robbert van den Berg, "God the Creator, God the Creation: Numenius' Interpretation of Genesis 1:2 (frg. 30)", in: *The Creation of Heaven and Earth: Re-interpretation of Genesis I in the Context of Judaism, Ancient Philosophy, Christianity, and Modern Physics*, ed. George H. van Kooten, Leiden/Boston 2005, 109 – 123, here 113 – 114, 121.
24 For this task, Rashid al-Din used the Pentateuch and various other historical and theological works. See the Edinburgh-Khalili manuscript of *Jāmi al-tawārīkh*, fol. 282v.

prophet and the Prophet Muhammad.²⁵ Wheeler further states that "Muslim exegetes use this contrast between Moses and Muhammad to conceptualize the differences between themselves and the other People of the Book, particularly the Jews [...]."²⁶ Therefore, it is clear that Rashid al-Din's visual portrayal of Moses stands in contrast to that Muslim view.

In the Edinburgh-Khalili manuscript, death completes the Moses cycle of illustrations. After the patriarch's farewell speech to his people, God calls him to Mount Nebo alone, where he shows Moses the Promised Land from afar; Moses then passes away in an unknown location on the mountaintop.²⁷ The text preceding the image narrates his last sermon and his final directive and advice to the Israelites. The narrative following the picture describes his last moments on earth and his death. Terry Allen claims that the scene depicted corresponds to the description of his death a few lines later, and not to the immediate breaking point in the calligraphed text.²⁸ The placement of the illustration on the page and the space designated for its insertion between text lines are both important features in Islamicate illustrated manuscripts. I would like to argue that the painting reflects a deeper understanding of the story and narrates a complex moment suggested by the narrative.

The painting emphasizes Moses' singular presence through a horizontal position, with his eyes closed and his hands relaxed (fig. 1). His figure is larger than the others, as he becomes one with nature, in complete harmony with it. The Israelites, on the other hand, appear anxious, their long, busy fingers articulating their difficult mental state while one of them, probably Joshua, points towards Moses. Rashid al-Din states in the *Jami al-Tawarikh* that up to his death Moses did not lose his mental vigor and that even afterwards his body did not decay or age.²⁹ He further writes that Moses died without any distress or effort, in a state of tranquillity, "and then God ordered for an angel to take his soul."³⁰

In the scene, the figure of Moses becomes like a part of the hills that surround him. His body and clothes form a continuum of the landscape, with sim-

---

25 Q18:60–82; 83–101. Brannon M. Wheeler, *Moses in the Quran and Islamic Exegesis*, New York 2002, 120–121, 125.
26 Ibid.
27 Rashid al-Din's text is based on Deuteronomy 34:6.
28 Terry Allen, "Byzantine sources for the 'Jāmi al-Tawārīkh' of Rashīd al-Dīn", in: *Ars Orientalis*, 15, 1985, 121–136, here 124.
29 It seems that Rashid al-Din is repeating some of the ideas that are written in the Hebrew Bible. See, for example, Deuteronomy 34:7–8. The non-decaying body of Moses appears in Midrash Tannaim, 227; Sifre D., 357. Louis Ginzberg, *Legends of the Jews*, 7 vols, Philadelphia 1909–1938, vol. 2, 148 and n. 953.
30 Nasser D. Khalili Collection, MS 727, K33 (reconstructed by Blair as fol. 294v).

ilar tones and linear treatment of the folds and the mountains (fig. 4). This image, which blends with the universe in the most harmonious and balanced way, is different from the one we find in Jewish legends, or in rabbinic *Aggadah* and *midrashim*. For example, one of the most popular stories regarding Moses death relates that he does not die but ascends to Heaven, from where he continues to protect and safeguard Israel. Another story tells of how Moses, anxiously regarding his death, argues with the angels and God about the time of his departure from this world.[31] Therefore, the death scene as described and painted in Rashid al-Din's *Jami al-Tawarikh* is quite distinct from the eschatological activities of Moses in other Jewish sources.

Fig. 4: The death of Moses, detail, *Jami al-Tawarikh* of Rashid al-Din. London, Nasser D. Khalili Collection of Islamic Art, MSS 727, fol. 54v [reconstructed by Blair as fol. 294v]

A comparable description of the death of Moses, however, was made by Maimonides. In his *Guide for the Perplexed*, Maimonides describes Moses – his perfect man – as if he died by "the kiss of God"[32] by a means parallel to the intimate

---

31 Ginzberg, *Legends of the Jews* (as in n. 29), vol. 3, 442, 448, 450–452, 47; Wayne A. Meeks, *The Prophet–King. Moses Traditions and the Johannine Christology*, Leiden 1967, 209–214.
32 Maimonides relies on the *Bava Batra* with respect to this tradition. Mosheh ben Maimon (Moses Maimonides), *Sefer Moreh ha-Nevukhim*, trans. into Hebrew by R. Shemu'el b. r. Yehudah Ibn Tibon, vol. 3, Jerusalem 2000, 51 and n. 2. Moses Maimonides, *The Guide of the Perplexed*, trans. by Shlomo Pines, vol. 3, Chicago 1963, 51 (p. 628).

way in which God communicated with the biblical law-giver when he was alive. Maimonides further argues that upon his death, Moses was at peace and in a state of contemplation because he had attained a deep closeness to God and the highest knowledge of the divine.[33] This description similarly resounds with the powerful illustration in the *Jami al-Tawarikh:* The image's aesthetic transmits the loss of the body's materiality, suggesting the unification of Moses' intellect with the divine. Hence, the viewer might recognize that he has achieved a state of human perfection.

In no other illustration from the Edinburgh-Khalili manuscript does Moses' body seem to blur with the surroundings in the same way (fig. 4). The composition captures the power of the moment. An enclosure of bare mountains and curving trees emphasizes the state of contemplation and solitude attending Moses at his last moments, separating him from the Israelites. Epitomizing the border-crossing, this moment symbolizes the transition of Moses' soul to the Hereafter and the Israelites to the Promised Land (fig. 1).

Visual representations of the Death of Moses are not very common in Islamicate visual tradition. The singularity of the subject matter makes the illustration in Rashid al-Din's text even more unusual, as the artist has consciously conflated and repurposed visual idioms, relating the scene of death to representations of birth, meditation or deep sleep, dreaming and compassion. Upon a closer look, however, the painting entices us to seek more intricate possibilities about the identification of the specific subject matter, as well as the exact moment that the artist and patron chose to portray.

The slanted position of Moses' body undermines the reality of his death. His pose, with knees bent and head slightly raised, is certainly not suitable for a dead person. Compared with other depictions of death and burial scenes from the Muslim Medieval period, we may notice that something else is happening in the *Jami al-Tawarikh* illustration.

An interment scene from the eleventh *Maqamat* of al-Hariri, which was painted in 1237, shows a shrouded body being lowered into a grave.[34] In contrast to Moses, the deceased is positioned diagonally, headfirst, and the body is almost flat. In several funerary episodes from the so-called Great Mongol *Shahna-*

---

33 Moses Maimonides, *Moreh ha Nevukhim* (as in n. 32), vol. 3, 51. See also Howard Kreisel, *Maimonides' Political Thought*, New York 1999, 137.
34 Burial scene, folio 29v, *Maqamat* al-Hariri, Baghdad, copied and illustrated by Yahya ibn Mahmud al-Wasiti. Paris, Bibliotheque Nationale. Ms. arabe 5847. The image is reproduced in the facsimile edition, *al-Maqāmāt al-Ḥarīrīyah*, illustrated by Yahya ibn Mahmud Al-Wasiti, London 2003.

ma (Book of Kings)³⁵, the body of the dead hero or king is invisible, as it is placed in a coffin carried by an animal or by mourners. According to Grabar and Blair, these images represent some of the mourning rituals that were also carried out at the Ilkhanid court.³⁶ Thus it is clear that the representation of the body of Moses does not follow the formal convention of depicting deceased heroic figures in Mongol Iran or earlier.

Some discussions of the picture postulate that it relates to illustrated Byzantine Bibles.³⁷ More specifically, Terry Allen argues that Moses' stance in the *Jami al-Tawarikh* composition "[...] is not inspired, but makes use of a pose commonly employed for deathbed scenes in Byzantine manuscript painting, substituting the rock ledge for a bed".³⁸ Considering the framework of contact between cultures, such as the Ilkhans in Iran and the Byzantines, it seems that representations of the death of Moses in twelfth- to thirteenth-century Byzantine Bibles share only limited features with Rashid al-Din's scene. In Byzantine illustrations, Moses is represented as a younger man, haloed, with his hands crossed over his chest and his body partially hidden by a mountain.³⁹ Often he is accompanied by an angel, or the Hand of God appears in the sky, radiating light. None of these elements can be found in the *Jami al-Tawarikh* picture.

In comparison to Byzantine representations of the Virgin's death (the Dormition), important differences appear: Mary is shown lying flat on a bed, her body balanced, not slanted; her legs are straight, not bent; and her hands are folded on her chest, not on her thighs.⁴⁰ She is usually surrounded by the apostles, angels, and Christ, who holds her soul.⁴¹ Moreover, the event takes place in an

---

35 This luxurious copy of the *Shahnama* was probably made around the 1330s in Ilkhanid Iran, and might have been commissioned by the vizier Ghiyath al-Din, son of Rashid al-Din. See *Legacy of Genghis Khan*, eds. Carboni/Komaroff (as in n. 14), 155–167, 227–228.
36 For example, in the *Shahnama*, at least one king, Iraj, and two champions, Isfandiyar and Zavara, are all buried in coffins. For black-and-white pictures of these illustrations, see Oleg Grabar/Sheila Blair, *Epic Images and Contemporary History*, Chicago 1980, 71, 101, 105.
37 Allen, Byzantine Sources (as in n. 26), 124; G. M. Meredith-Owens, "Some Remarks on the Miniatures in the Society's 'Jami al-Tawarikh'", in: *Journal of the Royal Asiatic Society*, 1970, 195–199.
38 He claims that since there were no matching painted Jewish manuscripts that could have been used as models for Rashid al-Din's artists, the choice of using Christian sources to depict Jewish subject matter is of no surprise. Allen, Byzantine Sources (as in n. 26), 124.
39 For example: *Menologion* of Basil II, Byzantine, ca. 1025; Smyrna Octateuch, Byzantine, 12th century. A.1; Smyrna Octateuch, Byzantine, 12th century, fol. 219v, Ms. #A.1; Mount Athos Monastery, Vatopedi, 602. Byzantine, Constantinople, 13th century.
40 See the left wing from icon 379 from Mount Sinai, 13th century, Byzantium.
41 As seen on a plaque from Mount Athos, Vatopedi monastery, steatite feast cycle icon, 14th century.

urban setting, as indicated by the architecture in the background.⁴² These pictorial divergences are purposeful and open up possibilities of linking Moses' death depiction with Mary's miraculous birth giving scene.

In Byzantine representations of the Nativity of Christ, such as in a mosaic from the Church of the Savior in Chora in Constantinople (ca. 1310–1320), a late-thirteenth-century Cypriot psalter, and a mid-thirteenth-century Byzantine illustrated Gospel, the Virgin Mary appears in a comparable body pose. She is depicted lying on her back in a diagonal-horizontal position, with her knees bent – similar to Moses – and her head is also slightly elevated.⁴³ Even the position of her hand is similar to Rashid al-Din's Moses and the figure of Mary in the Hamilton Greek psalter. Furthermore, the setting of the Nativity is often outside, in nature, in front of a grotto in a hilly landscape. In both cases the protagonists are isolated from the rest of the figures depicted in the scene.

Likewise we may recognize the same figural attitude in contemporary Ilkhanid illustrations of royal births, as evident in a folio from the Diez Album where a high-ranking Mongol woman reclines diagonally on a mattress with her knees bent and her head a bit elevated, while her newborn lies by her side (fig. 5).⁴⁴ In an illustration depicting the birth of the Prophet Muhammad from the Edinburgh-Khalili *Jami al-Tawarikh*, too, the mother (Amina) is shown in a pose similar to that of Moses, even though the scene takes place indoors (fig. 3). The composition of this same *Birth of the Prophet* intentionally evokes scenes of the Nativity of Christ, which were available to artists either via manuscripts or liturgical objects that became part of the Mongol court treasury in Tabriz.⁴⁵ In the

---

42 Such an example can be found in fol. 13v from a thirteenth-century Byzantine Gospel book. J. Paul Getty Museums, Los Angeles, Ludwig II.5 83.MB.49.

43 The mosaic on the east wall of the outer narthex represents the Virgin Mary reclining on a mattress and turning toward a maidservant (Constantinople, Church of the Savior in Chora [Kariye Camii], early 14th century). Similarly, in the Nativity of Christ from a mid-thirteenth-century Byzantine illustrated Gospel, Mary reclines on a mattress in a grotto. Paris, Bibliothèque Nationale, gr. 54, fol. 13v. In the Hamilton Greek Psalter from Cyprus, dated to the late thirteenth to early fourteenth century, the Virgin lies against a hilly mountain. Staatliche Museen, Berlin, Kupferstichkabinett, 78.A.9, fol. 46r.

44 This might be Quthluq Khatun giving birth to Ghazan Khan, Ilkhanid Iran, 14th century. *Staatsbibliothek, Berlin*, Preussischer Kulturbesitz, Orientabteilung (Diez Album A, fol. 70). On the right side, three Muslim men of learning, perhaps astrologers, are busy prognosticating the infant's horoscope.

45 Sheila Blair argues that "the artists turned to Western models" for inspiration. However, beyond offering simple compositional solutions, she does not explain why the birth of Muhammad was modelled specifically after that of Christ. Sheila Blair, Jāme' al-Tawārik: Illustrations, *Encyclopaedia Iranica* online, URL: <http://www.iranicaonline.org/articles/jame-tawarikh-ii> [26.06. 2012]. Christian artifacts were brought to the Mongol courts as diplomatic gifts, booty, commer-

Quran, the miraculous birth of Jesus, albeit stripped of Christological meaning, is considered to be one of God's signs. Like Moses, Jesus partakes in a divinely-crafted genealogy of prophets, ranging from Adam to Muhammad.[46] Therefore, we may argue that the visual juxtaposition between the death of Moses and the births of Jesus and Muhammad was conscious, setting implicit parallels between the three main representatives of the Abrahamic religions. It also conflates the death of Moses with the act of birth.[47] In doing so, Rashid al-Din's artists recast Moses' image in a transitory state, that is, a figure suspended between the two worlds, negotiating time, space and the boundaries of a Beginning and an End.

Visual concepts of levitating or floating between thresholds may be suggested by iconographic parallels between the posture of Moses and those of sleeping figures. Terry Allen invokes the figure of Alexander the Great sleeping on a pallet spread on the ground, from a fourteenth-century Byzantine manuscript painting of the *Romance of Alexander*, which he believes could have inspired the atelier in Tabriz.[48] Following a convention developed from the Classical tradition, Alexander is shown crossing his legs and with his head resting on his arm – a position distinct from that of Rashid al-Din's Moses. However, in contemporary

---

cial exchanges, or by the Christian communities living in these areas. See, for example, The Journey of William of Rubruck in Christopher Dawson, *Mission to Asia*, Toronto/Buffalo 1980, 162–180. Peter Jackson, *The Mongols and the West, 1221–1410*, Harlow, England/New York 2005, 98–100.

46 Q 3:84: "We believe in Allah and what has been revealed to us, and what was revealed to Ibrahim and Ismail and Ishaq and Yaqoub and the tribes, and what was given to Musa and Isa and to the prophets from their Lord; we do not make any distinction between any of them, and to Him do we submit." Also see Angelika Neuwirth, "The House of Abraham and the House of Amran: Genealogy, Patriarchal Authority, and Exegetical Professionalism", in: *The Quran in Context*, ed. Angelika Neuwirth/Nicolai Sinai/Michael Marx, Leiden 2009, 499–531, here 506; Rubin, Prophets and Caliphs (as in n. 22), 80–81.

47 Scholars have often noted the accurate rendition and faithful usage of Christian idioms in other paintings of the *Jami al-Tawarikh*. See Thomas Walker Arnold, *The Old and New Testaments in Muslim Religious Art*, London 1932, 14–15; Güner Inal, "Some Miniatures of the 'Jāmi al-Tavārīkh' in Istanbul, Topkapı Museum, Hazine Library no. 1654", in: *Ars Orientalis*, 5, 1963, 163–176; David T. Rice, *The Illustrations to the "World History" of Rashīd al-Dīn*, ed. Basil Gray, Edinburgh 1976; Basil Gray, *The World history of Rashīd al-Dīn: A study of the Royal Asiatic Society manuscript*, London 1978. Allen, Byzantine Sources (as in n. 26), 121–33; Blair, *Compendium of Chronicles* (as in n. 10), 60–90; Hillenbrand, Arts of the Book in Ilkhanid Iran (as in n. 14), 145–150.

48 *Alexander Sleeping*, manuscript painting in Pseudo-Callisthenes: *The Romance of Alexander*. The manuscript is housed at the Hellenistic Institute in Venice, fol. 131r. Allen, Byzantine Sources (as in n. 26), 124.

Fig. 5: Birth scene, Ilkhanid Iran, 14th century. Berlin, Staatsbibliothek – Preussischer Kulturbesitz, Orientabteilung, Diez Album A, fol. 70, S. 8

Ilkhanid renditions of sleeping persons, the resemblance in the bodily pose of Moses to the figures of four sleeping kings is revealing (fig. 6).[49] In this painting, there are four kings sleeping on low beds in a vaulted space. Their elevated heads rest on large pillows, and their knees are slightly bent, like the knees of Moses. Three of the four dormant rulers have their hands placed on their thighs; the one in the upper left corner even folds his hands together, rather like the Hebrew Bible Prophet.

Through this visual and semantic parallelism we may infer that the moment represented in the *Jami al-Tawarikh* image reinforces links to representations of birth and sleep rather than death, therefore placing the image of Moses in a liminal space, alternating between a corporal, identifiable body and a metaphysical image that is in a state of oneness with nature. Consequently, the tension created between these two dimensions is reflected in the potential of the figure to move

---

49 The folio, probably removed from an Ilkhanid manuscript, was pasted into an album. See *Legacy of Genghis Khan*, ed.by Carboni/Komaroff (as in n. 14), cat. 26, 251; David J. Roxburgh, "Heinrich Friedrich Von Diez and His Eponymous Albums: Mss. Diez A. Fols. 70 – 74", in: *Muqarnas*, 12, 1995, 112 – 136, here 116 – 117; Mazhar Şevket Ipsiroglu, *Saray-Alben: Diez'sche Klebebände aus den Berliner Sammlungen*, Wiesbaden 1964, 40. Ipsiroglu argues that the kings are dead. However, this idea stands in contrast to the kings' perfectly preserved bodies and their poses. Moreover, displaying cadavers before their burial was not a common practice of that period, hence the notion of deep sleep, coma or some kind of unconsciousness, as argued by Carboni and Komaroff, makes sense here.

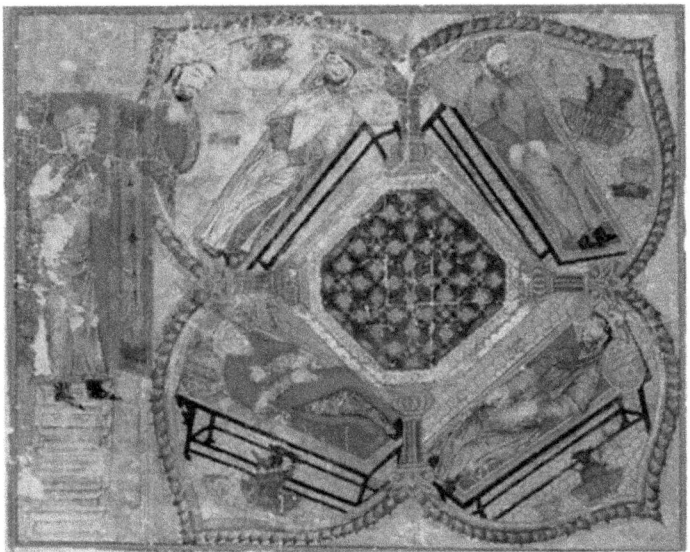

Fig. 6: Four kings in an underground vault, Ilkhanid Iran, 14th century. Berlin, Staatsbibliothek – Preussischer Kulturbesitz, Orientabteilung, Diez Album A, fol. 72, S. 29

or wake up, since he is not clearly deceased. Moreover, the placement of the image a few lines before the statement about the angel taking his soul further augments the concept of an intermediary state of being.

During his lifetime, Moses was accustomed to crossing borders between the mundane and the divine, and he did so quite often.[50] Since he had very close, not to say intimate, relationship with God, he could move easily about these worlds as if it were natural. He saw God's image and they spoke often, even "mouth to mouth" (Nm 12:8).[51] This passage is also mentioned by Rashid al-Din, and he writes that "God said that to others he speaks through angels, but with Moses I speak mouth to mouth (*mushafahatan*)"[52] – an idea that also appears in at least one other painting from the Moses cycle in the *Jami al-Tawar-*

---

50 For example, Moses went to the mountain twice to meet with God (Exodus 19:3, 9; 24:16), they spoke back and forth (Exodus 19:3, 19, 20) and he encountered God's image (Exodus 3:1–15).
51 This section is translated in English as "face to face"; however, the original Hebrew text clearly states "mouth to mouth".
52 *Jāmiʿ al-tawārīkh*, fol. 294v, Arabic. This idea appears in the Bible and to a certain extent also in the Qur'an (7:144); also see Cornelia Schöck, "Moses", in: *Encyclopedia of the Quran*, vol. 3, Leiden 2003, 419–426.

ikh.⁵³ It was this special status with the Almighty that resulted in Moses' ability to traverse the different spheres of the divine and the mundane.

The illustration of his death scene in the *Jami al-Tawarikh* translates these extraordinary qualities into visual terms: his torso becomes so flat that it is difficult to tell whether we are looking at the mountain plain or his chest (fig. 4). The use of transparent washes in depicting both his body and the mountains creates a porous effect in the image. There is much fluidity of pictorial elements, such as the folds of his garment around the arms and below the knees that reverberate and appear in continuity with the hilly range that uplifts and holds him. In addition, the painting's sophisticated composition further enhances the notion of intellection beyond borders. Via an innovative translation of different religious visual idioms the illustration reveals its circulatory nature, one that synthesizes intercultural encounters.

Notably, based on his specific body position, I would like to suggest that the image of Moses in Rashid al-Din's painting depicts a dying and not a deceased person. Such a representation of a dying (or languishing) hero may be seen in a painting from the Persian love story of Warqah and Gulshah.[54] In this illustration Warqah's father, Humam, is dying while resting his head on his offspring's lap.[55] Comforting his father and lamenting his loss, Warqah offers physical and mental support to the wounded body. The position of the dying Humam resting in the lap of his son is manifestly similar to that of Moses, fashioned with a slightly elevated head, bent knees, and a slanted angle of the body. How are we to understand this parallelism?

From the text of the Jewish Bible it is understood that God buried Moses (Deuteronomy 34:6), an idea of which Rashid al-Din is well aware as he explains the absence of Moses' tomb.[56] Hence Moses spent the last moments of his earthly life and his departure from this world in the company of God and an angel. The figure in Rashid al-Din's painting appears as if he is being lifted or held in someone's arms – perhaps God's own. His elusive body is thus being attended by an invisible, divine presence. This very last interpretation may explain the preroga-

---

[53] A sense of conversation between Moses and God can be seen in *Moses on Mount Sinai Hearing God's Voice*, fol. 10r, *Jami al-Tawarikh* of Rashid al-Din, Edinburgh University Library (Arab Ms. 20).
[54] This poem was written in verse by the eleventh-century poet Ayyuqi. Djalal Khaleghi-Motlagh, "'Ayyūqī," in: *Encyclopaedia Iranica*, vol. 3, fasc. 2, 167–168.
[55] Warqah grieves over his father, *Warqah and Gulshah*, ca. 1200–1250. Topkapı Palace Library, Hazine 841, f.15/16b.
[56] See fol. 54v (reconstructed by Blair as fol. 294v), *Jami al-Tawarikh* of Rashid al-Din. MS London, Nasser D. Khalili Collection, MS 727.

tive of the image's condition, portraying the moment in which God held Moses and buried him in an unknown location on the mountain. The artist has thus creatively invented a way of reiterating in visual terms a concept of something unseen, a moment of intersection between Heaven and Earth.

In several illustrated manuscripts of Rudolf von Ems' *Weltchronik* (World History) produced in thirteenth- and fourteenth-century Germany, we find paintings representing the end of Moses' life.[57] In these pictures, the moment chosen for illustration is Christ burying Moses on the mountaintop. Conversely, in these illustrations Moses has already passed away, while in the *Jami al-Tawarikh* image he lingers between the two worlds.

The idea that the painting represents God attending Moses in his last moments of transition is supported by Maimonides' description that Moses died by "the kiss of God".[58] The man and his Creator shared these last moments intimately together, reflecting how God communicated with Moses when he was alive, that is, "mouth to mouth".

Additionally, the notion of Moses' meditative, perhaps even levitating state, is further indicated by the landscape that cradles the Old-Testament prophet. His body is supported by a particular background that transforms into an emblematic setting. Priscilla Soucek argues that the mountains and trees in the death scene derive from cartographical works that were printed in China in the twelfth and thirteenth centuries.[59] This observation explains the technique behind the visual aspect and the precise means of representing these landscape elements. I would like to suggest an additional dimension to the picture: the setting in which Moses rests recalls scenic views in Chinese Buddhist landscape themes, where mountains and trees are traditionally connected to the experience of far-reaching insights or enlightenment and the practice of meditation.[60] Thus the landscape forms a meeting ground with the transcendent world. These specific surroundings have a dual iconography in the *Jami al-Tawarikh* painting: One is a schematic indication of a specific geographical place (the terrestrial Mount Nebo), as mentioned in the text. The second is a mode, a metaphor for a spiri-

---

57 I would like to thank Annette Hoffmann for bringing these images to my attention.
58 Maimonides relies on the *Bava Batra* with respect to this tradition. Maimonides, *Moreh Nevochim*, vol. 3, 51 and n. 2; and *Guide of the Perplexed*, trans. Pines (as in n. 30), vol. 3, 51 (p. 628).
59 Priscilla Soucek, "The Role of Landscape in Iranian Painting to the 15th Century", in: *Landscape Style in Asia*, ed. William Watson, London 1979, 86–110, here 91, n. 36 and 100.
60 William Watson argues that "[...] Chinese translators substitute mountain and forest [...]" for the Bodhisattvas meditating in caves. William Watson, "Landscape elements in the early Buddhist art of China", in: *Landscape Style in Asia*, Percival David Foundation of Chinese Art Colloquies on Art and Archaeology, 8 (1979), London 1980, 1–29, here 2.

tual/religious momentum symbolic of Moses' transition. These ideas may have reverberated in Rashid al-Din, since he was interested, among other things, in Buddhism and he translated philosophical and religious Buddhist texts into Persian.[61]

The setting of a meditative landscape and the choice of specific pose for Moses may further allude to an active moment in the story rather than to the passivity of death. Since the burial place of Moses remained a secret, as Rashid al-Din tells us, for God (via an angel) buried his chosen man, the artist had to depict what could not be depicted, creating a delicate balance between the painted and the unpaintable. I would like to suggest that in this illustration we may be witnessing Moses' ultimate reality, the moment in which God enveloped him with compassion, the point of transit between the two worlds. Thus, we may be looking at a hallowed ground, a portal, an "un-place" of transformation.

In the *Jami al-Tawarikh*, Rashid al-Din constructed a very specific image of Moses, trumpeted by Maimonides' vision of the biblical law-giver. For them, the patriarch was the singular servant of God who was involved in matters of government, religion and knowledge – the ultimate ruler and prophet-king. The death of Moses, like the man himself, has been a loaded and complex issue that symbolizes the completion of the Exodus. This intricate painting embodies the idea of transition; the loss of the corporeal body; and the concept of Moses as a mediator between high and low, between divine and mundane. The illustration of his extraordinary death further recalls other divine miracles, such as the Nativity of Jesus, linked to Muhammad's birth. Hence, Moses' death is related to the chain of prophets and the transmission of the divine legacy.[62] Moses does not cross the river to the Promised Land, but he crosses nobler and more divine frontiers – those between God and men. This illustration blurs various boundaries of death, birth, dormancy, compassion and meditation, using the innovative transformations of religious and visual idioms, which Rashid al-Din, as the patron of this book, would have recognized. As an image of transition, it epitomizes the special position of Moses as a man who walked between worlds, crossing extraterrestrial borders.

---

[61] Rashid al-Din wrote on the life of the Buddha in the *Jami al-Tawarikh*.
[62] The concept of hereditary authority and a monotheistic "universal code of religious laws" appears in the Jewish Bible and in Quranic tradition. Rashid al-Din was also aware of it via the work of al-Tabari. In his turn, Tabari takes these materials from Ibn Ishaq, who used Jewish sources, which he calls "people of the first book" (*ahl al-kitāb al-awwal*), i.e. the Torah." Quoted from Rubin: "Prophets and Caliphs" (as in n. 22), 80–81.

Angelika Neuwirth
The Prophet Muhammad's Visionary Journey to Jerusalem – a Spiritual Exodus

It may appear pretentious to claim an analogy between the Biblical Exodus and the Qur'anic "night journey". How does the historically paramount event of Moses' deliverance of an entire ethnic group, the Israelites, from captivity, and his clearing the way for their immigration into the Promised Land, compare to Muhammad's individual experience of a visionary journey to Jerusalem? It is common knowledge that the Exodus marks the essential beginning of Israel's life story, despite the fact that the text of the Hebrew Bible in its transmitted form begins with the Creation and subsequently focuses on the time of the Patriarchs. Yet substantially, Biblical history starts with the crucial experience of the Exodus that made the Israelites a self-conscious historical community, an event so decisive that earlier and subsequent experiences were seen in its light. The Qur'anic night journey is a case in point: it is designated as an "exodus", *isrā'*, and thus labeled with the same term used for Moses' Exodus. How is this analogy to be understood? The Biblical exodus is a complex event, comprised of at least four major stages: the Israelites' deliverance, i.e., their exit from Egypt which is preceded by punitive measures against the Pharaoh; the people's migration through the wilderness; the reception of divine instruction, i.e., their being granted the Giving of the Torah, *Matan Torah*, on Mount Sinai, an event followed by their temporal relapse into idolatry; and their immigration into the Promised Land. Which of these events is reflected in the Prophet's *isrā'* experience, so as to suggest a comparable impact on the earliest Muslim community's self-consciousness? What is the contribution of the *isrā'* to Qur'anic identity politics? These questions will be pursued on two levels: a discussion of the biographical event of the Prophet's nocturnal journey, *al-isrā'*, within the Qur'an and in early exegesis, and a discussion of the mythically adorned ascension story, *al-miʿrāj*, which in Islamic tradition was to supersede the "sober" Qur'anic notion of a visionary journey.

A Hermeneutical Turn

The Qur'an, which will be our main reference, must be credited with a special status. Unlike Judaism and Christianity, Islam does not emerge from religio-historical developments, but enters the history of religions as a latecomer at an advanced stage of Late Antiquity.¹ Two crucial events that had brought about a turn in religious history had long passed: the crucifixion of Christ and the destruction of the Jewish Temple with the Jews' losing their political autonomy. Both Jewish and Christian exegesis in Late Antiquity had achieved a reconfiguration of these events sublimating them into spiritually meaningful experiences with universal significance. Thus not only has the destruction of the Temple caused the "end of sacrifice"², but Christ's crucifixion was received as the terminating sacrifice after which no meaningful sacrifice could be offered. The destruction of the Temple and the end of the Jewish sacrificial cult contributed to the breakdown of the notion of a privileged cultic institution that, by being located in the centre of the earth³ and graced with continuous divine attention and care, can claim unique closeness to God. Once the sanctuary was physically lost, it was sublimated to become a universally significant spiritual Temple⁴, by some identified with the human soul⁵, by others translocated from the earthly Jerusalem to a heavenly Jerusalem⁶ to mention only two of the numerous re-interpretations. Transformation, however, did not only apply to historical events of Late Antiquity; events reported in the Hebrew Bible were equally re-read in terms of spiritual experiences. We may speak of a "hermeneutical turn" here, where the physical manifestations of divine interventions in history have ceded their significance to their spiritual meaning, "built on the 'trace of sanctity'" they left behind. Though some of the transformations of the Temple may be classified as allegorical interpretations, much more frequent was the establishment of a typological relation between a Biblical narrative and particular events in Jewish or, more often, Christian experience. Thus, in Christian eyes, the Biblical Exodus was thought to have re-materialized in the earliest history of Christianity. Particularly, the Gospel of Luke (and the same author's Acts of the Apostles) reflects a messianic reading of Exodus.⁷ Not unlike other Jewish writings of the time, Luke's double oeuvre presents a metaphorical reading: Christ's, that is, the Messiah's, life, death,

---

1 For the notion of Late Antiquity see *Denkraum Spätantike. Reflektionen von Antiken im Umfeld des Koran*, ed. Nora Schmidt/Nora Katharina Schmid/Angelika Neuwirth, Wiesbaden 2016.
2 See Guy G. Stroumsa, *Das Ende des Opferkults. Die religiösen Mutationen der Spätantike*, Berlin 2011.
3 Jon Levenson, *Sinai and Zion. An Entry into the Hebrew Bible*, New York 1987.
4 See Guy G. Stroumsa, "Mystical Jerusalems", in: *Jerusalem. Its Sanctity and Centrality in Judaism, Christianity, and Islam*, ed. Lee I. Levine, New York 1999, 349–370.
5 Ibid.
6 For the visionary journeys ascribed to individual saintly figures in Late Antiquity, see Peter Schäfer, *Die Ursprünge der jüdischen Mystik*, Berlin 2011.
7 Kerstin Schiffner, *Lukas liest Exodus. Eine Untersuchung zur Aufnahme ersttestamentlicher Befreiungsgeschichte im lukanischen Werk als Schrift-Lektüre*, Stuttgart 2008.

and resurrection constitute a narrative of deliverance which mirrors the Exodus and can be seen as its fulfillment since it extends the covenant with the Israelites to a covenant with mankind in general. In many cases a real event narrated in the Hebrew Bible became reconsidered as the "typus", the prefiguration of the theologically decisive messianic event, which received the status of an "antitypus", a fulfillment. It is noteworthy that this hermeneutical step was only rarely pursued in Qur'anic exegesis. But what about the Exodus?

The Israelite Exodus in the Qur'an

Is there a re-narration of the Biblical Exodus in the Qur'an? The Qur'an is known to entail a vast number of Biblical narratives, many of them retold in slightly different forms on various occasions. If we look for the plot of the Biblical Exodus, however, we will be disappointed. Those texts that are predominantly narrative, often focusing on Moses – the so-called middle Meccan suras[8] – seem to marginalize the Exodus.[9] Elements of the Biblical narrative are dispersed over the entire Meccan Qur'anic corpus, but nowhere do they form one coherent story that describes the four main stages explained above: the deliverance of the people, the wandering in the desert, the reception (and temporarily rejection) of the Torah, and the entry into the Promised Land. It is only through the accumulation of details in various suras that the narrative elements crystallize into an image of the Exodus. The earliest mention of Moses and Pharaoh are restricted to verbal exchanges between the prophet and the tyrant – evidently meant to mirror the conflict between the Prophet Muhammad and his powerful Meccan foes. The essential mission of Moses to free the Israelites and initiate the exodus is absent from most of the Meccan Moses-Pharaoh stories.

Even in the few cases in which the basic dates of the story are given, Q 20, Q 26, and Q 44, the event is related in an essentially different way from that of the Book of Exodus. The Qur'anic exodus is strikingly anticlimactic. There is no detailed account of the ten plagues and, moreover, there is no mention of the Israelites' wandering in the wilderness. The climactic events, such as the presenta-

---

8 The articles follow the diachronic approach, which – based on stylistic criteria – distinguishes between "early Meccan", "middle Meccan", "late Meccan", and Medinan texts.
9 For an overview over the Exodus-references in the Qur'an, see Nicolai Sinai, "Inheriting Egypt. The Israelites and the Exodus to Egypt in the Meccan Qur'an", in: *Islamic Studies Today. Essays in Honor of Andrew Rippin*, ed. Majid Daneshgar/Walid Saleh, Leiden 2016, 198–214. See also the commentaries on Q 20 and 26 in Angelika Neuwirth, Der Koran, vol. II/1: Frühmittelmekkanische Suren, Berlin 2017, 303–447.

tion of the Torah on Mount Sinai, and the people's subsequent temporary lapse into idolatry with the adoration of the Golden Calf, are briefly mentioned, but they do not coalesce to reflect the drama of the conclusion and subsequent break of the covenant that they constitute in the biblical account. The issue of divine instruction, the *Matan Torah*[10], which in the biblical account is inseparable from the Exodus, is not represented as an integral part of the venture. Though there is an exit from the site of oppression – the Israelites are led out of Egypt – there is no clear image of their entrance into the Promised land. Some Qur'anic texts rather seem to presuppose the Israelites inherited Egypt rather than Palestine.[11] Their itinerary thus remains ambiguous. What matters in the Qur'anic rendering is less the Exodus as a historical event than its typological significance: having been promised deliverance, the Israelites finally experience the fulfillment of the promise, even inheriting the possessions of their foes and suppressors. God's promise of his assistance to the faithful holds true.

The exodus in the Qur'an is reconstructed as a universally valid example that proves the reliability of the prophetical message. It is read typologically, although not in the same vein as in the Christian tradition: there is no claim to the perfection of the biblical event by instilling it with a messianic dimension. Typological readings of Biblical narratives in the Qur'an in most cases serve a more modest purpose: to allow the Qur'anic faithful – who suffer oppression as did the Israelites, to derive a dimension of hope from the fate of their Biblical precursors. The Qur'anic community does not restage the Biblical events to supersede them by imbuing them with a new theology, but rather refers to such events as reflections of their own situation. The restriction of the Exodus narrative to the events that fit into this analogy-pattern, however, has a momentous side effect: it implies a de-politicization of the Israelite Exodus story. There is no trace left of the almost world historical significance that is assigned to the Exodus in the Biblical account: the drama in which the Egyptian empire was shocked by the divinely inflicted ten plagues has faded. Instead, the strife is essentially between two figures: Pharaoh and the Prophet, that is, between the suppressor and the divine messenger charged with the protection of the oppressed.

There seems to be, however, a second typology hidden in the Qur'anic treatment of the Exodus. This is signaled by a linguistic allusion. The peculiarity of the Exodus, when it is finally introduced in some middle Meccan suras, is sig-

---

10 See Dirk Hartwig, " 'Der Urvertrag' (Q 7:172). Ein rabbinischer Diskurs im Koran", in: *'Im vollen Licht der Geschichte'. Die Wissenschaft des Judentums und die Anfänge der kritischen Koranforschung*, ed. Dirk Hartwig/Walter Homolka/Michael J. Marx/Angelika Neuwirth, Würzburg 2008, 191–202.
11 Sinai, "Inheriting Egypt" (as in n. 9).

naled by a stereotypical prefatory formula: *asri bi-'ibādī*, "Lead out my servants". In Q 26:52 it is *wa-awḥaynā ilā Mūsā an asri bi-'ibādī innakum muttabaʿūn,* "we instructed Moses: 'lead out my servants! You will be followed'". This divine instruction is repeated almost verbatim in Q 20:77 and in Q 44:23, where the nocturnal frame is made doubly explicit: although the verb *asrā* as such means "to lead out by night" the temporal determinant *laylan* "by night" is added. Obviously, Moses is urged to lead the people out clandestinely; he is to stage a "collective night journey", an *isrāʾ*. From this strikingly identical use of terms, the biblical event of Moses' and his people's exodus, (*isrāʾ*) and the Prophet Muhammad's night journey (*isrāʾ*), we may deduce that Moses' Exodus in the Qur'an is understood as a prototype of the Prophet's night journey. As such, it is not the Biblical event that endows real history with a mythical undercurrent, but the reverse: a Biblical event is relived not physically, but in a mythical, spiritual guise.

The notion of an axis of sanctity

Since this volume concerns movements in space, a few remarks about the sacred topography which is to be presupposed for the Qur'an are in place. In a recent article on *Ṭuwā*,[12] Uri Rubin shed light on the intricate typological character of Qur'anic perceptions of space. *Ṭuwā,* usually taken to be a toponym, appears in the introductory formula of one of the earliest stories about Moses: *hal atāka ḥadīthu Mūsā / idh nādāhu rabbuhu bi-l-wādi l-muqaddasi Ṭuwā* (Q 79:15–16 and compare 20:12) "Did the story of Moses come to you / when the Lord called upon Moses in the Holy Valley Ṭuwā". *Ṭuwā* had long been taken as a phonetically smoothed form of *ṭūrā*, "the Mount", to denote Sinai. But as Rubin shows, according to both Islamic exegesis and to rabbinic parallel texts, *Ṭuwā* is not related to *ṭūr/ā*, but constitutes an independent lexeme derived from ṬWY, "to fold", denoting something like "folded together". It refers to a theologically sophisticated perception of sacred space according to which Sinai, the holy site *par excellence*, has absorbed into itself the notion of the Holy Land. *Bi-l-wādi l-muqaddasi Ṭuwā* therefore needs to be rendered: "in the twice sanctified valley". In Sinai the sanctity of the Holy Land is already encapsulated, it is therefore twice holy. The idea of a "migration of sanctity" from Sinai to the Holy Land – later epitomized in Zion, Jerusalem – and back, indeed has

---

[12] Uri Rubin, "Moses and the Holy Valley Ṭuwan: On the Biblical and Midrashic Background of a Qur'anic Scene", in: *Journal of Near Eastern Studies,* 73/1, 2014, 73–81.

been claimed by Biblical scholars to be underlying the Hebrew Bible as an overall subtext.[13] Since Sinai during this process never loses its significance as the primary site of the sanctification of the Israelites it is possible to incorporate here Rubin's idea of an "axis of sanctity", whereby sanctity 'moves' from one site to another and back again.

The notion of a place that in an enigmatic way imbues another place with its sanctity, thus constituting an "axis of sanctity", seems to be presupposed already in the earliest Qur'anic texts: Q 95 opens with a mantic oath: *wa-l-tīn wa-l-zaytun / wa-ṭūri Sīnīn / wa-hādhā l-balad al-amīn*. "By the fig, by the olive, by Sinai and this town secure". By claiming a relationship between the two topographical sites as close as that between the two biblical sorts of fruit, these verses construct an axis of sanctity between Sinai, here called *ṭūr Sīnīn*, and Mecca which is represented as a place secured by its sacred precinct. The sanctity of the first mentioned Biblical site, Sinai, so-to-speak spills over into the second mentioned site (Mecca) which still needs to be established as a sacred place in the Biblical vein. A further, somewhat later, reference to a Sinai-Mecca axis would be Q 52:1–6 *wa-l-ṭūr / wa-kitābin masṭūr / fī raqqin manshūr / wa-l-bayti l-maʿmūr / wa-l-saqfi l-marfūʿ / wa-l-baḥri l-masjūr*, "By the Mount (Sinai)/ by a scripture inscribed/ in an unrolled parchment/ by the much frequented temple (i.e., the Kaaba)/ by the raised canopy/ by the ocean ever filled". Here "the Mount", mentioned together with the paraphernalia of scripture is juxtaposed with the Kaaba, which is introduced in association with the cosmic layers of heaven and earth (represented by the sea). Through their contexts both sites are given momentous significance: Sinai participates in the world of scripture, Mecca resonates with the cosmic dimensions of creation. Here again, Sinai serves as the origin of sanctity, mentioned before Mecca which partakes in its sanctity. The allusion to an axis that binds Mecca to Sinai seems to have been part of the Prophet's project to 'biblicize' the Meccan sanctuary, which was otherwise an ordinary ancient Near Eastern temple, and to reconsider Mecca's sanctity typologically in Biblical terms.

The mention of Sinai does not of course presuppose precise geographical knowledge by the community. Topography in the Qur'an is somewhat ambiguous, to the degree that – as we have seen – it is not clear if at the end of their exodus the Israelites inherit Palestine or take possession of Egypt. Egypt, however, does not open up an axis of sanctity; unlike Sinai and the Holy Land, it is never called *maqaddas*, "holy", or *mubārak*, "blessed", while in the Middle Meccan sura 28:20 Moses' call is staged in "the Blessed Valley" *fī l-buqʿati l-mubāra-*

---

[13] Jon Levenson, *Sinai and Zion. An Entry into the Hebrew Bible*, New York 1987.

ka. Similarly, Abraham and Lot escape to the "Blessed Land", *al-arḍ allatī bāraknā fīhā*, Q 21:71. The Israelites are invited to enter the "Holy Land", *al-arḍ al-muqaddasa*, Q 5:21. "Blessed" and "holy", *mubārak* and *muqaddas*, seem to be reserved as attributes of the Promised Land, including Sinai, the home of the prophets among the Israelites.

I. Isrā' – "Exodus" / Nocturnal Journey
Al-masjid al-aqṣā

Let us now leave the "ancient" Israelites and turn to the Prophet's night journey, a visionary experience typical of the new epistemic space of Late Antiquity. In a sura that can be dated to the middle Meccan phase of the Prophet's ministry, a single verse, semantically and formally (through a rhyme of its own) clearly detached from its context, speaks of a visionary night journey of the Prophet. Sura 17, *Al-isrā'*, opens with the verse:

> *subḥāna lladhī asrā bi-'abdihi laylan*
> *mina l-asjidi l-ḥarāmi ilā l-masjidi l-aqṣā*
> *lladhī bāraknā ḥawlahu*
> *li-nuriyahu min āyātinā*
> *innahu huwa l-samī'u l-'alīm.*
>
> Glory be to him who led his servant out by night
> from the sacred place of prayer (*al-masjid al-ḥarām*) to the farther place of prayer (*al-masjid al-aqṣā*)
> of which we have blessed the precincts
> so that we may show him some of our signs,
> surely he is the hearing, the seeing.

Although *al-masjid al-aqṣā* is not a toponym denoting Jerusalem in the Qur'an, the destination of the Prophet's *isrā'*, his night journey, "the farther place of worship", in Islamic tradition has been unanimously identified with Jerusalem. This is not least due to its attribute "of which we have blessed the precincts", *alladhī bāraknā ḥawlahu,* which entails an allusion to the Blessed Land. The short hymn related to the journey speaks of an *isrā'*, an "exodus" – thus employing the term used for the exodus of Moses – that starts from the familiar sacred place of worship (the Kaaba, named in the Qur'an since the middle Meccan period *al-masjid al-ḥarām*, that is, "the place of worship situated in the midst of a *ḥaram*, a sacred precinct"). It leads to a similar, though "more remote place of worship", *al-masjid al-aqṣā*. Yet what kind of *masjid* is this? The concept of *masjid* is new in Q 17, it points – contrary to *bayt*, "house of God" – to a place of "human worship". Yet *al-masjid al-aqṣā* does not need to be a physical place, let alone a building. It is true that, *al-masjid al-aqṣā*, "the farther place of prayer", if imagined in Jerusalem, must be related to the Jewish Temple. But since the Temple is destroyed, *al-masjid* seems to point less to a concrete sanctuary than to the site where the Temple has left "traces of sanctity". As a "sign of sanctity" it is suitable to function as the destination of the visionary night journey, one that culminates in the communication of spiritual "signs" to the Prophet. Within the sacred topography documented in the Qur'an, Jerusalem fits comfortably as the destination of the visionary journey: it is a "station" on the biblically established Sinai-Holy Land axis. Whereas in the Biblical frame the axis is bipolar – Sinai, the site of the Mosaic covenant, as the starting point of the axis, and Zion, the site of the Davidic covenant, as its terminal[14] – in the Qur'an the axis is extended to encompass Mecca as well.

But why a spiritual journey to Jerusalem? Scholars have pointed to earlier journeys of visionaries to the earthly Jerusalem, first and foremost to Ezechiel, and Henoch as well. Journeys to the heavenly Jerusalem are even more numerous.[15] Yet such precedents do not fully explain why such a visionary journey should have been undertaken in seventh-century Mecca and performed by a person deeply rooted in a true and active social life. The incident needs to be explained from the Qur'anic context. Let us try to embed the verse in its Qur'anic and sura context.

The Visionary Journey and Its Sura Context

The introduction of the visionary journey into the Qur'anic discourse certainly marks a leap in development: the earlier established Sinai-Mecca axis of sanctity had been presented as a given, a static, timeless relationship between the two sacred places, Sinai – virtually the Holy Land – and Mecca. In Q 17:1 the axis is set in motion. The Prophet himself is moved along the axis of sanctity between Mecca and the Holy Land. The axis thus forms part of a new construct of identity, where Jerusalem plays a role as the antipode of the Kaaba. Was this new axis open to the Prophet exclusively? There is no Qur'anic information about the Meccan community's prayer rites that the worshippers should have carried out facing a particular direction, a *qibla*. The topic of the *qibla* is raised only in Medina

---

14 See Levenson, *Sinai and Zion* (as in n. 13).
15 See Schäfer, *Die Ursprünge* (as in n. 6), 126.

when a previously followed direction was relinquished. This earlier *qibla* according to Islamic tradition faced Jerusalem. The only feasible alternative, the east, is not supported by Qur'anic evidence. But information about the Jerusalem *qibla* is equally scarce. Only the date of its abolition, less than two years after the Hidjra, is roughly agreed upon; its introduction, which remained unmentioned in the Qur'an, is not discussed. According to the most plausible hypothesis, the Jerusalem *qibla*, with its Biblical point of reference, should have been introduced together with the vast amount of narrative Biblical lore that became part of the Qur'anic community's religious education in middle Mecca, and moreover with the rite of prayer which was developed simultaneously. The analogy between the visionary journey as a most intimate encounter with the divine and the daily prayer, another form of encountering God, is clear. So why not associate the Prophet's Mecca-Jerusalem axis of the *isrā'* with the ordinary worshippers' pursuit of the same axis in their prayers? Considered as a kind of extension of the prayer rite, the nocturnal journey loses some of its enigmatic features.

A further point of reference corroborating Jerusalem as the destination of the *isrā'* is political. It is perhaps no mere coincidence that the sura, chronologically classified from the middle Meccan period, emerged at a time of political turmoil. In 614, a year that may be close to that of the composition of the sura (which cannot be determined), Jerusalem was wrested from the Byzantines by the Persians, who favored the Jews over the Christians and allowed them to participate in the administration of the town. This development, which to many seemed to reverse the religious-political status quo that had favored the Christians, is known to have triggered apocalyptic speculations. Jerusalem thus became the subject of public debate. The defeat of the Byzantines is more explicitly mentioned in Q 30, *al-Rūm*, equally a middle Meccan sura, and the controversies about it likely occupied the minds of the community at this time.

It is no surprise then that the topic of the Jerusalem *masjid* is not only raised in the initial verse about the Prophet's personal nocturnal journey, but is also revisited a few verses later with reference to Israelite history and the real Jewish Temple. The verse group Q 17:4–8 narrates the subsequent destructions of the first and the second Temple of Jerusalem.

> We decreed to the Israelites in the Scripture:
> You shall corrupt the earth twice
> And shall soar to a great height./
> When the time came for the first of two promises
> We sent against you servants of ours of great might
> And they marched against your habitations, shedding blood –
> A promise fulfilled./
> Then we granted you the counter-attack against them

> And provided you with wealth and progeny
> And made you more numerous as a troop./
> If you do good you do good to your own selves
> And if you do evil, likewise./
> When the second promise arrived,
> We sent against you servants of ours
> To abase your faces
> To break into the Temple as they did once before
> And to destroy utterly whatever they laid their hands upon./
> Perhaps your lord will show you mercy;
> But if you begin again, we shall begin again.
> We have made hell a dungeon for the unbelievers.

Yet how does this report relate to the visionary journey?

The ill fortunes of the Temple, its final devastation, is the essential backdrop for the visionary journey, the *isrāʾ*. Uri Rubin[16] has suggested that *masjid* in verse 1 reflects the Christian perception of a "New Jerusalem", cleansed from the memory of its sinful history alluded to in verse 17:4–8. Though the irenic Christian notion of a New Jerusalem may have been current, it is noteworthy that the report of the destruction is in no way partisan, let alone biased. It is devoid of any theologically grave accusation: it is no more than the usual hubris familiar from the Qur'anic stories about bygone nations, who perished because of their arrogance, which in turn led to the Israelites' loss of the Temple. No allusion is made to the Christian triumphalist verdict against the Jews, known from Origen and Eusebius, the latter of whom claimed that the destruction of the Temple was the punishment for the Jews' participation in the execution of Christ. What matters is not a review of history, but simply the erasure of the Temple, since the visionary journey leads to a non-spatial place of sanctity, to a "unräumlicher Ort"[17], a notion which only emerged after the disappearance of the Temple as an institution. This notion of a non-spatial site of sanctity is in accordance with the journeys of Jewish visionaries that led them to the heavenly Jerusalem. But why is the Prophet Muhammad transferred to the earthly Jerusalem? His case is unlike that of Ezechiel's transfer from Babylon to the earthly Jerusalem Temple, Ezk 8:1–3:

---

16 Uri Rubin, "Muḥammad's Night Journey (*isrāʾ*) to al-Masjid al-Aqṣā. Aspect of the Earliest Origins of the Islamic Sanctity of Jerusalem", in: *Al-Qantara*, XXIX 1, 2008, 147–164.
17 Klaus Bieberstein, " 'Eine Abbildung des an sich Unräumlichen im Raume'. Mythischer Raum und mythische Zeit im Symbolsystem Jerusalems", in: *Communio*, 41, 2012, 522–534, 537–538.

> And it came to pass in the sixth year, in the sixth month, in the fifth day of the month, as I sat in my home, and the elders of Judah sat before me, that the hand of the Lord God fell upon me. Then I beheld and lo a likeness as the appearance of fire [...] And he put forth the form of a hand, and took me by a lock of my head. And the spirit lifted me up between the earth and the heaven, and brought me in visions of God to Jerusalem, to the door of the inner gate that looks towards the north [...]

For Ezechiel the Temple was the emblem of his people's exilic memory and the direction of their prayers. In the Prophet's case no political recovery of the Temple is at stake.

A new sensitivity: exile and prayer as an exit from exile

The Prophet's and his community's relationship with Jerusalem is neither historically founded nor politically motivated. It is related instead to a very different epistemic universe. The middle Meccan suras display a new sensitivity developed by the community in face of their situation of siege, where two issues, the malaise of one's exilic situation in a hostile Mecca and the anticipation of release through prayer, are frequently expressed. While scholars are aware of the community's increasing estrangement from their Meccan milieu, they have seldom pursued study of the community's change in orientation, their endeavor to substitute Mecca for an "imagined homeland". This homeland is recovered in the Biblical abode of the Israelites, whom they typologically perceived to be their forerunners, a people guided and protected by a messenger, like themselves. It is marked by attributes such as "blessed" or "sanctified". Although the Holy Land already bore these qualifications in Christian tradition, their incorporation into Qur'anic discourse is noteworthy, particularly since there are no other places celebrated in the Qur'an as "blessed" – an expression of preference for the Holy Land over other areas that should be understood to point to the community's unusual relation to it.[18]

---

[18] Uri Rubin, "Between Arabia and the Holy Land: a Mecca-Jerusalem Axis of Sanctity", in: *Jerusalem Studies in Arabic and Islam*, 34, 2008, 345–362. Rubin of course is right to mention (345): "Apart from the land that derives its sacredness from God's blessing, the Qur'an knows of other precincts whose sacredness is described differently, by means of the Arabic root ḥ-r-m which means forbidding or declaring something sacred. The Qur'an describes the Kaaba as al-bayt al-ḥarām, i.e. \the sacred house" (Qur'an 5:2, 97), while the term al-mash'ar al-ḥarām \the sacred place of worship" (Qur'an 2:198), stands for a station of the ḥajj near 'Arafat."

Together with exile, prayer moves into the focus of the community's attention. It is no surprise to find that the introduction of the prayer rite as such is presented as already imposed on Moses: in Q 20:14, Moses is addressed: *innanī anā llāhu lā ilāha illā anā fa-ʿbudnī wa-aqimi l-ṣalāta li-dhikrī*, "I am God – no God but I – so serve me and perform the prayer in my remembrance". And so is the respecting of a *qibla*, which is first practiced by the Israelites: Q 10:87 has: *wa-jʿalū buyūtakum qiblatan wa-aqīmū l-ṣalāta*, "make your houses directions of prayer", although this verse does not yet specify the *qibla* locally. The importance of prayer in Middle Mecca may be deduced furthermore from the triumphant statement in Q 15:87 to dispose of a community prayer, the *Fātiḥa*, in addition to reading the Qur'an: *laqad ataynāka sabʿan mina l-mathānī wa-l-qurʾāna l-ʿaẓīm*, "We have given you seven verses to be repeated and [i.e.: in addition to] the mighty reading, to the *qurʾān*".

In the Qur'an, a number of biblical figures are portrayed praying, among them Noah, Moses, Zachariah, Mary, and Abraham. But not only the practice of prayer, also its most characteristic feature, the spiritual movement underlying prayer, the praying person's entry into a "state of sacredness", his entrance, *mudkhal*, into the spiritual world and his exit, *mukhraj* from it – in technical terms: his status of sanctity, the *iḥrām* – obviously plays an important role. As Q 17:80 shows: *aqimi l-ṣalāta [...] wa-qul rabbi adkhilnī mudkhala ṣidqin wa-akhrijnī mukhraja ṣidqin wa-jʿal lī min ladunka sulṭānan naṣīrā*, "Perform the prayer [...] and say: My Lord, lead me in with a just ingoing, and lead me out with just outgoing, grant me authority from Thee, to help me".

But to what space is the praying person being transferred? What is the realm of sacredness outside his real place? Moses' liberating exodus, *isrāʾ*, led him and his people out from physical plight, the oppression exercised by Pharaoh, and promised him deliverance in the blessed land. Such a physical exit was denied to the Prophet and his community, yet he was granted a micro-image of it, the one-time visionary journey to the centre of the blessed land, equally perceived as an experience of liberation. As for the community, a temporary, spiritual exit was open to them in prayer. There is no explicit word about the *iḥrām* transferring the worshippers to the blessed land, let alone to Jerusalem, before the Prophet's own transfer to *al-masjid al-aqṣā* in Q 17:1. Yet, why should their exit in prayer not have led them to their spiritual homeland, the Israelites' imagined abode, what the exegetes call the *qiblat al-Shām*, the Syrian, that is, the direction to the north? The assumption is plausible since it is precisely the remoteness of the worshippers from the sanctuary, intended as their point of orientation, that underlies the notion of a *qibla*. The very fact of its material inaccessibility makes a search for its direction necessary and enhances its significance. This understanding of a *qibla* would have resounded with Solomon's prayer in 1Kings 8, especially verses 33–34, where the direction of prayer towards Jerusalem is institutionalized:

> When thy people Israel be smitten down before the enemy, because they have sinned against thee, and shall turn again to thee, and confess thy name, and pray, and make supplication unto thee in this house:/then hear thou in heaven, and forgive the sin of thy people Israel and bring them again unto the land which thou gavest unto their fathers.

This Israelite/Jewish direction of prayer is to be considered as the prototype of the Qur'anic community's *qibla* towards Jerusalem. Going a step further, one could perceive of the visionary journey as a kind of imagined materialization of the Prophet's pursuit of the Jerusalem *qibla* in prayer. The experience of the *isrā'* is closely connected to prayer.

The Isrā' as the Target of Polemics in the Qur'an

Some of the listeners of the Prophet were less sensitive towards the spiritual dimension of the visionary experience. Looking for a *Sitz im Leben* for Q 17:1, for a social embedding of the verse, one might hypothesize that its proclamation came as a response to a public provocation. As the sura itself documents, the topic of supernatural translations of saintly men was an issue of discussion among the listeners to the Qur'an. Muhammad himself was challenged to perform an ascension to heaven in the vein of some visionaries known from Jewish tradition. He was also challenged to bring down a scripture – as Moses had done. These challenges are part of a longer polemical address that enumerates diverse miraculous signs enacted by earlier prophets, all of them recorded in the same sura 17. In verses 90–92 the opponents say:

> We will not trust you unless you cause a spring to gush forth for us from the ground,
> Or else you come to own a garden of palm trees and vines,
> and you cause rivers to gush forth in torrents through it all,/
> Or you make the sky fall upon us in bits and pieces, as you allege,
> or you summon God and the angels in our presence,/
> Or else you come to own a house made of gold,
> or you ascend to the sky,
> – nor will we trust your ascent (*ruqiy*) unless you bring down upon us a scripture we can read.

The prophet is to answer (verse 93b):

> "Say: Glory be to my lord! Am I anything other than a human being, a messenger?"

The idea of a physical ascension (*ruqiy*) that the prophet should carry out, thus occupied an important place in the debates of the time. The attestation of the visionary journey in verse 1 affirms that such expectations are in vain, that in the spiritual journey he experienced no magic dimensions were involved.

Early Exegetic Views of the Isrā'

It fell to the exegetes to re-connect the *isrā'* verse with its cultic context. The traditional reports about the communication of Q 17:1 embed the verse in a scenario of prayer. The most popular among the 'plain' and 'sober' references to the nocturnal journey – in contrast to the miraculously adorned ones, to be discussed below, is a narrative, transmitted by al-Ṭabarī from Ibn Isḥāq that dispenses entirely with mythical trends of interpretation. Here the destination of the Prophet's nocturnal journey is the town of Jerusalem. Umm Hāni', a cousin of the Prophet, reports:

> The nocturnal journey [*isrā'*, a term derived from the Qur'anic *asrā*, 'he made him depart by night'] of the Messenger of God took place as follows: He was staying at my house [indication of an ordinary place in Mecca instead of the precise location of the Kaʿba, a strikingly free exegesis of the Qur'anic *al-masjid al-ḥarām* [19]] where he spent the night (interpretation of the Qur'anic *laylan* – 'by night']. When he had performed the final evening prayer he went to sleep and so did we. In the early morning God's Messenger woke us for the morning prayer and when we had concluded it together he said to me: 'Umm Hāni', I have been praying here together with you the evening prayer, as you remember. But then I was in *Bayt al-Maqdis* [Jerusalem; an explication of the Qur'anic 'remote temple' – *al-masjid al-aqṣā*] and prayed there ['prayer' being an explication of the Qur'anic allusion to the vision of divine 'signs' *āyātinā*]. And now I have been praying with you the morning prayer in this place.[20]

Although we are not entitled to take this report as first hand testimony about the experience of the Prophet – the term *Bayt al-Maqdis* (the Arabic rendering of the Hebrew *bēt ha-miqdash*, 'Temple') does not yet figure in the Qur'anc is remarkable not least for the paucity of its semantic preconceptions. It does not display any ideological tendency, nor does it refer to any supernatural power or experience irreconcilable with the Qur'anic self-image, that is, the perception of the

---

[19] For the gradual evolution of topographical attributions such as individual place names in connection with a sanctuary, see Gerald R. Hawting, "The Origins of the Islamic Sanctuary at Mecca", in: *Studies of the First Century of Islamic History*, ed. Gautier H. A. Joynboll, Carbondale 1982, 25–47.
[20] al-Ṭabarī, *Jāmiʿ*, XV, 3.

Prophet. Also in favour of its genuineness is the observation that the Qur'anic text is not interpreted verbatim but is dealt with like a specimen of ordinary discourse so that *al-masjid al-ḥarām*, taken *pars pro toto* for Mecca, can be represented by a private house. The transmitter relates that the event occurred within a specific time frame, the limited hours between two periods of prayer. No supernatural agency is thus demanded, since the vision should have happened in a dream.

The 'sobriety' of the report, however, completely erases any trace of the Prophet's claim to a major spiritual experience, which is resounding in the Qur'anic verse with its triumphant tenor (*subḥāna*), its expressive mention of a locomotion between the two momentous sanctuaries of the oecumene – an event felt to have taken place 'out of time'. The performance of prayer is central, and unsurprisingly so, since prayer in most of the exegesis of Q 17:1 is not only the starting point of the experience, but, as we shall see, also its culmination, and, finally, the conclusion of the venture.

Exegesis is less interested in the typological dimension of the event. Its Qur'anic perception as an *isrā'*, as an exodus, is however a telling reference to Moses, who ascended Mount Sinai to receive the tablets during an encounter with God himself. The *Matan Torah* is a core part of the exodus and a formative event in the Israelites' achievement of a national identity. Such an ascension of a mountain relates to Jesus as well, who, on the occasion of his transfiguration, ascended Mount Tabor where he was to receive divine confirmation of his mission. His story – staged no longer in Antiquity, but in Late Antiquity – is different from that of Moses. Jesus no longer encountered God himself but found himself flanked by divine messengers: the first prophet of the Bible, Moses, and the last, Elija. Jesus was not granted a written scripture on Mount Tabor, but received oral words. The Prophet Muhammad by his very claim to have been granted an *isrā'*, an exodus-like deliverance, relates his experience to that of Moses. But similar to Jesus rather than to Moses he is no more honored by an encounter with God, but granted traces of the divine presence, *āyāt*, signs. What are these signs like?

The Ascension, al-Mi'rāj

New approaches to the meaning of the enigmatic signs, āyāt

The visionary journey in the Qur'an is only alluded to in Q 17:1 and thus remained enigmatic; it was thus a challenge to later readers of the Qur'an to interpret its meaning. The question is finally answered in the *mi'rāj* story, Muhammad's "ascension" to heaven (fig. 1).

Fig. 1: The Prophet mounted on the Buraq passing over the Kaaba, the *Khamsah* of Nizami, Herat, late 15th century. London, The British Library, Ms. Or. 6810, fol. 5v

Against the plain and sober report of Umm Hāni, who only attests the Prophet's transfer to a remote place of worship between two prayer periods, there stands a narrative richly adorned with images and fantastic features in which the nocturnal departure culminates in an ascent to heaven and – as we shall see – in a kind of Giving of the Torah. It has found visual expression in numerous miniatures throughout the Islamic world.[21] The narrated story first appears combined with the visionary journey (*isrā'*) report in the eighth century.[22] By this time, the miraculous character of the *mi'rāj* had infiltrated the erstwhile sober account of the *isrā'*. Already the classical biography of the Prophet by Ibn Isḥāq (d. 768), the *sīra* par excellence,[23] which transmits different versions of the nocturnal journey, contains a miraculous ride of the Prophet to Jerusalem culminating in a detailed description of an ascent to heaven. Both movements, the longitudinal leading to the earthly sanctuary and the vertical leading to the heavenly spheres, though ascribed to different transmitters (al-Ḥasan al-Baṣrī and 'Abdallāh b. Mas'ūd, respectively), are dealt with as successive phases of the same event. Although the reports arose only a few generations after the death of the Prophet, the perspectives of these presentations differ radically from that of the 'plain' report.

In the transmission of al-Ḥasan al-Baṣrī, which is adduced as representative of the accounts of a completely revised, miraculously adorned journey to Jerusalem, the event is framed as an initiation rite. The novice, Muhammad, sleeping in the sanctuary, is awakened with three strokes by the initiator, the angel Gabriel, who led him out and subjected him to a test. Inserted between these steps is a scene staged in Jerusalem, one in tune with the Qur'anic notion of a 'succession of Prophets' (Q 19:36–37):[24] a gathering of the prophets and patriarchs familiar to Jewish and Christian salvation history, among whom, the Prophet Muhammad must assert his rank. Finally, the story returns to the 'real' scenario at Mecca, where the report of the nocturnal journey with its supernatural traits has provoked criticism and even derision among the Qurayshites:

---

21 See *The Prophet's Ascension. Cross-Cultural Encounters with the Islamic Mi'rāj Tales*, ed. Christane Gruber/Frederick Colby, Bloomington 2010.
22 See Frederick Colby, *Narrating Muhammad's Night Journey. Tracing the Development of the Ibn 'Abbas Ascension Discourse*, New York 2008.
23 Muḥammad Ibn Sa'd, *al-Ṭabaqāt al-kubrā*, ed. Eduard Sachau, Leiden 1904 (reprint, Beirut 1960), vol. II/1, 142–145, could be quoted; see Heribert Busse, "Jerusalem in the Story of Muhammad's Night Journey and Ascension", in: *Jerusalem Studies in Arabic and Islam*, 14, 1991, 1–40.
24 See Angelika Neuwirth, *Der Koran als Text der Spätantike. Ein europäischer Zugang*, Berlin 2010, vol. II/1, 619–620.

> I was told that al-Ḥasan said that the Prophet said: While I was sleeping [interpretation of the Qur'anic *laylān*] in the *Ḥijr* [narrow understanding of the *masjid al-ḥarām*] Gabriel came and stirred me with his foot. I sat up but saw nothing and lay down again. He came a second time and stirred me with his foot. I sat up, but saw nothing and lay down again. He came to me a third time and stirred me with his foot. I sat up and he took hold of my arm and I stood beside him and he brought me out to the door of the mosque and there was a white animal, half mule, half donkey [indication of an interpretation of the Qur'anic *asrā* as a movement on horseback], with wings on its sides with which it propelled its feet, putting down each forefoot at the limit of its sight and he mounted me on it. Then he went out with me keeping close to me.[25]

Al-Ḥasan relates the continuation of the story:

> The apostle and Gabriel went their way until they arrived at the Temple [narrow understanding of the Qur'anic *al-masjid al-aqṣā*] at Jerusalem. There he found Abraham, Moses and Jesus among a company of the prophets [as bearers of the divine blessings, a representation of the Blessed Land, the Qur'anic *al-arḍ allatī bāraknā fīhā*]. The apostle acted as their imām in prayer [identification of the Qu'ranic *āyāt* with the performance of a prayer in the community of the prophets]. Then he was brought two vessels, one containing wine and the other milk. The apostle took the milk and drank it, leaving the wine. Gabriel said: 'You have been rightly guided to the way of nature and so will your people be, Muhammad. Wine is forbidden you.' Then the apostle returned to Mecca and in the morning he told the Quraysh what had happened. Most of them said: 'By God, this is a plain absurdity! A caravan takes a month to go to Syria, and a month to return and can Muhammad do the return journey in one night?' Many Muslims gave up their faith.[26]

Ibn Isḥāq, reporting on the authority of Abū Saʿīd al-Khuḍrī, then includes the ascension story directly following that of the miraculous journey to Jerusalem: "I heard the apostle say: 'After the completion of my task in Jerusalem a ladder (*miʿrāj*) was brought to me finer than any I have ever seen [...] My companion mounted it with me until we came to one the gates of heaven.'" This report is followed by visions of hell, then further climbings across the spheres, each occupied by one prophet until the seventh sphere is reached, from which a vision of Paradise opens up. The further description of the ascension attributed by Ibn Isḥāq to ʿAbdallāh b. Masʿūd, a scribe of the Prophet, concludes with the following scene:

---

[25] ʿAbd al-Malik Ibn Hishām, *al-Sīra al-nabawiyya*, ed. Aḥmad Muḥammad Shākir, Cairo 1373/1954; Muḥammad Ibn Isḥaq, *The Life of Muhammad: A Translation of Ibn Isḥaq's Sīrat Rasūl Allāh*, trans. by Alfred Guillaume, Lahore 1974, 181.
[26] Ibn Hishām, *al-Sīra al-nabawiyya* (as in n. 24), vol. I, 398; Ibn Isḥaq, *The Life of Muhammad* (as in n. 24), 181f.

(Finally) they reached the seventh heaven and his Lord. There the duty of the fifty prayers was laid upon him. The apostle said: 'On my return I passed by Moses and what a fine friend of yours he was! He asked me how many prayers had been laid upon me and when I told him fifty he said, 'Prayer is a weighty matter and your people are weak, so go back to your Lord and ask him to reduce the number for you and your community.' I did so and He took off ten. Again I passed by Moses and he said the same again; and so it went on until only five prayers for the whole day and night were left. Moses again gave me the same advice. I replied that I had been back to my Lord and asked him to reduce the number until I was ashamed and I would not do it again. Any one of you who performs them in faith and trust will have the reward of fifty prayers.'[27]

At this stage of the exegetical development, we finally learn about the meaning of the "signs" that in Q 17:1 had been left unexplained. What takes place as the culmination of the *mi'rāj* is nothing else than a *Matan Torah*. The Prophet is charged with the imposition of prayer on his community. Though he receives neither written words, like Moses, nor words explicitly affirming his status, like Jesus, he does receive – in the shape of the injunction to establish a certain number of obligatory daily prayers – a kind of vocal, melodic Torah, Prayer is not only the spiritual backbone of Islam, it also entails scriptural texts; indeed, prayer is widely composed of Qur'anic readings. If we assume that the Qur'an has from the beginning been articulated with a cantilena, the task that Prophet Muhammad was charged with in heaven was to bring down a "chanted Torah".

Thus, two of the plural elements of the Biblical exodus have materialized a second time in its Qur'anic and post-Qur'anic reconfiguration. First, the attainment of a new consciousness, of a liberating "exit" – not through a guided collective movement from a geographic site, but through an introverted, personal act, prayer. It was in the context of prayer that the Prophet was granted his visionary exit, his *isrā'*. The liberating event in the history of the Israelites, the historical exodus, was turned into a spiritual exodus.

The second element from the Biblical exodus story to be reconfigured in Islamic tradition is the *Matan Torah*, the divine instruction of the people through words "given" to Moses on Mount Sinai. Though the Qur'an only alludes to this analogy, it unfolded in exegesis. The climax of the *mi'rāj* narrative, which in Islamic tradition has superseded the Qur'anic *isra'*, is to become the crucial token of the Prophet's closeness to the divine. The Prophet during his sojourn in the seventh heaven is "given" the institution of prayer, the most important cultic practice of Islam. It is no coincidence that the *mi'rāj* started from Jerusalem, which had been the destination of the Qur'anic *isrā'*. Jerusalem is no terminal,

---

27 Ibn Hishām, *Al-Sīra al-nabawīya* (as in n. 24), vol. I, 407; Ibn Isḥaq, *The Life of Muhammad* (as in n. 24), 187.

but the starting point of manifold ascensions, be it those of elect individuals, be it those of the prayers universally articulated by the pious. The *miʿrāj* is an important stratagem within early Islamic identity politics, a complex image through which the Qur'anic community has expressed its claim to participate in Biblical tradition and lore.

Susanne Talarbadon
The Paradigm of a Second Exodus in Jewish Tradition

The paradigm of Exodus runs throughout the narratives of the Hebrew Bible. Reflection upon Abraham's curious departure from Haran, the difficult return of Jacob, and the adventurous journeys of Moshe reveals that the idea of Exodus is always lurking between the lines. This observation is neither astonishing nor revolutionary, however, when one considers that many biblical texts were written under the impression of the Babylonian Exile.

I

The anonymous biblical poet who was labelled Second Isaiah by sober-minded theologians[1] gave the paradigm of a *Second* Exodus its classical outline. His grandiose visions of an impressive departure from Babylonia to return to the Holy Land may have sounded too florid to his astonished contemporaries. Even to his contemporary audience it should have been evident that their return to Judaea would not turn out like this:

> Yea, you shall leave in joy and be led home secure./ Before you, mount and hill shall shout aloud, and all the trees of the field shall clap their hands. (Is 55, 12 JPS translation)

Indeed, this magnificent picture of a Second Exodus had little to do with rational judgement of reality: the poet's imagination allowed him to not only depict the great return of Israel's children accompanied by nature's attendance, but to imagine that gentile[2] rulers, convinced by these events, would eagerly submit

---

[1] The first authors who developed the idea of two authors being responsible for Is 1–39 and 40–66, respectively, were Johann Christoph Döderlein and Johann Gottfried Eichhorn by the end of the eighteenth century. They held that chapters 40–66 (then assigned to the anonymous Second Isaiah) stem from the time of the Babylonian Exile. Bernhard Duhm (1847–1928) was the first who attributed Is 56–66 to a third hypothetical post-exilic author called Trito-Isaiah. Recently, some scholars tend to see the Second or Third Isaiahs not as the authors of distinct 'books' but of two redactions working up the First Isaiah.

[2] Modern English language lexically distinguishes between *gentile(s)* and *pagan(s)* to describe ethnicity (gentile) or religious (pagan) aspects of a certain person or community. Until Christianity drastically began to challenge late-antique identity patterns, 'gentile' and 'pagan' – ethnic

to Israel's God and His might. (Is 49:7). The overall impression of gentiles acknowledging Israel's supremacy in Isaiah 40–55 has little to do with the peaceful metaphors of First Isaiah's vision of Zion (Is 2:2–4). The exilic writer rather sketched a global upheaval during which hills get even and military superpowers lost all their strength – just to pave the path for the once lost and now found tribes of Israel.

Second Isaiah's concept of a Second Exodus was inspired by the approaching breakdown of Babylon's rule (539 CE) when the Persian king Cyrus II succeeded in building his empire. Shortly thereafter, in 538 CE, Cyrus issued his famous edict[3] which promised the exiled would be released. This announcement should have set the Second Exodus in motion. In actual fact, the few former Judaeans who decided to return dropped rather haltingly back into their home country. Manifestly, they did not find a land flowing with milk and honey, but a wretched country without much political and economic perspective.[4] Furthermore, this poetic misjudgement not only brought about individual disappointment but a very important new theological paradigm. Second Isaiah interpreted the Persian king as the Lord's Messiah, who should, in the name of Israel's God, put an end to the kingdom of Babylonia:

> Thus said the LORD to Cyrus, His anointed one – Whose right hand he has grasped,/ Treading down nations before him/ Ungirding the loins of kings,/ Opening doors before him/ And letting no gate stay shut:/ I will march before you/ And level the hills that loom up;/ I will shatter doors of bronze/ And cut down iron bars./ I will give you treasures concealed in the dark/ And secret hoards – So that you may know that it is I the LORD, / the God of Israel, who call you by name. (Is 45:1–3)[5]

At first sight, choosing a Persian king to liberate exiled Israel from Babylonian bondage sounds like a much more realistic scenario than a Second Exodus envisioned with trees clapping their hands. But upon closer examination, the prophetic concept of a pagan Messiah turns out to be even less convincing than the alternative.

---

and religious identity generally went together. The following essay will, thus, use both terms synonymously – at least as far as the time before the spread of Christianity is concerned.

3 The 'Edict of Liberation' gained enormous importance for postexilic Israel. It was included twice in the biblical book of Ezra, once in Aramaic (Ezra 6:3–5), and once in Hebrew (Ezra 1:1–4).

4 See Rainer Albertz, *History of Israelite Religion*, vol. 2, Louisville 1994, 414–426 (Second Isaiah); 437–458 (early postexilic period).

5 The Bible is quoted here and elsewhere according to the New JPS Translation (Philadelphia 2003).

> That [Y'] should have commissioned in distant Media a foreign king who did not even know him (cf. 45.5) to lead a great revolution in world politics solely because of a marginal colony of Jewish exiles sounded completely improbable; indeed it had all of the official tradition against it. [...] Thus the message of the Deutero-Isaiah group was not only politically incredible but also theologically highly offensive.[6]

As for political plausibility, the prophet did not have much by way of argument. Dealing with tradition and theological reasoning vis-à-vis his compatriots should have been all the more compelling. The problems with Israelite tradition were at hand. Anointing Cyrus would presuppose that Israel's Lord would be entitled to give orders to Persian kings, speaking in theological terms: Second Isaiah's ground breaking assignment requires monotheism. Consequently, the text which declares Cyrus a Messiah of Israel continues:[7]

> I am the Lord and there is none else;/ Besides Me, there is no god./ I engird you, though you have not known Me,/ So that they may know, from east to west,/ That there is none but Me./ I am the Lord and there is none else. (Is 45:5–6)

The exiled Jerusalem theologians, who rallied around the anonymous master called Second Isaiah, were, thus, determined to take every necessary step to confirm their overall vision of Israel's future. As a result, a tiny group of a subjected people at the edge of the nascent Persian Empire proclaimed the absolute power of their (national) God over the entire world.

Consequently, the concept of Second Exodus is deeply intertwined with gentiles – they will reluctantly submit to set Israel free of their bondage (Is 43:1–9) and will be forced to accept the Lord of Israel to be the world's only God. But this concept of theological universalism – inescapable if one were to establish Cyrus' election – brought about an inner antagonism between the strict particularism of Israel's pre-exilic tradition and the universal notions of monotheism.[8] Even against their intentions, Israel's theologians had to develop some idea of what the Heavenly Father would finally plan for His pagan children. One of those concepts, perhaps the most prominent one, predicts a pilgrimage of the gentiles to Mount Zion at the end of time (Is 2:2–4):

> In the days to come, The Mount of the LORD's House/ shall stand firm above the mountains/ and tower above the hills;/ And all the nations/shall gaze it with joy./ And the

---

6 See Albertz, *History* (as in n. 4), 415–416.
7 The mission of Cyrus is nevertheless mentioned throughout Second Isaiah, see for instance, Is 41:2.25; 43:14–15; 44:28; 48:15.
8 See Gerd Theißen, *The Religion of the Earliest Churches*, Minneapolis 1999, 212–216.

many peoples shall go and say:/ "Come, let us go up to the Mount of the LORD,/ To the house of the God of Jacob; / That He may instruct us His ways, And that we may walk His paths."/ For instruction shall come forth from Zion,/ the word of the LORD from Jerusalem. (Is 2:2–3)[9]

Simultaneously, the special relationship of a 'national' God to his people Israel – the covenants with Abraham and at Sinai – had to be strictly maintained. Monotheism, an inevitable consequence of exilic theology, created an inner aporia, which was not to be eased. Over the course of time, it led to the emergence of divergent movements inside Judaism, such as Christianity.[10]

II

Immediate reactions to Second Isaiah's concept proved to be extremely disheartening, and the same holds true for later periods. After two disastrous defeats against the Roman Empire, the Rabbis tried to downplay any idea of an (immediate) messianic restoration. Moreover, (Second) Isaiah's vision seemed to be split up between emergent Judaism and emergent Christianity: While the Rabbinic movement maintained the importance of the Holy Land within the eschatological drama without emphasizing the conversion of pagans, early Christianity took over the concept of universal conversion of gentiles without sticking to the Land of Israel or Exodus.

Moreover, the Rabbis insisted on the concept of Israel's particularity, connecting it explicitly to the Exodus paradigm. Mekhilta, one of the oldest halakhic Midrashim, accentuates that the Torah was presented in the public sphere of the Sinai desert, thereby providing access to revelation for the whole mankind:

> They encamped in the Wilderness.[11] The Torah was given in public, openly in a free place. For had the Torah been given in the land of Israel, the Israelites could have said to the na-

---

9 Joseph Blenkinsopp (*Isaiah 1–39*, New York et al. 2000, 191) suggests that Is 2:2–5 could be "a collage of Zion themes that we encounter in all sections of the book". Willem A. Beuken, *Jesaja 1–12*, Freiburg/Basel/Wien 2003 (Herders theologischer Kommentar zum Alten Testament) 89, maintains a similar point of view: Is 2:2–5 "bündelt von Anfang an die Aufmerksamkeit der Leser des Jesajabuches auf das überraschende Heilsangebot Deuterojesajas an die Völker (42,1–4; 45,22–25; 49,1–6), wobei deren Kommen zum Zion eine große Rolle spielt".
10 See Theißen, *Religion* (as in n. 8), 214: "It is an inner aporia of Judaism, which produces universalistic groups in its midst. Here, too, it needs to be added that this aporia is not 'resolved' in Christianity but continues to be active in it."
11 Ex 19:2.

tions of the world: You have no share in it. But now it was given in the wilderness publicly and openly in a place that is free for all, everyone wishing to accept it could come and accept it.¹²

But the gentile peoples refused to accept the Torah for different reasons of their own. Therefore, the election of Israel remained the Lord's only way to pass his message to the sons of men. That Israel's particularity becomes, thus, something like a divine *second-rate quality* could be seen as an ironic by-product of that new paradigm of salvation history (Heilsgeschichte).

After the Jewish War and Bar Kokhba, Christianity took over the Roman Empire and began to discover the Holy Land. When Christian pilgrims began to occupy Biblical landscape – in the course of the third and fourth century – a paradigm shift between Second Isaiah and his rabbinical interpreters became manifest. This change of attitude is clearly to be detected in the Babylonian Talmud Avoda Zara 2a–3b. The text, probably a third-century Palestinian homily delivered at Sukkot,¹³ imitates the literary trial device which is very prominent in Biblical prophecy. It is also present in Isaiah 43:9 which functions as the main biblical point of departure.

> All the nations assemble as one,/ The Peoples gather./ Who among them declared this, Foretold to us the things that happened?/ Let them produce their witnesses and be vindicated,/ That men, hearing them may say, "It is true!" (Is 43:9)

Gentile nations fail to recognize the divinity of Israel's Lord; their priests were not able to foretell the Second Exodus. In reaction to that failure, Israel is named the principal witness of God's supremacy. The Talmud and Isaiah 43 share the scenario of a High court trial. But a closer look on the subsequent cast reveals a profound difference between the Biblical original and its Rabbinic interpretation: Who serves as a witness for whom? ¹⁴ In Isaiah we see Israel witnessing the divinity of God, because – as discussed above – the Nations failed to recognize it. In Avoda Zara, the gentiles have already recognized the Lord of Is-

---

12 Mekhilta Bachodesch I, Translation by Jacob Z. Lauterbach, Mekhilta de-Rabbi Ishmael, vol. 2, Philadelphia 2004, 293–294.
13 The bulk of the homily is written in Hebrew; the Talmudic text contains several Aramaic interpolations. See Jeffrey L. Rubenstein, "An Eschatological Drama: Bavli Avodah Zarah 2a–3b", in: *AJS Review*, 21/1, 1996, 1–37. The homily is preserved in different versions: Tanhuma Schoftim § 9; Midrasch Tanhuma, ed. Salomon Buber, Vilna 1885, vol. 2, Schoftim § 9; PRK (Mandelbaum) 2, 452; Yalqut ha-Makhiri on Isaiah, ed. R. Machir b. Abba Mari, Berlin 1893, 138–140; Yalqut Shim'oni ad Is § 452; BHM VI, 50.
14 See Rubenstein, "An Eschatological Drama" (as in n. 13), 15.

rael but fail to fulfil Torah. Therefore, the commandments, God Himself and the nations are named witnesses for Israel's fulfilment of Torah:

> R. Hanina b. Papa – some say R. Simlai – expounded [the foregoing verse] thus: In times to come, the Holy One, blessed be He, will take a scroll of the Law in His embrace and proclaim:
> 'Let him who has occupied himself herewith, come and take his reward.' Thereupon all the nations will crowd together in confusion, as it is said: All the nations are gathered together, etc. [...] Thereupon the Kingdom of Edom[15] will enter first before Him. [...] The Holy One, blessed be He, will then say to them: 'Wherewith have you occupied yourselves?' They will reply: 'O Lord of the Universe, we have established many market-places, we have erected many baths, we have accumulated much gold and silver, and all this we did only for the sake of Israel, that they might [have leisure] for occupying themselves with the study of the Torah.' The Holy One, blessed be He, will say in reply: 'You foolish ones among peoples, all that which you have done, you have only done to satisfy your own desires. You have established marketplaces to place courtesans therein; baths, to revel in them; [as to the distribution of] silver and gold, that is mine, as it is written: Mine is the silver and Mine is the gold, saith the Lord of Hosts; [Hag 2:8] are there any among you who have been declaring this?' And 'this' is nought else than the Torah, as it is said: And this is the Law which Moses set before the children of Israel. [Deut. 4:44] They will then depart crushed in spirit. On the departure of the Kingdom of Rome, Persia will step forth. [...] The Holy One, blessed be He, will ask of them: 'Wherewith have ye occupied yourselves?'; and they will reply 'Sovereign of the Universe, we have built many bridges, we have captured many cities, we have waged many wars, and all this for the sake of Israel, that they might engage in the study of the Torah. Then the Holy One, blessed be He, will say to them: 'You foolish ones among peoples, you have built bridges in order to extract toll, you have subdued cities, so as to impose forced labour; as to waging war, I am the Lord of battles, as it is said: The Lord is a man of war [Exod. 15:3] are there any amongst you who have been declaring this? 'and 'this' means nought else than the Torah, as it is said: And this is the Law which Moses set before the Children of Israel [Deut. 4:44]. They, too' will then depart crushed in spirit. [...] R. Johanan says: This teaches us that the Holy One, blessed be He, offered the Torah to every nation and every tongue, but none accepted it, until He came to Israel who received it. (bAZ 2a.b)[16]

The trial in the Talmud develops in two stages: First, Rome and Persia, leading powers in Late Antiquity, attempt to defend themselves before the God's High Court. They claim to have built up their imperia to the greater benefit of all mankind. They have thus had no time to fulfil the Torah but request from the Divine Judge to accept their interventions as a kind of vicarious merit. Their arguments, however, are rejected.

In a second step, the gentile nations take an offensive position: they doubt *Israel's* fulfilment of the Torah. The Holy One pronounces himself witness as do

---

15 The Rabbis often use "Edom" as a code name for Rome; in later times for Christianity.
16 The Talmud is quoted according to the Soncino translation (Isidore Epstein, ed.).

Heaven and Earth, but the Nations declare them biased; therefore, The Eternal names biblical personal of *gentile* origin as witnesses of Israel's faithfulness, a decision that, finally, silences the self-defending prosecutors:

> Then the Holy One, blessed be He, will say, 'Some of yourselves shall testify that Israel observed the entire Torah. Let Nimrod come and testify that Abraham did not [consent to] worship idols; let Laban come and testify that Jacob could not be suspected of theft; [Gen 31,37] let Potiphar's wife testify that Joseph was above suspicion of immorality; let Nebuchadnezzar come and testify that Hanania, Mishael and Azariah did not bow down to an image; let Darius come and testify that Daniel never neglected the [statutory] prayers; let Bildad the Shuhite, and Zophar the Naamathite, and Eliphaz the Temanite [and Elihu the son of Barachel the Buzite] testify that Israel has observed the whole Torah; as it is said, Let them [the nations] bring their [own] witnesses, that they [Israel] may be justified.' (bAZ 3a)

As this shows, the fulfilment of the Torah replaces biblical monotheism. The Nations must not only recognize the God of Israel but do his Torah. Their rejection in the Last Judgement seems thus inevitable. In their desperation, the gentiles decide to plead for a second chance, which they are granted. Told to try an easy commandment – to dwell in a sukkah at the Feast of Tabernacles – the request could be interpreted as an ironic reply to the infrastructure projects of the Romans and Persians that they used as an apology for not having accepted the Torah. As was to be expected, the pagans also missed their second chance.

Nevertheless, the sages expect the peoples of the world to press their case another time in sight of the imminent messianic era.

> R. Jose says, In time to come idol-worshippers will come and offer themselves as proselytes. But will such be accepted? Has it not been taught that in the days of the Messiah proselytes will not be received; likewise were none received in the days of David or of Solomon? – Well, they will be self-made proselytes, and will place phylacteries on their foreheads and on their arms, fringes in their garments, and a Mezuzah on their doorposts, but when the battle of Gog-Magog will come about they will be asked, 'For what purpose have you come?' and they will reply: 'Against God and His Messiah' as it is said, Why are the nations in an uproar, and why do the peoples mutter in vain, etc. [Ps. 2:1] Then each of the proselytes will throw aside his religious token and get away, as it is said, Let us break their bands asunder, [Ps. 2:3] and the Holy One, blessed be He, will sit and laugh, as it is said: He that sitteth in heaven laugheth. [Ps. 2:4] (bAZ 3b)

The Talmudic text presents a straightforward correction of Isaiah's vision of gentile's pilgrimage to Zion by the end of the days (Is 2:2–5). According to the sages, the Nations were offered the chance to join Israel repeatedly – but failed each attempt, even under imminent eschatological pressure. Compared to the biblical model, the conditions of judgement have changed. Monotheism or conversion to Israel's God ceased to mark the borderline between Israel and the pagans. A simple pilgrimage to Zion will not meet Divine expectation (particularly since the Temple lied in ruins): The yardstick set out by rabbinic sages is the Torah and the fulfilment of the commandments.

It could be asked (but not easily answered), whether this eschatological drama constructs a polemic against Christianity. Qualifying Jewish monotheism as an identity marker between Israel and the heathen might point towards that direction. Early Christian misrepresentations of Paul, for example by Deutero-pauline authors,[17] seemed to suggest that it would be either impossible (for Jews) or useless (for Christians) to do the commandments. Avoda Zarah, on the other hand, specifies that it might be generally impossible for gentiles to get along with the Torah, but they will, nevertheless, be punished for not doing so. The pronounced judgement on the dominating pagan nations made Avoda Zarah 2a–3b "clearly a favourite among Jews throughout the Middle Ages, preserved in the later midrashic collections and cited by medieval authors".[18] Interestingly, a second exodus is not part and parcel of the eschatological scenery presented by Avoda Zarah – neither for Israel, nor for the heathen.

III

A second paradigm shift, also presented in the Babylonian Talmud (bKet 111a), replaces the Palestinian perspective by a Diaspora view, precisely, that of Babylonian Jewry. The concept of a Second Exodus, as mentioned above, originated from the experience of an exile to end soon. Over the course of time, hundreds of years after the destruction of the Second Temple, living in exile or diaspora did not, however, seem to end. Every rebellion against the Romans had proven disastrous. A vast majority of Jews had lived outside Israel for generations. The rabbinic sages, eager to disfavour any new provocation against the gentile empires, had to adapt themselves to that reality.

The lengthy but very interesting discussion in bKetubot 110b–111a serves these purposes. It starts with the traditional Palestinian conviction that a worthy Jewish life can only be lived in Israel. But it concludes with the suggestion that a pilgrimage to Israel is sufficient as well. In the middle of debate, the following lines are presented:

> R. Zera was evading Rab Judah because he desired to go up to the Land of Israel while Rab Judah had expressed [the following view:] Whoever goes up from Babylon to the Land of

---

[17] See Eph. 2:11–16; Kol 2:9–17.
[18] Rubenstein, "An Eschatological Drama" (as in n. 13), 3.

Israel transgresses a positive commandment, for it is said in Scripture, They shall be carried to Babylon, and there shall they be, until the day that I remember them, saith the Lord. [Jer. 27:22] And R. Zera? – That text refers to the vessels of ministry. [cf. Jer. 27: 19 ff.] And Rab Judah? – Another text also is available: I adjure you, O daughters of Jerusalem, by the gazelles, and by the hinds of the field, [that ye awaken not, nor stir up love, until it please]'. [Cant. 2:7] And R. Zera? – That implies that Israel shall not go up [all together as if surrounded] by a wall. And Rab Judah? – Another 'I adjure you' [Cant. 2:7] is written in Scripture. And R. Zera? – That text is required for [an exposition] like that of R. Jose son of R. Hanina who said: 'What was the purpose of those three adjurations? [Cant 2:7; 3:5; 5:8] – One, that Israel shall not go up [all together as if surrounded] by a wall; the second, that whereby the Holy One, blessed be He, adjured Israel that they shall not rebel against the nations of the world; and the third is that whereby the Holy One, blessed be He, adjured the idolaters that they shall not oppress Israel too much'. And Rab Judah? – It is written in Scripture, That ye awaken not, nor stir up. And R. Zera? – That text is required for [an exposition] like that of R. Levi who stated: 'What was the purpose of those six adjurations? – Three for the purposes just mentioned and the others, that [the prophets] shall not make known the end, that [the people] shall not delay the end, and that they shall not reveal the secret to the idolaters'. (bKet 11a)

We find two sages arguing about whether one should stay in exile or return home. In the course of history, the state of affairs had already altered so greatly that a return to Israel had to be defended – all the more so for a Second Exodus. The most important passage of the Talmudic debate is based on Canticles 2:7.

I adjure you, O maidens of Jerusalem,/ By gazelles or by hinds of the field:/ Do not wake or rouse/Love until it please!

In Jewish and Christian tradition the Canticum is meant to speak allegorically of the love between God and Israel or Jesus and the Church, respectively.[19] Therefore, the sleeping beauty which may not be stirred up is supposed to be Israel; the lover adjuring the maidens of Jerusalem should be God. The Talmud resumes that the very same request not to 'wake or rouse' is repeated three times (Cant 2:7; 3:5; 5:8) – which, according to the hermeneutical rules of the Rabbis, has to be interpreted.[20] The first meaning adjusted to the verse, therefore, forbids a mass

---

19 See Midrash Shir ha-Shirim (compiled during the second half of the 6th century but containing older material) or the famous homilies on the Canticum of Origen (184–235). Compare Marc Hirshman, *A Rivalry of Genius: Jewish and Christian Biblical Interpretation in Late Antiquity*, New York 1996, 84–94.
20 The sages hold that no single word, not even a letter, in the Bible was superfluous (principle of omnisignificance). Repetitions thus concealed specific meanings. For the term omnisignificance as a hermeneutical principle compare James Kugel, *The Idea of Biblical Poetry*, New

immigration to the Holy Land: You should not motivate all Israel to go up to Israel 'as a wall', as the Talmud has it. This ruling is undisputed even to Rabbi Zera who urgently wants to emigrate. Only individuals might decide to leave the Diaspora for Israel. The second and third meanings of the 'Do not wake' reveal the motivation behind the Talmudic dictum: Israel should not fight the gentile domination again – and the heathen peoples are requested to oppress Israel not too hard.

Notwithstanding the ritual ardent desire for Zion, the idea of a Second Exodus seemed to be shattered in view of political reality: 'The Holy One, blessed be He, adjured Israel that they shall not rebel against the nations of the world.' Not even to think of pagans who could join the pilgrimage to Zion, to a Zion where no Temple existed for centuries. The gentiles might stay where they are, as do the majority of the Jewish people.

IV

The Talmudic dictum not to go up 'as a wall' is cited time and again by medieval rabbis. Like their Babylonian predecessors, they attempted to establish their respective home country, be it Ashkenas or Poland or Spain, as a proper Jewish dwelling place. They did so by telling legends about German or Ukrainian or English towns and they singled out holy places where Jewish heroes were buried. They did so while interpreting the Talmud and creating new codices of Halakha.[21]

During the Middle Ages, two of the most important Jewish sages, Judah Halevi (before 1075–1141) and Moshe ben Maimun (1135–1204), each developed a very influential concept of emigration to the land of Israel. Both left their home in al-Andalus: Halevi did so more or less because he yearned for Zion; Maimonides emigrated because he was forced to leave. Their motivations were as different as their philosophies.

Haven 1981, 103–104; Christoph Dohmen/Günter Stemberger, *Hermeneutik der Jüdischen Bibel und des Alten Testaments*, Stuttgart 1996, 75–83.

[21] Cf. Marc Saperstein, "The Land of Israel in Pre-Modern Jewish Thought", in: The *Land of Israel. Jewish Perspectives*, ed. Lawrence. A. Hoffman, Notre Dame 1986, 188–209, Shalom Rosenberg, "The Link to the Land of Israel in Jewish Thought: A Clash of Perspectives", in: ibid., 139–169.

Judah Halevi expounded his ideas in his philosophical chef d'oeuvre, the Sefer ha-Kuzari,[22] just as he did in his wonderful poetry.[23] The Kuzari, formally a set of dialogues between a Jewish rabbi (חבר) and the king of the Khazars which is framed by a conversion narrative,[24] was (and is) most influential and widely read from the medieval period onwards. Over the years, a broad majority of scholars felt bemused by what they called the hodgepodge nature of the work. This judgement gave way to a great many concepts regarding the development and purpose of the Kuzari.[25] The spectrum is dominated by notions of a successive expansion of the work,[26] beginning with Book Three which was completed by the final Book Five. Mainstream scholars maintain that the Kuzari was meant to be an anti-rationalist rejection of the "project of Jewish philosophy" in al-Andalus.[27]

Developing an integrated concept of human nature, Halevi gestured towards the influences of the physical and spiritual environment upon an individual's fate[28] – such as experience while living in Eretz Israel. Halevi holds that, corresponding to the election of the Jewish people, the Land of Israel should be considered superior to every other country in the world. On account of the beneficial climate and soil, the land possesses an unusual power (Kuzari, IV,17) which adds

---

22 The book, in its Arabic original *Kitab al Khazari* or *Kitab al-Ḥujjah wal-Dalil fi Nuṣr al-Din al-Dhalil*, had been completed around 1140. English translations have been provided by Hartwig Hirschfeld, *Judah Hallevi's Kitab al Khazari*, New York 1905, and, more recently, Yehuda Halevi, *The Kuzari: In Defense of the Despised Faith*, trans. N. Daniel Korobkin, ed. David Kahn, Jerusalem ²2009 (first published Northvale 1998).
23 A selection of his Pilgrim's songs is to be found (both in their Hebrew and English translations) in Raymond P. Scheindlin, *The Song of the Distant Dove: Judah Halevi's Pilgrimage*, Oxford 2008. The book provides an interpretation of Halevi's pilgrimage poetry. A small selection of his poetry, brilliantly translated into English by Gabriel Levin, can be found in Yehuda Halevi, *Poems from the Diwan*, London 2002.
24 For a short and instructive description of the content see Adam Shear, *The Kuzari and the Shaping of Jewish Identity,1167–1900*, Cambridge 2008, Viii–Xii.
25 For a summary of research history see ibid., 3–12 or Michael S. Berger, Toward a New Understanding of Halevi's Kuzari, in, *The Journal of Religion*, 72, 1992, 201–211.
26 This turns out to be the main assumption of Yohanan Silman, *Philosopher and Prophet: Judah Halevi, the Kuzari, and the Evolution of His Thought*, Albany 1995, Viii: "An analysis of Halevi's thought on key issues, supplemented by external evidence, indicates that these currents express two stages in the evolution of his thought at the time he wrote the Kuzari: In the earlier stage, Halevi still adhered to many tenets of Aristotelian philosophy […]. Later, though, he broke with many of these tenets and placed the emphasis on the unique experiences of the Jewish people." Since the book has been published, many scholars and reviewers (such as Robert Eisen in: *Speculum*, 73, 1998, 596–598) have seriously doubted Silman's thesis.
27 See Shear, *The Kuzari* (as in n. 24), 3.
28 See Silman, *Philosopher* (as in n. 26), 240.

to the purification of man's soul (Kuzari, II,14). Closely connected to the Land of Israel is prophecy, the highest level humans can attain, and the one needed to experience God's revelation 'face to face' (I, 103.109):

> Anyone who prophesied did so either in Israel, or for Israel's sake. [...] Note that Abraham – who was the heart of the elite – was removed from his land when he began to excel spiritually and became worthy of attaching to Divinity [ha-Injan Ha-elohi[29]] He was transplanted to the place where his development could be completed. [...] So, too, did prophecy and prophets abound in Abraham's progeny, as long as they were living in Canaan, and as long as they used the tools for spirituality, namely, the preservation of purity, the performance of the commandments, and the sacrifices. (Kuzari, II,14)[30]

Although prophecy ceased to exist with the destruction of the First Temple of Jerusalem in 586 BCE, living in the Land of Israel still benefits Jewish life enormously. Only there, Halevi boldly expounds, the commandments can be fulfilled perfectly:

> Nevertheless, the land of Canaan is especially reserved for the God of Israel, and one's deed cannot be entirely complete in any place except there. Many commandments are not practicable for one who does not live in the land of Israel. Furthermore, one's heart and soul cannot be entirely pure and refined except in a place that one knows is especially reserved for God. (Kuzari, V,23)[31]

Accordingly, the master (חבר) of the Kuzari (probably the alter ego of Halevi) decides to immigrate to Israel at the end of the book. But the unusual power of the Holy Land extends much farther. If the Jews presently living in the Diaspora would only follow the master's example, redemption could be at hand earlier. A Second Exodus would be, according to the Kuzari, of paramount importance – notwithstanding the poor condition of Eretz Israel which suffered from Crusader domination.[32]

> When people become aroused to love this holy place and to press for the anticipated event, this, too, generates great reward. [...] This means that Jerusalem will be rebuilt, when the

---

29 The term ha-Injan ha-Elohi (האניןהאלהי) /'amr-ilahi, literally "divine thing", is crucial for Halevi's concepts. It denotes something like the divine power or presence as such or as immanent in prophets, in Israel or in the Holy Land. See Ignatz Goldziher, "Le amr ilâhî (ha-Injan ha-elohi) chez Jehuda Halevi", in: *Revue des Études Juives*, 50, 1905, 32–41.
30 Korobkin, "The Kuzari" (as in n. 22), 64–67.
31 Ibid., 308–309. See Rosenberg, "The Link" (as in n. 21), 151.
32 The yearning for Israel is expressed even more intensely in Halevi's poetry. See the famous poem "My heart is in the East". A Hebrew-English version of it is to be found in *The Penguin Book of Hebrew Verse*, ed. T. Carmi, Harmondsworth/Middlesex et al. 1981, 347.

Jewish people yearn for it to the ultimate degree, to the point where they favour its stones and dust (Kuzari V, 27)[33]

Against the Talmud, Judah Halevi resolutely opted for a Jewish mass immigration into the Holy Land to live there according to the Torah and to hasten redemption. By contrast, the most influential medieval Jewish philosopher and halakhist Moshe ben Maimon (Maimonides, 1135–1204) did not urge any Second Exodus. In the last part of his Talmudic compendium Mishneh Torah,[34] the Hilkhot Melakhim (Doctrines of the Kings),[35] Maimonides refers approvingly to the aforementioned discussion bKetubot 110b ff. The Jews should, thus, live in Eretz Israel, if possible. On the other hand, they should not emigrate to the Holy Land "as a wall".[36]

This leads to the assumption that Maimonides would promulgate a much more traditional messianic scenario. Actually, the Mishneh Torah ascribes the gathering of the "dispersed of Israel" to the essential mission of the Messiah:

> If a king will arise from the House of David who diligently contemplates the Torah and observes its mitzvot as prescribed by the Written Law and the Oral Law as David, his ancestor, will compel all of Israel to walk in (the way of the Torah) and rectify the breaches in its observance, and fight the wars of God, we may, with assurance, consider him Mashiach. If he succeeds in the above, builds the Temple in its place, and gathers the dispersed of Israel, he is definitely the Mashiach. He will then improve the entire world, motivating all the nations to serve God together, as Tzephaniah 3:9 states: 'I will transform the peoples to a purer language that they all will call upon the name of God and serve Him with one purpose.' (MT Schoftim, Hilkhot Melakhim XI,4)[37]

---

[33] Korobkin, "The Kuzari" (as in n. 22), 311.
[34] The Mishneh Torah (MT), completed between 1170 and 1180, found a controversial echo among contemporary rabbis because it often fails to cite its Talmudic sources. Nowadays, the Mishneh Torah is held in great esteem as one of the greatest Talmudic codes ever composed.
[35] After presenting the laws of the king proper (Hilkhot Melakhim I–4; following Deut 17: 14–20), Maimonides passes on to the rules of warfare (Hilkhot Melakhim V). Discussing which peoples could or should be conquered in a campaign of conquest (Milchemet ha-Reschut) leads him to question which countries Jews were supposed to dwell in (Hilkhot Melakhim V, 6–12).
[36] The practical relevance of the rules codified by Maimonides (even to himself) could nevertheless be scrutinized. True to the sources, he includes the interdict to live in Egypt in the MT (ibid., V,7) – even if he himself lives in Egypt, having left Eretz Israel behind.
[37] For the translation see: http://www.chabad.org/library/article_cdo/aid/1188356/jewish/Chapter-11.htm (25/12/2012; 12:30), which was published in print: Moses Maimonides, Ramba"m, *Mishneh Torah*, ed. Eliyahu Touger, 31 volumes, New York 1998. Similar and more exhaustive statements to the messianic scenario are to be found in Maimonides' Iggeret Teman (Epistle to Yemen), composed around 1172.

Maimonides closely links the return to Israel with the messianic reinstitution of the kingdom of David. The king-Messiah will lead the people of Israel back to Israel. By doing so, Israel's striving for individual and collective sanctification will be sealed and rewarded. Halevi, on the contrary, maintains that only the land of Israel itself will provide the power of sanctification to the Jewish people. Therefore, Jews should not wait in the lands of Exile until the king-Messiah passes. They should emigrate to Israel because only there will they find the means to sanctify, which is seen as a prerequisite for redemption by both Jewish philosophers.

This dispute certainly adds new aspects to the actualization of Second Exodus. Yet, the Talmud presents an unresolved tension: Does the land of Israel contribute to the fulfilment of the Torah, or not? Is it, therefore, possible to stay in Exile while awaiting redemption? Moreover, in the medieval debate any gentile claim to a portion of the Torah or redemption seems to be silenced. There is no Second Exodus. The only question that remains is: should some individual Jews emigrate or not.

V

Let us have a look at a very last example of Exodus motives in the history of the Jewish religion, which is an admittedly strange one: the exoduses of Nahman Brazlawer, a Hasidic Rebbe, who lived from 1772 until 1810. These however, do not appear in Jewish mainstream thought. As Arthur Green has convincingly shown,[38] Nahman's pilgrimage to the Holy Land in 1798/1799 marked a turning point in his short life. After returning home he bravely tackled his great mission: a reform of the Hasidic reform. He attacked popular "wunderrebbes," as well as elitist mystics, and, as a kind of second biblical Joshua, Nahman forced his way into the territory of Arje Leib of Spolje (1725–1812). Arje Leib, called the "Shpoler Zejde" (the grandfather of Shpola) was considered a disciple of the Ba'al Shem Tov (around 1700–1760) – the great-grandfather of Nahman. The Zejde, who was much older than Nahman, was the very paradigm of a popular rebbe. Therefore, he was a highly provocative example of a (false) Hasidic leader who – in Nahman's eyes – distorted the heritage of his holy ancestor. After two frustrating years of exile in the Zejde's lands, Nahman decided to undertake a new conquest and invade Brazlaw, a small Ukrainian town after which Nahman's Hasidic

---

[38] Arthur Green, *Tormented Master. The Life and Spiritual Quest of Rabbi Nahman of Bratslav*, Woodstock 1992.

group was later named. The Brazlaw project was carefully justified either in Nahman's homilies or in his biographical books. The invasion during Summer 1802 presents itself as a spiritual conquest following the models of Abraham and Joshua, and, as the Chosen Land, Brazlaw emerges as an (unexpected) axis mundi.

To conquer the town, Nahman resorted to the same method as Joshua in Jericho: he entered Brazlaw with dance and music, using not trumpets or trombones, but his own hands. This new method was spiritually well-founded:

> It is known that the air in the lands of Gentile peoples is impure. But the air inside Eretz Israel is holy and pure. That is to say, the Holy One, blessed be He, lead it out from under the hands of the star worshippers and gave it to us. [vgl. BerR; Rasch"i ad Gen I,1] Or, the land of the Gentiles is outside the Holy land, the air is impure there. But if we clap hand to hand, the power of 28 [כ"ח] will be raised which is inside creation, the power [כח] of His works. And so you find that this is the way we are given the heritage of the Gentiles because everything belongs to the Holy One, blessed be he. We possess, therefore, the power in our hands to clean up the air of the land of the Gentile peoples so that the land of the Gentile peoples comes under the dominion of the Holy One, blessed be He, again. (Liqquté Mohara"n I, 44)

The sanctification of impurity is founded here upon the kabbalist premise that the powers of Good beneath correspond to the powers of Good above. The 28 joints in Jewish hands and fingers correspond to the works of creation and can, thus, reduce the powers of Evil. Therefore, Ukrainian land can be transformed into Eretz Israel. The Ukrainian town of Bratzlaw gained a new, Hebrew name: Bres-lev, alluding to 'heart of flesh'. At the same time, the concept of Second Exodus seems fully transformed: instead of leaving gentile lands to regain Eretz Israel and instead of transforming the Heathen to pious pilgrims yearning for Zion, the land of the pagans was transformed into Israel. The heathen peoples were disinherited and lost their spiritual claim over their countries. The Holy One, thus, regained dominion over the entire world.

At the end of his short life, Nahman left Brazlaw for one last conquest, settling in Uman, where he died five months later. There, he wished to redeem the souls of secular Jews (maskilim) – but that is a story for another time.

VI

Surveying the Jewish tradition in different ages, a complete change in the concept of Second Exodus may be witnessed. The idea of gentile peoples flocking to Zion seems to have been abandoned early on, perhaps on account of a wish to discourage nationalist groups and early Christian universalism. Across the centuries, the political reality of a small minority did not require any change of agenda. The somewhat difficult standing of the Jewish people under foreign rule overshadowed any attempt to care for the fate of the pagans. In due distance to any military adventures, the medieval sages discussed the impact of Zion on the redemption of the Jewish people again. Two contradictory positions were developed which dominated the debate until the 19th century: the land of Israel was seen either as a means of redemption or as its reward. Finally, apart from Jewish mainstream, Nahman of Brazlaw, one of the most original Jewish thinkers, wished to transfer the holiness of Israel to Ukrainian lands. He used the setting of biblical history to "restore" pagan towns in order to prepare for the coming of the Messiah.

Ute Holl
„Du hast die Greuel gesehen...".
Zum Exodus als ästhetischer
Unterscheidungskraft[1]

Gegen Macht

In den Künsten und der Popkultur ist der Exodus im zwanzigsten Jahrhundert zur Signatur für Befreiungsprozesse und -bewegungen geworden, für religiöse und für säkulare[2]. Aufstand und Auszug des israelitischen Volks aus der ägyptischen Gefangenschaft, die Moses und sein Bruder Aron durch ihre Inszenierung von Plagen oder, je nach Standpunkt, von Wundern, initiierten, gilt als Muster und Modell jeder Befreiung aus Unterdrückung oder Versklavung. Zumindestens gilt das für Kulturen im Umfeld aller drei monotheistischer Religionen, in denen von Moses als von einem Befreier und Mediator zwischen Menschen und divinen Mächten berichtet wird. In dieser Tradition antwortet der Exodus stets auf ein Modell der Macht, das als hierarchisch, autoritär und von oben über die Leute herrschend vorgestellt ist.

Die Oper *Moses und Aron* von Arnold Schoenberg und deren eigensinnige Verfilmung durch Danièle Huillet und Jean-Marie Straub verhandeln und reformulieren dieses Konzept der Macht für das 20. Jahrhundert, Schoenberg kurz vor, und Straub/Huillet nach dem Zweiten Weltkrieg. Beide Werke stellen die Möglichkeit politischer Befreiung erstens deutlicher und, wenn man so will, bibeltreuer in den Kontext von Gesetzlichkeit und Gewalt. Zweitens entwickeln sowohl Oper als auch Film ein Konzept der Befreiung, das nicht mehr als Gegenbewegung gegen einen einzigen autoritären Repressionsapparat begriffen werden kann, wie es im Modell „das Volk Israel gegen den Pharaoh" vorgestellt ist. Vielmehr entwickeln sowohl Oper als auch Film einen Raum der Erfahrung von komplexen und vielfältigen Formen von Machtbeziehungen. Jeder Befreiung, jedem Exodus setzen sie die Einsicht voraus, dass jede und jeder selbst in die Exekution von Macht verstrickt ist, und das gerade da – wie Michel Foucault zeigt – wo wir es am wenigsten wissen wollen: im Begehren und auch in ästhetischen Erfahrungen, in

---
[1] Der Text beruht auf Überlegungen aus meinem Buch *Der Moses-Komplex. Politik der Töne, Politik der Bilder*, Zürich/Berlin 2014.
[2] Vgl. Michael Walzer, *Exodus und Revolution*, Frankfurt am Main 1995.

der Kunst, der Musik, den Bildern, die unsere sinnlichen Verhältnisse, Wahrnehmung reorganisieren.

In beiden Werken beginnt die Befreiung daher damit, neue Räume des Hörens und, im Film, des Sehens unter Bedingungen der Migration und des Exils zu eröffnen. Das geschieht im Musikalischen durch das von Schoenberg in der Oper radikal durchgeführte Verfahren der Zwölftonmusik, der Gleichverteilung mithin aller Töne im Raum, die nach der Regel einer Reihe ohne jede Privilegierung durch Leittöne, Dominanten oder Harmonien „nur aufeinander bezogen"[3] gespielt werden. Das ist nicht nur eine strukturelle, sondern eine ästhetische Setzung: Nicht um die Ordnung der Töne geht es Schoenberg, sondern um die Desorganisation aller Hörkonventionen und die Eröffnung neuer Klangräume, in denen ein gleichschwebendes oder ein, im ästhetischen wie im juristischen Sinne, ungerichtetes Hören möglich wird.

Arnold Schoenberg eröffnet mit der Zwölftonmusik zunächst ein akustisches Feld neuer und unerhörter Klangfarben. Er beginnt mit dem Komponieren nach dem Verfahren, zwölf Töne gleichwertig aufeinander zu beziehen, bereits in den zwanziger Jahren, aber eine theoretische Durchdringung des Konzepts wird er erst in den vierziger Jahren vorlegen, prominent im Text „Komposition mit zwölf Tönen", der auf einen Vortrag im Jahr 1935 an der University of Southern California in Los Angeles, wo er damals wohnte, zurück geht (Abb. 1). Im Zuge der Komposition von *Moses und Aron*, einer Oper des Exodus mithin, realisiert Schoenberg die strenge Form zum ersten Mal in einem umfassenden Werk. In der Oper werden damit die Begründung einer Gesetzesform und Visionen der Befreiung mit der eben auch mosaischen Frage des Medialen, der Einschreibung, des Aufschreibens und Abbildens auf Tafeln, Notenpapier oder dann bei Huillet/Straub auf Leinwänden eng geführt. Medien und Migration, Exil und Befreiung sind die Komplexe, die das Thema des Exodus mit der politischen Wirklichkeit des zwanzigsten Jahrhunderts verbinden. In der Oper *Moses und Aron* und deren Verfilmung aus dem Jahr 1974 wird der Exodus daher auf avancierte Weise als grundlegende Konstellation kultureller Opposition oder, wie Danièle Huillet formulierte, als Ästhetik des Widerstands unter Medienbedingungen verhandelt.

---

[3] Arnold Schönberg, „Komposition mit zwölf Tönen", in: id., *Stil und Gedanke*, Frankfurt am Main 1992, 105–137, hier 110.

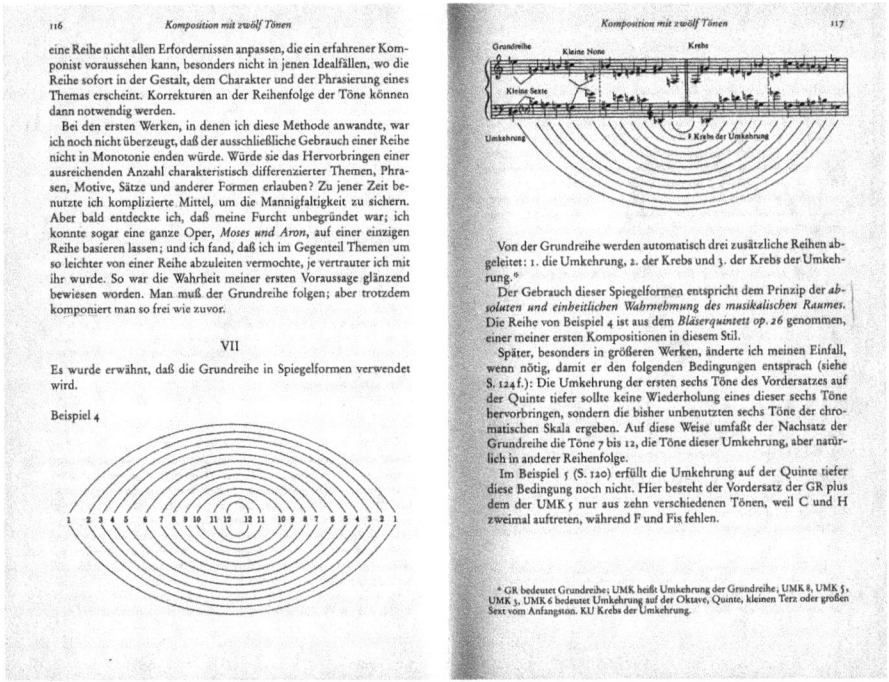

Abb. 1: Arnold Schönbergs Diagramm der Grundreihe, Komposition mit zwölf Tönen

Gleichverteilung

Das Experiment, um das es den Exodus-Projekten sowohl von Arnold Schoenberg als auch von Danièle Huillet und Jean-Marie Straub zu tun war, hieß, eine Wahrnehmung herzustellen, die nicht hierarchisch und nicht berechenbar ist, die mit dem Unwahrscheinlichen kalkuliert und selbst Verwantwortung übernimmt.

Für Schoenberg ist die Zwölfton-Oper *Moses und Aron* zuerst und vor allem die Eröffnung eines neuen, und im Sinne des Exodus ließe sich sagen, versprochenen Klangraums als eines Möglichkeitsraums. Der ergibt sich aus der Gleichheit aller Töne im doppelten Sinne „vor dem Gesetz". Das ist kein einfach theoretisches Konzept. Schoenbergs musikalische Formen verdanken sich zwar, insofern sie auf dem Papier notierte sind, zunächst der Symbolisierung und daher der Mathematisierbarkeit von Klängen, und als symbolisierte kann Schoenberg Töne durch Permutationen, Kombinatoriken und Inversionen drehen, wenden und spiegeln. Aber nach dieser symbolischen Prozessierung gibt er die Musik dem Realen eines Klangraums zurück, den er nicht ganz und gar kontrollieren kann.

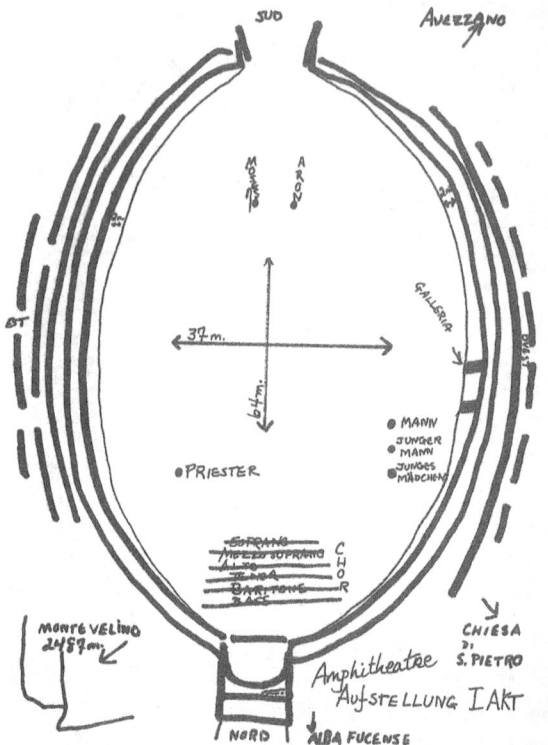

Abb. 2: Gregory Woods Zeichnung des Amphitheaters von Alba Fucense (Filmkritik Heft 221/222, Mai/Juni 1975, 256)

Hier beginnt für Schoenberg, der ja auch leidenschaftlicher Tennisspieler im Wind der Pacific Palisades, seines kalifornischen Exils, war, die Kunst als wirklich mosaische: Nicht das Gesetz selbst, sondern seine Implementierung und deren Effekte in eine wirkliche Welt interessierten ihn.

Danièle Huillet und Jean-Marie Straub werden jene Gleichverteilung der Elemente, die Schoenberg als akustische Körnung der Einzeltöne in eine wüstenhafte Ebenmässigkeit des Klangs verfolgt hatte, in der Bearbeitung von Räumen und Zeiten ins Filmische transponieren. Durch ein komplexes Verfahren der Aufzeichnung von Stimmen, Klängen und Geräuschen im Akustischen des Films und im Visuellen durch Einstellungen, in denen es keine *establishing shots* gibt, keine Einstellungen, die Überblick oder Orientierung etablieren oder fingieren und in denen die horizontale Kamerabewegung des Schwenks heterogene Elemente des Bildes gleichförmig und gleichgültig verbindet, übertragen sie die kompositorischen Prinzipien ins Kino. Auf diese Weise löschen sie etablierte

Abb. 3: Danièle Huillet und Jean-Marie Straub, *Moses und Aron:* Der Chor der Frauenstimmen in der Arena

kulturelle und räumliche Ordnungen und versetzen das Kinopublikum ebenfalls in die Orientierungslosigkeit eines Übergangsraums, der im Alten Testament ebenso wie in allen Kinogeschichten Wüste heißt. Trotz der titelgebenden Namen richten beide Werke, Oper und Film, die Aufmerksamkeit nicht auf Objekte, Dinge oder Figuren, sondern auf Verhältnisse, Verteilungen, Verbindungen und Übertragungen, auf Intervalle möglicher Übergänge. Beide Arbeiten thematisieren damit die prekäre Lage vor dem Gesetz. Diese erweist sich als ungerichteter Raum der Offenheit, zugleich aber auch als ein ungesicherter Raum, in dem jene Gewalt herrscht, die, wie Jacques Derrida formuliert, „uns von innen her daran erinnert, daß das Recht stets eine Gewalt ist."[4] Um die Frage der Gleichheit als eine des Verhältnisses von Selbst und Anderem zu begreifen und als je historischen und kulturellen Akt der Unterscheidung, breiten Oper und Film zunächst die Frage nach Differenzsystemen überhaupt aus. Die Feststellung des Moses: „Ich bin ein Fremdling geworden im fremden Land" (Ex 2:22), die sowohl Schoenberg als auch

---

4 Jacques Derrida, *Gesetzeskraft. Der ‚mystische Grund der Autorität'*, Frankfurt am Main 1991, 12.

Huillet und Straub in ihren Arbeiten als eigene Erfahrung des Exils mitführen, wird als ästhetische Erfahrung möglicher Fremdheit, als Möglichkeit der Fremdwahrnehmung ausgebreitet. Anstatt also die in rezenten Debatten um Exodus und Moses-Figur erneut aufgesprungene Frage nach dem Verhältnis von Theologie und Politik aufzuwerfen[5], lassen sich anhand der Arbeiten von Schoenberg und Huillet/Straub ästhetische Strategien darlegen, die unter gegenwärtigen Bedingungen ubiquitärer Migration erneut und möglicherweise neue Bedeutung entfalten könnten.

Die Erfahrung des Exils strukturiert die Oper. Schoenberg wird im Laufe der Arbeit an der Oper Österreich, dann Deutschland und schließlich Europa verlassen. Dabei wird er 1933 in der Pariser Synagoge und unter der Zeugenschaft Marc Chagalls in die jüdische Gemeinschaft zurückkehren, aus der er als Jugendlicher ausgetreten war. „Wie Du sicherlich bemerkt hast", schreibt er am 16. Oktober 1933 an Alban Berg, „ist meine Rückkehr zur jüdischen Religion schon längst erfolgt und ist in meinem Schaffen sogar in den veröffentlichten Teilen erkennbar (‚Du sollst nicht.... Du mußt...') und in Moses und Aron, von dem Du seit 1928 weißt, der aber wenigstens fünf Jahre zurückliegt".[6]

Jean-Marie Straub und Danièle Huillet, die seit den späten fünfziger Jahren unter weniger prekären, aber dennoch explizit politischen Gründen Frankreich verlassen mussten, nahmen die Arbeit am *Moses und Aron*-Film auf, nachdem sie 1959 in Berlin die Aufführung der Oper gesehen hatten, die Hermann Scherchen, seit 1937 im Exil in der Schweiz, dirigierte. Straub und Huillet fanden die Berliner Inszenierung jedoch „épouvantable", eine nachkriegsdeutsche „abstraction théâtrale". Der Straub/Huillet'sche Film markiert einen Widerstand gegen falsche Ästhetik. Der Film *Moses und Aron* wurde anlässlich der Hundertjahrfeier zu Schoenbergs Geburtstag schließlich doch von deutschen Fernsehanstalten realisiert, dann aufgrund einer Widmung an Holger Meins jedoch zensiert, blockiert, verschoben und schließlich zum christlichen Osterfest in den „wieder wie Weihnachten zusammengeschalteten dritten Programmen der Bundesrepublik"[7] gesendet. Ob 1975 in den Redaktionen jemand daran dachte, dass damit auch das Pessachfest, der Auszug aus Ägypten und das Exil aufgerufen wurden, bleibt dahingestellt. *Moses und Aron* komprimiert eine Kritik deutscher Nachkriegskul-

---

5 Vgl. anlässlich der Arbeiten Jan Assmanns den Kommentar von Gerhard Kaiser: „War der Exodus ein Sündenfall?", in: Jan Assmann, *Die Mosaische Unterscheidung oder der Preis des Monotheismus*, München 2003, 239–271.
6 Arnold Schoenberg, *Briefe*, ausgewählt und hrsg. von Erwin Stein, Mainz 1958, 200–201.
7 Brigitte Jeremias, „Ein sakraler Monolith, mitten in die Landschaft gestellt. Jean-Marie Straubs Moses und Aron-Verfilmung", in: *Frankfurter Allgemeine Zeitung*, Nr. 49, 27.2.1975, 21.

Abb. 4: Danièle Huillet und Jean-Marie Straub, *Moses und Aron:* Der Chor der Frauenstimmen in der Arena

tur von den fünfziger bis in die siebziger Jahre, bezieht diese aber wiederum präzise auf die Zeit der Entstehung der Oper.

Verwüstung

Arnold Schoenbergs Oper *Moses und Aron* beginnt mit einer in den dunklen Opernsaal hinaus erklingenden Vokalise, einem langen O___. Fast unbeabsichtigt entwickelt Schoenberg einen ungerichteten und hybriden Klang, wenn er Schwingungen, die zum Teil aus Körpern kommen, zum Teil aus Instrumenten, sich vermischen und überlagern lässt. War anfangs der Einsatz der Instrumente zur Stützung der Stimmen geplant, so setzt Schoenberg dann die Mischung von Klängen, deren Quellen ununterscheidbar bleiben, als Form ein:

> Daß die Sechs Solost. immer von sechs Instrumenten begleitet sein sollen, geschah wohl aus praktischen Gründen: ihre Sicherheit zu verbürgen. Aber ich bitte, sie auch dann nicht wegzulassen, wenn man glaubt, daß die Sänger sie entbehren können. Denn nun ist dieser

Abb. 5: Danièle Huillet und Jean-Marie Straub, *Moses und Aron:* Der Chor der Frauenstimmen in der Arena

Klang hier hineingearbeitet und soll nicht mehr fehlen. NB: Wo Sänger und Instrumente sich im Vortrag unterscheiden sollen (insbesondere Dynamik) wird das deutlich angemerkt sein, sonst sollen die Klänge sich möglichst vollkommen miteinander verschmelzen.⁸

Der erste Klang der Oper ergeht damit als unmenschlich polyphoner, der sich dann ausdifferenziert in viele Stimmen, Klänge und Geräusche, darunter vier, die in der Partitur später explizit als „Stimme aus dem Dornbusch" ausgewiesen werden.⁹ Sie fordern Moses auf, das Volk zu befreien. Gottes Stimme und die Stimme des – überhaupt erst zu gründenden und noch zu befreienden – Volkes

---

8 Vgl. Schoenberg, *Moses und Aron Partitur*, 1958, Anmerkung auf Seite 4. Das hörbare Schwingen der Luft, das die menschlichen und instrumentellen Klänge zu einem neuen, befremdlichen Klang synthetisiert, ist in der Einspielung der Oper durch Pierre Boulez sehr viel deutlicher ausgeführt als in der von Michael Gielen für den Film. Vgl. Pierre Boulez, *Arnold Schoenberg, Moses und Aron*, aufgenommen in West Ham Central Mission, London, 30. November und 3., 5. und 6. Dezember 1974, Sony Classical 1993 (Audio-CD).
9 Arnold Schoenberg, *Moses und Aron. Oper in drei Akten. Studien Partitur*. B. Schott's Söhne, Mainz o. J., Akt I Takt 9 (ohne Paginierung).

kommen aus einem einzigen, aber in seinen Farben und Nuancen wiederum sehr komplexen Klangkörper. Wenn Moses diesen hört und dann als Anruf und Auftrag wahrnimmt, lässt er ihn gewissermaßen ausdifferenzieren: zu Gott und Volk, Kreatur und Wüste. Verantwortlich dafür, dass dies geschieht, ist zuerst das Hören der Zu- oder Aufhörenden.

Abb. 6: Danièle Huillet und Jean-Marie Straub, *Moses und Aron:* Erste Einstellung mit der Figur des Moses

Die Wüstenhaftigkeit dieses Klangraums verdankt sich der konzeptionellen Struktur der Schoenbergschen Zwölfton-Musik. Darin gibt es keinen Grund-Ton, keinen Leit-Ton, keine Harmonien oder Disharmonien, sondern einen Klangraum, der aus den regelmäßig nacheinander erklingenden Elementen einer festgelegten Reihe aus zwölf chromatischen Tönen entsteht. Pierre Boulez hat diesen Raum deshalb als einen glatten Raum vom gekerbten und metrisierten, vom kulturtechnisch geordneten Wahrnehmungsraum unterschieden. Gilles Deleuze und Félix Guattari haben diesen glatten Raum, im Anschluss an Boulez, der Wüste verglichen und diejenigen, die sich darin zu bewegen wissen, als Nomaden bezeichnet, als Leute vor dem Gesetz, zwischen Staats- und Kriegsapparat.[10] Unter denen, die sich im 20. Jahrhundert mit dem Moses-Komplex beschäftigt haben, finden sich auffallend viele Exilanten, Flüchtlinge oder Migranten, Heinrich Heine im 19. Jahrhundert, und dann Schoenberg oder Sigmund Freud, Martin Buber oder Bluma Goldstein und auch Danièle Huillet und Jean-Marie Straub.[11] Sie alle verhandeln den Übergang, den ästhetische Erfahrung als Erwartung kommender Gesellschaften öffnet, zugleich auch als Begegnung mit Bedrohung und Gewalt.

Die glatte Struktur der Wahrnehmung gleichwertiger und gleichverteilter Elemente realisieren Danièle Huillet und Jean-Marie Straub im kinematographisch Räumlichen. Sie haben ihren Film *Moses und Aron* in den Abruzzen, in der Nähe von Rom, gedreht, im griechischen Amphitheater von Alba Fucense, das noch kein szenisches Theater der griechischen Polis ist, in dem aber bereits das Agonale des römischen Stadions aufscheint (Abb. 2). In dieser Arena, also buchstäblich in einem – wie es im Lateinischen hieße –, Sand-Raum, einer Wüste also, sind die Sänger und Chöre so aufgestellt und so gefilmt, dass jeder Überblick über die Anlage systematisch entzogen wird (Abb. 3–5). Der Raum entwickelt sich aus der Verbindung der einzelnen Elemente. Genau wie die Musik Schoenbergs sich aus Beziehungen unter den Tönen, nicht aus präfigurierten Harmonien entwickelt, ersetzen die filmischen Einstellungen von Huillet und Straub die Gesamtschau durch ein Netz von Relationen. Nirgends ist dieser Raum im Film durch einen Überblick, einen *establishing shot*, oder durch die raumkonstituierende Logik von Schuss-Gegenschuss Verfahren zum Beispiel gesichert.

Der Film von Huillet und Straub erhält seine ungewohnte Wirkung nicht nur durch die karge Inszenierung, sondern ist irritierend auch in seiner Synchronisation von Bild und Ton. Die Strategie, ein Nomadisches und Wüstenhaftes herzustellen, beginnt mit der ersten Einstellung auf die Figur des Moses (Abb. 6). Sie zeigt diesen von hinten, über die Schulter als Großaufnahme gefilmt, vor dem Sand, und so, dass nicht klar wird, wie sich die Musik, die dann zu hören ist, zum Körper dieses Mannes verhält. Ununterscheidbar ist, ob Klang und Sprechgesang ein Außen oder ein Inneres realisieren. Die Sänger und der Chor treten im wüsten Raum der Arena auf, sind im direkten, offensichtlich nicht nachsynchronisierten O-Ton zu hören, und dazu erklingt ein brillant aufgenommenes Orchester, das

---

10 Gilles Deleuze/Félix Guattari, „Das Glatte und das Gekerbte", in: *Tausend Plateaus. Kapitalismus und Schizophrenie II*, ed. Günther Rösch, Berlin 1992, 657–693 (= 14. Kapitel, „1440").
11 Vgl. dazu vor allem: Sigmund Freud, „Der Mann Moses und die monotheistische Religion", in: id., *Gesammelte Werke, chronologisch geordnet*, Bd. 16: Werke aus den Jahren 1932–1939, Frankfurt/Main 1981, 101–246; Bluma Goldstein, *Reinscribing Moses: Heine, Kafka, Freud, and Schoenberg in a European Wilderness*, Cambridge 1992.

jedoch nirgends sichtbar wird. Die Verfilmung der Oper ist kein Abfilmen einer bereits bestehenden Inszenierung, sondern die ästhetische Realisierung eines neuen Raums. Dieser verdankt sich der Montage einzelner und nur aufeinander bezogener filmischer und akustischer Elemente, deren synästhetische oder symphonische Wirkung niemals ganz und gar vorauszusehen ist.

Abb. 7: Danièle Huillet und Jean-Marie Straub, Moses und Aron: Einstellung aus der Serie der Himmelsbilder

Wie der akustische Raum der Oper sich erst in der Aufführung realisiert – weil er Elemente des realen Raums als Modulationen und Transformationen der aufgeschriebenen Partitur umfasst –, so entsteht auch der akustische Raum des Films *Moses und Aron* erst in der Kinoprojektion, das heißt im Hören und Sehen des Publikums. Der synthetische akustische Raum, den Huillet und Straub zusammen mit dem musikalischen Leiter Michael Gielen und dem Tonmeister Louis Hochet konstruierten, beruht auch nicht auf ausgefallenen elektroakustischen Effekten, sondern auf radikaler Reduktion der akustischen Parameter – ganz ähnlich der visuellen Dramaturgie. Während Schoenberg in seiner Eröffnung die Überblendung von Stimmen und Instrumenten zum Einklang verlangt, nehmen Straub und Huillet diesen Eindruck zunächst systematisch auseinander. Sie zerlegen und differenzieren den Klang aus, bevor sie erst am Ende der Prozessierung von menschlich und technisch erzeugten Klängen alle gleichwertig wieder zusammensetzen.

In ihrer Verfilmung der Oper, die genau deshalb als einzigartig gilt, entwickelten Straub und Huillet aufnahmetechnische Verfahren für eine Trennung aller Klangebenen und -formen. Die einzelnen Parts der Partitur wurden einzeln und ohne übergeordnetes Prinzip – der Zeit, der Stimmenhierarchien oder Priorität des Klangs vor dem Geräusch – aufgenommen, um ebenso gleichwertig wieder zusammengefügt zu werden. So wurde zuerst im Studio des Wiener ORF eine trockene, hallfreie Mono-Fassung der Orchestermusiken für den Film angefertigt, die den Sängerinnen und Sängern während ihrer Auftritte im Freien der Arena als stützende Töne über kleine Monitore, die unter den Choristen angebracht waren, zur Verfügung standen. Deren Emission durfte freilich nicht in den Empfindlichkeitsbereich der Mikrofone kommen, da es sonst Rückkopplungen gegeben hätte, die – das unterscheidet die ästhetischen Strategien der Filmproduktion von Popmusik – ausgeschlossen wurden. Auch die Solisten sangen mit winzigen Kopfhörern, um sich an der Orchestermusik orientieren zu können. Dirigent Gielen, der auf einem fahrbaren Podest stand, hatte ebenfalls einen Kopfhörer aufgesetzt „und schlug den Takt fast ohne zu hören, was gesungen wurde".[12] Damit blieb auch der verkabelte Dirigent einer unter vielen, *pars inter pares*, und nicht Herrscher über die Partitur.

Komplementär zur vielfachen Auflösung eines kollektiven akustischen Raums durch die technische Isolierung der einzelnen Mitwirkenden stellten Aufnahme und Mischung auf dem Set einen Klangraum aus verteilten Elementen her. Es ließe sich hier bereits vom Konzept eines distribuierten Netzwerks *ante letteram* sprechen. Der Gesang des Chores und der Solisten in der Arena mit allen Hall- und Nebengeräuschen – allerdings ohne signifikante Geräusche wie Vogelgezwitscher oder Flugzeuglärm – wurde mit mehreren Mikrofonen aufgenommen.[13] Toningenieur Hochet legte die Aufnahmen der Sänger und Sängerinnen während der Dreharbeiten im Amphitheater – als Live-Synchronisation – an die Studioaufnahmen an. Die Stimmen wurden damit erst auch untereinander und natürlich mit den Orchesterklängen auf dem Tonband wieder zusammengeführt. Nach den Dreharbeiten blieb, das bereits synchronisierte Material dynamisch abzumischen. Dass in einer Theaterruine im Italien der frühen siebziger Jahre die Regelmäßigkeit der Frequenz des per Kupferkabel verlegten Stroms ständig kontrolliert werden musste, bleibt Hinweis auf die anfällige und volatile

---

12 Michael Gielen, *Unbedingt Musik. Erinnerungen*, Leipzig 2005, 180.
13 Ibid., „Abbruch bei jedem Flugzeug, ja sogar bei Vogelgezwitscher".

Situation, in der hier Synchronizität etabliert wurde. In einer Rückkopplungsschlaufe von Techniken und Körpern konstruierten Huillet und Straub damit einen Klangraum, der keine vorgeschriebenen Unterteilungen kennt, sondern sich in ständiger Abhängigkeit von Umgebungen, menschlichen, unmenschlichen, musikalischen und technischen, klanglichen und geräuschhaften, ausdifferenziert. Aus dem kollektiven Raum der Oper oder des Kinos wurde über dieses Verfahren der systematischen Verwüstung dann ein vielfach vernetzter, modularer, der Leute und historische Umgebungen verbindet, ein im strengen Sinne ökologischer Raum.

Unterscheiden

Texte und künstlerische Arbeiten, die sich mit dem Moses-Komplex beschäftigen, sind fast alle in hohem Maße selbstreflexiv. Sie zeichnen sich dadurch aus, dass sie die Bedingungen der Möglichkeit untersuchen, Unterscheidungen zu treffen, die kultur- und wirklichkeitsstiftend sind und diese Unterscheidungen in ihren Verfahren zugleich erst zu establieren. Es sind ontologische Operationen im Sinne der Kulturtechnikforschung: „Jede Kultur beginnt mit der Einführung von Unterscheidungen: innen/außen, rein/unrein, heilig/profan, Sprache/Sprachlosigkeit, Signal/Rauschen. Ihre weltstiftende Kraft ist der Grund dafür, dass wir die Kultur, in der wir leben, als Wirklichkeit erleben und oft genug als die natürliche Ordnung der Dinge."[14]

Das Insistieren dieser vermeintlich natürlichen Ordnung tritt dann besonders deutlich hervor, wenn sie aufgelöst wird. Dafür steht die Situation des Lagers als Ort eines Übergangs, klassischerweise eines kriegerischen, vor dem Gesetz. Deutlich wird das zuerst in der Störung aller Verhältnisse und in der Wahrnehmung der Störungen als diffuses Unbehagen an der Kultur. Entsprechend verfolgen medienanalytische Untersuchungen, wie sich die Verlagerung der Aufmerksamkeit vom Rauschen eines Kanals, das nicht einmal richtig von einem allgemeinen Umweltgeräusch zu trennen ist, zu einem Signal und einer bevorstehenden Kommunikation verschiebt, vollzieht oder vollziehen kann.[15] Andersherum sind es genau die Störungen in der Botschaft, an der sich der Kanal als Medium der Übertragung, das normalerweise überhört wird, erst zu erkennen gibt: Das Knistern des Dornbuschs, das Kratzen einer Schallplatte oder das hör-

---

14 Bernhard Siegert, „Kulturtechnik", in: *Einführung in die Kulturwissenschaft*, hrsg. von Harun Maye/Leander Scholz, München 2011, 95–117, hier 100.
15 Vgl. Friedrich Kittler, „Signal-Rausch-Abstand", in: id.: *Draculas Vermächtnis, Technische Schriften*, Leipzig 1993, 161–181.

bare Atmen der Sänger unter der Sonne eines Amphitheaters im August machen uns darauf aufmerksam, dass Nachrichten nie aus dem Nichts oder Jenseits kommen. Jede Mitteilung ist angewiesen auf einen Kanal und seine Materialität, die die Botschaft zugleich formt und verändert. Aus einem Rauschen muss ein Verhältnis von Kanal und Botschaft unterschieden werden, aus dem Rauschen ist ein Geräusch zu destillieren, das einen, das uns angeht. Hier beginnt jede Geschichte des Exodus.

Abb. 8: Danièle Huillet und Jean-Marie Straub, *Moses und Aron:* Einstellung auf Aaron vor dem Goldenen Kalb

In diesem Sinne hört Moses aus dem Geräusch des brennenden Busches eine Stimme, die ihn mit Namen anruft: „Mose, Mose!" (Ex 3:4), und ihm befiehlt, die Schuhe auszuziehen, denn er stehe – jetzt beginnt Kommunikation – auf heiligem Boden. An dieser Stelle weist Bluma Goldstein auf die erste Verschiebung zwischen Bibel und Libretto hin: Während nach dem Buch Exodus der Bibel Gott selbst das Leiden seiner Leute, seines Volkes gesehen und gehört hat, – „ich habe gesehen das Elend meines Volks in Ägypten und habe ihr Geschrei gehört über die, so sie drängen; ich habe ihr Leid erkannt." (Ex 3:7) – ist es in Schoenbergs Libretto Moses selbst, der gesehen und gehört haben muss, was geschieht:

Du hast die Greuel gesehen, die Wahrheit
erkannt; so kannst du nicht anders mehr:
du musst dein Volk daraus befreien![16]

Nachdem also Moses zunächst selbst Rauschen und Signal unterschieden hat, oder, in ethischen Begriffen, Gewissen und Verantwortung gebildet hat, meldet sich der akustische Gott darauf zunächst als historisch bestimmter, als Gott der Väter, Gott Abrahams, Isaaks und Jakobs, und befiehlt Moses, die unterdrückten Kinder Israels aus der Knechtschaft des Pharao zu befreien und ins Gelobte Land zu führen. Daraufhin fragt Moses, wie er den Israeliten erklären solle, wer der Gott sei, der Befreiung verspricht: „Da werden sie mich fragen: wie heisst er? Was soll ich ihnen darauf sagen? Da antwortete Gott dem Mose: Ich bin der ‚ich-bin-da'". (Ex 3:15) In der Lutherübersetzung heißt es: „Ich werde sein, der ich sein werde". Es sind wiederum rekursive Formeln, in deren Mitte eine Differenz gesetzt ist. Häretischer ließe sich das ausdrücken als ein Gottesbegriff, der selbst erst nach einer Einführung von Differenz verlangt, wie Gregory Bateson das für einen kybernetischen formuliert hat: Götter seien „entities, being fictitious persons, more or less endowed with cybernetic and circuit characteristics",[17] die den Menschen helfen, kurzfristige Intentionen in langfristige kulturelle Prozesse zu übersetzen. Götter schließen kurz, was Menschen, um zu handeln, wieder unterscheiden müssen. Jeder Exodus setzt diesen Prozess der Differenzierung voraus. Damit daraus die Möglichkeit einer Transition oder Transgression wird, müssen die Differenzen jedoch in ihrer Gleichwertigkeit offengehalten werden. Regeln der Produktion dürfen noch nicht zum Gesetz geworden sein. Und ökologisches Denken setzt da ein, wo das Verhältnis von Figur und Grund, von Objekt und Umwelt wieder umkippen kann, wo also Gottes Stimme sich ins Rauschen einer verwüsteten Umgebung rückübersetzt. Kulturell, machtpolitisch und eben auch ästhetisch heißt das, die Wahrnehmung von Dingen und Figuren nicht mehr vor jener der Verbindungen, Verhältnisse oder Kanäle zu priorisieren. Sean Cubitt hat das epistemologisch im Sinne einer medienökologischen Analyse beschrieben:

The microcosmic density of ecosystems, human societies and their interweaving moves towards increasing mutual mediation of all lives, all deaths. The assertion that the world is composed of things is based on the rejection of this connectedness. Such an ontology of

---

16 Bluma Goldstein, „Schoenberg's Moses und Aron. A Vanishing Biblical Nation", in: *Political and Religious Ideas in the Works of Arnold Schoenberg*, ed. Charlotte M. Cross/Russell A. Berman, New York 2000, 159–192, hier 159.
17 Gregory Bateson, „Letter to Warren McCulloch, 20.12. 1967", in: id., *They threw God out of the garden: letters from Gregory Bateson to Philip Wylie and Warren McCulloch*, CoEvolution Quarterly, 32 (Winter), 1982, 62–67, hier 65.

objects would be merely metaphysical were it not for the fact that it describes so accurately the way we see and understand the world. The question is how we, especially in the West, came to see the world this way.[18]

Die Befreiung aus der Sklaverei und aus den Ketten Ägyptens, den der Exodus realisiert, wäre weiterzutreiben als Anerkennung einer mikrokosmischen Verkettung aller Dinge der Welt, wie wir sie als Geräusche wahrnehmen können. Straub und Huillet haben genau das als kommunistische Wahrnehmung entworfen.

Störungen

Sowohl Schoenbergs Oper als auch Straub/Huillets Film führen in die Wahrnehmung einer Umgebung, in der Töne und bildliche Elemente gleichmäßig verteilt sind, in eine neue gesellschaftliche Lage, deren rechtmäßige Verfassung noch nicht ausgehandelt wurde. Beide Werke führen buchstäblich „vor das Gesetz", wie es der Musikwissenschaftler Matthias Schmidt für die Komposition der Oper formuliert hat.[19] Beide Werke entziehen uns systematisch den bekannten Boden der Wahrnehmung, den gewohnten Hörraum, führen uns in ein Unbestimmtes und fordern uns auf, selbst Unterscheidungen zu setzen, aus dem Unbekannten heraus, ins Blaue. Zuerst wäre das die Setzung der Differenz zwischen Rauschen und Signal, die uns aufruft, Leute, die unterdrückt sind, keinen Ort, keinen Platz, kein Lager haben und noch nicht einmal ein Volk sind, zu retten. Dann aber verlangt das Exodusmotiv im 20. Jahrhundert auch, Signale immer wieder auf ihr Rauschen zu beziehen.

Systematisch entzieht der Film *Moses und Aron* einen übersichtlichen Raum des Sehens. Das Bilderverbot, das im Zentrum der mosaischen Verhandlungen um eine neue Gesellschaft und ein neues Gesetz steht, strukturiert den Exodus. Es stellt uns auf unbekannten, nicht-menschlichen und deshalb „heiligen" Boden, konfrontiert uns mit unerhörten Klängen und ungesehenen Einstellungen. Die Bilder von Straub und Huillet zeigen Landschaften, Licht und Bewegung, liefern jedoch keine hierarchisch organisierten Blickstrukturen. Vor allem geben oder gestatten die Einstellungen und ihre Montage keinen Überblick. Sie wirken vielmehr als Aufforderung, sich selbst zu orientieren.

---

18 Sean Cubitt, *Finite Media, Environmental Implications of Digital Technologies*, Durham/London 2017, 4.
19 Matthias Schmidt, „Vor dem Gesetz. Zur religiösen Dimension eines musikalischen Begriffs bei Schönberg", in: *Arnold Schönberg und sein Gott. Bericht zum Symposium 26.–29. Juni 2002*, hrsg. von Christian Meyer, Wien 2003, 299–310.

Insofern ist die erste Szene des Films eine Anrufung aus dem Dornbusch in doppeltem Sinne: Einmal ist Moses' Berufung dargestellt, das heißt die Situation, in der er herausgefordert ist, zu unterscheiden, einen Anruf zu vernehmen, Verantwortung zu übernehmen, ein Volk zu befreien. Zum Zweiten aber werden wir, Zuhörer und Zuschauerinnen, selbst konfrontiert mit einem Kino als Dornbusch, einem rauschenden Klang und unkonventionellen Einstellungen, die uns, parallel zu Moses, zwingen, uns dazu zu entscheiden, in dieser Wüste der Bilder und Töne eine Botschaft zu hören, zu sehen, anzunehmen. Botschaften kommen aus dem Diesseits, aber sie müssen relativiert werden, in Beziehung gesetzt zum Übertragungsapparat und zu den Umwelten, die sie ermöglichen.

Der Film von Huillet und Straub wird die erste Sequenz der Anrufung, wie alle anderen, in eine sehr konkrete jedoch historisch geschichtete Umgebung setzen, einen historisch und herrschaftsgeladenen Zwischenraum: die Abruzzen, einer Gegend der Armut mitten im Europa der siebziger Jahre. Wo Schoenberg den Raum der biblischen Erzählung zunehmend zu einer asketischen Anordnung von Reinheit und reinen Gedanken destillieren will, der von der Begleitung aller Vorstellungen befreit sein muss, führen Straub und Huillet den Konflikt zurück in eine Geschichtlichkeit des Physischen, die freilich auch im Sinne Schoenbergs stets und musikalisch mitschwingen muss.

Diese Herausforderung nehmen Straub und Huillet exakt an der Stelle an, an der es in der Oper um die Produktion eines Bildes geht, das nicht einfach nur repräsentieren, sondern Zeugenschaft für die Anwesenheit Gottes geben soll: die Bildung des Goldenen Kalbs. In den Szenen der Verwandlung von Volksvermögen in eine goldene Statue und dann in der Darstellung des Tanzes und der Opferriten folgen sie ganz entschieden nicht mehr den Anweisungen Schoenbergs. Wo Schoenberg hoffte, seine Visionen möglicherweise „mit modernen Mitteln als Suggestionen ausführen"[20] zu lassen – und er dachte konkret an Kinolösungen und elektronische Klangerzeugung – analysieren Straub und Huillet Suggestibilität selbst mit filmischen Mitteln. In ihrer Montage des Films nehmen sie damit einerseits die Position Arons gegen Moses ein, nämlich die Medialität der Bilder auch unter dem Monotheismus und seinem kontrollierenden Bilderverbot für Augen und Ohren sichtbar werden zu lassen, anstatt einen reinen Geist anzunehmen, der sich unter Menschen nicht erweisen lässt. Andererseits stärken sie die Position Moses' gegen Aron, dass nämlich Bilder niemals Ersatz sind, niemals nur Repräsentation, Metapher oder Gotteszeichen, sondern stets unmittelbar

---

20 Arnold Schoenberg, „Brief an Herrmann Scherchen vom 16.1.1950", in: id., *Moses und Aron, Oper in 3 Akten. Entstehungsgeschichte, Texte und Textentwürfe zum Oratorium und zur Oper*, hrsg. von Christian Martin Schmidt, Mainz 1998, 17.

stratifizierende Machtstruktur, der sich nur Nomaden, unüberwindlich in der „Wunschlosigkeit der Wüste"[21], entziehen können. Im Film *Moses und Aron* wird solch ein verwüstetes Bild realisiert durch ein Stück leeren Films. Welche Art der Leere das ist, ist nicht einfach zu bestimmen. Licht selbst, Bedingung, Rauschen und Kanal des Kinos, werden hier in Szene gesetzt. Etwas strahlt, bevor das Gold als Kalb glänzende Form wird. Etwas wird „alltäglich sichtbar" (Takt 196), wie Aron meint, bevor er den ganzen Zauber der Macht der Götter zuschlägt.

„Bringt Gold herbei", singt Aron. Er übernimmt in diesem Moment die Führung des verzweifelten Volks und gibt der populären Forderung nach einer verlässlichen und zuverlässigen Vorstellung und Vorstellbarkeit nach, „ihr sollt glücklich werden" (Takt 200 ff). Dann folgt im Film jener Schnitt ins Blaue, der auf den ersten Blick und in alten Kopien wie Blankfilm, Weißbild, aussieht und von Danièle Huillet in ihrem Protokoll des Films auch so bezeichnet ist; „Einstellung 50: Weißfilm".[22] Die Transformation von Immateriellem ins Materielle und zurück, von Bewegung in Licht, von Stoff in Form zeigt sich, während der Chor aus dem Off zu hören ist, als fast dreiminütiger bilderloser Film auf der Leinwand. Eigentlich aber ist diese Einstellung vielmehr ein Bild des Lichts selbst, Licht gefilmt unter italienischer Sonne, das auf den neuen DVD-Editionen tatsächlich wie ein Bild in der Serie der Himmelsbilder des Films bläulich schimmert (Abb. 7). Ein Bild ohne Motiv, Struktur oder Figuren ist im Kino jedoch immer noch ein Lichtbild, kein Nichts. Kinolicht sucht sich immer einen Ort diesseits der Transzendenz.

In diesem Licht bildet sich das Volk als Soziales. Es ist glücklich, dass endlich etwas sichtbar werden soll. Der Chor verfällt in einen Dreivierteltakt, fühlt „durch die leibliche Sichtbarkeit, Gegenwart" seine „Sicherheit verbürgt" und walzt sich durch das Glück, mitzuwirken an der Konstruktion vorstellbarer Götter und Welten. Hier lässt Schoenberg den Takt ins Gleiten kommen. Zuerst wird „Juble Israel", Takt 250, staatstragend, im Viervierteltakt gekerbt, aber ab Takt 245 wechselt die Musik phasenweise von einem Takt zum nächsten zwischen zweiviertel, dreiviertel und viertviertel, sodass das Maß ins „lisse", ins Ungekerbte, Glatte, Unberechenbare der Klangschichten übergeht. Diesem Überschwang und der konstatierten Sicherheit entziehen Straub und Huillet das figürliche Bild und damit den Grund. Sie lassen das Volk noch eine Weile vor dem Gesetz im glatten Raum der Wünsche gleiten, bis alles mit dem letzten Ausruf „Juble, freue dich Israel" (Takte 301–307) wieder im gekerbten Raum und also zum Viervierteltakt

---

21 Danièle Huillet, „Moses und Aron. Das Drehbuch. Beschreibungen – Texte – Photogramme, redigiert und eingerichtet für den Druck von Helmut Färber", in: *Filmkritik*, 221/222, 1975, 203–252, hier 251.
22 Ibid., 230.

geordnet wird. Dann steht mit einem wunderbar offenen Akkord und einem weiteren Beckenschlag, das Goldene Kalb materiell, wirklich, unmetaphorisch, selbst und ganz authentisch als kleine Statue auf einem Sockel im Bild, immer noch als Lichtbild freilich. Wenn Aron, halbnah, von unten als „Quasi Recit", wie Schoenberg anweist, in die Kamera singt: „Dieses Bild bezeugt, daß in allem, was ist, ein Gott lebt" (Takt 308–310), steht hinter ihm das Kalb, in gleißendem Goldschein, vor dem jetzt enorm azurblauen Himmel der Abruzzen und sprengt jegliche Farbdramaturgie und Oberflächenstruktur des bisherigen Films (Abb. 8). Wie ein Panzer liegt metallisches Licht über dieser einen Szene und kehrt den Blick gegen das Auge. Das Wort „Bild" ist schon in Schoenbergs Komposition auf zwei Töne, genauer, auf ein Intervall gesetzt, auf den Sprung vom d' auf das fis, also –8 Halbtöne, und initiiert damit eine Schichtung im Akustischen, eine Differenz und Differenzierung, die die Montage im Visuellen dann durchsetzt.

Wenn sich der Film *Moses und Aron* im Akustischen aller seiner Tonaufnahmen und -mischungen erst im Kino realisiert, gewinnt dasselbe für das Visuelle in der Szene des Weiß- oder Blankfilms noch einen anderen Aspekt: Mit der Projektion von hellem Licht wird die Gemeinde der Kinogänger selbst für einander sichtbar – eine praktische Analyse dessen, was in der frühen Kinotheorie zum Teil pathetisch als Kollektiv im Dunkel der Projektion beschworen wurde. Das vermeintlich Kollektive des Kinos zerfällt hier wieder in eine Vielheit von Partikularitäten, die Gesamtheit wird zum Modularisierten. Der Raum der Wahrnehmung wird zu einem Ensemble von Potentialqualitäten, die erst noch realisiert werden müssen – und zwar durch jede und jeden, der bereit ist, in einem unübersichtlichen Geräusch der Welt einen Anruf als Aufruf zu hören.

In diesem Sinne führen Huillet und Straub die Bildung des Goldenen Kalbs, einem Lichtbild im strengen Sinne, und die Bildung eines Volkes als Prozess ästhetischer Verräumlichung riskant zusammen. Ohne Führer, ohne Sonne, ohne Bild allein gelassen, formiert sich das Volk, zugleich allerdings stagniert der Exodus. Als Moses im Film schließlich vom Berg Sinai zurückkehrt und das goldene Idol sieht, ruft er – bezeichnenderweise aus dem Off des Films, das ja zugleich auf eine Präsenz jenseits der Leinwand und auf die Anwesenheit der Leute im Kinosaal selbst verweist – „Vergeh, du Abbild des Unvermögens, das Grenzenlose in ein Bild zu fassen!" (II. Akt, Takt 980–982). Während es bei Schoenberg schlicht heißt: „Das Goldene Kalb vergeht, das Volk weicht zurück und verschwindet rasch von der Bühne", womit das Verschwinden von Volk und Abbildungsfunktion in ein und demselben Prozess gefasst wäre, treiben Straub und Huillet die Anweisung wiederum filmisch und wahrnehmungsanalytisch weiter in eine konkrete Wahrnehmungsform, dann eine dingliche Realität und ihre filmische Realisierung: Sie lassen exakt auf das „Vergeh!" hin durch eine schnelle Aufblende das Bild des Kalbs wieder im grellen Weiß des reinen Lichts auf der Leinwand verschwinden, so dass sich für eine kurze Dauer das Bild des Kalbs und das Nachbild, das sich mit dem blendenden Weißfilm auf der Netzhaut zeigt, ununterscheidbar vermischen (Abb. 9): ein visueller Anruf mithin, den Schrecken des Grenzenlosen als Bedingung jeder Ordnung des Sehens wahrzunehmen. Wenn sie das Licht des Kinos und die optische Augentäuschung mit dem Bild der Leinwand verbinden, verweisen Straub und Huillet in einer aufklärerischen Geste auf die Macht, die Medien selbst jenseits aller Figürlichkeit unwillkürlich auf Körper ausüben. Aufklärung wird durch Blendung hergestellt, das wäre die Dialektik des Verfahrens.[23]

Aber dann setzen Huillet und Straub gegen die Einschübe von Schwarz- und Weißfilm die extreme Materialität der Dinge, wie sie von Kamera und Tonband aufgenommen und übertragen werden. Die nächste Einstellung nämlich zeigt in einer Totalen in extrem kurzer Brennweite im Hintergrund die hohen Berge, im Vordergrund die Arena, in der eine große Tierherde – Esel, Ochsen und ein sehr schönes weißes Kamel – durch ihre eigentümlichen und eigensinnigen Bewegungen den Film als spezifische Realitätsform zu sehen geben (Abb. 10). Dazu sind die Töne, das Schnauben und Scharren der Tiere unter die Bilder und unter die Musik gelegt. Eine doppelte oder sogar dreifache Referentialität spaltet und transformiert das Wahrnehmungsbild: „Dieses Bild", von dem Aron singt, könnte an dieser Stelle sowohl das Goldene Kalb sein als auch das weiße Strahlen, das so deutlich aus dem farblichen und textuellen Rahmen des Filmes fällt, und ebenso könnte der Hinweis auf „dieses Bild" die sehr lebendige Einstellung mit den wirklichen Tieren ankündigen. Arons gewitzter Hinweis auf ein Bild als eine changierende Wahrnehmung, das heißt als changierende Aufmerksamkeit für die Sinnlichkeit der Dinge, setzt dem Sehen als metaphorischem oder signifizierenden einen entschiedenen Widerstand entgegen. Alle einfach ikonologischen und ikonoklastischen Kontexte werden damit zerrissen, um das Gewebe der Wirklichkeit durch das Kino sichtbar zu machen.

Die spezifische Realität und Geschichtlichkeit der Bilder wird in der folgenden Einstellung durch eine historische und eine historisierende Schicht gebrochen. Durch ein Tor des Theaters treiben Hirten, die in archaisierenden Kostümen auftreten, weitere Tiere, Schafherden und Ochsen in die Arena, mit Bewegungen, die kulturtechnisch eine jahrtausendalte Geschichte aufrufen. Diese historischen Schichten machen deutlich, dass es Straub und Huillet nicht um Datierungen geht, sondern darum, Abstände von historischen Wirklichkeiten zu ermessen.

---

23 Diese Verkörperung der Bildgewalt ist eine interessante Variante der biblischen Erzählung, in der Moses das Kalb, nachdem er die Tafeln zerbrochen hat, im Feuer schmilzt, zu Pulver zermalmt, in Wasser auflöst und den Kindern Israel zu trinken gibt. In der monotheistisch bildlosen Welt tauchen magische Praktiken auf. Vgl. Ex 32:20.

Diese Einstellung führt Kultur- und Naturgeschichten zusammen an aufgenommenen Gesten, Spuren und Stimmen. An dieser Stelle im Film wird die Schoenberg'sche Musik zum zweiten Mal deutlich von Geräuschen überlagert, diesmal von vielfältigen Tiergeräuschen, die sich aber am Ende des langen Orchestersatzes – der extreme und unerhörte Glissandi gegen den orientalisierenden Rhythmus setzt – mit Instrumenten, mit Klavier und Schlagzeug, Bläsern und Streichern mischen: Ochsen und Kontrafagott vermischen sich in ihren Klangfarben, wie zuvor die Stimme aus dem Dornbusch eine aus Instrumenten und Menschenstimmen gemischte war.

In dieser Szene mit den aufgetriebenen Herden, in der Bild und Ton, wie Danièle Huillet schreibt, auf den Rhythmus aus der Einstellung warteten,[24] ergeht eine aus Tierstimmen und Instrumenten synthetisierte Anrufung, die aber nicht mehr aus dem Jenseits angenommen wird, aus der Transzendenz, sondern als Anrufung aus dem Leben und seiner konkreten Klangfarbenmischung von Wesen, Dingen, Instrumenten und vermutlich von Aufzeichnungsmaschinen. An dieser Einstellung werden die Zuschauenden, wir, selbst der Probe unterzogen, zu unterscheiden. Der Anruf aus dem Dornbusch ergeht als ästhetische Aufforderung, zu erkennen, und das heißt, nicht an Stimmen oder Götter zu denken, sondern an lebendige Verhältnisse. Dazu brauchen wir Zeit, denn dieses hörende Unterscheiden ist ein rekursiver Prozess, der dauert. Die filmische Strategie hat Danièle Huillet sehr schön formuliert als „dem Leben seine Zeit geben", mit der sie genau die andauernden und nicht linearen Prozesse des Erkennens unter Medienbedingungen beschreibt. In der Verfilmung wird insistierend die Frage nach dem, was ein Bild sei, ersetzt durch die Frage, wie ein Bild die Wahrnehmung vom Material her transformiert, so dass historische und soziale Schichten sichtbar werden. Hier lässt sich noch Sean Cubitts Aufforderung anführen, Aufmerksamkeit für „microcosmic densities" im Kino zu provozieren, die Aufmerksamkeit für Beziehungen, Verhältnisse, Verbindungen und Übertragungen, die in westlichen Konventionen von der Wahrnehmung der Figuren verdeckt bleiben.

---

24 Danièle Huillet, „Appunti sul giornale di lavorazione di Gregory", in: *Filmkritik*, 225, 9/1975, 398–419, hier 418.

Abb. 9: Danièle Huillet und Jean-Marie Straub, *Moses und Aron:* Einstellung auf das vergehende Kalb

In einem bekannten Kommentar zu den Filmen von Danièle Huillet und Jean-Marie Straub kommt Gilles Deleuze, wenn er deren Kunst als Widerstandsakt beschreibt, auf das Fehlen des Volkes zu sprechen. Ausgehend von einer Bemerkung Paul Klees ‚Das Volk fehlt', erklärt er Studierenden der Pariser Filmhochschule: „Das Volk fehlt und fehlt gleichzeitig nicht. Das Volk fehlt: das will heißen, daß diese grundlegende Affinität zwischen dem Kunstwerk und einem Volk, das noch nicht existiert, nicht klar ist und nie klar sein wird. Es gibt kein Kunstwerk, das sich nicht an ein Volk wendet, das noch nicht existiert."[25] Kunst also hätte zugleich das hervorzurufen, was sie erst zur Wahrnehmung macht. Das Volk wäre zunächst eine konstitutive Leerstelle, die aufmerksam macht auf die zirkulär-kausale Produktion von kultureller Wahrnehmung. Gegenwärtige Formen der Migration lassen sich vielfältig in Begriffen des Ökologischen fassen. „Ecological crisis [...] is not the fault of individuals, but of the communicative systems, most of all the tyranny of the economy, of money as the dominant medium of the

---

25 Gilles Deleuze, „Was ist ein Schöpfungsakt?", in: id., *Schizophrenie und Gesellschaft: Texte und Gespräche 1975–1995*, Frankfurt/Main 2005, 298–308, hier 308.

twenty-first century intercourse between humans and the world."²⁶ Exodus heißt in diesem Kontext, Mikroverbindungen wahrzunehmen. Die Herausforderung an das Kino wäre, Sehen und Hören so zu differenzieren, dass alle Migrationen und Fluchtbewegungen der Leute als Exodus aus einem Gewaltzusammenhang wahrnehmbar werden.

Abb. 10: Danièle Huillet und Jean-Marie Straub, *Moses und Aron:* Einstellung der Herde mit dem weißen Kamel

---

26 Cubitt, *Finite Media* (wie in Anm. 13), 7.

Bibliography

Abrams, Daniel. "From Germany to Spain: Numerology as a Mystical Technique", in: *Journal of Jewish Studies*, 47, 1996, 85–101.

Abrams, Daniel/Ta-Shema, Israel, eds. *Sefer Gematriot of R. Judah the Pious: Facsimile Edition of a Unique Manuscript*, Los Angeles 1998 [in Hebrew].

Abrams, Daniel. *Kabbalistic Manuscripts and Textual Theory: Methodologies of Textual Scholarship and Editorial Practice in the Study of Jewish Mysticism*, Jerusalem/Los Angeles 2010.

Académie des inscriptions et belles lettres. *Corpus Inscriptionum Semiticarum (CIS)*, pars II: *Inscriptiones Aramaicas continens*, Paris 1902.

Albertz, Rainer. *Religionsgeschichte Israels in alttestamentlicher Zeit*, vol. 1: *Von den Anfängen bis zum Ende der Königszeit*, Göttingen 1992 (ATD Erg. 8/1).

Albertz, Rainer. *History of Israelite Religion in the Old Testament Period*, vol. 2: *From the Exile to the Maccabees*, Louisville 1994.

Albrecht, Karl-Dieter. *Rechtsprobleme in den Freilassungen der Böotier, Phoker, Dorier, Ost- und Westlokrer, untersucht mit besonderer Berücksichtigung der gemeinschaftlich vorgenommenen Freilassungsakte*, Paderborn 1978 (Rechts- und staatswissenschaftliche Veröffentlichungen der Görres-Gesellschaft, N.F. 26).

Allen, Terry. "Byzantine sources for the 'Jāmi al-Tawārīkh' of Rashīd al-Dīn", in: *Ars Orientalis*, 15, 1985, 121–136.

Al-Otaibi, Fahad Mutlaq. *From Nabataea to Roman Arabia: Acquisition or Conquest*, Oxford 2011.

Al-Hariri, *Al-Maqāmāt al-Ḥarīrīyah*, illustrated by Yahya ibn Mahmud Al-Wasiti, London 2003 (facsimile edition).

Ambrose, Saint. *'On the Mysteries' and the Treatise, 'On the Sacraments', by an Unknown Author*, trans. Tim Thompson, edited by J. H. Srawley, New York 1919 (Translations of Christian Literature, ser. 3, Liturgical Texts).

Ameisenowa, Zofia. "The Tree of Life in Jewish Iconography", in: *Journal of the Warburg Institute*, 2, no. 4, 1939, 326–345.

Ameisenowa, Zofia. "Die hebräische Sammelhandschrift Add. 11639 des British Museum", in: *Wiener Jahrbuch für Kunstgeschichte*, 24, 1971, 10–48.

Amitai, Reuven. Il–Khanids: "Dynastic History", in: *Encyclopaedia Iranica*, vol. 12, fasc. 6, 645–654.

Anastasius of Sinai. "Collection I": *Tales of the Sinai Fathers, (Diegemata paterika); Selections from Collection II: Edifying Tales (Diegemata steriktika)*, trans. by Daniel F. Caner, in: History and Hagiography from the Late Antique Sinai, Liverpool 2010 (Translated Texts for Historians, 53), 172–199.

Andreae, Bernard/Settis, Salvatore, eds. *Colloquio sul reimpiego dei sarcofagi romani nel medioevo*, conference proceedings (Pisa, Scuola Normale Superiore, 1982), Marburg 1984.

Assmann, Jan. *Moses der Ägypter. Entzifferung einer Gedächtnisspur*, München/Wien 1998.

Assmann, Jan. *Die mosaische Unterscheidung: oder der Preis des Monotheismus*, München/Wien 2003.

Assmann, Jan. "Monotheismus und Gewalt. Eine Auseinandersetzung mit Rolf Schieders Kritik an 'Moses der Ägypter'", in: *Die Gewalt des einen Gottes. Die Monotheismus-Debatte zwischen Jan Assmann, Micha Brumlik, Rolf Schieder, Peter Sloterdijk und anderen*, edited by Rolf Schieder, Berlin 2014, 36–55.

Assmann, Jan. *Exodus. Die Revolution der Alten Welt*, München 2015.

Attias, Jean-Christophe/Hoog, Anne Hélène, eds. *Moïse. Figures d'un prophète*, exhibition catalogue (Musée d'Art et d'Histoire du Judaïsme, Paris), Paris 2015.

Bachmann-Medick, Doris. *Cultural Turns. Neuorientierungen in den Kulturwissenschaften*, Reinbek 2006.

Baert, Barbara. "Marble and the Sea or Echo Emerging (A Ricercar)", in: *Espacio, tiempo y forma*, ser. VII, Historia del arte, 5 (2017), 35–54.

Banterle, Gabriele, ed. and trans. *Delle varie eresie, San Filastrio di Brescia; Trattati, San Gaudenzio di Brescia*, Milan/Rome 1991 (Scrittori dell'area Santambrosiana, 2).

Barry, Fabio. "Walking on Water: Cosmic Floors in Antiquity and the Middle Ages", in: *The Art Bulletin*, 89 (4), 2007, 637–656.

Barry, Fabio. *Painting in Stone: The Symbolism of Colored Marbles in the Visual Arts and Literature from Antiquity until the Enlightenment*, PhD thesis, Columbia University, New York 2011.

Bateson, Gregory. "Letter to Warren McCulloch, 20.12. 1967", in: id. *They Threw God out of the Garden: Letters from Gregory Bateson to Philip Wylie and Warren McCulloch*, CoEvolution Quarterly, 32 (Winter), 1982, 62–67.

Baumgarten, Elisheva/Mazo Karras, Ruth/Mesler, Katelyn, eds. *Entangled Histories: Knowledge, Authority, and Jewish Culture in the Thirteenth Century*, Philadelphia 2017.

Baur, P.V.C./Rostovtzeff, Michael I. *The Excavations at Dura-Europos, Conducted by Yale University and the French Academy of Inscriptions and Letters. Preliminary Report of Second Season of Work*, New Haven/CT 1931.

Beal, Jane, ed. *Illuminating Moses: A History of Reception from Exodus to the Renaissance*, Leiden et al. 2014 (Commentaria, 4).

Becker, Erich. "Protest gegen den Kaiserkult und Verherrlichung des Sieges am Pons Milvius in der altchristlichen Kunst der konstantinischen Zeit", in: *Konstantin der Grosse und seine Zeit*, edited by Franz J. Dölger, Freiburg im Breisgau 1913 (Römische Quartalschrift für christliche Altertumskunde und Kirchengeschichte, supp. 19), 155–190.

Beer, Eduard Friedrich Ferdinand. *Inscriptiones Veteres litteris et lingua hucusque incognitis ad Montem Sinai magno numero servatae quas Pocock, Niebuhr,... aliique descripserunt*, Leipzig 1840.

Beit–Arié, Malachi. "The Making of the 'Miscellany'", in: *The North French Hebrew Miscellany: British Library Add. MS 11639*, edited by Jeremy Schonfield, London 2003, 62–64.

Ben-Amos, Dan. "Talmudic Tall Tales", in: *Folklore Today: A Festschrift for Richard M. Dorson*, ed. Linda Degh/Henry Glassie/Felix Oinas, Bloomington/IN 1976, 25–43.

Ben Eliezer, Tobias. *Lekah Tov*, edited by Solomon Buber, Jerusalem 1960 (first published Vilna 1880).

Berger, Michael S. "Toward a New Understanding of Halevi's Kuzari", in: *The Journal of Religion*, 72, 1992, 201–211.

Berlin, Adele. "Interpreting Torah Traditions in Psalm 105", in: *Jewish Biblical Interpretation and Cultural Exchange. Comparative Exegesis in Context*, edited by Natalie B. Dohrmann/David Stern, Philadelphia 2008, 20–36.
Beuken, Willem A. *Jesaja 1–12*, Freiburg/Basel/Wien 2003 (Herders theologischer Kommentar zum Alten Testament).
Bialik, Hayyim Nahman. *Poems*, Tel Aviv 1973 [in Hebrew].
Bieberstein, Klaus. "'Eine Abbildung des an sich Unräumlichen im Raume'. Mythischer Raum und mythische Zeit im Symbolsystem Jerusalems", in: *Communio*, 41, 2012, 522–534, 537–538.
Birkhan, Helmut. *Geschichte der altdeutschen Literatur im Licht ausgewählter Texte*, Teil II: *Mittelhochdeutsche vor- und frühhöfische Literatur*, Wien 2002.
Blair, Sheila. *A Compendium of Chronicles*, London 1995.
Blair, Sheila. "Patterns of Patronage and Production in Ilkhanid Iran. The Case of Rashid al-Din", in: *The Court of the Il-Khans, 1290–1340*, edited by Julian Raby/Teresa Fitzherbert, Oxford 1996, 39–62.
Blair, Sheila. "Calligraphers, Illuminators, and Painters in the Ilkhanid Scriptorium", in: *Beyond the Legacy of Genghis Khan*, edited by Linda Komaroff, Leiden/Boston 2006, 167–182.
Blenkinsopp, Joseph. *Isaiah 1–39. A New Translation with Introduction and Commentary*, New York et al. 2000.
Blidstein, Gerald J. *The Death of Moses: Readings in Midrash*, Alon Shvut/Israel 2008 [in Hebrew].
Blinn, Hans-Jürgen. *Die Altdeutsche Exodus. Strukturuntersuchungen zur Zahlenkomposition und Zahlensymbolik*, Amsterdam 1974.
Boehrer, Stephen L. *Gaudentius of Brescia: Sermons and Letters*, PhD thesis, The Catholic University of America, Washington DC 1965 (Studies in Sacred Theology, 2nd series 165).
Böttrich, Christfried/Ego, Beate/Eißler, Friedmann. *Mose in Judentum, Christentum und Islam*, Göttingen 2010.
Borger, Rykle. *Die Inschriften Asarhaddons, Königs von Assyrien*, Graz 1956 (Archiv für Orientforschung, Beih. 9).
Borghini, Gabriele, ed. *Marmi antichi*, Rome 2001 (Materiali della cultura artistica, 1).
Borselli, Camillo. "Gli scavi nella chiesa inferiore di S. Afra e la ecclesia Sancti Faustini ad sanguinem", in: *Commentari dell'Ateneo di Brescia*, 154, 1955 [1956], 71–86.
Borselli, Camillo. "Gli scavi nella chiesa inferiore di S. Afra", in: *Miscellanea di studi bresciani sull'alto medioevo*, edited by the Comitato bresciano per l'ottavo congresso internazionale dell'arte dell'alto medioevo, Brescia 1959, table II.
Botti, Andrea/Gomez Serito, Maurizio. *Pietre bresciane: il manuale del marmo e del porfido bresciano*, Roccafranca 2005.
Boulez, Pierre. *Arnold Schoenberg, Moses und Aron*, recorded in West Ham Central Mission, London, November 30th and December 3rd, 5th and 6th, 1974, Sony Classical 1993 (Audio-CD).
Bowersock, Glenn Warren. *Roman Arabia*, Cambridge, MA 1983.
Bradley, Mark. "Colour and Marble in Early Imperial Rome", in: *The Cambridge Classical Journal*, 52, 2006, 1–22.
Branham, Joan. "Sacred Space under Erasure in Ancient Synagogues and Early Churches", in: *Art Bulletin*, 74 (3), 1992, 384–386.

Brilliant, Richard. *Visual Narratives: Storytelling in Roman and Etruscan Art,* Ithaca/NY 1984.
Brin, Gershon. "An Inquiry into the Commentaries to the Torah of R. Judah the Pious", in: *Sinai,* 88, 1980, 1–17 [in Hebrew].
Brin, Gershon. "Linguistic Inquiries into Judah the Pious' Commentary to the Torah", in: *Leshonenu,* 44, 1980, 314–315 [in Hebrew].
Brin, Gershon. "Studies in R. Judah the Pious' Exegesis to the Pentateuch", in: *Teudah 3 = Studies in Talmudic Literature in Post-Biblical Hebrew and in Biblical Exegesis,* edited by Mordechai A. Friedman/Abraham. Tal/Gershon Brin, Tel Aviv 1983, 215–226 [in Hebrew].
Brinker von der Heyde, Claudia. "Der implizite Autor als (Re)creator: Legitimations- und Erzählstrategien im Schöpfungsbericht der 'Wiener Genesis'", in: *Gottes Werk und Adams Beitrag. Formen der Interaktion zwischen Mensch und Gott im Mittelalter,* edited by Thomas Honegger/Gerlinde Huber–Rebenich/Volker Leppin, Berlin 2014, 313–325.
Brockmeyer, Norbert. *Antike Sklaverei,* Darmstadt 1979 (Erträge der Forschung, 116).
Brosh, Naʿama with Rachel Milstein. *Biblical Stories in Islamic Painting,* exhibition catalogue (The Israel Museum, Jerusalem), Jerusalem 1991.
Bruni, Giancarlo. *Pasqua primavera della storia: teologia del tempo nei testi omiletici di Gaudenzio di Brescia,* Rome 2000 (Scripta Pontificiae Facultatis Theologicae "Marianum", 55).
Buber, Solomon, ed. Midrash *Tanchuma,* Vilna 1885, 2 vols.
Bugini, Roberto/Folli, Luisa. "Sull'uso di marmi colorati antichi in Lombardia (Italia settentrionale)", in: *Marmora: An International Journal for Archaeology, History and Archaeometry of Marble and Stones,* 1, 2005, 145–168.
Burckhardt, John Lewis. *Travels in Syria and the Holy Land,* London 1822.
Busse, Heribert. "Jerusalem in the Story of Muhammad's Night Journey and Ascension", in: *Jerusalem Studies in Arabic and Islam,* 14, 1991, 1–40.
Campbell, Patricia J./MacKinnon, Aran/Stevens, Christy R., eds. *An Introduction to Global Studies,* Chichester et al. 2010.
Caner, Daniel F., ed. *History and Hagiography from the Late Antique Sinai,* Liverpool 2010 (Translated Texts for Historians, 53).
Carmi, T., ed. *The Penguin Book of Hebrew Verse,* Harmondsworth/Middlesex et al. 1981.
Cartlidge, David R. /Elliot, J. Keith. *Art and the Christian Apocrypha,* London/New York 2001.
Clayton, Robert. *A Journal from Grand Cairo to Mount Sinai, and back again. Translated from a manuscript, written by the Prefetto of Egypt,* London 1753.
Coburn Soper, Alexander. "The Latin Style on Christian Sarcophagi of the Early Fourth Century", in: *The Art Bulletin,* 19 (2), 1937, 148–202.
Cohen, Mordechai Z./Berlin, Adele, eds. *Interpreting Scriptures in Judaism, Christianity and Islam: Overlapping Inquiries,* Cambridge 2016.
Colby, Frederick. *Narrating Muhammad's Night Journey. Tracing the Development of the Ibn ʿAbbas Ascension Discourse,* New York 2008.
Collier, Paul. *Exodus. How Migration is Changing our World,* Oxford et al. 2013.
Collins, Andrew. "The Biblical Pithom and Tell el-Maskhuta, A Critique of Some Recent Theories on Ex 1,11", in: *Scandinavian Journal of the Old Testament: SJOT,* 22, 2008, 135–149.
Corsato, Celestino. "Il battesimo nei "Tractatus" di Gaudenzio di Brescia", in: *Sul sentiero dei sacramenti: scritti in onore di Ermanno Roberto Tura nel suo 70° compleanno,* edited by Celestino Corsato, Padua 2007, 203–234.

Cosmas Indicopleustes, *Christian Topography* (Topographica christiana) V, selections, trans. by Daniel F. Caner in: *History and Hagiography from the Late Antique Sinai*, Liverpool 2010 (Translated Texts for Historians, 53), 246–251.

Cosmas Indicopleustes. *Topographie chrétienne*, edited by Wanda Wolska-Conus, 3 vols., Paris 1968–1973 (Sources chrétiennes, 141, 159, 197).

Couzin, Robert. *Death in a New Key: The Christian Turn of Roman Sarcophagi*, PhD thesis, University of Toronto, Toronto 2013.

Cubitt, Sean. *Finite Media, Environmental Implications of Digital Technologies*, Durham/London 2017.

Czerwinski, Peter. "Das Nibelungenlied. Widersprüche höfischer Gewaltreglementierung", in: *Einführung in die deutsche Literatur des 12. Bis 16. Jahrhunderts*, vol. 1: *Adel und Hof – 12./13. Jahrhundert*, edited by Winfried Frey et al., Opladen 1979, 49–87.

Dahari, Uzi. *Monastic Settlements in South Sinai in the Byzantine Period: the Archaeological Remains*, Jerusalem 2000.

Dalachanēs, Angelos. *The Greek Exodus from Egypt. Diaspora Politics and Emigration, 1937–1962*, New York 2017.

Damgaard, Finn. *Recasting Moses: The Memory of Moses in Biographical and Autobiographical Narratives in Ancient Judaism and 4th-Century Christianity*, Frankfurt am Main 2013 (Early Christianity in the Context of Antiquity, 13).

Daniélou, Jean. *Sacramentum futuri: études sur les origines de la typologie biblique*, Paris 1950 (Études de Théologie Historique, 8).

Daube, David. *The Exodus Pattern in the Bible*, London 1963 (All Souls Studies, 2).

Davidson, Israel. *Thesaurus of Mediaeval Hebrew Poetry*, 4 vols., New York, 1924–1933.

Dawson, Christopher. *Mission to Asia*, Toronto/Buffalo 1980.

De Nuccio, Marilda/Lucrezia Ungaro, eds. *I marmi colorati della Roma imperiale*, exhibition catalogue (Rome, Mercati di Traiano, 2002–2003), Venice 2002.

De Silvi, Gianluigi. "La chiesa paleocristiana dei Santi Faustino e Giovita 'ad sanguinem'", in: *Angela Merici: la società, la vita, le opera, il carisma*, edited by Gianpietro Belotti, Brescia 2004, 261–280.

De Troyer, Kristine. "Doing Good and Bad: Links between Exodus and the Deutero-canonical Books", in: *Exodus. Rezeption in Deuterokanonischer und Frühjüdischer Literatur*, edited by. Judith Gärtner/Barbara Schmitz, Berlin/Boston 2016, 89–99.

Deckers, Johannes. "Die Wandmalerei des tetrarchischen Lagerheiligtums im Ammon-Temple von Luxor", in: *Römische Quartalschrift* 68, 1973, pp 1–34.

Deckers, Johannes. "Die Wandmalerei im Kaiserkultraum von Luxor", in: *Jahrbuch des Deutschen Archäologischen Instituts*, 94, 1979, 600–652.

Deleuze, Gilles /Guattari, Félix. "Das Glatte und das Gekerbte", in: *Tausend Plateaus. Kapitalismus und Schizophrenie II*, edited by Günther Rösch, Berlin 1992, 657–693.

Deleuze, Gilles. "Was ist ein Schöpfungsakt?", in: id., *Schizophrenie und Gesellschaft: Texte und Gespräche 1975–1995*, Frankfurt am Main 2005, 298–308.

Demaris, Richard E. "Water Ritual", in: *The Oxford Handbook of Early Christian Ritual*, edited by Risto Uro et al., Oxford 2019, 391–408.

Derrida, Jacques. *Gesetzeskraft. Der 'mystische Grund der Autorität'*, Frankfurt am Main 1991.

Dölger, Franz J. "Der Durchzug durch das Rote Meer als Sinnbild der christlichen Taufe", in: *Antike und Christentum*, 2, 1931, 63–69.

Döring, Jörg/Thielmann, Tristan, eds. *Spatial Turn. Das Raumparadigma in den Kultur- und Sozialwissenschaften*, Bielefeld 2008.

Dohmen, Christoph /Stemberger Günter. *Hermeneutik der Jüdischen Bibel und des Alten Testaments*, Stuttgart 1996, 75–83.

Dohmen, Christoph/Ederer, Matthias. "Wie Exodus zum Exodus wurde. Ein Buch und sein Thema", in: *Exodus. Rezeption in Deuterokanonischer und Frühjüdischer Literatur*, edited by Judith Gärtner/Barbara Schmitz, Berlin/Boston 2016, 1–16.

Dohrmann, Natalie B./Stern, David, eds. *Jewish Biblical Interpretation and Cultural Exchange. Comparative Exegesis in Context*, Philadelphia 2008.

Donner, Herbert. *Geschichte des Volkes Israel und seiner Nachbarn in Grundzügen*, vol. 1: *Von den Anfängen bis zur Staatenbildungszeit*, Göttingen ³2000 (ATD Erg. 4/1).

Downey, Susan B. *The Stone and Plaster Sculpture. The Excavations at Dura-Europos Conducted by Yale University and the French Academy of Inscriptions and Letters*, Final Report III, Part I, Fascicle 2, Los Angeles 1977.

Dresken-Weiland, Jutta, ed *Repertorium der christlich-antiken Sarkophage*, vol. 2, *Italien mit einem Nachtrag Rom und Ostia, Dalmatien, Museen der Welt*, Mainz 1998.

Du Mesnil du Buisson, Robert Comte. *Les Peintures de la synagogue de Doura–Europos 245–56 Après J.-C.*, Rome 1939.

Egeria, *Travelogue (Itinerarium)*, I–IX, with abridgements by Peter the Deacon, trans. by Daniel F. Caner in: *History and Hagiography from the Late Antique Sinai*, Liverpool 2010 (Translated Texts for Historians, 53), 211–231.

Ego, Beate. *Targum scheni zu Ester: Übersetzung, Kommentar und theologische Deutung*, Tübingen 1996.

Eisen, Robert. Review of: "Yochanan Silman, Philosopher and Prophet: Judah Halevi, the 'Kuzari', and the Evolution of His Thought", Albany/NY 1995, in: *Speculum*, 73, 1998, 596–598.

Elschazlī, ʻAbd-Elṣamad. *Der Dialog zwischen Mose und Pharao über Gott im Koran und bei ausgewählten Korankommentatoren*, Göttingen 2015.

Elsner, Jaś. "Cultural Resistance and the Visual Image: The Case of Dura Europos", in: *Classical Philology*, 96 (3), 2001, 282–283.

Elsner, Jaś. *Roman Eyes: Visuality and Subjectivity in Art and Text*, Princeton/NJ 2007.

Elsner, Jaś. "The Christian Museum in Southern France: Antiquity, Display, and Liturgy from the Counter-Reformation to the Aftermath of Vatican II", in: *Oxford Art Journal*, 32 (2), 2009, 181–204.

Elsner, Jaś. "'Pharaoh's Army Got Drownded': Some Reflections on Jewish Narrative and Roman Genealogies in Early Christian Art", in: *Judaism and Christian Art: Aesthetic Anxieties from the Catacombs to Colonialism*, edited by Herbert L. Kessler/David Nirenberg, Philadelphia/Oxford 2011, 10–44.

Elsner, Jaś/Wu Hung. Editorial, in: *RES: Anthropology and Aesthetics*, 61/62, special issue: *Sarcophagi*, 2012, 5–21.

Eusebius. *Ecclesiastical History*, vol. II: books 6–10, trans. by John Ernest Leonard Oulton, Cambridge, MA 1932 (Loeb Classical Library, 265).

Faino, Bernardino. "Catalogo delle chiese di Brescia (Manoscritti Queriniani E. VII. 6 ed E. I. 10)", in: *Supplement: Commentari dell'Ateneo di Brescia*, edited by Camillo Borselli, Brescia 1961.

Ferguson, Everett. *Baptism in the Early Church: History, Theology, and Liturgy in the First Five Centuries*, Grand Rapids/Cambridge 2009.
Ferrua, Antonio. *Le pitture della nuova catacomba di via Latina*, Vatican City, 1960 (Monumenti di antichità cristiana, 2nd series, 8).
Fine, Steven. *This Holy Place. On the Sanctity of the Synagogue During the Greco-Roman Period*, Notre Dame/IN 1997 (Christianity and Judaism in Antiquity Series, vol. 11).
Fine, Steven. *Art and Judaism in the Greco-Roman World: Toward a New Jewish Archaeology*, Cambridge 2005.
Fink, Robert O. "An Addition to the Inscription of the Arch of Trajan (Rep. IV, no. 167)", in: *The Excavations at Dura-Europos*, Final Report VI, New Haven/CT 1949, 480–482.
Finkelstein, Louis. *Sifre on Deuteronomy (Siphre ad Deuteronomium)*, New York/Jerusalem 1993 (first published in Berlin 1939) [in Hebrew].
Finley, Moses I. *Ancient Slavery and Modern Ideology*, Princeton 1998 [1980].
Fischer, Elizabeth L. *Streams of Living Water: The Strigil Motif on Late Antique Sarcophagi Reused in Medieval Southern France*, MA thesis, University of North Carolina, Chapel Hill, 2011.
Frankel, Jona. "Bible Verses Quoted in Tales of the Sages", in: *Studies in Aggadah and Folk Literature*, edited by J. Heinemann/D. Voy, Jerusalem 1971 (Scripta Hierosolymitana, 22), 80–99.
Freidenreich, David M./Goldstein, Miriam, eds. *Beyond Religious Borders: Interaction and Intellectual Exchange in the Medieval Islamic World*, Philadelphia 2012.
Freud, Sigmund. "Der Mann Moses und die monotheistische Religion", in: id., *Gesammelte Werke, chronologisch geordnet*, vol. 16: Werke aus den Jahren 1932–1939, Frankfurt am Main 1981, 101–246.
Freytag, Hartmut. *Die Theorie der allegorischen Schriftdeutung und die Allegorie in deutschen Texten besonders des 11. und 12. Jahrhunderts*, Bern/München 1982.
Gärtner, Judith /Schmitz, Barbara, eds. *Exodus. Rezeption in Deuterokanonischer und Frühjüdischer Literatur*, Berlin/Boston 2016.
Galinsky, Judah. *'Arba'ah Turim': Four Turim and the Halakhic Literature of 14th Century Spain*, PhD thesis, Bar-Ilan University, Ramat-Gan 1999 [in Hebrew].
Gaudenzio di Brescia. *I sermoni*, trans. Carlo Truzzi, Rome 1996 (Collana di testi patristici, 129).
Gall, Lothar/Willoweit, Dietmar, eds. *Judaism, Christianity, and Islam in the course of history: exchange and conflicts*, Plymouth 2011.
Gellis, Jacob. *Sefer Tosafot Hashalem: Commentary on the Bible*, 9 vols., Jerusalem 1982 [in Hebrew].
Genette, Gérard. *Paratexts: Thresholds of Interpretation*, Cambridge 1997 (originally published in French as *Seuils*, Paris 1987).
Gerhards, Meik. *Die Aussetzungsgeschichte des Mose, Literar– und traditionsgeschichtliche Untersuchungen zu einem Schlüsseltext des nichtpriesterlichen Tetrateuch*, Neukirchen-Vluyn 2006 (Wissenschaftliche Monographien zum Alten und Neuen Testament, 109).
Gerstel, Sharon E. J./Nelson, Robert S., eds. *Approaching the Holy Mountain: Art and Liturgy at St. Catherine's Monastery in the Sinai*, Turnhout 2010 (Cursor Mundi, 11).

Geula, Amos. *Lost Aggadic works known only from Ashkenaz: Midrash Abkir, Midrash Esfa and Devarim Zuta*, PhD thesis, The Hebrew University of Jerusalem, Jerusalem 2006 [in Hebrew].

Gielen, Michael. *Unbedingt Musik. Erinnerungen*, Leipzig 2005.

Ginzberg, Louis. *Legends of the Jews*, 7 vols., Philadelphia 1909–1938.

Gold, Avie, ed. *Baal Haturim Chumash: The Torah with the Baal Ha-Turim's Classic Commentary Translated, Annotated, and Elucidated*, trans. Eliyahu Touger, 5 vols., Brooklyn 2000–2004.

Goldschmidt, Daniel. *Mahzor for the High Holy Days: Rosh Hashanah*, 2 vols., Jerusalem 1970 [in Hebrew].

Goldstein, Bluma. *Reinscribing Moses: Heine, Kafka, Freud, and Schoenberg in a European Wilderness*, Cambridge 1992.

Goldstein, Bluma. "Schoenberg's Moses und Aron. A Vanishing Biblical Nation", in: *Political and Religious Ideas in the Works of Arnold Schoenberg*, edited by Charlotte M. Cross/Russell A. Berman, New York 2000, 159–192.

Goldziher, Ignatz. "Le amr ilâhî chez (ha–Injan ha–elohi) chez Jehuda Halevi", in: *Revue des Études Juives*, 50, 1905, 32–41.

Goodenough, Erwin R. *Jewish Symbols in the Greco–Roman Period*, 13 vols., New York 1953–68 (Bollingen Series, 37).

Grabar, André. "Le theme religieux des fresques de la synagogue de Doura (245–256 apres J.-C.)", in: *Revue de l'histoire des religions*, 123 (2–3), 1941, 143–192, and 124 (1), 1941, 5–35.

Grabar, Oleg/Blair, Sheila. *Epic Images and Contemporary History*, Chicago 1980.

Gray, Basil. *The World history of Rashīd al-Dīn: A study of the Royal Asiatic Society manuscript*, London 1978.

Green, Arthur. *Tormented Master. The Life and Spiritual Quest of Rabbi Nahman of Bratslav*, Woodstock 1992.

Green, Dennis H. *The Millstätter Exodus. A Crusading Epic*, Cambridge 1966.

Green, Dennis H. "The Millstätter Exodus and its Bibical Source", in: *Medium Aevium*, 38, 1969, 227–238.

Grimm, Jacob/Grimm, Wilhelm. *Der digitale Grimm*, edited by Hans-Werner Bartz, Frankfurt am Main 2005.

Grossfeld, Bernard. *The Two Targums of Esther*, Edinburgh 1991.

Gruber, Christane/Colby, Frederick, eds. *The Prophet's ascension. Cross-Cultural encounters with the Islamic Mi'rāj Tales*, Bloomington 2010.

Guerrini, Paolo. "Notizie e bibliografia", in: *Memorie storiche della diocesi di Brescia*, 16 (4), 1949, 185–187.

Guerrini, Paolo. "La basilica paleocristiana di San Faustino 'ad sanguinem'", in: *Miscellanea di studi bresciani sull'alto medioevo*, edited by the Comitato Bresciano per l'ottavo congresso internazionale dell'arte dell'alto medioevo, Brescia 1959, 39–44. (Reprinted from the *Giornale di Brescia* 16 February 1953).

Günzel, Stephan. *Raum. Eine kulturwissenschaftliche Einführung*, Bielefeld 2017.

Gutmann, Joseph. "Programmatic Painting in the Dura Synagogue", in: *The Dura–Europos Synagogue: A Re–Evaluation (1932–72)*, edited by Joseph Gutmann, Missoula/MT 1973, 137–154.

Gutmann, Joseph. *Hebrew Manuscript Painting*, New York 1978.

Hachlili, Rachel. "The Niche and the Ark in Ancient Synagogues", in: *Bulletin of the American Schools of Oriental Research*, 223, 1976, 43–53.
Halevi, Yehuda. *Poems from the Diwan*, London 2002.
Halevi Yehuda. *The Kuzari: In Defense of the Despised Faith*, trans. Korobkin, N. Daniel, edited by David Kahn, Jerusalem ²2009 (first published Northvale 1998).
Hartwig, Dirk. "'Der Urvertrag' (Q 7:172). Ein rabbinischer Diskurs im Koran", in: *'Im vollen Licht der Geschichte'. Die Wissenschaft des Judentums und die Anfänge der kritischen Koranforschung*, edited by Dirk Hartwig/Walter Homolka/Michael M. Marx/Angelika Neuwirth, Würzburg 2008, 191–202.
Hawting, Gerald R. "The Origins of the Islamic Sanctuary at Mecca", in *Studies of the First Century of Islamic History*, edited by Gautier H. A. Joynboll, Carbondale 1982, 25–47.
Haykin, Michael A. G. "'In the Cloud of the Sea': Basil of Caesarea and the Exegesis of 1 Cor 10:2", in: *Vigiliae Christiancae*, 40 (2), 1986, 135–144.
Heintel, Martin/et al. "Grenzen – eine Einführung", in: *Grenzen. Theoretische, konzeptionelle und praxisbezogene Fragestellungen zu Grenzen und deren Überschreitungen*, edited by Martin Heintel/Robert Musil/Norbert Weixlbaumer, Wiesbaden 2018, 1–15.
Heintel, Martin/Musil, Robert/Weixlbaumer, Norbert, eds. *Grenzen. Theoretische, konzeptionelle und praxisbezogene Fragestellungen zu Grenzen und deren Überschreitungen*, edited by Martin Heintel/, Wiesbaden 2018.
Helfers, James Peter, ed. *Multicultural Europe and cultural exchange in the Middle Ages and Renaissance*, Turnhout 2005.
Henning, Ursula. *"Altdeutsche Exodus"*, in: *Verfasserlexikon*, vol. I., 2nd ed., Berlin/New York 1978, coll. 276–279.
Hillenbrand, Robert. "The Arts of the Book in Ilkhanid Iran", in: *The Legacy of Genghis Khan*, edited by Linda Komaroff/Stefano Carboni, New Haven 2003, 134–162.
Hirschfeld, Hartwig. *Judah Hallevi's Kitab al Khazari*, New York 1905.
Hirshman, Marc. *A Rivalry of Genius: Jewish and Christian Biblical Interpretation in Late Antiquity*, New York 1996.
Hoffmann, Birgitt. *Waqf im mongolischen Iran: Rašīduddīns Sorge um Nachruhm und Seelenheil*, Stuttgart 2000.
Holl, Ute. *Der Moses-Komplex. Politik der Töne, Politik der Bilder*, Zürich/Berlin 2014.
Holladay, John S. "Judaeans (and Phoenicians) in Egypt in the Late Seventh to Sixth Centuries B.C.", in: *Egypt, Israel, and the Ancient Mediterranean World, Studies in Honor of Donald B. Redford*, edited by Gary N. Knoppers/Antoine Kirsch, Leiden 2004, 405–437.
Holly, Michael Ann. "Notes from the Field: Materiality", in: *The Art Bulletin*, 95 (1), 2013, 15–17.
Hoogland Verkerk, Dorothy. "Exodus and Easter Vigil in the Ashburnham Pentateuch", in: *The Art Bulletin*, 77 (1), 1995, 94–105.
Hoogland Verkerk, Dorothy. *The font is a kind of grave: Remembrance in the Via Latina Catacombs*, in: *Memory and the Medieval Tomb*, edited by Elizabeth Valdez del Alamo, with Carol Stamatis Pendergast, Aldershot 2000, 157–171.
Horovitz, Hayyim Saul, ed. *Siphre d'be Rab*, Jerusalem 1992 (first published Leipzig 1917).
Huillet, Danièle. "Appunti sul giornale di lavorazione di Gregory", in: *Filmkritik*, 225, 9/1975, 398–419.

Huillet, Danièle. "Moses und Aron. Das Drehbuch. Beschreibungen – Texte – Photogramme, redigiert und eingerichtet für den Druck von Helmut Färber", in: *Filmkritik*, 221/222, 1975, 203–252.
Huskinson, Janet. *Roman Strigillated Sarcophagi: Art & Social History*, Oxford 2015.
Ibn Hishām, 'Abd al-Malik. *al-Sīra al-nabawiyya*, edited by Aḥmad Muḥammad Shākir, Cairo 1373/1954.
Ibn Isḥaq, Muḥammad. *The Life of Muhammad: A Translation of Ibn Isḥaq's Sīrat Rasūl Allāh*, trans. Alfred Guillaume, Lahore 1974.
Ibn Sa'd, Muḥammad. *al-Ṭabaqāt al-kubrā*, edited by Eduard Sachau, Leiden 1904 (reprint, Beirut 1960).
Idel, Moshe. *Absorbing Perfections: Kabbalah and Interpretation*, New Haven/London 2002.
Idel, Moshe. "On Angels and Biblical Exegesis in Thirteenth-Century Ashkenaz", in: *Scriptural Exegesis – The Shapes of Culture and the Religious Imagination: Essays in Honour of Michael Fishbane*, edited by Deborah A. Green/Laura Lieber, Oxford 2009, 211–244.
Inal, Güner. "Some Miniatures of the 'Jāmi al-Tavārīkh' in Istanbul, Topkapı Museum, Hazine Library no. 1654", in: *Ars Orientalis*, 5, 1963, 163–176.
Ingold, Tim. *Being Alive: Essays on Movement, Knowledge and Description*, London/New York 2011.
Ipsiroglu, Mazhar Şevket. *Saray-Alben: Diez'sche Klebebände aus den Berliner Sammlungen*, Wiesbaden 1964.
Jackson, Peter. *The Mongols and the West, 1221–1410*, Harlow, England/New York 2005.
Jahn, Karl. *Die Geschichte der Kinder Israels des Rašīd ad-Dīn*, Vienna 1973.
Janowski Bernd/Wilhelm Gernot, eds. *Texte zum Rechts- und Wirtschaftsleben*, (Texte aus der Umwelt des Alten Testaments, Neue Folge, 1).
Jellinek, Adolph, ed. *Bet ha-Midrasch*: Sammlung kleiner Midraschim und Vermischter Abhandlungen aus der älteren Jüdischen Literatur, 6 vols., Jerusalem 1967.
Jensen, Robin M. *Living Water: Images, Symbols, and Settings of Early Christian Baptism*, Leiden/Boston 2011 (Supplements to Vigiliae Christianae. Texts and Studies of Early Christian Life and Langauage, 105).
Jensen, Robin M. *Baptismal Imagery in Early Christianity: Ritual, Visual, and Theological Dimensions*, Grand Rapids 2012.
Jeremias, Brigitte. "Ein sakraler Monolith, mitten in die Landschaft gestellt. Jean-Marie Straubs Moses und Aron-Verfilmung", in: *Frankfurter Allgemeine Zeitung*, Nr. 49, 27.2.1975, 21.
Jordan, William Chester. "A Jewish Atelier for Illuminated Hebrew Manuscripts at Amiens?", in: *Wiener Jahrbuch für Kunstgeschichte*, 37, 1984, 155–156.
Josephus, Flavius. *Jewish Antiquities*, trans. Henry St. John Thackeray, London/New York 1930.
Julian. *Orations 6–8. Letters to Themistius, To the Senate and People of Athens, To a Priest. The Caesars. Misopogon*, vol. 2, trans. by Wilmer C. Wright. Cambridge, MA 1913 (Loeb Classical Library, 29).
Kaiser, Gerhard. "War der Exodus ein Sündenfall?", in: Jan Assmann, *Die Mosaische Unterscheidung oder der Preis des Monotheismus*, München/Wien 2003, 239–271.
Kaiser, Otto, ed. *Texte aus der Umwelt des Alten Testaments (TUAT)*, Alte Folge, 3 vols., Gütersloh 1982–1997.

Kalavrezou-Maxeiner, Iole. "The Imperial Chamber at Luxor", in: *Dumbarton Oaks Papers*, 29, 1975, 227–251.
Kanarfogel, Ephraim. *Jewish Education and Society in the High Middle Ages*, Detroit 1992.
Kanarfogel, Ephraim. "On the Role of Bible Study in Medieval Ashkenaz", in: *The Frank Talmage Memorial Volume*, edited by Barry Walfish, 2 vols., Haifa 1993, vol. I, 151–166.
Kanarfogel, Ephraim. *Peering Through the Lattices: Mystical, Magical and Pietistic Dimensions in the Tosafist Period*, Detroit 2000.
Kanarfogel, Ephraim. *The Intellectual History and Rabbinic Culture of Medieval Ashkenaz*, Detroit 2013.
Kawatoko, Mutsuo, ed. *Archaeological Survey of the Rāya/al-Ṭūr Area on the Sinai Peninsula, Egypt, 2004*, Tokyo 2005.
Kawatoko, Mutsuo/Tokunaga, Risa. "Arabic Rock Inscriptions of South Sinai", in: *Proceedings of the Seminar for Arabian Studies*, 36, 2006, 217–227.
Kazuhiko, Shiraiwa. *Rashid al-Din's 'Compendium of Chronicles': a Bibliography of Extant Manuscripts*, Tokyo 2000 [in Japanese].
Keech, Dominic. *Gaudentius of Brescia on Baptism and the Eucharist*, Norwich 2013 (Joint Liturgical Studies, 76).
Kerkeslager, Allen. "Jewish Pilgrimage and Jewish Identity in Hellenistic and Early Roman Egypt", in: *Pilgrimage and Holy Space in Late Antique Egypt*, edited by David Frankfurter, Leiden 1998 (Religions in the Graeco–Roman World, 134), 99–225.
Khaleghi-Motlagh, Djalal. "'Ayyūqī", in: *Encyclopaedia Iranica*, vol. 3, fasc. 2, 167–168.
Kimelman, Reuven. "The Literary Structure of the Amidah and the Rhetoric of Redemption", in: *Echoes of Many Texts: Reflections on Jewish and Christian Traditions*, edited by William G. Dever/J. Edward Wright (Essays in Honor of Lou H. Silberman), Missoula/MT 1977, 171–230.
Kittler, Friedrich. "Signal-Rausch-Abstand", in: id., *Draculas Vermächtnis, Technische Schriften*, Leipzig 1993, 161–181.
Klugmann, Joel, ed. *Rabbeinu Ephraim: A Twelfth Century Biblical Commentary*, 2 vols. Jerusalem 1992 [in Hebrew].
Koch, Guntram. *Frühchristliche Sarkophage*, Munich 2000.
Kogman-Appel, Katrin. "Coping with Christian Pictorial Sources: What Did Jewish Miniaturists Not Paint?", in: *Speculum*, 75, no. 4, 2000, 816–858.
Kogman-Appel, Katrin. *Jewish Book Art Between Islam and Christianity. The Decoration of Hebrew Bibles in Medieval Spain*, Leiden/Boston 2004.
Kogman-Appel, Katrin. "Sephardic Ideas in Ashkenaz. Visualizing the Temple in Medieval Regensburg", in: *Jahrbuch des Simon–Dubnow–Instituts*, 8, 2009, 245–277.
Kraeling, Carl H. "The Synagogue", in: *The Excavations at Dura–Europos Conducted by Yale University and the French Academy of Inscriptions and Letters*, edited by Michael I. Rostovtzeff et al, New Haven/CT 1936, 337–383.
Kraeling, Carl H. *The Synagogue: The Excavations at Dura–Europos*, Final Report VIII, Part I, New Haven/CT 1956.
Krause, Joachim J. *Exodus und Eisodus: Komposition und Theologie von Josua 1–5*, Leiden et al. 2014 (Vetus Testamentum, Supplements, 161).
Krawulsky, Dorothea. *The Mongol Īlkhāns and their Vizier Rashīd al-Dīn*, Frankfurt am Main et al. 2011.
Kreisel, Howard. *Maimonides' Political Thought*, New York 1999.

Kugel, James. *The Idea of Biblical Poetry*, New Haven 1981.
Kushelevsky, Rella. "The Longings for the Land of Israel in the Midrashim on the Death of Moses", in: *Alei Siah*, 31–32, 1993, 189–196 [in Hebrew].
Kushelevsky, Rella. *Moses and the Angel of Death*, trans. by Ruth Bar–Ilan, New York 1995.
Laderman, Shula. "A New Look at the Second Register of the West Wall in Dura Europos", in: *Cahiers Archeologiques*, 45, 1997, 5–18.
Laderman, Shulamit. "Two Faces of Eve: Polemics and Controversies Viewed through Pictorial Motifs", in: *Images*, 2, 2008, 1–20.
Laderman, Shulamit/Furstenberg, Yair. "Jewish and Christian Imaging of the 'House of God': A Fourth-Century Reflection of Religious and Historical Polemics", in: *Interaction between Judaism and Christianity in History, Religion, Art and Literature*, edited by Marcel Poorthuis/Joshua J. Schwartz/Joseph Turner, Leiden 2008 (Jewish and Christian Perspectives, 17), 433–456.
Lambert, Wilfred G. *Babylonian Wisdom Literature*, Oxford 1969 (reprint Winona Lake 1996).
Lange, Isaac, ed. *The Commentaries to the Torah of R. Judah the Pious*, Jerusalem 1975 [in Hebrew].
Larison, Kristine M. *Mount Sinai and the Monastery of St. Catherine: Place and Space in Pilgrimage Art*, Ph.D., University of Chicago, Chicago 2016.
Lassus, Jean. "Quelques représentations du 'Passage de la Mer Rouge' dans l'art chrétien d'Orient et d'Occident", in: *Mélanges d'archéologie et d'histoire*, 45, 1928, 159–181.
Laubscher, Hans Peter. *Der Reliefschmuck des Galeriusbogens in Thessaloniki*, Berlin 1975.
Lausberg, Heinrich. *Der Hymnus 'Veni Creator Spiritus'*, Opladen 1979.
Lauterbach, Jacob Z./Stern, David M., eds. *Mekhilta de-Rabbi Ishmael*, 2 vols., Philadelphia 2004.
Lawrence, Marion. "City-Gate Sarcophagi", in: *The Art Bulletin*, 10 (1), 1927, 1–45.
Lazzarini, Lorenzo. "Rosso Antico and Other Red Marbles Used in Antiquity: A Characterization Study", in: *Marble: Art Historical and Scientific Perspectives on Ancient Sculpture*, conference proceedings (Malibu, J. Paul Getty Museum 1988), Malibu 1990, 237–252.
Le Blant, Edmond. *Étude sur les sarcophages chrétiens antiques de la ville d'Arles*, Paris, 1878.
Lehnard, Andreas. "'Seder Yom ha–Kippurim kakh hu': Zur Entwicklung der synagogalen Liturgie des Versöhnungstages", in: *The Day of Atonement: Its Interpretations in Early Jewish and Christian Traditions*, edited by Thomas Hieke/Tobias Nicklas, Leiden 2012, 257–269.
Lemche, Niels Peter. "Andurārum and Mīšarum: Comments on the Problem of Social Edicts and their Application in the Ancient Near East", in: *Journal of Near Eastern Studies*, 38, 1979, 11–22.
Leveen, Jacob. *The Hebrew Bible in Art*, London 1944.
Levenson, Jon. *Sinai and Zion. An Entry into the Hebrew Bible*, New York 1987.
Levy, M. A. "Über die nabathäischen Inschriften von Petra, Hauran, vornehmlich von Sinai-Halbinsel und über die Münzlegenden nabathäischer Könige", in: *Zeitschrift der Deutschen Morgenländischen Gesellschaft*, 14, 1860, 363–484, 594.
Lewis, N. N. /MacDonald, Michael. "W. J. Banks and the Identification of the Nabataean Script", in: *Syria*, 80, 2003, 41–110.

Lindbeck, George A. *The Nature of Doctrine. Religion and Theology in a Postliberal Age*, Philadelphia 1984.
Loewe, Raphael. "Description of the Texts", in: *The North French Hebrew Miscellany: British Library Add. MS 11639*, edited by Jeremy Schonfield, London 2003, 188–287.
MacCormack, Sabine. *Art and Ceremony in Late Antiquity*, Berkeley 1981.
Maimonides, Moses. *The Guide of the Perplexed*, trans. Shlomo Pines, Chicago 1963.
Maimonides, Moses (Ramba"m): *Mishneh Torah*, edited by Eliyahu Touger, 31 vols., New York 1998.
Maimonides, Moses (Mosheh ben Maimon). *Sefer Moreh ha-Nevukhim*, trans. into Hebrew R. Shemu'el b. r. Yehudah Ibn Tibon, vol. 3, Jerusalem 2000.
Mainenti, Antonio. "Il sarcofago di S. Afra (frammento in onice)", in: *Commentari dell'Ateneo di Brescia* 165, 1966, 177–206.
Malachi, Zvi. *The Avodah for Yom Kippur: Its Characteristics, History and Development in Hebrew Poetry*, PhD thesis, The Hebrew University of Jerusalem, Jerusalem 1974 [in Hebrew].
Manafis, Konstantinos A., ed. *Sinai: Treasures of the Monastery of Saint Catherine*, Athens 1990.
Marchini, Maurizio. *Un tesoro della ecclesia di Brescia: La Confessione di fede di Tommaso sul sarcofago da S. Afra nel Museo di S. Giulia*, Brescia 2014.
Marcus, Ivan G. "Introduction", in: *Sefer Hasidim: Ms. Parma H 3280*, Jerusalem 1985, 9–31 [in Hebrew].
Marcus, Ivan G. "Exegesis for the Few and for the Many: Judah he-Hasid's Biblical Commentaries", in: *The Age of the Zohar: Third International Conference on the History of Jewish Mysticism*, ed. Joseph Dan, Jerusalem 1989, 1–24.
Marcus, Ivan G. *Rituals of Childhood: Jewish Acculturation in Medieval Europe*, New Haven/London 1996.
Margoliouth, George. *Catalogue of the Hebrew and Samaritan Manuscripts in the British Museum*, London 1899.
Margoliouth, George. "An Ancient Illuminated Hebrew MS. at the British Museum", in: *The Jewish Quarterly Review*, 17, 1905, 193–197.
Martinengo, Ascanio. *Vite de' gloriosi santi martiri Faustino, et Giovita, & di Sant'Affra et d'altri santi bresciani gli cui sacri corpi, & reliquie si conservano in diverse chiese di Brescia*, Brescia 1602.
Matthews, Thomas F. *The Clash of Gods: A Reinterpretation of Early Christian Art*, Princeton 1999.
Maul, Stefan M. "Der assyrische König – Hüter der Weltordnung", in: *Gerechtigkeit. Richten und Retten in der abendländischen Tradition und ihren altorientalischen Ursprüngen*, edited by Jan Assmann/Bernd Janowski/Michael Welker, München 1998, 65–77.
Mayerson, Philip. "The Pilgrim Routes to Mount Sinai and the Armenians", in: *Israel Exploration Journal*, 32 (1), 1982, 44–57.
Meeks, Wayne A. *The Prophet-King. Moses Traditions and the Johannine Christology*, Leiden 1967.
Melville, Charles. "Jāmeʿ al-Tawārīḳ", in: *Encyclopaedia Iranica*, vol. 14, fasc. 5, 462.
Meredith-Owens, G. M. "Some Remarks on the Miniatures in the Society's 'Jami al-Tawarikh'", in: *Journal of the Royal Asiatic Society*, 1970, 195–199.

Meshel, Ze'ev. "Were the Sinai Rock Inscriptions Really Inscribed by 'Nabateans?'", in: *Sinai: Excavations and Studies*, Oxford 2000 (BAR International Series, 876), 143–151.

Metzger, Mendel. "Illustrations Bibliques d'un Manuscrit Hébreu du Nord de la France (1278–1340 environ)", in: *Mélanges Offerts à René Crozet à l'occasion de son soixante-dixième anniversaire*, edited by Pierre Gallais/Yves–Jean Riou, Poitiers 1966, 1237–1253.

Metzger, Thérèse. "Les Enluminures du Ms. Add. 11639 de la British Library, un Manuscrit Hébreu du Nord de la France (fin du 13e siècle – premier quart du 14e siècle): Problèmes Iconographiques et Stylistiques", in: *Wiener Jahrbuch für Kunstgeschichte*, 38, 1985, 59–113, 281–290.

Michel, Karl. *Gebet und Bild in frühchristlicher Zeit*, Leipzig 1902 (Studien über christliche Denkmäler, 1).

Millar, Fergus. *The Roman Near East, 31 B.C. – A.D. 337*, Cambridge, MA 1993.

Milstein, Rachel. "The Iconography of Moses in Islamic Art", in: *Jewish Art*, vol. 12/13, 1986/1987, 199–212.

Milstein, Rachel. *La Bible dans l'art islamique*, Paris 2005.

Milwright, Marcus. "'Waves of the Sea': Responses to Marble in Written Sources (Ninth-Fifteenth Centuries)", in: *The Iconography of Islamic Art: Studies in Honour of Robert Hillenbrand*, edited by by Bernard O'Kane, Edinburgh 2005, 211–221.

Mirsky, Aharon, *The Poems of Yosse ben Yosse*, Jerusalem 1977 [in Hebrew].

Mitchell, John. "Believing is Seeing: The Natural Image in Late Antiquity", in: *Architecture and Interpretation: Essays for Eric Fernie*, edited by by Jill A. Franklin/T. A. Heslop/Christine Stevenson, Woodridge 2012, 16–41.

Montfaucon, Bernard de, ed. *Collectio Nova Patrum et Scriptorum Graecorum*, vol. II, Paris 1707.

Montville, Joseph V., ed. *History as Prelude: Muslims and Jews in the Medieval Mediterranean*, Lanham MD 2011.

Moon, Warren. "Nudity and Narrative: Observations on the Synagogue Paintings from Dura-Europos", in: *Polykleitos, the Doryphoros, and Tradition,* edited by Warren Moon, Madison 1995, 283–316 [originally published as Warren Moon: Nudity and Narrative: Observations on the Frescoes from the Dura Synagogue, in: *Journal of the American Academy of Religion* 60, 1992, 587–658].

Morandini, Francesca. "Fronte di sarcofago frammentario", in: *Constantino 313 d.C.: l'editto di Milano e il tempo della tolleranza*, exhibition catalogue (Milan, Palazzo Reale/Rome, Colosseo and Curia Iulia, 2012–2013), edited by Gemma Sena Chiesa, Milan 2012, 190, cat. 29.

Morgan, David. "Rashīd al-Dīn Ṭabīb", in: Encyclopaedia of Islam, *vol.* 8, Leiden, ²1994, 443–444.

Morgan, David. *The Mongols*, Malden, MA/Oxford, UK 2007.

Morris-Suzuki, Tessa. *Exodus to North Korea. Shadows from Japan's Cold War*, Lanham/ MD et al. 2007.

Municipio di Brescia. *Civico Museo Cristiano: breve guida alle opere esposte*, Brescia 1949.

Narkiss, Bezalel. *Hebrew Illuminated Manuscripts*, Jerusalem 1969.

Natif, Mika. "Rashid al-Din's Alter Ego: The Seven Paintings of Moses in the 'Jami al-Tawarikh' ", in: *Rashid al-Din as an Agent and Mediator of Cultural Exchanges in*

Ilkhanid Iran, edited by Anna Akasoy/Charles Burnett/Ronit Yoeli-Tlalim, London 2013, 15–37.
Negev, Avraham. "New Dated Nabatean Graffiti from the Sinai", in: *Israel Exploration Journal*, 17 (4), 1967, 250–255.
Negev, Avraham. *The Inscriptions of Wadi Haggag, Sinai*, Jerusalem 1977 (Qedem, 6).
Negev, Avraham. *Nabatean Archaeology Today*, New York/London 1986.
Negev, Avraham. *Personal Names in the Nabatean Realm*, Jerusalem 1991 (Qedem, 32).
Netzer, Amnon. "Rashīd al-Dīn and His Jewish Background", in: Irano-Judaica: Studies Relating to Jewish Contacts with Persian Culture throughout the Ages, edited by Shaul Shaked/Amnon Netzer, *vol.* 3, Jerusalem 1994, 118–126.
Neubauer, Adolf. *Catalogue of the Hebrew Manuscripts in the Bodleian Library*, Oxford 1886.
Neuwirth, Angelika. "The House of Abraham and the House of Amran: Genealogy, Patriarchal Authority, and Exegetical Professionalism", in: *The Quran in Context*, edited by Angelika Neuwirth/Nicolai Sinai/Michael Marx, Leiden 2009, 499–531.
Niebuhr, Carsten. *Travels through Arabia, and other countries in the East performed by M. Neibuhr*, trans. Robert Heron, Edinburgh 1792.
Noga-Banai, Galit. "The Sarcophagus of Louis the Pious at Metz: A Roman Memory Reused", in: *Frühmittelalterliche Studien*, 45, 2011, 37–50.
Noga-Banai, Galit. *Sacred Stimulus: Jerusalem in the Visual Christianization of Rome*, Oxford 2018 (Oxford Studies in Late Antiquity).
Nordström, Carlo-Otto. "The Water Miracles of Moses in Jewish Legend and Byzantine Art", in: *Orientalia Suecana*, 7, 1958, 78–109.
Nordström, Carl-Otto. The *Duke of Alba's Castilian Bible. A Study of the Rabbinical Features of the Miniatures*, Uppsala 1967.
Offenberg, Sara. *Expressions of Meeting the Challenges of the Christian Milieu in Medieval Jewish Art and Literature*, PhD thesis, Ben-Gurion University of the Negev, Beer Sheva 2008 [in Hebrew].
Offenberg, Sara. "Crossing over from Earth to Heaven: The Image of the Ark and the Merkavah in the North French Hebrew Miscellany", in: *Kabbalah*, 26, 2012, 135–158.
Offenberg, Sara. *Illuminated Piety: Pietistic Texts and Images in the North French Hebrew Miscellany*, Los Angeles 2013.
Oswald, Wolfgang. *Staatstheorie im Alten Israel, Der politische Diskurs im Pentateuch und in den Geschichtsbüchern des Alten Testaments*, Stuttgart 2009.
Oswald, Wolfgang. "Auszug aus der Vasallität – Die Exodus-Erzählung (Ex 1–14*) und das antike Völkerrecht", in: *Theologische Zeitschrift*, 67, 2011, 263–288.
Otto, Eckart. "Programme der sozialen Gerechtigkeit, Die neuassyrische *(an-)durāru*-Institution sozialen Ausgleichs und das deuteronomische Erlaßjahr in Dtn 15*", in: *Zeitschrift für altorientalische und biblische Rechtsgeschichte*, 3, 1997, 26–63.
Otto, Eckart. "Mose und das Gesetz. Die Mosefigur als Gegenentwurf Politischer Theologie zur neuassyrischen Königsideologie im 7. Jh. v. Chr.", in: *Mose, Ägypten und das Alte Testament*, edited by Eckart Otto, Stuttgart 2000, 43–83 (Stuttgarter Bibelstudien, 189).
Otto, Eckart. *Mose. Geschichte und Legende*, München 2006.
Panazza, Gaetano. *La Pinacoteca e i musei di Brescia*, new edition, Bergamo 1968.
Panazza, Gaetano. "Le manifestazioni artistiche dal secolo IV all'inizio del secolo VII", in: *Storia di Brescia*, edited by Giovanni Treccani degli Alfieri, vol. 1, *Dalle origini alla caduta della signoria viscontea (1426)*, Brescia 1963, 361–391.

Papp, Edgar. *D[enis] H[ovard] Green, The Millstätter Exodus. A Crusading Epic [Rez.]*, in: *Beiträge zur Geschichte der Deutschen Sprache und Literatur*, 89, 1967, 356–363.
Papp, Edgar, ed. *Die Altdeutsche Exodus. Untersuchungen und kritischer Text*, München 1968.
Pekáry, Thomas. "Das Opfer vor dem Kaiserbild", in: *Bonner Jahrbücher*, 186, 1986, 91–103.
Piacenza Pilgrim, *Travels from Piacenza*, in: *Jerusalem Pilgrims before the Crusades*, trans. John Wilkinson, 2nd edition, Warminster 2002, 129–151.
Pniower, Otto. *Die Abfassungszeit der Altdeutschen Exodus*, in: *Zeitschrift für deutsches Altertum und Literatur*, 33, 1889, 73–97.
Pococke, Richard. *A Description of the East and Some Other Countries*, London 1743–1745.
Porten, Bezalel/Yardeni, Ada. *Textbook of Aramaic Documents from Ancient Egypt*, vol. II: *Contracts*, Jerusalem/Winona Lake 1989.
Preminger, Alex/Brogan, T.V. F., eds. *The New Princeton Encyclopedia of Poetry and Poetics*, Princeton/NJ 1993.
Ragusa, Isa. *The Re-use and Public Exhibition of Roman Sarcophagi during the Middle Ages and the Early Renaissance*, BA thesis, New York University, New York 1951.
Rice, David T. *The Illustrations to the "World History" of Rashīd al_Dīn*, edited by Basil Gray, Edinburgh 1976.
Riesener, Ingrid. *Der Stamm 'bd im Alten Testament, Eine Wortuntersuchung unter Berücksichtigung neuerer sprachwissenschaftlicher Methoden*, Berlin 1979 (Beihefte zur Zeitschrift für die alttestamentliche Wissenschaft, 149).
Rizzardi, Clementina. *I sarcofagi paleocristiani con rappresentazione del passaggio del Mar Rosso*, Faenza 1970 (Saggi d'arte e d'archeologia, 2).
Roberts, Alastair John. *The Red Sea Crossing and Christian Baptism: A Study in Typology and Liturgy*, PhD thesis, Durham University, Durham 2015. URL: http://ethesis.dur.ac.uk/10977/ [02.08.2018].
Rosenberg, Shalom. "The Link to the Land of Israel in Jewish Thought: A Clash of Perspectives", in: The *Land of Israel. Jewish Perspectives*, edited by Lawrence. A. Hoffman, Notre Dame 1986, 139–169.
Rostovtzeff, Michael I. *Dura–Europos and Its Art*, Oxford 1938.
Rostovtzeff, Michael I./Brown, Frank E./ Welles, Charles B., eds. *The Excavations at Dura–Europos. Preliminary Report of the Seventh and Eighth Seasons of Work 1933–1934 and 1934–1935*, edited by, New Haven/CT/London 1939.
Roth, Martha T. *Law Collections from Mesopotamia and Asia Minor*, Atlanta ²1997 (Writings from the Ancient World, 6/Society of Biblical Literature, 39).
Rothenberg, Beno. "An Archaeological Survey of South Sinai", in: *Palestine Exploration Quarterly*, 102, 1970, 4–29.
Roxburgh, David J. "Heinrich Friedrich Von Diez and His Eponymous Albums: Mss. Diez A. Fols. 70–74", in: *Muqarnas*, 12, 1995, 112–136.
Rubenstein, Jeffrey L. "An Eschatological Drama: Bavli Avodah Zarah 2a–3b", in: *AJS Review*, 21/1, 1996, 1–37.
Rubin, Uri. "Prophets and Caliphs: The Biblical Foundations of the Umayyad Authority", in: *Method and Theory in the Study of Islamic Origins*, edited by Herbert Berg, Leiden, Brill 2003, 73–99.
Rubin, Uri. "Between Arabia and the Holy Land: a Mecca-Jerusalem Axis of Sanctity", in: *Jerusalem Studies in Arabic and Islam*, 34, 2008, 345–362.

Rubin, Uri. "Muhammad's Night Journey (*isrāʾ*) to al-Masjid al-Aqsa. Aspect of the Earliest Origins of the Islamic Sanctity of Jerusalem", in: *Al-Qantara*, XXIX 1, 2008, 147–164.

Rubin, Uri. "Moses and the Holy Valley Tuwan: On the Biblical and Midrashic Background of a Qur'anic Scene", in: *Journal of Near Eastern Studies*, 73/1, 2014, 73–81.

Rudy, Kathryn. *Piety in Pieces: How Medieval Readers Customized their Manuscripts*, Cambridge/UK 2016.

Saperstein, Marc. "The Land of Israel in Pre-Modern Jewish Thought", in: The *Land of Israel. Jewish Perspectives*, edited by Lawrence. A. Hoffman, Notre Dame 1986, 188–209.

Savio, Fidèle. "La légende des SS. Faustin et Jovite", in: *Analecta Bollandiana*, 15, 1896, 5–72, 113–159, 377–400.

Schäfer, Peter. *Die Ursprünge der jüdischen Mystik*, Berlin 2011.

Schaper, Joachim. "Exodus – die LXX-Fassung und ihre Rezeption in der deuteronkanonischen und frühjüdischen Literatur", in: *Exodus. Rezeption in Deuterokanonischer und Frühjüdischer Literatur*, edited by Judith Gärtner/Barbara Schmitz, Berlin/Boston 2016, 17–31.

Scheindlin, Raymond P. *The Song of the Distant Dove: Judah Halevi's Pilgrimage*, Oxford 2008.

Schenk, Kära. "Temple, Community, and Sacred Narrative in the Dura-Europos Synagogue", in: *Association for Jewish Studies Review*, 34 (2), 2010, 195–229.

Schiffner, Kerstin. *Lukas liest Exodus. Eine Untersuchung zur Aufnahme ersttestamentlicher Befreiungsgeschichte im lukanischen Werk als Schrift-Lektüre*, Stuttgart 2008.

Schipper, Bernd Ulrich. "Egypt and the Kingdom of Judah under Josiah and Jehoiakim", in: *Tel Aviv*, 37, 2010, 200–226.

Schirolli, Paolo. "Il passato geologico della 'terra dei marmi': l'evoluzione del paesaggio e l'assetto attuale", in: *Il marmo bresciano: territorio, vicende, economia*, edited by Antonio Porteri/Carlo Simoni, Brescia 1997, 13–44.

Schmidt, Matthias. "Vor dem Gesetz. Zur religiösen Dimension eines musikalischen Begriffs bei Schönberg", in: *Arnold Schönberg und sein Gott. Bericht zum Symposium 26.–29. Juni 2002*, edited by Christian Meyer, Wien 2003, 299–310.

Schmidt, Nora/Schmid, Nora Katharina/Neuwirth, Angelika, eds. *Denkraum Spätantike. Reflektionen von Antiken im Umfeld des Koran*, Wiesbaden 2016.

Schmitz, Barbara. "Gotteshandeln. Die Rettung am Schilfmeer als Paradigma göttlichen Handelns (Ex 13,17–14,31; Ex 15; Jes 43,14–21; Weish 10,15–21; Jdt)", in: *Exodus. Rezeption in Deuterokanonischer und Frühjüdischer Literatur*, edited by Judith Gärtner/Barbara Schmitz, Berlin/Boston 2016, 33–69.

Schneider, Rolf Michael. "Coloured Marble: The Splendour and Power of Imperial Rome", in: *Apollo*, 154 (473), 2001, 3–10.

Schöck, Cornelia. "Moses", in: *Encyclopedia of the Quran*, vol. 3, Leiden 2003, 419–426.

Schoenberg, Arnold. *Briefe*, edited by Erwin Stein, Mainz 1958.

Schoenberg, Arnold. *Moses und Aron.Oper in drei Akten. Studien – Partitur*, Mainz 1958.

Schoenberg, Arnold. "Komposition mit zwölf Tönen", in: id.: *Stil und Gedanke*, Frankfurt am Main 1992, 105–137.

Schoenberg, Arnold. *Moses und Aron, Oper in 3 Akten. Entstehungsgeschichte, Texte und Textentwürfe zum Oratorium und zur Oper*, edited by Christian Martin Schmidt, Mainz 1998.

Schonfield, Jeremy, ed. *The North French Hebrew Miscellany: British Library Add. MS 11639*, London 2003.

Schröder, Edward. *Zur ‚Exodus': Termin und Publicum*, in: *Zeitschrift für deutsches Altertum und Literatur*, 72, 1935, 239–240.

Schumacher, Leonhard. *Sklaverei in der Antike, Alltag und Schicksal der Unfreien*, München 2001.

Schwarzbaum, Haim. *Biblical and Extra-Biblical Legends in Islamic Folk Literature*, Walldorf-Hessen 1982.

Sed–Rajna, Gabrielle. "The Paintings of the 'London Miscellany', British Library Add. Ms 11639", in: *Journal of Jewish Art*, 9, 1982, 18–30.

Sed–Rajna, Gabrielle. "Ateliers de manuscrits hébreux dans l'Occident medieval", in: *Artistes, Artisans et Production Artistique au Moyen Age: Colloque International, Université de Rennes II – Haute–Bretagne, 2–6 mai 1983*, edited by Xavier Barral i Altet, 2 vols., Paris 1986, vol. I. 339–352.

Sed–Rajna, Gabrielle. "Images of the Tabernacle/Temple in Late Antique and Medieval Art: The State of the Research", in: *The Real and Ideal Jerusalem in Jewish, Christian and Islamic Art*, edited by Bianca Kühnel (Studies in Honor of Bezalel Narkiss on the Occasion of His Seventieth Birthday), *Journal of the Center of Jewish Art*, 23/24, 1997/8, 42–53.

Segovia, Carlos A. *The Quranic Noah and the Making of the Islamic Prophet. A Study of Intertextuality and Religious Identity Formation in Late Antiquity*, Berlin/Boston 2015 (Judaism, Christianity, and Islam – Tension, Transmission, Transformation, 4).

Segovia, Carlos A. *The Quranic Jesus. A New Interpretation*, Berlin/Boston 2018 (Judaism, Christianity, and Islam – Tension, Transmission, Transformation, 5).

Shalev-Eyni, Sarit. *The Tripartite Mahzor*, PhD thesis, The Hebrew University of Jerusalem, Jerusalem 2001 [in Hebrew].

Shalev-Eyni, Sarit. "Obvious and Ambiguous in Hebrew Illuminated Manuscripts from France and Germany", in: *Materia Giudaica*, 7, 2002, 249–271.

Shalev-Eyni, Sarit. *Jews among Christians: Hebrew Book Illumination from Lake Constance*, London 2010.

Shatzmiller, Joseph. *Cultural Exchange: Jews, Christians, and Art in the Medieval Marketplace*, Princeton 2013.

Shear, Adam. *The Kuzari and the Shaping of Jewish Identitx, 1167–1900*, Cambridge 2008.

Shinan, Avigdor. "On the Wilderness in the Rabbinical Literature", in: *'When You Went after Me in the Wilderness...'*, edited by Yair Zakovitch/Avigdor Shinan, Jerusalem 1995 (The President's Study Group on the Bible and Sources of Judaism, 3), 34–35 [in Hebrew].

Siegert, Bernhard. "Kulturtechnik", in: *Einführung in die Kulturwissenschaft*, edited by Harun Maye/Leander Scholz, München 2011, 95–117.

Silman, Yohanan. *Philosopher and Prophet: Judah Halevi, the Kuzari, and the Evolution of His Thought*, Albany 1995.

Sinai, Nicolai. "Inheriting Egypt. The Israelites and the Exodus to Egypt in the Meccan Qur'an", in: *Islamic Studies Today. Essays in Honor of Andrew Rippin*, edited by Majid Daneshgar/Walid Saleh, Leiden 2016, 198–214.

Soloveitchik, Haym. "Two Notes on the Commentary on the Torah of R. Yehudah he-Hasid", in: *Turim: Studies in Jewish History and Literature Presented to Dr. Bernard Lander*, edited by Michael A. Shmidman, 2 vols., New York 2007–2008, vol. II, 241–251.

Solzbacher, Rudolf. *Mönche, Pilger und Sarazenen: Studien zum Frühchristentum auf der südlichen Sinaihalbinsel – Von den Anfängen bis zum Beginn islamischer Herrschaft*, Altenberge 1989 (Münsteraner Theologische Abhandlungen, 3).
Sonne, Isaac. "The Paintings of the Dura Synagogue", in: *Hebrew Union College Annual*, 20, 1947, 255–362.
Soucek, Priscilla. "The Role of Landscape in Iranian Painting to the 15th Century", in: *Landscape Style in Asia*, edited by William Watson, London 1979, 86–110.
Stahl, Jacob Israel. *Sefer Gematriot of R. Judah the Pious*, 2 vols., Jerusalem 2004 [in Hebrew].
St. Clair, Archer. "The Torah Shrine at Dura–Europos: A Re-Evaluation", in: *Jahrbuch für Christentum und Antike*, 29, 1986, 109–117.
Stein, Dinah. "Different Perspectives: A Reading of Bava Batra 73a–75b", in: *Jerusalem Studies in Hebrew Literature*, 17, 1999, 18–21 [in Hebrew].
Stella, Clara. "Fronte di sarcofago frammentaria", in: *Milano capitale dell'impero romano, 286–402 d.C.*, exhibition catalogue (Milan, Palazzo Reale, 1990), edited by Maria Paola Lavizzari Pedrazzini/Maria Pia Rossignani, Milan 1990, 157–158, cat. 2b.2c.
Stone, Michael E. *Armenian Inscriptions from Sinai: Intermediate Report*, Sydney 1979.
Stone, Michael E., ed. *The Armenian Inscriptions from the Sinai*, Cambridge, MA 1982.
Stone, Michael E. "Sinai Armenian Inscriptions", in: *Biblical Archaeologist*, 45 (1), 1982, 27–31.
Straub, Jean-Marie/Huillet, Danièle. "Conversation avec Jean-Marie Straub et Danièle Huillet (Moïse et Aaron). Par Jacques Bontemps, Pascal Bonitzer et Serge Daney", in: *Cahiers du cinema*, 258/259, 1975, 5–24.
Stroumsa, Guy G. "Mystical Jerusalems", in: *Jerusalem. Its Sanctity and Centrality in Judaism, Christianity, and Islam*, edited by Lee I. Levine, New York 1999, 349–370.
Stroumsa, Guy G. *Das Ende des Opfers*, Berlin 2011.
Stuckenschmidt, Hans Heinz. *Arnold Schönberg – Leben, Umwelt, Werk*, Zürich 1974.
Sukenik, Eleazar L. *The Synagogue of Dura–Europos and Its Paintings*, Jerusalem 1947.
Swartz, Michael D. /Yahalom, Joseph. *Avodah: An Anthology of Ancient Poetry for Yom Kippur*, University Park, PA 2005.
Taylor, Jane. *Petra and the Lost Kingdom of the Nabataeans*, Cambridge, MA 2002.
Taylor, Jane. "The Writing on the Rocks", in: *Al-Ahram Weekly Online*, 620, 9–15 January 2003, URL:<http://weekly.ahram.org.eg/Archive/2003/620/heritage.htm>[19.03.2017].
Teixidor, Javier. "Les Nabatéens du Sinai", in: *Le Sinaï durant l'antiquité et le Moyen Age: 4,000 ans d'histoire pour un desert*, edited by Dominique Valbelle/Charles Bonnet, Paris 1998, 83–87.
Theißen, Gerd. *The Religion of the Earliest Churches*, Minneapolis 1999.
Tronzo, William. *The Via Latina Catacomb: Imitation and Discontinuity in Fourth Century Roman Painting*, University Park, PA/London 1986.
Turner, Victor W. *The Ritual Process: Structure and Anti-Structure*, New York 1969.
Turner, Victor W. "Liminalität und Communitas", in: *Ritualtheorien. Ein einführendes Handbuch*, edited by Andréa Belliger/David J. Krieger, Opladen/Wiesbaden 1998, 247–260.
Van den Berg, Robbert. "God the Creator, God the Creation: Numenius' Interpretation of Genesis 1:2 (frg. 30)", in: *The Creation of Heaven and Earth: Re-interpretation of Genesis*

I in the Context of Judaism, Ancient Philosophy, Christianity, and Modern Physics, edited by George H. van Kooten, Leiden/Boston 2005, 109–123.

Van Gennep, Arnold. *Les rites de passage*, Paris 1981 (first published in 1909).

Van Gennep, Arnold. *The Rites of Passage*, trans. by Monika B. Vizedom/Gabrielle L. Caffee, Chicago 1960.

Van Seters, John. "The Geography of the Exodus", in: *The Land that I Will Show You. Essays on the History and Archeology of the Ancient Near East in Honour of J. Maxwell Miller*, edited by John Andrew Dearman/Matt Patrick Graham, Sheffield 2001, 255–276 (Journal for the Study of the Old Testament, Supplement Series, 343).

Verkerk, Dorothy. "Life after Death: The Afterlife of Sarcophagi in Medieval Rome and Ravenna", in: *Roma Felix – Formation and Reflections of Medieval Rome*, edited by Éamonn ó Carragáin/Carol Neuman de Vegvar, Aldershot 2007, 81–96.

Vezzoli, Giovanni. "Cimeli paleocristiani e altomedioevali di S. Faustino ad sanguinem", in: *Miscellanea di studi bresciani sull'alto medioevo*, edited by the Comitato bresciano per l'ottavo congresso internazionale dell'arte dell'alto medioevo, Brescia 1959, 9–18.

Vollmann-Profe, Gisela. *Geschichte der deutschen Literatur von den Anfängen bis zum Beginn der Neuzeit. Band I: Von den Anfängen zum hohen Mittelalter, Teil 2: Wiederbeginn volkssprachlicher Schriftlichkeit im hohen Mittelalter (1050/60 – 1160/70)*, Königstein 1986.

Walker Arnold, Thomas. *The Old and New Testaments in Muslim Religious Art*, London 1932.

Walzer, Michael. *Exodus und Revolution*, Frankfurt am Main 1995.

Watson, William. "Landscape elements in the early Buddhist art of China", in: *Landscape Style in Asia*, Percival David Foundation of Chinese Art Colloquies on Art and Archaeology, 8 (1979), London 1980, 1–29.

Weill, Raymond. *La presqu'île du Sinai: étude de géographie et d'histoire*, Paris 1908.

Weinfeld, Moshe. *Social Justice in Ancient Israel and in the Ancient Near East*, Jerusalem 1995.

Weitzmann, Kurt/Kessler, Herbert. *The Frescoes of the Dura Synagogue and Christian Art*, Washington DC 1990 (Dumbarton Oaks Studies, 28).

Welker, Michael /Schweiker, William, eds. *Images of the Divine and Cultural Orientiations. Jewish, Christian, and Islamic Voices*, Leipzig 2015.

Wharton, Annabel J. "Good and Bad Images from the Synagogue of Dura Europos: Contexts, Subtexts, Intertexts", in: *Art History*, 17, 1994, 1–25.

Wharton, Annabel J. *Refiguring the Post Classical City. Dura Europos, Jerash, Jerusalem and Ravenna*, Cambridge 1995.

Wheeler, Brannon M. *Moses in the Qur'an and Islamic Exegesis*, New York 2002.

Wilkinson, John, ed. *Egeria's Travels*, 3rd edition, Oxford 1999.

Wilkinson, John, ed. *Jerusalem Pilgrims before the Crusades*, 2nd edition, Warminster 2002.

Wille, Christian. "Räume der Grenze – eine praxistheoretische Perspektive in den kulturwissenschaftlichen Border Studies", in: *Praxeologie. Beiträge zur interdisziplinären Reichweite praxistheoretischerAnsätze in den Geistes-und Sozialwissenschaften*, edited by Friederike Elias et al., Berlin 2014 (Materiale Textkulturen, 3), pp 53–72.

Wilson, Thomas M./Donnan, Hastings, eds. *A Companion to Border Studies*, Chichester 2016.

Winter, Irene. "After the Battle Is Over: *The Stele of the Vultures* and the Beginning of Historical Narrative in the Art of the Ancient Near East", in: *Pictorial Narrative in*

Antiquity and the Middles Ages, edited by Herbert L. Kessler/Marianna S. Simpson, Washington DC 1985, 16–21 (*Studies in the History of Art* 16).

Wischnitzer, Rachel. *The Messianic Theme in the Paintings of the Dura Synagogue,* Chicago 1948.

Wolfson, Elliot R. "The Mystical Significance of Torah Study in German Pietism", in: *The Jewish Quarterly Review,* 84, 1993, 43–78.

Yahalom, Joseph. *'Az be-en kol' Priestly Palestinian Poetry: A Narrative Liturgy for the Day of Atonement,* Jerusalem 1996 [in Hebrew].

Yitzhak bar Yehudah HaLevi. *Paneach Razah,* Warsaw 1932 [in Hebrew].

Zirlin, Yael. "The Decoration of the 'Miscellany', Its Iconography and Style", in: *The North French Hebrew Miscellany: British Library Add. MS 11639,* edited by Jeremy Schonfield, London 2003, 75–161.

Zirlin, Yael. "The Jewish Christian Polemic in Pictures: The North French Miscellany (BL. Add. MS. 11639)", in: *Timorah,* edited by Bracha Yaniv, Ramat Gan 2006, 61–72 [in Hebrew].

Zohar, Zvi. "'Ve–mi Metaher Ethem' – Your Father in Heaven, the 'Seder Avodah' Prayer: Context, Function, and Meaning", in: *AJS Review,* 14, 1989, 1–28 [in Hebrew].

Zunz, Leopold. *Zur Geschichte und Literatur,* Berlin 1845.

Index

Aaron   12, 42 f., 91, 114 f., 118, 121, 123 – 125, 129 f., 199 – 201, 203 – 209, 212 – 218, 220 f.
Abraham   97 – 99, 112, 119, 148, 157, 169, 174, 180, 183, 186, 189, 194, 197, 213
Abruzzi   208, 215, 217
Abu Sa'id Khan   147
Adam   118, 157
Adar   113
aggadah   131 f., 134 – 136, 138 f., 144, 153
Ahasuerus   125
Ain Huderah   91
Aix-en-Provence, Musèe des Beaux Arts   61
alabaster, alabastro fiorito   55
Alba Fucense   202, 208
Albertz, Rainer   20, 184 f.
Alexander the Great   59, 157
Al-Andalus   192 f.
Allah   1, 141, 157
allegory   94, 96
Allen, Terry   77, 152, 155, 157, 203, 210
al-Tabari   142, 162, 176
Altdeutsche Exodus (Middle High German poem)   10, 11, 93 – 107
Altdeutsche Genesis (Middle High German poem)   94, 100 f., 107
Ältere Judith (Middle High German poem)   95
Amalek   109, 125 – 127, 129 f.
Ambrose, Saint (archbishop)   59, 68 f.
Ameisenowa, Zofia   110, 114, 123
amora   134 f.
Amram   139
angel   3, 34, 42, 63, 109, 111 f., 131, 137 f., 140 – 142, 152 f., 155 f., 159 f., 162, 175, 179, 200
Arab   6, 79, 92, 134, 148, 151, 154, 160
Arabic   7, 77 f., 84, 86, 90 – 92, 147 – 150, 159, 173, 176, 179, 193
Aramaic   26, 30, 34, 78 f., 84, 86 – 90, 110, 184, 187
Aristotle   65
Arles   50, 57, 59, 61

Armenian   10, 29, 42, 47, 77 – 92, 114
Asher, Jacob ben   113
Ashkenaz   11, 109, 111 – 114, 123 f., 129
Assmann, Jan   7 f., 27, 204
Assyrian   21
Augustine, Saint   59
Avoda Zara (Mishnah)   187

Ba'al Shem Tov   196
Baal-Zephon   32
Babylon   21, 25, 38, 126, 140, 183 f., 187, 190 – 192
Baraita   140 f.
Bar Kokhba Revolt   46
Barry, Fabio   65 f., 112
Bateson, Gregory   213
Bava Batra (Mishnah)   11, 131, 134 f., 153, 161
Beal, Jane   6 f.
Becker, Erich   59
Beer, Eduard   86, 123
Ben Gamla, Joshua   125
Benjamin (scribe)   110, 123, 130
Berg, Alban   150 f., 193, 204, 217 f.
Bethel   35 f.
Beuken, Willem A.   186
Bible
– Genesis   30, 35 – 37, 62, 93 f., 100 – 103, 107, 111, 151
  – Gn 5:24   138
  – Gn 49:15   18
– Exodus   passim
  – Ex 1:11   18, 20 f.
  – Ex 1 – 13   9
  – Ex 1 – 14   15 f.
  – Ex 1 – 15   16
  – Ex 2:22   203
  – Ex 3:4   212
  – Ex 3:7   212
  – Ex 3:15   213
  – Ex 4:23   17
  – Ex 5:1   23
  – Ex 5:15   17

- Ex 7:16   23, 126, 129
- Ex 8:5   17
- Ex 8:16   23
- Ex 8:18–19   23
- Ex 9:1   23
- Ex 9:13   8, 30, 63, 239
- Ex 9:14   23
- Ex 10:1–3   23
- Ex 11:2   30
- Ex 12:31   23
- Ex 12:34–36   30
- Ex 13:3–8   30
- Ex 13:18   30, 63
- Ex 13–14   32
- Ex 14   33, 35
- Ex 14:9   32
- Ex 14:10–11   32
- Ex 14:15–22   63
- Ex 14:19–20   33
- Ex 14:22   24
- Ex 14:23   24
- Ex 14:24   33
- Ex 14:26–29   60
- Ex 14:26–45   132
- Ex 14:28   24
- Ex 14:30   24
- Ex 15:3–6   188
- Ex 15:5   64
- Ex 15:8   64
- Ex 15:15   25
- Ex 15:16   64
- Ex 17:6   63
- Ex 17:8–16   125
- Ex 17:16   126, 129
- Ex 20:2   15
- Ex 28:31–34   124
- Ex 28:36   124
- Ex 30:11–16   113
- Ex 31:18   83
- Ex 32:16   83
- Ex 49:15   18
- Numbers   113, 143
  - Nm 11:35–12:16   91
  - Nm 12:8   159
  - Nm 14:1–37   131
  - Nm 20:7–13   131 f.
  - Nm 33:17–18   91
- Deuteronomy   19, 84, 137, 139, 141, 143, 152, 160
  - Dt 1:34–39   132
  - Dt 6:6–9   84
  - Dt 15:12   23
  - Dt 20:10–15   19
  - Dt 20:11   18
  - Dt 20:14   19
  - Dt 32:48–54:12   131
  - Dt 32:52   143
  - Dt 34:6   140 f.
- Joshua   8, 57, 137, 140, 142 f., 149 f., 152, 196 f.
  - Jos 6:3–4   38
  - Jos 16:10   18
  - Jos 17:13   18
- Judges
  - Jdg 1:28   18
  - Jdg 1:33   18
  - Jdg 1:35   91
- 2Samuel
  - 2Sam 12:31   18
- 1Kings
  - 1Kgs 5:27–28   19
  - 1Kgs 15:27   22
- 2Kings
  - 2Kgs 17:4   22
  - 2Kgs 18:5   22
  - 2Kgs 18:7   22
  - 2Kgs 20   22
  - 2Kgs 21:1–18   21
  - 2Kgs 23:33–35   21
  - 2Kgs 24:1   22
- 2Chronicles
  - 2Chr 8:8   18
- Ezra   25, 184
  - Ezr 1:1–4   18
  - Ezr 6:3–5
- Esther   109, 118, 125, 129
  - Est 10:1   18
- Psalm   1, 33, 58, 101
  - Ps 2:1–4   189
  - Ps 18:13   34
  - Ps 50:5   133
  - Ps 113   58
- Isaiah   139, 183–187, 189
  - Is 1–39   183

– Is 2:2–3   186
– Is 2:2–4   184 f.
– Is 2:2–5   186, 189
– Is 40–66   183
– Is 41:2–25   185
– Is 43:1–9   185
– Is 43:9   187
– Is 43:14–15   185
– Is 44:28   185
– Is 45:1–3   184
– Is 45:5–6   185
– Is 45:13   23
– Is 48:15   185
– Is 49:7   184
– Is 51:6   139
– Is 55:12   183
– Is 56–66   183
– Jeremiah
– Jer 27:19–22   191
– Jer 34   26
– Jer 34:9   17
– Jer 36:24   17
– Lamentations
– Lam 1:1   18–21
– Lam 1:3–5   20
– Ezekiel
– Ezk 1:28   126
– Ezk 8:1–3   172
– Joel
– Jl 4:20–21   46
– Gospels   156, 164
– Acts
– Ac 2:4   101
– Ac 2:25–32   105
– 1Corinthians
– 1Cor 10:1–2   56
Blair, Sheila   146–148, 151–153, 155–157, 160
Blenkinsopp, Joseph   186
border studies   2
Boulez, Pierre   206 f.
Brescia
– Arca di San Felice   9 f., 49–55, 57, 60, 62, 65–75
– Museo di Santa Giulia   9 f., 49–55, 57, 60, 62, 65–75
– Sant'Afra   9 f., 49–55, 57, 60, 62, 65–75

– Sarcophagus, Crossing of the Red Sea   49–75
Bruni, Giancarlo   68–70
Buber, Martin   17, 132, 138, 141, 187, 208
Burckhardt, John Lewis   89
burning bush   77, 206, 211, 215, 219

Canaan   194
Carchemish (city)   21
Chagall, Marc   204
China   161
Clayton, Robert   83–85, 89
Clement of Alexandria   83
clerical   95 f.
column of fire   33, 50, 67, 73
Constantine (emperor)   58 f., 62
Corsato, Celestino   70, 73
corvée (labour)   18–21, 24, 27
Cosmas Indicopleustes   78, 80, 82–84, 87, 89
creation   23, 75, 118 f., 125, 151, 163, 168, 197
Cubitt, Sean   213 f., 219, 221
Cyprian of Antioch, Saint   58
Cyrus II (king)   184

David (king)   1, 3, 16, 38, 45, 58, 63, 77, 105, 114, 117 f., 125, 129, 145, 147 f., 157 f., 161, 189, 193, 195 f.
Deleuze, Gilles   207 f., 220
Derrida, Jaques   203
Döderlein, Johann Christoph   183
Dohmen, Christoph   2 f., 192
Duhm, Bernhard   183
Dura-Europos, synagogue   9, 29–48, 56

Easter   9 f., 25, 59, 68 f., 73, 75, 77, 90 f., 94, 101, 125, 167 f., 204
Easter vigil   57, 59, 69
Ebenezer, Battle of   38–40
Ederer, Matthias   2 f.
Edom   188
Egeria   80, 82, 84, 89 f.
Egypt   1–3, 6, 8 f., 11, 15–17, 19–24, 26, 29–32, 38, 42, 44 f., 69–71, 73, 77, 83 f., 89–91, 102 f., 131–133, 135, 163, 165 f., 168, 195, 204, 212, 214

– Elephantine 26
– Meribah 131f. 131–132
Egyptians 3, 9, 18, 24, 29f., 32–35, 42, 61, 63, 71f., 75
Eichhorn, Johann Gottfried 183
Eisenbeiss, Anja 13
Eliezer 140f.
Eljakim 22
Elsner, Jaś 42, 57f., 60–62, 68, 74f., 79
epilogue 97, 100–102, 104–106
eschatological 47, 50, 104, 106, 109, 118, 123, 139, 144, 153, 186, 187, 189, 190, 238
establishing shot 12, 202, 208
Ethiopian 141f.
Eucharist 69, 71
Eusebius of Caesarea 58f., 172
exile 20, 37, 139f., 144, 173f., 183, 185, 190f., 196, 200, 202, 204
Exodus Rabbah 34, 133
Exultet 3, 5
Ezekiel 170, 172, 173,

Faustino and Giovita (martyrs) 52–54
Felice, Saint (bishop) 54, 74
Flavius, Josephus 59, 136
Foucault, Michel 199
France 5, 11, 63, 75, 109f., 118, 204
Freud, Sigmund 96, 104, 208

Gad 141
Gaudentius (bishop) 10, 68–75
Gehinnom 133, 137
Gematriot (numerological associations) 11, 111f.
Genette, Gérard 119
Gennep, Arnold van 2f., 60, 131
Ghazan Khan 156
Gielen, Michael 206, 209f.
Gog Magog 189
golden calf 83, 133, 148, 166, 212, 215, 217f.
Goldstein, Bluma 1, 208, 212f.
Goliath 118, 125
Grabar, Andre 29, 32, 43, 155
grace 70, 98, 101, 104f., 114, 118

Great Mongol Shahnama (Book of Kings) 155
Greek 6, 10, 17, 36, 71, 78, 83f., 90, 92, 151, 156
Green, Arthur 94–96, 98, 100, 112, 125, 196
Green, Dennis 94–96, 98, 100, 112, 125
Guattari, Félix 207f.

Halevi, Judah 190–195
Haman 125
Haran 183
Hartmann von Aue 98
Hashanah, Rosh 118, 129
Heine, Heinrich 208
Hidjra 171
High Priest 114, 118f., 122–125, 129f.
Hillel the Elter (school of) 134f.
Hochet, Louis 209f.
Holly, Michael Ann 75
Holy Land 1–3, 8, 11f., 46, 80, 89, 131, 149, 152, 154, 162f., 165–170, 173f., 180, 183, 186f., 192, 194–197
Holy Spirit 99
Huillet, Danièle 12, 199–212, 214–221

Ilkhanid 11, 145, 147, 148, 155–159, 225, 231, 237,
Incredulity of Saint Thomas 50, 73
Ingold, Tim 75
inscriptions 10, 29, 42, 47, 77–92, 114
inspiration 104, 132f., 138, 156
interdiction of images 214f.
Isaac 29, 112, 118f.
Isaiah 139, 183, 184, 185, 187, 225
isrā᾽ 163, 167, 169, 171f., 174–177, 179, 181
Israelites 2f., 9–11, 17–20, 22f., 30, 32–35, 39, 43, 45f., 50, 58, 61, 67f., 71, 75, 77, 82, 84, 95, 97, 99, 101–103, 106, 126, 132f., 135, 138, 143–145, 149, 152, 154, 163, 165f., 168f., 171–174, 177, 181, 186, 213
Israel (Land of Israel) 1, 3, 8f., 11, 15–17, 19–24, 27, 29f., 35–37, 41–43, 45f., 48, 63f., 71, 80, 84, 90, 103, 106, 109, 111, 113f., 118, 123, 126, 130, 132f., 137,

139, 142–144, 147, 149, 151, 153, 163, 175, 183–199, 213, 216, 218
Italy   49, 210

Jacob   35f., 99, 103, 110f., 183, 186f., 189
Jami al-Tawarikh (World History)   11, 145–158, 160–162
Jehoiakim (king)   21
Jericho   38f., 197
Jerusalem   7, 12, 18–21, 23, 26, 29f., 36, 38, 42, 45–48, 58f., 78f., 82, 87f., 90f., 102, 104–106, 109–112, 114, 118f., 123, 132f., 135, 137, 139, 141–143, 147, 153, 163f., 167, 169–176, 179–181, 185f., 191, 193f.
– Al-Aqsa   169–180
– Heavenly Jerusalem   58, 102, 104–106, 164, 170, 172
– Temple   30, 36, 38, 42, 45–48, 113, 125f., 130, 164, 170, 171–173, 180, 190, 192, 194f.
 – Temple implements   118, 120, 125
– Zion   12, 36, 46, 139f., 164, 167f., 170, 184–186, 189f., 192, 197f.
Jesus   7, 69f., 105, 157, 162, 177, 180f., 191
– Nativity of Christ   7, 69f., 105, 156f., 162, 177, 180f., 191
– Raising of Lazarus   7, 50, 57, 69f., 105, 157, 162, 177, 180f., 191
Jewish Hellenistic   136
Joahas (king)   22
John, Saint (Evangelist)   71
Jordan, Mount Nebo   11, 38, 69f., 110, 131, 143, 152, 161
Jordan River   2, 131
Joseph   1, 16, 29, 38, 57, 102–106, 110, 112, 119, 189
Joshua   8, 57, 137, 140, 142f., 149, 150–152, 196f., 234
Josiah   21f.
Judah   21f., 26
Judeans   20f.
Judith   2, 8, 93, 95
Julian the Apostate (emperor)   66

Kaaba   168–170, 173, 178
Klee, Paul   220

Kohen   130
Kraeling, Carl   29–34, 36, 38f., 41, 47
Krause, Joachim   8
Kurigalzu II (king)   24

laical   95f.
Latin   78, 84, 87–90, 95f., 98, 100f., 208
lay theology   96, 106
Lebanon   19
Le Blant, Edmond   57f.
Leib of Spolje, Arje   196
Lekah Tov   141
Leviticus Rabbah   133
liturgical poem   118
liturgy   10, 45, 47, 57f., 75, 77, 118f.

Mahzor   109, 114, 118f., 123, 129
Maimonides (Rabi Moshe ben Maimon)   150, 153f., 161f., 192, 195f.
Malachi, Zvi   110, 119, 124f.
Manasseh (king)   21
manumission   25–27
manuscripts
– Berlin, Staatsbibliothek – Preussischer Kulturbesitz, Orientabteilung (Diez Album A)   158f.
– Budapest, Magyar Tudomanyos Akademia, MS. Kaufmann A 384 (Tripartite Mahzor)   114
– Edinburgh, University Library, Arab. Ms. 20 (Jâmi' al-tawârîkh)   6, 148f., 151f., 154, 156
– London, British Library, Add. MS 11639 (London Miscellany)   109–130
– London, The British Library, Ms. Or. 6810 (Khamsah)   178
– Oxford, Bodleian Library MS Opp. 202 (commentary on Exodus)   109–130
– Paris, Bibliothèque Nationale de France, Ms. nouv. acq. fr. 710 (Exultet)   3, 5
Maqamat of al-Hariri   154
marble   49f., 53, 55, 60–68
– Breccia damascata   55
– Breccia oniciata   55
Marchini, Maurizio   49, 53–55, 73f.
Martinengo, Ascanio   54f.
Mary   155f., 174

– Dormition of 155 f., 174
Marys at the Tomb of Christ 50
Matan Torah 163, 166, 177, 181
materiality 49, 62, 75, 154
Matthews, Thomas 59, 73
Maxentius (emperor) 58 f.
Mecca 12, 165, 168–171, 173 f., 176 f., 179 f.
Meins, Holger 204
Mekhilta 30, 32–34, 46, 186 f.
menorah 114 f., 121, 123
Meribah 131 f., 132
Merkavah (chariot) 106, 126
Meshel, Ze'ev 79 f., 87 f.
Messiah 129 f., 164, 184 f., 189, 195 f., 198
Messianic 11, 29, 38, 45, 47, 129 f., 133, 164–166, 186, 189, 195 f.
Metzger, Mendel 110, 123, 125
Middle High German 78, 84, 87–90, 95 f., 98
Middle Meccan suras 165 f., 173
Midrash 11, 34, 109, 118, 126, 129, 132 f., 141–144, 152 f., 186, 191
midrashic 9, 32, 129, 131, 136, 138, 141, 167, 190
Midrash Tanhuma 132, 138 f., 187
migration 1, 6, 8, 10, 16, 163, 167, 200, 204, 220 f.
Milan, Santa Maria dei Miracoli 49, 63, 65, 68 f., 112
Milvian Bridge 58
Mishnah 11, 38, 45, 123, 133, 140
mishnaic 136
Misopogon 66
Mitaka, Middle Eastern Culture Center in Japan (MECCJ) 91, 92
Moab 2, 11, 136–138, 141
Mongols 145, 147, 157
Moon, Warren 29, 42 f., 138
Mordecai 1, 112, 125
Moses passim
– death of Moses 131–162
– grave of Moses 11, 136, 139–141, 144
– kiss of God 153, 161
– Moses striking the rock 50, 65, 72
– Perfect Man 150 f., 153
Moses-Komplex 199, 208, 211

mosque 169–172, 174, 176 f., 180
Mota Mussah 141
movement 4, 11, 38, 75, 78, 93, 97, 99, 101–106, 167, 174, 179–181, 186, 199, 214, 216, 218
Muhammad 1, 7, 12, 145, 150–152, 156 f., 162 f., 165, 167, 172, 175, 177, 179–181
– birth of the Prophet 150 f., 156 f., 162 f.

Nabataean 77–80, 82–84, 86–90, 92
Nahman of Brazlaw 196
Nebuchadnezzar 189
Necho II 21, 27
Nedarim (tractate) 133
Neo-Assyrian 18
Neoplatonic philosophy 73
Nimrod 189
Nineveh 18 f., 21
Noah 118 f., 174,
– Noah's Ark 118

Onyx, African or red 9, 49, 51 f., 54 f.
Origen 59, 172, 191

Panazza, Gaetano 49, 53 f.
paradise 119, 180
Pardes, Ilana 3
Paul, Saint 6, 56 f., 66, 156, 190
penitence 70, 98
Pentecost 100, 105 f.
People of the Book 152
Persian 7, 43, 45, 147, 149–151, 160, 162, 171, 184 f., 189
Peter, Saint 63, 105
Peter the Deacon 80
Petirat Moshe (narrative) 136, 142 f.
Pharaoh 4, 7, 10, 17 f., 21, 23 f., 27, 32, 35, 58 f., 63 f., 67, 69, 71 f., 98, 148, 163, 165 f., 174, 199, 213
Philistines 39–42, 45
Phrygia 66
Pietists 111
Pi-hahiroth 32 f.
pilgrimage 77–80, 87–92, 185, 189 f., 192 f., 196
Pithom (city) 18, 21 f.
piyyut 114, 118 f., 124 f., 129

Poland 192
Pre-exilic 185
prologue 22
Psammetichus I 21
Pseudo-Jonathan 32, 33
Purim 109, 113, 126, 129

Qibla 170f., 174f.
Qur'an 8, 12, 151, 163–182
- Q 5:21 169
- Q 10:87 174
- Q 15:87 174
- Q 17 169, 174
- Q 17:1 170, 174–177, 181
- Q 17:4–8 171
- Q 17:80 174
- Q 20 165
- Q 20:12 167
- Q 20:14 174
- Q 20:77 167
- Q 21:71 169
- Q 26 165
- Q 26:52 167
- Q 28:20 168
- Q 30 171
- Q 44 165
- Q 44:23 167
- Q 52:1–6 168
- Q 79:15–16 167

Rabbah bar Bar Hana 134–136
Rabbi Asher ben Yehiel 113
Rabbi Eleazar ben Moshe 11, 29, 109–114, 126, 129f.
Rabbi Eleazar of Worms 112
Rabbi Judah the Pius 109, 111, 112, 114,
Rabbi Zera 190–192
Rabbinic 8, 12, 47, 112, 131f., 136, 142, 153, 167, 186f., 190
Rab-i Rashidi 147f.
Rameses (city) 18, 21
Ramperto (bishop) 53
Rashid al-Din 6, 11, 145–157, 159f., 162
Red Sea 1, 3–5, 9f., 30, 32–36, 43, 49–75, 91, 138, 148
- Reed Sea 16, 23, 27
Rephidim 125, 127

Reuben 141
Rizzardi, Clementina 49, 58–61
Romance of Alexander 157
Rome 3f., 29, 46, 49, 55–57, 59, 61f., 66, 68f., 75, 188, 208
- Museo Pio Cristiano Vaticano 61, 64f.
- Via Latina, catacombs 3f., 56f., 68
Rudolf von Ems 161

salvation history 179, 187
Samuel 39
Sanhedrin (tractate) 126, 133, 136
sarcophagi, Red Sea sarcophagi 49–75
Saurma, Liselotte 13
Schipper, Bernd Ulrich 21
Schmidt, Matthias 164, 214f.
Schönberg, Arnold 200f., 214
Schröder, Edward 94–96, 100
Scroll of Esther 125
Seder Avodah (order of worship) 118, 125f., 129f.
Sefer ha-Kuzari 193–195
Serabit El Khadim 77
Shammai (school of) 134f.
Shekalim (tractate) 113f., 125, 130
sifre 137, 139, 141, 152
Sinai 1, 3, 10, 12, 36, 77–92, 112, 133, 137, 148, 155, 157, 160, 163–170, 177, 181, 186, 217
- Monastery of St. Catherine 77, 90
- Mount Naqus 91f.
- Mount Sinai 90–92, 137, 148, 163, 166, 177, 181
- Rāya/al-Ṭūr 91f.
- Wadi Mughara 87
- Wadi Mukattab 83, 89, 92
sinfulness 105
slavery 17f., 71, 136
Solomon (king) 19, 36, 38, 47, 114, 116, 118, 129, 132, 141, 189
Song of Moses and Miriam 64
Song of Roland 95f.
Song of the Sea 46
Soucek, Priscilla 161
Spain 192
Split, Archaeological Museum 61, 186
SS Exodus 4, 6

Straub, Jean-Marie   12, 199–212, 214–218, 220f.
synagogue   9, 29–48, 56, 125
Syria, eastern   29, 84, 89, 174, 180

Tabriz   6, 145–147, 151, 156f.
Talmudic   112, 131–134, 136, 138, 144, 187, 189, 191f., 195
Talmud (Jerusalem Talmud)   30, 38, 126, 133, 140f., 187f., 190–192, 195f.
Targum Pseudo-Jonathan   32f.
Tertullian   59
Theißen, Gerd   185f.
Theodosian   60, 62
Theodosius (emperor)   60
Theophrastus   65
Thessaloniki, Arch of Galerius   44f.
Throne of God   126, 129
Torah   1, 12, 35f., 46–48, 111–114, 118, 133, 137f., 145, 162f., 165f., 179, 181, 186–190, 195f.
Trajan (emperor)   43, 79
transitus   10, 68, 72, 74
translation   10f., 17, 25, 30, 68f., 78, 84, 86, 89, 93, 97, 99, 101, 103–106, 118f., 124, 160, 175, 180, 183f., 187f., 193, 195
Troyer, Kristine De   8
Turner, Victor   3, 57, 131

Ṭuwā (Holy Valley)   167
Tzitziyot   134

Uljaytu Khan   147
Uman   197

vassal treaty   22
vernacular   10f., 93, 95, 97, 104, 106
Vulgata   94, 96, 103

wall of water   10, 24, 34, 64, 71–73
Warqah and Gulshah   160
water   3f., 10, 24, 34, 49, 51, 56, 60–67, 69–72, 79, 131f., 143
Weinfeld, Moshe   23, 25
Weitzmann, Kurt   29, 33, 38, 56
Wheeler, Brannon   7, 147, 151f.
wilderness   3f., 10f., 16, 33, 36–38, 77, 83f., 88, 131–144, 163, 165, 186f., 208
Paran   132
Shur   132
Sin   132
Woods, Gregory   202

Yahweh   15, 17, 23f., 27, 184, 189, 194
Yom Kippur   109, 113, 118f., 124–126, 130

Zedekiah   22
Zirlin, Yael   110, 123

Photo Credits

Annette Hoffmann: fig. 1: © foto Pontificia Commissione di Archeologia Sacra; fig. 2: Paris, Bibliothèque Nationale de France; fig. 3: Edinburgh, University Library

Kära Schenk: fig. 1–8, 10: Yale University Art Gallery, Dura-Europos Collection; fig. 9: Athen, Deutsches Archäologisches Institut

Jessica Richardson: figs. 1–3: Brescia, Fondazione Brescia Musei (photos: Michele Luigi Vescovi); fig. 4: photo Finoskov © Creative Commons; fig. 5: photo: Lanmas / Alamy Stock Photo; fig. 6: Milan, Civiche Raccolte Grafiche e Fotografiche del Castello Sforzesco, Civico Archivio Fotografico, RI inv. 8738 (photo: Ugo Zuecca; by kind permission of the Santuario di S. Maria dei miracoli presso S. Celso, Milan)

Kristine Larison: fig. 1: New York, Public Library Digital Collections; fig. 2: Los Angeles, The Getty Research Institute

Sara Offenberg: figs. 1–8: © The British Library Board, London

Mika Natif: fig. 1, 4: © Nour Foundation, courtesy of the Khalili Family Trust; fig. 2: reproduced with the permission of the Topkapi Palace Museum, Istanbul; fig. 3: Edinburgh, University Library; figs. 5–6: Berlin, Staatsbibliothek – Preußischer Kulturbesitz

Angelika Neuwirth: fig. 1: © The British Library Board, London

Ute Holl: fig. 1: from Schönberg, Arnold. "Komposition mit zwölf Tönen", in: id. *Stil und Gedanke*, ed. Ivan Vojtech, Frankfurt/Main 1992, 105–137, 116; fig. 2: from Gregory Woods. "Ein Arbeitsjournal", in: Filmkritik 221/222, 1974, 254–273, 256; figs. 3–10: photographed from the film "Moses und Aron", BRD 1974, direction: Jean-Marie Straub, Danièle Huillet (reproduced with the permission of Jean-Marie Straub)

www.ingramcontent.com/pod-product-compliance
Lightning Source LLC
Chambersburg PA
CBHW052056230426
43662CB00037B/1933